D0791843

Produced in cooperation with the
Grand Rapids Area Chamber of Commerce

Windsor Publications, Inc.
Northridge, California

Ellen Arlinsky & Marg Ed Kwapil

RAPIDS

In Celebration of **GRAND**

Windsor Publications, Inc.—History Book Division

Vice-President of Publishing: Hal Silverman
Editorial Director: Teri Davis Greenberg
Design Director: Alexander D'Anca

Staff for *In Celebration of Grand Rapids*
Senior Editor: Gail Koffman
Senior Production Editor: Susan L. Wells
Assistant Production Editor: Laura Cordova
Director, Corporate Biographies: Karen Story
Assistant Director, Corporate Biographies: Phyllis Gray
Editor, Corporate Biographies: Judith Hunter
Editorial Assistants: Kathy M. Brown, Nina Kanga, Susan Kanga, Pat Pittman
Proofreader: Susan J. Muhler
Design and layout: Ellen Ifrah
Layout Artist, Corporate Biographies: Barbara Moore
Sales Representative, Corporate Biographies: Glenn Edwards

Library of Congress Cataloging-in-Publication Data

Arlinsky, Ellen, 1940-
    In celebration of Grand Rapids.

    "Produced in cooperation with the Grand Rapids Area Chamber of Commerce."
    Bibliography: p. 409
    Includes index.
    1. Grand Rapids (Mich.)—History. 2. Grand Rapids (Mich.)—Description.
3. Grand Rapids (Mich.)—Industries. I. *Kwapil, Marg Ed, 1931-* II. Grand Rapids
Area Chamber of Commerce. III. Title.
F574.G7A77   1987   97734'56   87-10697
ISBN 0-89781-210-7

© 1987 Windsor Publications, Inc.
All rights reserved
Published 1987
Printed in the United States of America
First Edition

The following are affiliated with the Grand Rapids Camera Club: Pat Bulthuis, Marian L. Carter, Doug Diekman, J. Phillip Haven, Larry Heydenburg, Boots Schmidt, Jack Standley, Gerrit J. Tepastte, Marie Velting

Frontispiece: Fourth of July fireworks burst over Grand Rapids. Photo by William Hebert

Facing page: One of Grand Rapids' many agricultural products is shown here, illuminated by early morning sunlight. Photo by William Hebert

Page six: The promise of rich farmland attracted many settlers to the Grand Rapids area. Photo by Boots Schmidt

Page eight: The sun setting over Lake Michigan is always a spectacular sight. Photo by William Hebert

Part openers: Sunset on Lake Michigan is a heart-warming and awe-inspiring spectacle. Photo by Scott Corder

Table of Contents

Dedication

As the Grand Rapids Area Chamber of Commerce celebrates its centennial anniversary, we are mindful of the fact that for the past fifteen years, Stuart Cok has served ably and tirelessly as its president. Fair minded, even tempered, and considerate of others' views, Stu is a man of high principles, a local community leader well known and highly regarded in communities and Chambers of Commerce far beyond Grand Rapids' borders. During his tenure as president, the Grand Rapids Chamber has become one of the most widely respected Chambers of Commerce in the country.

After a decade and a half of dedicated service, Stu Cok has retired from the Chamber presidency. We wish him good fortune and every success in the years to come and we dedicate this book to him and to all of those committed individuals—staff and volunteers—who have served the Chamber of Commerce over the past one hundred years. We will follow the example they have set for us and build on it for generations to come.

G. Jack Cooper, Chairman of the Board
Grand Rapids Area Chamber of Commerce

Acknowledgments

The authors are grateful to all of those individuals and organizations who supplied us with informal interviews, photographs, research assistance and technical information.

We extend special thanks for their invaluable advice, guidance, assistance and support to Jack Cooper, chairman of the board, Grand Rapids Area Chamber of Commerce; Stuart Cok, president, Grand Rapids Area Chamber of Commerce; Ann LaReau, vice president, marketing, Grand Rapids Area Chamber of Commerce; Gordon Olson, Grand Rapids City Historian; William Black, Grand Rapids City Archivist; Pam Boynton, Helen Bisbee, Dan McCullough and Bruce Siebers, Michigan Room staff, Grand Rapids Public Library; David Miller, volunteer, Grand Rapids Public Library; W.D. Frankforter, director, Grand Rapids Public Museum; and Marilyn Merdzinski, registrar, Grand Rapids Public Museum.

Our appreciation also goes to photographers William Hebert and John Strauss for the speed and skill with which they undertook assignments; to the "Partners in Progress" for their time and always gracious cooperation; and to the members of the Grand Rapids Camera Club for their enthusiasm and for the many superb photographs which grace the pages of this book. Organized in 1898 as an outgrowth of the Valley City Photographic Society, the Grand Rapids Camera Club is the oldest camera club in the United States in continuous and uninterrupted existence.

Finally, we thank our editors at Windsor Publications, Gail Koffman and Karen Story, for their patience and support.

Introduction

GRAND RAPIDS: IN CELEBRATION OF A CITY

In many respects, Grand Rapids is not much different than its sister cities in the Midwest. It was first settled in the late 1820s, and the first permanent settlers were mainly easterners moving west to new lands and new opportunities. Next came Europeans, for the same reasons the first settlers arrived in the region—new lands, new opportunities, hope for economic gain, and a better life for themselves and their children.

Many of the settlers realized their dreams. They put down roots, raised families, and established businesses. They built on their dreams, and in doing so, became a part of the story of West Michigan growth and prosperity.

Grand Rapids is the pulse beat of West Michigan. As the largest metropolitan area on the west side of the state, it is the keystone of the region's economy and a business, convention and cultural center as well. A tradition of diligence, hard work, and enterprise, plus superb environmental features, and maybe just a little good luck, have made Grand Rapids one of the premier cities of the Midwest.

And so, in observing the 100th anniversary of its founding, the Grand Rapids Area Chamber of Commerce, which has always been dedicated to the welfare of the city, has much to celebrate. Descendants of families who were respected citizens contributing to the welfare and culture of the community in 1887 still play active roles in the community. Newcomers in every decade have made their own special contributions to the flavor and spirit of the city. Many of the businesses that were fledgling enterprises in 1887 or before are themselves celebrating 100 years or more of serving West Michigan.

We are only a little more than a decade away from a new century. As we look forward to the progress of new eras, the promise of new technologies, and the challenge of new opportunities, we look back with a special nod to all those who have brought us to this point—the visionaries, the risk-takers, the foot soldiers. We acknowledge the debt and pledge to build on their legacy.

Preface

I always enjoy the excitement of introducing Grand Rapids, the jewel in Michigan's crown. As Michigan's second largest metropolitan area, Grand Rapids enjoys the diversity and amenities of an urban environment. At the same time, the Grand Rapids area maintains a sense of community pride and civic participation associated with grass-roots America. Grand Rapids is a community that works!

The Grand Rapids economy is diverse, providing protection and moderation from cyclical swings in the national economy. And the economy is expanding. Grand Rapids, in fact, is one of the few "snowbelt" cities in the entire nation projected for substantial population and economic growth into the twenty-first century.

Our local school systems—both public and private—rank among the best in Michigan. And yet, the effective rate of taxation in the region is among the lowest of all of Michigan's urban areas. An abundant and affordable housing stock, along with hospitalization and health-care costs which are among the lowest in the nation, contribute to the well-being of employer and employee alike.

Served by several outstanding public and private colleges, Grand Rapids is the site of a new cooperative Research and Technology Center, pointing our economy toward the development of automated manufacturing technologies. Home to one of the largest community arts festivals in the nation, a regional symphony orchestra which has received national recognition, and only half an hour's drive from the splendors of Lake Michigan, Grand Rapids offers a diverse range of opportunities which enrich the lives of its citizens.

The strong faith of its religious communities and the cultural richness of its ethnic diversity reinforce the excitement of a city on the move. Grand Rapids is second to none as a place to raise a family, to do business, and to live life at its best. This is a community where old values and new opportunities cross paths. Grand Rapids—there's no place like home.

Paul B. Henry, Member of Congress
Fifth District, Michigan

A sparkling blue sky over a field of flowers is a common sight in Grand Rapids. Photo by William Hebert

PART

1

A Place of Promise

1 The Community and the River

Through the richly varied and complex tapestry of Grand Rapids' history runs the ever-present thread of the Grand River. Created by the glacial movement and flowing meltwater of the last Ice Age—some 15,000 years ago—the wide, fast-moving river and its fertile valley have been home to man for more than 10,000 years.

As the intense cold of the Ice Age gave way to warmer temperatures, Michigan's climate came to resemble that of today's northern Canada—and spruce forests grew where the glaciers once held sway. Fish and other marine creatures lived in glacier-fed lakes. Bears larger than grizzlies prowled the forests, 200-pound beavers swam in the rivers, and great mammoths and mastodons grazed along their banks. Camels, horses, caribou, bison, saber-toothed tigers, and giant wolves all moved into what is now Michigan, following the glacial retreat. Behind them, eventually, came man, drawn to the region—as later inhabitants would also be—by the abundance of game and the lush, green, glacial valley of the Grand.

This scene east of Johnson Park provides a glimpse of the stark beauty of the Grand Rapids area in winter. Photo by Gerrit J. Tepastte

The earliest humans in North America migrated from Asia some 30,000 to 40,000 years ago over a land bridge that crossed the Bering Sea. By the year 10,000

15

B.C., their descendants, the people archaeologists call Paleo-Indians, had made their way into Michigan in search of game.

The Paleo-Indians, Michigan's oldest inhabitants, were hunters and gatherers who lived in small, nomadic groups. They occupied the region for some 3,000 years, chipping tools and weapons out of stone and tracking big game for their sustenance. The remains of an 11,000-year-old mastodon unearthed in nearby Grandville in 1986 bear evidence, according to one archaeologist, that the huge beast was slain and then butchered, perhaps with its own sharp bones, by human hands.

The elephant-like mastodon, who rooted around in the brush of the post-glacial forest, and its cousin, the mammoth, who grazed on the grassy plains, became extinct some 8,000 years ago. But the human population was in the region to stay.

Like their Paleo-Indian ancestors, the people of the Archaic period, which began about 6,000 B.C., depended on the resources of the Grand River valley for their sustenance. They modified their weapons to kill elk, deer, and other smaller, faster-moving game; they fished for sturgeon and gathered mussels in the lakes and rivers; and they learned to gather the hickory nuts, acorns, wild grapes, grass seeds, and other foodstuffs that were in plentiful supply.

Over the 5,000 years that the Archaic period lasted, life became more settled as populations increased. Less nomadic than their Paleo-Indian predecessors, Archaic peoples grew more technologically sophisticated. They used grooved stone axes to build wooden

shelters and hollow logs into dugout canoes, and they made pestles and grinding stones to prepare plants and seeds into food.

Sometime during the Archaic period, about 3,000 years ago, northern Michigan people began mining copper, hammering it into tools, weapons, and ornaments, and trading the fruits of their labor for shells and other goods from the south. Soon a vast network of trade began extending from the Gulf of Mexico in the south to Lake Superior in the north.

As the centuries passed, cultural patterns continued to change. During the Woodland period, ca. 1,000 B.C. to A.D. 1650, the people of the Grand River valley learned to grow plants for food on the rich soils of glacial floodplains that were the legacy of a far earlier age. And into the valley from Illinois, beginning in about 100 B.C., came the culture of the mound

builders.

Today known as the Hopewell, the mound builders of the Grand River valley lived in small, scattered villages beside the river and grew crops of sunflowers, squash, and corn. From time to time they gathered near the rapids which ran between present-day Leonard and Pearl streets. There, on the river banks, they buried their honored dead, and, over the gravesites, built mounds of earth and bark. Interred beneath the mounds, along with the human remains, were objects, some of them made from materials whose closest source was more than a thousand miles away. The variety of grave goods—obsidian and grizzly bear teeth from the Rocky Mountains, copper and silver from mines along Lake Superior, galena from Missouri and southern Illinois, pipestone and mica from Ohio, and conch shells from the Atlantic and Gulf coasts—pro-

Facing page, left: **Weather patterns have changed dramatically since the Ice Age, but Grand Rapids still enjoys an average of about seventy inches of snow per year. Photo by Pat Bulthuis**

Facing page, right: **The Grand River was a gathering place for man as early as 11,000 years ago. Photo by Gerrit J. Tepastte**

Above: **The first people to grow crops on West Michigan's fertile soil planted sunflowers, squash, and corn more than 3,000 years ago. The region's rich farmland still yields a variety of food crops. Photo by Scott D. Corder**

Above: **Many of Grand Rapids' early settlers were attracted to the area by news of abundant farmland. Photo by Jean Hoyle**

Facing page: **As if symbolizing good fortune, a rainbow shines above this quiet farm scene. Photo by William Hebert**

vides evidence of the mound builders' widespread and active trading network.

The mound builders' culture flourished in the Grand River valley for nearly 500 years, at the same time that the Roman Empire rose and fell. Then it vanished as new cultural patterns emerged. But the thirty to forty earthworks left by the mound builders on the west bank of the Grand River (later demolished for roadfill by early Grand Rapids settlers) and the seventeen remaining mounds on the east bank southwest of the city (today preserved as the Norton Group) testify to the fact that a sophisticated cultural and trade center existed in Grand Rapids at the time of Christ. As early as 2,000 years ago, Grand Rapids was a thriving place of culture and commerce.

For thousands of years, successive generations have looked to the resources of the Grand River valley for sustenance. Like their predecessors in the region, the Indians who succeeded the mound builders grew corn and other crops in the valley's fertile soil, fished in its waters, made pottery from its clay, hunted and trapped game, tapped maple trees for sap to make syrup and sugar, and constructed the bark canoes that made long-distance trade and travel possible. Whatever they needed they took from the land, and the land provided for all their needs. But those needs changed beginning in the sixteenth century as the nations of Europe embarked on their explorations of the New World. First the French, and then the British, laid claim to the territories they explored and established colonies on the North American continent, seeking the riches of empire and a fortune in furs.

By the early decades of the seventeenth century, felt hats made of beaver pelts and fur garments had become immensely fashionable in Europe, and furs from the New World were a major source of supply. The fur trade thus became increasingly important to

Europeans and Indians alike. Profits from the trade lined the pockets of Europe's colonial officials and helped support their New World empires. The Indians, for their part, trapped the furs and received in exchange the European pots and tools, cloth and knives, guns and ammunition that soon became essential to their way of life. As a result, seventeenth-century North America swiftly became a battleground for European territorial ambitions and Indian rivalries for furs. And with the arrival of Europeans along the Grand River, life in the valley was irrevocably changed.

The abundance of fur-bearing animals and the presence of skilled native trappers brought French traders to the Grand River valley late in the seventeenth century. Souls they regarded as ripe for conversion to Catholicism attracted the missionary priests. The Ottawa Indians, forced west by a series of fur-trading wars with the Iroquois, moved into Michigan's lower peninsula in the early 1700s to serve as mid-

dlemen in the fur trade with the French. Once their favorite hunting grounds, the lower peninsula became their permanent home, and they established year-round villages at the rapids of the Grand.

The fur trade in Michigan remained lucrative even after France lost its North American territories to Britain in the French and Indian War (1754-1763) and the American colonists were victorious in their own war for independence against the British in 1789. In 1755, Charles Langlade, half-French, half-Ottawa, established a trading post at the mouth of the Grand River at Grand Haven. Fur trader Joseph LaFramboise made annual trips to the Grand River valley beginning in the 1780s and, with his wife Magdelaine, established a trading post on the Grand River near Lowell in 1809. Widowed a year later, Madame LaFramboise ran the post until 1821, when pressure exerted by Rix Robinson, an agent of John Jacob Astor's American Fur Company, forced her to sell. Robinson, in turn, operated the post until 1837.

Even when demand declined in the face of changing fashions and the fur supply dwindled as a result of overtrapping, trading remained a profitable enterprise. Traders licensed by the United States government—including Louis Campau, who arrived in Grand Rapids in 1826 to do business with the Ottawa—continued to sell goods and whiskey to the Indians, on credit, expecting to be paid from the proceeds of treaties that had already begun moving Indians off their ancestral lands.

By 1833, six years after Louis Campau built his Grand Rapids trading post, furs were not the area's only attraction. Like iron filings moving toward a magnet, settlers and speculators were being drawn to the valley by the availability of land and the opportunity for profit.

The federal government paved their way—with treaties that called for the cession of Indian lands, territorial surveys followed by public land sales at low prices, and the opening of the Erie Canal in 1825. By 1835, nearly a hundred settlers had joined the local Ottawa Indians and their missionaries in calling Grand Rapids home.

On the west bank of the Grand River lived one group of Ottawa and their leader, Nawequageezhik (sometimes called Noonday), in the Baptist mission and model farm that had been established for them a year before Campau's arrival by the terms of the Treaty of 1821. While the Reverend Leonard Slater ministered to their spiritual needs, the Ottawa farmed the land, raised cattle, and operated a sawmill built with treaty funds. Half a mile downriver, also on the west bank, was another Ottawa village, led by Megisinini, and St. Mary's, the Roman Catholic mission established in 1833 by the Jesuit Father Frederic Baraga.

Opposite the Baptist mission, on the river's east bank, was Louis Campau's trading post, along with the "homes, arts and appliances" of a growing population. Many of the earliest settlers in the Grand Rapids area were farmers who moved onto what was still Indian territory, anticipating a new treaty that would place the land in the hands of the federal government and lead to a public sale. According to the federal pre-emption laws passed in 1828, any settler who occupied

Facing page: **The Grand River retains its beauty throughout the seasons of the year. Photo by Gerrit J. Tepastte**

Above: **Fur trader, land speculator, tavern owner, banker, and village trustee, Louis Campau was an important figure in Grand Rapids from 1826 until his death on April 13, 1871. Courtesy, Grand Rapids Public Library**

Right: This map depicts Michigan Territory in 1822, fifteen years before Michigan became a state. Courtesy, Grand Rapids Public Library

Facing page, top: This scene of Grand Rapids in 1856, from a painting by Sarah Nelson, is a view from the west bank of the river. Prospect Hill rises on the east bank and the old stone schoolhouse is visible on the right. Courtesy, Grand Rapids Public Library

Facing page, bottom: This sketch by the Reverend John Booth shows Grand Rapids as it was in 1831. The three buildings on the right are Louis Campau's cabin, trading post, and blacksmith shop (site of today's George Welsh Civic Auditorium). Across the river is the Baptist Indian Mission, and in the foreground is the camp of the Ottawa Chief Nawaquegeezhik. Courtesy, Grand Rapids Public Library

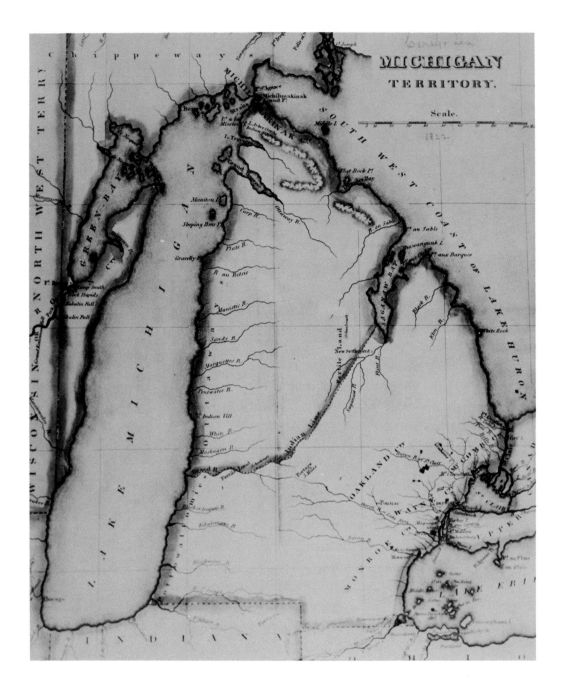

Indian land and made improvements by constructing buildings and clearing the land for farming had first claim to that parcel when it was placed on the open market. As they sought to make their living from the land, these early farming families needed clothing and supplies, and before long shopkeepers, craftsmen, artisans, and tradesmen were making their way to Grand Rapids, certain of finding customers for their products and markets for their wares. Opportunities for profit multiplied, and the population surged.

A great many of the newcomers in the 1830s and 1840s were New Englanders from Massachusetts and New Hampshire, and New Yorkers from the upstate cities of Troy and Albany. Improved roads and the Erie Canal not only eased their way west but provided the means for shipping their goods and cash crops to market. The Yankees who came to Grand Rapids were a dominant force in the community right from the first. They built a thriving city out of a little frontier town, and they and their descendants furnished the capital, owned the businesses, and held political sway from village days until well into the 1880s. What the first Yankee settlers found at the end of their journey west was a green valley through which flowed a turbid river with rapids that tumbled in a mile-long, eighteen-foot drop over a series of limestone outcroppings. The roar of the water, it was said, could be heard from a mile away. Parallel to the river, and seventy feet above it, rose Prospect Hill, located between Monroe and Ottawa, where the Waters Building stands today. Below the rapids were four islands—two at the foot of Pearl and Lyon streets and two more, one encompassing several acres further to the south.

Navigable most of the year on either side of the rapids—upriver to cities such as Jackson and downriver to Lake Michigan—the river was valuable to the early settlers as a means of transportation, as a highway on which to move their goods, and as a source of industrial power. Equally valuable, if not more so, were the hundreds of miles of thick virgin forests through which it flowed—forests of walnut, butternut, elm and cherry trees, black ash, sycamore, burr oak, hickory, soft maple, and pine.

As every generation since has done, the early Grand Rapids settlers looked to the resources of the

Above and facing page: **West Michigan's once-abundant forests supplied the raw materials for Grand Rapids' nationally renowned furniture industry. Above, photo by David Jackson; facing page, photo by William Hebert**

river and the valley to supply their needs. And like future generations, they often acted heedlessly. As local historian William Etten put it in his 1926 centennial history of the city, "The white man is a great civilizer and explorer, but he also interferes with and alters nature's work."

The early citizens of Grand Rapids, acting in the name of progress, saw the limestone ledges beneath the rapids as building blocks for a growing city. So they hauled away the limestone and obliterated the rapids. They also regarded the four islands in the

Right: St. Mark's Episcopal Church, located on Division Avenue, was built with limestone from the Grand River. Photo by Pat Bulthuis

Facing page: The Fourth Street dam was built in 1866 to channel the flow of water into the West Side Canal and to provide water power for riverside factories. Courtesy, Grand Rapids Public Library

Grand River as barriers to transportation. So they shifted the river's course westward and they eliminated the islands. As Albert Baxter reported:

Early days those islands, with their spreading elms and rich grassy verdure in the summer season, formed a handsome feature of the picturesque landscape in that part of the city. But the insatiate hand of improvement for proper uses has been laid upon them; the east channel has been cut off and filled from the upper end more than halfway down, the islands made part of the mainland, and on them and over the old channel bed are many valuable business blocks and other structures.

The "insatiate hand of improvement" also took aim at Prospect Hill, which was leveled, its remains carted off to supply fill for low-lying areas. For the sake of profit, the forests were cut down. Overtrapping seriously eroded the supply of beaver and other fur-bearing animals. By the late 1850s, bear and deer no longer crossed the river above the rapids, and by the turn of the century, with the ruin of their habitat, the wild geese, ducks, turkey, partridge, and quail once seen in such profusion had virtually disappeared.

Over the years the river continued to feel the impact of the hand of man. The mile-long East Side Canal project, begun in 1835 and completed in 1842, used a wing dam at its upper end, near Sixth Street, to divert current into the canal and create valuable mill properties along the riverbank. Locks were also planned as a means to facilitate transportation, but the funds ran out and the project was never completed. Another dam, two blocks south of the original one, was built in 1867 as part of the West Side Water Power Canal project.

To the early settlers, the Grand River was a highway to move their goods and a tool to be harnessed as an energy source to run their mills and factories. But by 1890, even these functions had lost their importance, and the once beautiful Grand was on its way to becoming an open sewer.

Above: As the city's population grew in the nineteenth century, the need for an adequate supply of drinking water increased. Already tainted by an assortment of pollutants, water from the Grand River would not serve, and in 1874 the city built a reservoir on Lookout Hill, in today's Belknap neighborhood. Six years later, a portion of the pipe below the reservoir eroded, and four million gallons of water rushed down to Ottawa Avenue, doing considerable damage along the way. Courtesy, Grand Rapids Public Library

Facing page: Sites along the banks of the Grand River have long been occupied by a variety of local industries. Courtesy, Grand Rapids Public Library

The disposition of sewage was a problem from the settlement's earliest days. The original city charter, adopted in 1850, gave the Common Council the authority to construct and repair sewers and drains. "There was at the time an abundant need of such work," according to Baxter, "but the city did not fully wake up to a realization of that fact during the first three or four years."

The city began sewer construction in 1865 and, with total disregard of the effects it would have, dumped the waste into the river. By 1881, as Albert Baxter noted, the city surveyor found it necessary to report to the Board of Public Works:

Nearly all the east side drainage from Fourth Avenue on the south to Coldbrook Street on the north, was by sewers having outlet near the Grand Rapids and Indiana Railroad bridge. This outlet was much complained of as a nuisance, on account of the stench arising therefrom. The surveyor reported two plans of relief, but it doesn't appear that his plans were adopted.

The situation was destined to grow worse. By 1889 the "population growth along the courses of Coldbrook and Carrier creeks had caused a contamination of their waters." And by 1891,

considerable difficulty has been encountered in the matter of the disposal of sewerage, or its discharge into the river. From the foot of Lyon Street down to near the steamboat landing, a large arched culvert receives the contents of several trunk sewers, and conducts them below. Yet there has been great complaint of the offensive odors arising from the comparatively still waters into which they discharge. To remedy this will require sometime a large outlay.

Even the large outlay predicted by Baxter did little to improve matters, because the 334 miles of sewers in operation by 1926 continued to empty their contents directly into the Grand. In 1911 Wyoming Township sued, and the Michigan Supreme Court ordered the city to cease polluting the river with sewage and industrial waste. Two years later Grand Rapids boasted a new water filtration plant—a model facility and the only one in the country, in fact, equipped with a lecture room—but sewage continued to pour into the river. In 1922 the state board of health ordered installation of a sewage disposal plant, which was completed in 1929, on the eve of the Great Depression.

Although the environment was changing, over the years Grand Rapids continued to attract newcomers. Between 1860 and 1870 the city's population doubled from 8,000 to 16,000 and over the next ten years doubled again to 32,000. The decade between 1880 and 1890 saw another doubling of the population, to 60,000. By the turn of the century, some 90,000 people were calling Grand Rapids home. These and succeeding generations were drawn to Grand Rapids not by the river but by the commercial and industrial opportunities available along and beyond its banks.

In time the city turned its back completely on the river, and by the 1960s, the once-grand river had become a victim of industrial waste. The high concentrations of cyanide and heavy metals pouring directly into the river or flowing into the sewage system for future discharge into the river prompted the City of Grand Rapids Environmental Protection Department to report that "few persons used the Grand as a recreational resource and fewer yet dared eat the fish caught from its waters." At the same time, according to the United States Public Health Service, Grand Rapids ranked fifty-second out of sixty-five industrial cities in terms of the severity of its air pollution.

By the late 1960s, however, in the wake of the heightened environmental concern that was sweeping the nation, the citizens of Grand Rapids once again turned their attention to the river, not just to use it for their own advantage, but to clean it up for the benefit of all. In 1969 the Grand Rapids City Commission

Above and facing page, bottom left: Fishing is an exciting sport along the Grand River. Above, photo by Marian L. Carter; facing page, photo by Pat Bulthuis

Facing page, top and bottom right: Designed by Joseph Kinnebrew III and dedicated in 1975, the Fish Ladder provides a close-up view of the salmon that battle their way upstream each fall to spawn and then to die. Facing page, top, photo by David Jackson; bottom, photo by Pat Bulthuis

enacted a strict sewer-use ordinance, regulating the discharge of possible pollutants into the sewer system and for the first time requiring the industrial pretreatment and detoxification of heavy metal wastes. By 1972 the river showed clear signs of improvement. Clean air likewise became a major priority, and by 1979 Grand Rapids was in the vanguard of cities with clean air, ranked second only to Honolulu in a survey of forty-two major cities.

One of the keys to the success of the environmental cleanup campaign was community-wide cooperation and commitment. Concerned citizens and members of such organizations as the Grand Rapids-based West Michigan Environmental Action Council devoted considerable time and energy to environmental issues. Federal, state, and local dollars were appropriated to implement clean air and clean water standards. And local industries invested millions of dollars in the construction of waste pretreatment facilities. These efforts paid off in a river where fish once again swam

and boaters and canoeists spent their leisure hours.

By the middle of the 1970s, the city was ready to move beyond mere cleanup to the restoration of the river as a focus of city life. As one community activist put it, "The Grand River is one of our greatest assets whose carefully planned development can turn it from a neglected area into its rightful place as our front yard."

Evidence of City Hall's commitment to that goal was the institution of an official "Grand River Edges" policy. Established in 1981, the policy aims to turn the Grand River into an "aesthetic backdrop" to the downtown by creating twelve miles of bicycle paths

Above: **These Grand Rapids sailors encounter the vastness of Lake Michigan. Photo by William Hebert**

Preceding pages: **Ah-Nab-Awen Bicentennial Park provides a peaceful setting for strolling. Photo by William Hebert**

Facing page: **The Gerald R. Ford Presidential Museum's distinctive triangular shape on the west bank of the Grand River stands in contemporary counterpoint to the George Welsh Civic Auditorium on the east bank, built during the Great Depression. Photo by David Jackson**

and pedestrian walkways on both sides of the river through the heart of the city and investing about three million dollars in ten major projects to improve riverfront sites. Plans include building a boardwalk, complete with a terraced walkway and dock projecting into the river, just north of the Pearl Street bridge on the east bank; transforming the old Conrail railroad bridge into a bench-lined pedestrian overpass linking the central downtown area with the west bank; and constructing a walkway along the floodwall in the Fulton Street area on the east side of the river. Although the Grand River's edges won't be fully developed for another five to ten years, the river itself has nevertheless regained its place of importance as an asset to

community life. Each year, gather at the Fish Ladder, bui salmon battle their way upstr Grand River yield more salm to one source, than all the W bined, but thanks to the clear once again safe to eat.

Parks bloom along the rive Park, built in 1978 on the sp Canal once flowed, pays tribu Native American inhabitants the nation's bicentennial centennial anniversaries. Eth regularly take place in the p are particularly inviting to pi office workers who enjoy a wa stroll along the river.

Overlooking the park and Ford Presidential Museum. rabilia of the city's longtime tive to the U.S. Congress w thirty-eighth president, the s ing was dedicated with grea today one of the city's prem

Above: These Grand Rapids sailors encounter the vastness of Lake Michigan. Photo by William Hebert

Preceding pages: Ah-Nab-Awen Bicentennial Park provides a peaceful setting for strolling. Photo by William Hebert

Facing page: The Gerald R. Ford Presidential Museum's distinctive triangular shape on the west bank of the Grand River stands in contemporary counterpoint to the George Welsh Civic Auditorium on the east bank, built during the Great Depression. Photo by David Jackson

and pedestrian walkways on both sides of the river through the heart of the city and investing about three million dollars in ten major projects to improve riverfront sites. Plans include building a boardwalk, complete with a terraced walkway and dock projecting into the river, just north of the Pearl Street bridge on the east bank; transforming the old Conrail railroad bridge into a bench-lined pedestrian overpass linking the central downtown area with the west bank; and constructing a walkway along the floodwall in the Fulton Street area on the east side of the river. Although the Grand River's edges won't be fully developed for another five to ten years, the river itself has nevertheless regained its place of importance as an asset to

community life. Each year, residents and tourists gather at the Fish Ladder, built in 1975, to watch the salmon battle their way upstream. Not only does the Grand River yield more salmon annually, according to one source, than all the West Coast streams combined, but thanks to the cleanup efforts, the fish are once again safe to eat.

Parks bloom along the river banks. Ah-Nab-Awen Park, built in 1978 on the spot where the West Side Canal once flowed, pays tribute to the area's original Native American inhabitants and also commemorates the nation's bicentennial and the city's sesquicentennial anniversaries. Ethnic festivals of all kinds regularly take place in the park, and its open spaces are particularly inviting to picnickers and downtown office workers who enjoy a warm-weather, lunch-time stroll along the river.

Overlooking the park and the river is the Gerald R. Ford Presidential Museum. Built to house the memorabilia of the city's longtime fifth district representative to the U.S. Congress who became the nation's thirty-eighth president, the striking triangular building was dedicated with great fanfare in 1981 and is today one of the city's premier tourist attractions.

Grand Valley State College's new Downtown Center, also on the west bank, just south of the Ford Museum, brings educational services to the riverfront, in keeping with city planning goals to develop river bank sites for a variety of uses. On the east side of the river on opposite sides of Pearl Street stand the Forslund Building, its upper floors given over to condominium apartments, and the twenty-nine-story Amway Grand Plaza Hotel Tower, completed in 1983. Both buildings afford their occupants access to the river and its pleasing riverfront views.

More housing and offices on both sides of the river remain a planning priority, as do additional hotels. Two development proposals have been given the go-ahead by the city commission. Construction of an $8.5 million hotel at Pearl Street on the west bank of the Grand River got underway in December 1986. The

175-room facility, which will be operated by Days Inn, is expected to be completed in 1988. At the same time, United Development Corporation has unveiled its plans for a three-tier tower complex of condominiums, rental apartments and hotel rooms on more than four downtown acres on the east bank.

Grand Rapids had its beginnings on the Grand River, and the river has played an important part in the history of the region, attracting Native American settlers to its banks some 2,000 years ago. For the past 150 years, the city has owed much to the river's role as a transportation artery, a source of power, and a focus of industrial development. Today reclaimed from the near-fatal pollution of years past, the Grand River represents a new beginning in the community's recognition of its heritage and its commitment to the future.

2
Riches From the Land

The roots of the place that is now Grand Rapids stretch far back into unrecorded time, leaving their traces in layers of rock and the scattered relics of ancient populations that have come and gone.

The earth's landforms and its climate have changed over the millennia. North America once lay much closer to the equator, and Michigan, hot and dry, was submerged beneath a shallow inland sea. Over time, the sea water evaporated, depositing beds of gypsum in its place.

Later, some 15,000 years ago, the great glaciers of the last Ice Age covered the land of present-day Grand Rapids with a sheet of ice two miles thick. As the glaciers advanced southward, they pushed sand and clay and gravel ahead of them and built moraines—glacial ridges—along their melting southern edge. One such moraine runs across today's Kent County, its high point along 92nd Street between Eastern and South Division avenues.

As the earth's climate continued to warm over the Ice Age's waning centuries, the glaciers inched their way north. Flowing meltwater washed away clay, leaving deposits of sand and gravel behind. The movement of the ice shaped the rolling hills and broad valleys of the landscape, and great puddles of meltwater formed the Grand River and the Great Lakes. Other lakes, created where water was trapped between ice and hills, gradually aged and disappeared, their beds of silt

Much of the land surrounding the Grand Rapids metropolitan area is still devoted to farming. Photo by William Hebert

transformed into rich, fertile soil.

Over the centuries, many more changes occurred. As glacial meltwater flowed south, rivers altered their courses. The Grand River, the longest river in Michigan, was once much wider than it is today, flowing south along South Division Avenue, and later shifting to just south of Hudsonville and Zeeland before running its present course.

The Grand Rapids of the nineteenth century owed much to its geology and to the natural resources created by climatic and geologic upheavals eons earlier in time. The area's salt basins and gypsum beds, limestone deposits, clay soil, and pine forests all became the basis of industries that took their prosperity directly from the land. And the waterpower of the Grand made much of that prosperity possible.

Salt mining was one of the city's earliest extractive industries. In 1841 Lucius Lyon sank a well and by the following year was advertising his willingness to exchange 450 pounds of salt for five cords of wood.

Eight years later the well caved in. As one early chronicler noted, "Salt making in Grand Rapids was at an end for the time being, and there was a great feeling of disappointment." Convinced that salt would pay, other entrepreneurs also sank time and money into holes in the ground. Richard Butterworth abandoned his salt mine in 1859 and, in a burst of ingenuity, used the brine to operate mineral bath houses for a few years. The Grand Rapids Salt Manufacturing Company and the Grand River Salt Company also tried and failed. "Considerable salt was manufactured there," according to early historian Baxter, "but the supply was insufficient for profit, and the works were operated but a short time." In light of the better resources and facilities in other parts of the state, salt making in Grand Rapids was "extinct" by 1891, "but those who tried it had the satisfaction of much experiment and great expectations."

Great expectations likewise greeted both the state geologist's report in 1838 of extensive gypsum deposits

south of the city and the subsequent tests proving that the gypsum could be profitably worked. Those who pinned their hopes on gypsum were not disappointed, for the demand for plaster and stucco would continue to be fueled by population growth—first in the city and then throughout the country.

In 1841 Daniel Ball and Warren Granger established their plaster mill on Plaster Creek, two miles south of Grand Rapids. The mill turned out over forty tons its first week in operation; by the winter of 1848-1849, demand had far outstripped supply. Other entrepreneurs got in on the act, and by 1852, sixty-ton shipments were being moved to market by horse teams every day.

In the years after the Civil War, with more and more settlers heading to the Far West, plaster had become big business. And with the post-war expansion of the nation's rail network, local companies were finding ready markets from Ohio to California. Grand Rapids plaster and stucco, for construction and ornamental work, and land plaster, used as "soil sweetener," were known for their superior quality and, as one early observer noted, "gypsum quarries are a mine of apparently inexhaustible wealth to our city."

Although Grand Rapids was still one of the country's foremost gypsum producers well into the twentieth century, the heyday of the local gypsum industry,

like that of so many other extractive industries, eventually passed. Today, however, with the resurgence of the building industry, local gypsum mines are enjoying a rebirth. In 1980, the Domtar Corporation of Canada purchased the Grand Rapids Plaster Company property, originally owned by Richard Butterworth, and the Georgia Pacific Corporation still maintains a mine site near Kent County International Airport and another one on Butterworth S.W. One local mine is already functioning, and a considerable quantity of gypsum remains to be unearthed from the rest. If demand becomes great enough, Grand Rapids may once again be a leading plaster producer, able to reclaim its former title as the "gypsum capital of the world."

Other mills besides plaster mills were important to the early Grand Rapids economy. To the new and growing community, sawn lumber was an essential product—needed to build homes and furnish them and construct the buildings and sidewalks of an emerging commercial center downtown. With heavily timbered forests nearby and an abundant supply of water power close at hand, Grand Rapids quickly became a sawmill center.

The earliest mill in the area, built in the 1820s at the Baptist Indian mission, was a primitive affair, "with an old-fashioned upright saw, capable of cut-

Left: The bandsaw used to process logs into lumber at this sawmill in the 1890s was considered a very modern piece of equipment. The walls were whitewashed as a fire preventative in the belief that the lime would cause any sparks generated by the saw to die out on contact. Courtesy, Grand Rapids Public Library

Facing page: Extractive industries continue to play a role in the Grand Rapids economy. Photo by J. Phillip Haven

Page thirty-eight: As the sun sets over Lake Michigan, the South Shore pier is silhouetted against an orange sky. Photo by J. Phillip Haven

Right: As illustrated here, logs were piled on the riverbanks to wait for the high water that would carry them to their destination. Courtesy, Grand Rapids Public Library

Facing page: The great log jam of 1883 destroyed one railroad bridge and damaged two others along its course. Courtesy, Grand Rapids Public Library

Below: In 1870 Reuben Wheeler's sawing, planing, and floor-dressing factory was powered by the water that flowed though the East Side Canal. Courtesy, Grand Rapids Public Library

ting, perhaps, from five to eight hundred board feet per day, when there was water sufficient to keep it in motion." Small though its output may have been, the Indian sawmill supplied lumber for the white settlers' building needs and was part of the reason that many of the early settlers tended to cluster around the mission. By the 1830s and 1840s, Grand Rapids sawmills were all water powered and capable of cutting only 1.5 to 2 million feet per season. A mill which would turn out 4,500 feet per day was then considered an especially good one; later mills would eventually cut ten times that much.

With completion of the East Side Canal's millrace in 1842, many more sawmills began springing up along the river, assured of a nearly steady supply of swift-running water to keep them operating. Later on, other mills set up operations on the opposite side of the river to take advantage of the water power supplied by the West Side Canal, completed in 1867.

In 1853 Powers, Ball and Company put up the first steam mill equipped with a circular saw. The many other innovations that soon followed improved goods, changed styles, and reduced prices. In addition to cutting lumber, many of the early sawmills turned out furniture and a host of other wood products, from pails and tub staves to sashes, doors, and blinds. As the city's population doubled, redoubled, and then doubled again over the course of three decades beginning in 1860, lumbering and associated industries boomed, supplying building materials not only to local customers but to a growing population further to the west.

The sawmill industry depended on the river not only as a source of power but as the only highway on which the uncut timber could be delivered. Tributaries flowing north and south to the Grand provided the means for transporting vast shipments of saw timber to the local mills or to Grand Haven for shipment across the lake to Milwaukee and Chicago. Pine was the most sought after product in the early days, and extensive tracts grew along rivers to the north of the city, furnishing millions of feet of timber to the mills. Later on, the hardwoods would be cut, to supply the needs of a growing furniture industry.

The Grand Rapids lumber trade started in 1838 with the first shipment of logs downriver, and for the next decade or so, growth was only moderate. But as more and more settlers pushed further and further west, demand increased and business flourished. In 1850 Michigan ranked fifth in lumbering nationally; fifteen years later the state was number one and would remain so throughout the 1880s.

The Grand Rapids Booming Company, organized in 1870, controlled the movement of all logs downriver to and below the city. Between 1871 and 1888, the company floated nearly 655 million feet of logs downriver to the mills. The biggest year was 1873, with over fifty-six million board feet bumping and sliding their way downstream, pushed and prodded and kept in motion by spike-booted rivermen expertly wielding the spiked poles known in the trade as peaveys. The worst season came a decade later in 1883—the year of the great log jam. Riding on rain-swollen waters, a vast uncontrolled tangle of logs swept through the city, taking out one railroad bridge and heavily damaging two others along its thunderous course. Only twenty-one million feet were delivered to Grand Rapids' mills that year; the rest were retrieved further downriver and shipped to western markets from the lake ports.

Just as the annual spring flotillas transformed the Grand and its tributaries into a rolling river of logs, the end of the logging season turned Grand Rapids into a brawling lumberjack town. The lumbermen, after a cold, lonely winter in the woods, were ready for a bit of high life, and there were plenty of saloons and other rowdy establishments more than willing to

oblige them.

From the 1840s to the late 1880s, lumbering and the sawmill industry were mainstays of the local economy. But like the local limestone quarries that were gradually played out and the brickyards that disappeared as the clay pits were exhausted, the forests did not last much beyond the turn of the century. The waste was enormous—and unnecessary. Cut down willy-nilly and with no thought for the future, the forests made fortunes for a few, and then they were gone—a renewable resource heedlessly destroyed.

The demise of lumbering spelled the end of the sawmill industry by the turn of the century. Flour mills, too, had only a short time left in which to enjoy their prosperity. Many of the area's first settlers were farmers who raised wheat and corn, and the city's first mills were built to serve their needs. Fertile soil made

for abundant crops, and the milling industry grew, supplying flour to ever-expanding markets. Kent Mills, between Canal and Bridge streets, had a thirty-year run, between 1842 and 1872, patronized by "wheat raisers" as well as consumers at home, and its product was in brisk demand abroad.

Just as water power from the Grand River ran the saws of the lumber mills, so the city's flour mills depended on the Grand to operate their grinding stones. Flour became a major commodity, and such brand names as "Lily White" and "Roller Champion," the products of Valley City Mills, one of the city's largest mills, became household words throughout the region and beyond. Over the years, the mills changed hands and names. Production processes were modernized as the old millstones were replaced by rollers and water power gradually gave way to steam. As long as the

Right: Grand Rapids was a sawmill center for much of the nineteenth century. Photo by Pat Bulthuis

Facing page: By the time these hardwood logs were cut down in the 1890s to be used for the manufacture of furniture, Michigan's forests were all but depleted. Courtesy, Grand Rapids Public Library

farmers kept producing, operations such as the Voigt Milling Company (earlier known as Crescent Mills), purveyor of "Star" and "Crescent" flour, remained profitable enterprises, shipping their products through Chicago or Detroit to New England or Southern markets.

What silenced the Grand Rapids millstones and brought a halt to the local flour industry was competition from the vast wheat fields of the West. With their more direct rail connections to national markets and their ability to grow both hard and soft wheat varieties, the plains states rose to preeminence in the grain business, and local farmers turned their efforts to growing the fruits and vegetables that in the long run have proven even more profitable than wheat.

Although by the turn of the twentieth century many of the resources of the land were exhausted, the land itself continued to have value, just as it did when Grand Rapids was first settled. Fur trader Louis Campau was certainly well aware of that fact. As soon as the lands ceded by Indian treaties to the federal government were surveyed and put on the block for public sale, Campau snapped up seventy-two acres at $1.25 each. For a total of ninety dollars, Campau was the owner of what would eventually become the heart of the city's downtown. Campau turned his first profit

in 1833 by selling two of his newly platted lots to Joel Guild for fifty dollars. Guild moved his wife and seven children onto the land and there, where the McKay Tower stands today, built the first frame home in the valley.

Government surveyor Lucius Lyon, who bought land to the north of Campau's, also had profit in mind. He and the other members of his Proprietors of Kent did a brisk business in land sales, as did Campau and the many other landlookers and speculators who descended on the little town in the early 1830s. Land sales—most of them on credit—soared. Prices skyrocketed to as much as fifty dollars per square foot, but seldom did cash payments for the transactions change hands.

As it was bound to do, the speculative bubble burst, punctured by the Panic of 1837. Recovery, almost a decade away, finally stabilized prices; a Canal Street lot between Lyon and Crescent, 25-foot frontage, sold in 1849 for $200 and was resold a few months later for $275. In 1887 the land purchased on Ottawa and Crescent as the site for the new county building went for a dollar a square foot; during the downtown urban renewal of the 1960s, Old Kent Bank purchased land in that same vicinity for $5.50 per square foot.

Although the days of wild land speculation had

come to an end by the 1840s, downtown land remained prime property. Proof of its importance as a salable and profitable commodity lies in the fact that the early citizens of Grand Rapids went to great lengths to level it, fill it in, raise it, and otherwise impress their will upon it to suit their residential, industrial, and commercial needs.

The first step was the nineteenth-century equivalent of moving a mountain. Prospect Hill's seventy-foot elevation of compacted clay and gravel rose between Monroe and Ottawa and extended northward beyond Lyon Street. Lacking the heavy earth-moving equipment of a more modern era, the citizens of Grand Rapids hacked away at the hill and cut streets through it with picks and shovels, using draglines to load the dirt into wagons drawn by oxen or horse teams.

Getting rid of the debris was no problem at all, because much of today's downtown was yesterday's swampy lowland and, when rainfall was heavy, "after a while mud flowed down Monroe like lava." The fill carted away from Prospect Hill raised some downtown spots—including today's lower Monroe—by as much as fifteen feet and changed the course of the Grand River by filling in the east channel which flowed where the Amway Grand Plaza Hotel stands today. In the process of filling, paving, and adding other improvements, the citizens of Grand Rapids turned what was originally swampland into some of the most expensive real estate in West Michigan.

According to unofficial estimates made by city assessors in 1985, the value of Louis Campau's original ninety-dollar downtown plot, bounded by Michigan Street on the north, Fulton Street on the south, Division Avenue on the east, and the Grand River on the west, has appreciated 280,000 times in 154 years. The worth of the land alone has risen to about twenty-five million dollars, while the current market value of land and buildings combined has been conservatively pegged at $500 million.

Real estate values throughout the city have likewise soared. The total assessed valuation of all the land and buildings within Grand Rapids city limits stands at more than $1.4 billion, which makes for a true market value of nearly $2.9 billion. Add to that the estimated value of all tax-exempt property within city limits, and Grand Rapids today is worth a grand total of over $3.7 billion.

Land has been a valuable commodity from the city's earliest days, and by 1890 Grand Rapids boasted a well-developed real estate industry, with a list of more than 100 dealers who organized themselves three years later into the Grand Rapids Real Estate Board; the national board would not be founded for another fifteen years. The original roster of 148 member realtors has grown to more than 800 members today, and total transactions add up to millions of dollars annually. Until the 1950s, the focus of real estate and land development remained, for the most part, within the city limits, which had grown from just four square miles in 1850 to forty-four square miles by 1966. But in the years following World War II, Grand Rapids began to feel the effects of a national phenomenon—suburbanization.

Earlier Grand Rapids suburbs had grown up along the streetcar routes that, beginning around the turn of the century, made it possible and practical for homes, shops, and businesses to spread outward from the center city. In the 1950s, however, the automobile was the ticket out of town. Freed from the necessity of living near public transportation or within walking

Facing page: **Agriculture and agribusiness form Michigan's second largest industry. In addition, crops from the farms of local growers supply the state's rapidly growing food-processing industry. Photo by Jean Hoyle**

Above: **Locally grown wheat and corn were ground in Grand Rapids' mills during the latter half of the nineteenth century. Photo by James Glessner**

distance from work, increasing numbers of Grand Rapids residents cast their eyes on more distant suburban locations, where the homes were newer, the lots larger, and the grass presumably greener. The fields and farms on the city's outskirts that had once supplied food to a growing population were now more valuable as potential sites for housing developments, and the postwar availability of low-interest home mortgages provided an additional impetus to continuing decades of suburban growth.

With the 1970s came a discernible change in housing patterns. Grand Rapids has long been a city of predominantly single-family homes, and the ratio of owner-occupied homes to rental apartments, in fact, remains one of the highest in the nation. But as the supply of residentially zoned land continued to shrink while the costs of development rose, the trend within city and suburbs shifted toward the construction of multi-family rental and condominium dwellings of all types.

Today, however, the revised federal tax code has eliminated many of the advantages that formerly accrued to the owners of multi-family dwellings, and builders are again concentrating on single-family homes. Declining mortgage rates and the creation of new jobs has led to an increased demand for single-family housing in the metropolitan Grand Rapids area, and residential construction in Kent and Ottawa counties grew at the rate of 39 percent in 1986. Nonresidential construction was up, too, with the value of building permits issued in 1986 showing a two-million-dollar increase over 1985.

Even today, with the real estate market rising, Grand Rapids remains a city of affordable housing. According to a national survey released in August 1986 by the National Association of Realtors, the median resale price of a home in Grand Rapids is $51,600, lowest of the fifty-three metropolitan areas surveyed. Officials attribute the area's affordable housing to land and construction costs that have stayed below the national average. As a result, the Grand Rapids residential real estate market has been described as the "hottest in the state," with a total sales volume over the first eight months of 1986 amounting to more than $356.2 million. The figures represent a 30 percent increase over the same time period in 1985, more than double the 14 percent rate of growth enjoyed throughout the state.

Close on the heels of suburban housing development over the past three decades came commercial development, and the commercial and retail corridors that grew up on the outskirts of Grand Rapids pulled business, tax revenues, and population away from the city's core. Between 1970 and 1980, Grand Rapids' population declined by 8 percent while Kentwood's population rose by nearly 50 percent. At the same time, Walker's population increased by 31 percent, and Wyoming enjoyed an increase of 5.4 percent.

The opening in 1961 of the area's first suburban shopping center—Rogers Plaza, one of the first enclosed malls in Michigan and one of the earliest in the nation—was followed in swift succession by Breton Village, Eastbrook, Woodland, and North Kent malls. Strip malls, small businesses, and fast-food establishments proliferated along such major thoroughfares as 28th Street and Plainfield Avenue, pushing development ever outward toward a burgeoning suburban population.

Entrepreneurs continue to be drawn to the 13.5-mile-long 28th Street because of the high-volume traffic, which is a plus as far as business owners are concerned. New strip malls have recently sprung up along the busy thoroughfare between Breton and Kalamazoo, and in 1987 developers proceeded to turn the last bit of undeveloped land on 28th Street's eastern end, between East Paris and Patterson avenues in Kentwood, into building sites for an automobile dealership, a 200,000-square-foot shopping mall, a restaurant, a 125-room motel, and a discount merchandise outlet. An integral part of the project was an extension of 29th Street, a roadway originally constructed to help alleviate the congestion on 28th Street and which is now becoming almost as heavily traveled and highly

Facing page: **Voigt House, built by mill owner Carl G.A. Voigt in the 1890s, is now operated as a museum by the Grand Rapids Public Museum. Photo by Jean Hoyle**

Above: **Joel Guild arrived in Grand Rapids in June 1833 and purchased the first lots sold in Grand Rapids from Louis Campau. Courtesy, Grand Rapids Public Library**

developed as its companion street.

The increasingly heavy traffic and the welter of unlovely facades on 28th Street and other streets like it offer stark testimony to the after-effects of uncontrolled development. And as those streets and other commercial corridors brought to life in the 1960s have themselves become more crowded, development has extended into such formerly unspoiled areas as the East Beltline, north of Plainfield. What kind and how much development is appropriate or necessary are questions with which citizens will have to grapple in the future.

Within a decade after the exodus from the city began, some of the new suburban communities incorporated themselves as separate municipalities—

Right: The McKay Tower occupies the site on which Joel Guild's frame house once stood. Photo by David Jackson

Facing page: The past twenty years have witnessed dramatic development in and around downtown Grand Rapids. Photo by David Jackson

Wyoming in 1959, Walker and Kentwood a few years later. Other localities—particularly Cascade, Ada, and Forest Hills, on the city's southeast side—followed suit, aware of their future growth potential and anxious to avoid annexation by the city of Grand Rapids.

Annexation was the process by which the city had increased its total area from just four square miles in 1850 to about 23.5 square miles by 1927. Further annexations of outlying areas were put on hold during the Great Depression and World War II, but the postwar surge in suburban development opened the door to expansion once again as new residential communities sought police and fire protection and other such municipal services from Grand Rapids. In 1959, the Grand Rapids City Commission and Mayor Stanley Davis announced that services would not be provided to unannexed areas. A flurry of annexations followed, increasing the city's total area to 44.07 square miles by 1966. Since then, the incorporation of surrounding communities as separate municipalities and East

Grand Rapids' rejection of annexation attempts in 1959 and 1963 have put an end to geographic expansion, and Grand Rapids' total land area stands at 44.9 square miles.

In order to establish a tax base from which to support their school systems and other municipal services, the separately incorporated suburbs began offering tax incentives to attract industry. Hard pressed to refuse such offers, a growing number of businesses and industries packed up and moved—lock, stock, and headquarters—to the greener suburban pastures.

As the scene of the action shifted to the suburbs, the city's downtown slowly and inexorably decayed. Urban renewal was the 1960s' response. Armed with a massive infusion of federal funds, the city went to work. Just as once the citizens of Grand Rapids leveled Prospect Hill to make way for homes and streets and businesses, so in the 1960s did the city proceed to tear down the remnants of eras past to clear a path for what was generally agreed to be progress. Keeping to another precedent established in the past, the rubble of

128 demolished buildings was used for lowland fill. Although in hindsight there are now regrets that more of the city's heritage was not preserved, there is no doubt that the urban renewal of the 1960s focused renewed attention on the value of downtown property for business, commercial, and even residential use.

Many citizens and civic officials have also come to accept the idea that the past itself has value and that previous development is in many instances well worth saving. As a result, while much new construction has taken place, downtown has also been undergoing extensive renovations of such historic sites as the 113-year-old Ledyard Building, whose Italianate iron cornices evoke the styles and tastes of an earlier age.

The city itself and the greater Grand Rapids metropolitan area continue to work to attract new business and commercial ventures, well aware that economic growth, wherever it occurs, benefits the region as a whole. Covering 1,429 square miles of Kent and eastern Ottawa counties, and home to 626,400 people, the Grand Rapids metropolitan area today is the site of six state-certified industrial parks and more than

seventy-five industrially zoned sites ranging in size from two to 400 acres. Much of the available land on 44th Street between Broadmoor and the Kent County International Airport has attracted industrial development as have properties further south in Kentwood.

Building within city limits has likewise increased. According to a recent Dun & Bradstreet survey, Grand Rapids showed a 57.9 percent increase in the value of its building permits during the first six months of 1986. Permits issued by the city during that period were valued at fifty-four million dollars, up significantly from 1985's six-month total of thirty-four million dollars. That increase has placed Grand Rapids thirty-first in building activity among the nation's 202 largest cities.

The first settlers who came to Grand Rapids saw their new home as a place of great potential, and they used its resources—wisely or otherwise—to carve for themselves and their city a prosperous future. From these roots has grown a city and a metropolitan area whose potential remains undiminished and whose future continues to look bright.

3
The Wheels of Industry

The wheels of industry have moved the Grand Rapids economy through several distinct and identifiable stages. From 1840 to 1880, the extractive industries—agriculture, milling, lumbering—carried the most economic weight. By 1880, Grand Rapids had become the nation's Furniture City, and the manufacture of residential furniture continued to dominate the local economy for the next forty years. Although office furniture production rose to prominence in the years after the residential furniture industry lapsed into decline, the Grand Rapids economy of today is built on a foundation of diversity, and the many industries located in the metropolitan area have gone from serving a limited local market to supplying an enormous array of manufactured goods to customers across the country and throughout the world.

Among the first manufacturing operations to locate in Grand Rapids were the small establishments that supplied the early settlers' immediate and basic needs—including wagons, harnesses, bedsprings, shoes, barrels in which to store foodstuffs and spirits, and beer to fill the barrels. The first local brewery, in fact, made its appearance in 1836, and beer was produced in the city until 1951, when the increased competition from St. Louis and Milwaukee finally spelled the demise of the Fox DeLuxe Brewing Company, the city's last local brewery.

With its rich forests, nearby farms, and abundant

The wheels of industry have made Grand Rapids a city on the move. Photo by William Hebert

supply of water power, Grand Rapids in its growing years became a milltown, with sawmills, lumberyards, and flour mills lining both banks of the river. Those early mills depended on local foundries for the castings and other iron parts so necessary to their operations. One of the area's first foundries, established by James McCray in 1843, became the Grand Rapids Iron Works two years later and advertised itself as being able to make "every variety of castings for flouring, grist, saw, and other mills on short notice." In 1869, after several changes of ownership and name, the company was still doing business, and had expanded its output to include heavy castings, engines, general machinery, and logging cars.

As the age of steam gradually supplanted the days of water power, foundries like the Valley City Iron Works, established by Adolph Leitelt in 1862, began manufacturing steam boilers and engines. Two years earlier, Joseph Jackoboice opened an iron works that specialized in band saws for the sawmill trade and fire escapes, many of them destined for the flour mills, no doubt, where the dust made fire an ever-present danger.

As the city grew, so did its industries, and the small shops of the 1800s gave way to larger enterprises that turned out a multiplicity of products for ever-expanding markets. The first shoemakers in the city, for example, Maxime and John Ringuette, were small-time entrepreneurs who had to supplement their shoe business earnings with work on the river boats in the summertime. By the 1880s and 1890s, however, the city boasted any number of sizable shoe factories, including the Grand Rapids Felt Boot and Shoe Company, a large operation that produced the kind of warm footwear so practical for the cold and slushy Grand Rapids winters. In 1859 Henry Schmidt started rolling cigars in a small shop on Canal Street. Within thirty years, there were fifty cigar shops in the city employing hundreds of workers, many of whom were women.

Women also found employment in the many knitting works that grew up around the city. The oldest knitting factory was the Star Knitting Works, which was organized in 1892; the longest lasting was the Globe Knitting Works, which was founded in 1897,

Facing page: Grand Rapids factories produce a remarkable diversity of goods. Photo by Jean Hoyle

Above: **Still in business after 125 years, Leitelt (originally Valley City) Iron Works began as a machine shop serving industry and continues to concentrate on heavy machine repair. Pictured here are chief engineer Dan Van Haften (left) and president Herbert Weidenfeller examining a repaired part from a punch press. Photo by William Hebert**

bought out by Aetna Industries in 1952, and moved to Rhode Island four years later. Wartime government contracts in 1917 and 1941 had assured a degree of prosperity to the knitting industry, but by the 1950s, with the rise of foreign competition, the knitting mills disappeared from the local economic scene as did the once-thriving cigar trade.

Another industry which loomed large on the economic horizon and then completely disappeared was bicycle manufacturing. According to a report by the Grand Rapids *Herald* in May 1897, the city's six bicycle factories were turning out 25,000 to 30,000 bicycles a year. In those long-ago days before the advent of an automobile in virtually every American garage, bicycles were a favored mode of transportation —both to get to school or to work and for recreation. Bicycles, in fact, had become a national craze, and bicycle manufacture was one of the city's leading industries. But by 1899, all of the bicycle companies were gone, swallowed up and shut down by a national bicycle trust that had been formed to protect its own interests from the type of competition that was being offered by the Grand Rapids firms.

Furniture, the product on which Grand Rapids' international reputation was built, not only came to dominate the city's economy but spawned dozens of support industries. Companies that produced brass trim, mirrors, mattresses, varnishes, veneers, and woodworking tools became integral parts of the residential furniture industry and continued to thrive even after office furniture rose to importance and the production of residential furniture declined in the years during and after World War I.

The furniture industry also gave a big boost to the local printing and engraving industry. The manufacturers who had turned Grand Rapids into the Furniture Capital of America during the 1880s and 1890s were expanding their markets into new and distant locations. Needing increasingly sophisticated marketing techniques, they turned to local printers for trade catalogs that pictured all of their products in painstaking detail and listed specifications and prices. Other manufacturers of other products also saw the benefit of catalogs as a marketing and advertising tool, and

Below: **Despite the demise of the local bicycle industry, cycling remained a popular pastime. Long cumbersome skirts did not seem to deter this group of cyclists, who posed for a picture in 1902 in Fulton Street Park. The elaborate fountain was removed in 1926. Courtesy, Grand Rapids Public Library**

Facing page: **A noon sing, led by the recreation secretary of the YMCA, took place at the Oliver Machinery Company in 1921. Courtesy, Grand Rapids Public Library**

by 1908 the city's engraving industry ranked fourth in the nation.

Today, printing is a multimillion-dollar industry, and Grand Rapids is the country's fifth largest printing center. Not only is the Grand Rapids graphic arts industry the largest area manufacturing industry in terms of number of establishments, but it also ranks sixth nationwide in the number of employees. The local printing industry ranges across the entire graphic arts spectrum—from small-job printing houses which specialize in business cards and invitations to nationally known color houses and producers of business forms and labels.

With a large and devout Dutch population whose religion has traditionally placed great emphasis on reading theological works, it is not surprising that

Grand Rapids has also become a world Christian religious publishing center. Four religious publishing companies—Baker, Eerdmans, Kregel, and Zondervan—are all headquartered here, and the combined annual sales of their Bibles, encyclopedias, religious classics, inspirational works, and mass market titles run into the millions of volumes.

Even before the turn of the century, an assortment of up-to-date products rolled out of the city's factories and into the nation's homes. Housewives throughout the country constituted a ready market for a number of Grand Rapids-made products—from the Leonard Cleanable Refrigerator, whose manufacturer was the acknowledged industry leader in 1925, to the Bissell Double Action Carpet Sweeper. Patented by Grand Rapids crockery shop owner Melville Bissell in 1876,

the new sweeper was designed primarily for use in the shop to clean up the sawdust scattered by crockery packaging. Customers, seeing how efficiently the new gadget performed, soon became more interested in the sweeper than in the crockery, and to satisfy demand the company began manufacturing the sweeper in a loft above the crockery shop. By 1883, the Bissell Company had abandoned its crockery business entirely and was producing a thousand sweepers a day to be marketed and sold throughout the United States and abroad.

Like the Bissells, other entrepreneurs were quick to seize the opportunity to move their businesses in new directions, taking advantage of changes in the marketplace. As the need for wooden barrels died out, coopers turned their hands to the manufacture of wooden boxes, metal containers, excelsior, and cardboard crates. The Jackoboice family, whose West Side Iron Works once produced band saws and fire escapes, branched out into the manufacture of power hydraulic control equipment. The company later incorporated as the Monarch Road Machinery Company and is today doing business as Monarch Hydraulics, Inc. Another onetime foundry, the Oliver Machinery Company, turned to the manufacture of bread-slicing machines as a way to recoup Depression-era losses. That decision ultimately led to a thriving specialty in the production of wrapping machines and labels.

Local companies continue to adapt their operations and extend their product lines in order to tap potential markets created in the wake of sweeping technological advances. High-tech industries, in fact, are assuming increasing importance in the West Michigan area, and a number of area companies, including Unique Tool in Kentwood, GWI Engineering and Anderson Automation in Grand Rapids, have jumped on the high-tech bandwagon. While continuing to manufacture such products as automotive tools and dies, specialized welding systems, and spray-painting equipment, these companies have branched out into the fast-growing field of automation and robotics. Applications for the high-tech systems emerging from Grand Rapids factories seem virtually limitless, and local products are already being used to weld mufflers to tailpipe assemblies in a California

Above: **Such technological advances as robotics will play an increasingly important role in many Grand Rapids area industries.**

Facing page: **On April 1, 1931, this custom sedan rolled out of the DeVaux-Hall Motor Corporation's Grand Rapids factory. Less than a year later, Grand Rapids' only automobile manufacturer was bankrupt, its assets sold to Continental Motor Corporation of Muskegon. Courtesy, Grand Rapids Public Museum**

factory, to assemble and perform quality checks on washing-machine bases, and to weld office-system panels together in a Georgia factory. According to one recently completed market survey, more than 800 West Michigan companies are likely candidates for some form of robotics or automation—and the area's automotive industry suppliers are certainly among them.

The automotive supply companies of today have their roots in the wagon works and carriage factories of yesterday. In the early 1900s, as automobiles set out on the road that would take them from luxury to necessity, the Harrison Wagon Company and the Belknap Wagon Works shifted the focus of their production to auto manufacturing. Harrison produced its first car in 1905, two years after local auto manufacturer Walter Austin came out with his extravagant prototype for a line of cars that would eventually be more expensive than the Cadillac.

Auto manufacturing rose to such prominence in

Grand Rapids that for many years, beginning in 1910, the city staged its own annual auto shows. Not only were local factories producing their own cars and trucks, during the 1910s and 1920s, but a growing number of support companies were supplying the local industry and its Detroit competitors with such adjunct products as headlight dimmers, safety signals, automobile tops, coil springs, rubber tires, and auto bodies. By 1929 the local Hayes Body Corporation, with contracts to produce auto bodies for Chrysler, Marmon, Reo, and Willys Overland, was Grand Rapids' largest employer, with more than 3,000 workers on its annual five-million-dollar payroll.

Never large enough to pose a serious threat to their competitors in Detroit and Lansing, the Grand Rapids auto makers were out of business by the time of the Great Depression. But the local firms that had made their marks as auto industry suppliers were here to stay. Today, West Michigan remains one of the prime suppliers of auto bodies, tools and dies, plating services, fabricated parts, and trim for Detroit's auto industry. And the three General Motors plants that have set up shop here—G.M. Stamping, which came to the city in 1935; G.M. Diesel, 1944; and Fisher Body Plant No. 2, 1950—have collectively become one of the largest employers in the Grand Rapids metropolitan area.

The automobile was not the only twentieth-century means of transportation to attract the attention of local manufacturers. Aircraft manufacturing, too, seemed to represent an opportunity for profit in the years following World War I. Although the city never did become the major aviation production center that some of its enthusiastic entrepreneurs envisioned, groups of Grand Rapids furniture manufacturers did form consortiums during both world wars to produce airplane parts for the military, and several other local companies made a specialty of aeronautic parts supply. The most successful of these was Lear, Inc., a Chicago firm which set up operations in Grand Rapids in 1943. Purchased nine years later by the Siegler Corporation of Centralia, Illinois, the Grand Rapids-based Lear Siegler, Inc., (LSI) became the largest unit in the parent company's worldwide operations, producing aircraft instruments, automatic flight control systems, gyroscopes and gyroscopic systems, and coupler accessories. By 1966 LSI had become the third largest employer in Grand Rapids and is still one of the largest today.

Throughout the years, Grand Rapids has owed its industrial success and accomplishments to a wide variety of factors: the availability of raw materials and water power; the many skilled craftsmen who have come to the city seeking opportunities to practice their trades; a labor force strongly committed to the work ethic; and a host of entrepreneurs whose ingenuity, inventiveness, and hard work have enabled them to foresee needs and capitalize on the demands of the marketplace. The need for fast and efficient materials handling during World War II, for example, created an enormous demand for the conveyor belts produced by Rapistan (now a division of LSI). During the mid-1930s, General Motors needed a new transformer that would make the assembly-line welding process more efficient. One-time electrical mechanic Russel Kirkhof rose to the occasion and made a fortune, designing a resistance welding transformer that not only revolutionized auto welding, but could also be applied to a wealth of other industries as well.

Other Grand Rapids industrialists have had similar success in gauging their markets and mobilizing the resources essential for profitable industrial ventures. As a result, Grand Rapids has come to enjoy an economy that owes much to diversity. The list of products is long and varied. Juke boxes, brushes, janitorial supplies, baked goods, asphalt shingles, prefabricated houses, books, Bibles, and even board games have all rolled off local assembly lines to be purchased by consumers far and wide.

Diversity continues to paint the city's industrial portrait. Today, every major industrial category except tobacco is represented here, and no single industry accounts for more than 6 percent of the area's total employment. While furniture—primarily the manufacture of office furniture—is the largest single industry in Grand Rapids, furniture making accounts for less than 19 percent of manufacturing jobs and less than 6 percent of all jobs. A number of local manufacturing firms do employ more than a thousand workers each: Steelcase, office furniture, 8,000; GM, transportation equipment, 7,850; Amway, personal and home-care products, 4,500; Lear Siegler, Inc., 2,900; Wolverine World Wide, shoes, 2,000; Keeler Brass, hardware, 1,800; American Seating, institutional and office furniture, 1,000; and Grand Rapids Manufacture, major home appliances, 1,000. But most of the city's workers—about 93 percent—are employed in firms with fewer than fifty employees. Only one-third of all the hourly and salaried workers in the core city and satellite areas are employed in manufacturing, and their jobs are spread out over all industries.

What these figures mean is that Grand Rapids' economy does not depend on a single industry for its prosperity. As a result, Grand Rapids emerged relatively unscathed from the recession of the late 1970s. In fact, while the production of goods in the state as a whole has declined since 1970, Grand Rapids manufacturing employment has risen by more than 18 percent.

Local industries large and small are widely regarded as good places to work, and over the past twenty years less than one percent of the labor force has been idled by strikes. The work force continues to have a large non-union base; 16 percent of local manufacturing companies are unionized. At the same time, organized labor has played an important role in the city's economic stability, and Grand Rapids enjoys its reputation as a place where labor and management have a cooperative rather than an adversarial relationship.

In addition to its diversity, Grand Rapids' industry is noteworthy for its high percentage of privately owned businesses. West Michigan, in fact, has one of the highest concentrations of privately held businesses of any region in the country, and two of the area's largest employers—Amway and Steelcase—remain in private hands.

Privately held or publicly owned, local industries contribute much to the area's overall quality of life. All of the city's cultural institutions, its annual arts festival, and countless civic groups and charitable organizations are the beneficiaries of corporate commitments of time, money, and expertise, all aimed at the betterment of the community.

Because of the area's exceptionally hospitable economic climate and its quality of life, many major companies continue to call the metropolitan Grand Rapids area home. Steelcase, Amway, General Motors, Wolverine World Wide, Bissell, Gerber Products, Squirt, Reynolds Metals, Westinghouse, Guardsman, McDonnell-Douglas, Gulf and Western, and many more all maintain headquarters or substantial branch operations here.

Grand Rapids has not become complacent about its wealth of industry, however, and continues to work actively to attract new business to the area. The Grand Rapids Economic Development Corporation (EDC),

The Autodie Corporation is one of many local companies that supply parts for the automotive industry. Today the largest die-making facility in North America, Autodie uses state-of-the-art equipment to produce complete sets of dies for automobile outer-body shells. Photo by William Hebert

for example, claims credit for hundreds of millions of dollars of business development, at least 12,000 new jobs, and more than a million dollars in both income tax and property tax revenues since 1976. Established in 1971, the EDC has a two-fold mission—to promote new business growth and to retain existing businesses.

One of the most important services provided by the Grand Rapids EDC and thirteen similar EDCs in surrounding communities is help with financing. According to statistics appearing in the *Grand Rapids Press,* the city EDC was responsible between 1979 and 1986 for arranging $241.5 million in bonding for 112 projects that created 5,499 new jobs; at the same time, EDC assistance in obtaining $426.6 million in loans for 225 projects accounted for the creation of 6,747 new jobs and the retention of 26,336 existing jobs.

Tax incentives are another device often used by local governments to encourage the construction of new industries, the expansion and renovation of existing facilities, and the remodeling of obsolete plants. Manufacturers who improve land, buildings, machinery, furniture, fixtures, and the like have become eligible for property tax relief. Eight such tax abatements,

totaling $7.8 million, were granted in Grand Rapids in 1984; the following year saw twenty-nine abatements for $15.7 million. Not only did these programs help enlarge the area's industrial base, according to officials, but they also created 2,000 new jobs.

Other local organizations such as the Grand Rapids Area Chamber of Commerce, The Right Place Program, and the Greater Grand Rapids Economic Area Team (GGREAT) are working to pull private and public forces together to pursue common economic goals. GGREAT, a nonprofit growth alliance made up of representatives of business, labor, education, and government, devotes its energies to attracting new businesses by helping to locate appropriate sites and buildings, arrange financing, and find and train workers. Working with The Right Place Program, GGREAT is also committed to retaining existing employers and helping their businesses expand and grow.

The wheels of industry have been in motion in Grand Rapids for nearly 150 years. Keeping those wheels continually working and in good repair is the best assurance that they won't stand still.

4

Minding the City's Business— The Chamber

Grand Rapids in 1887 was a prosperous young city, doing a volume of more than twenty-four million dollars annually in retail and manufacturing sales. The population stood at approximately 60,000 residents, with hundreds more arriving annually. Furniture manufacturing, the kingpin of the city's economy, was a $5.5 million industry. Some of the city's best known names in mercantiling—Herpolsheimer, Steketee, Houseman, May, Wurzburg—were well established, some in business for twenty years or more. A great diversity of industries and commercial endeavors thrived in the town, from iron foundries and gypsum mining to flour milling, banking, real estate, and construction. There were all the support services that citizens of a healthy and growing city might need, as well as educational institutions, three opera houses, and a variety of musical, literary, and other such societies dedicated to the arts and the pursuit of knowledge and culture.

Always ready for new challenges, the Grand Rapids Area Chamber of Commerce is helping to prepare the city and West Michigan for the twenty-first century. Photo by William Hebert

But there was trouble in River City—in a word, "transportation." As Henry D.C. Van Asmus, a local business leader at the time, put it, Grand Rapids was

Right: The O-Wash-Ta-Nong (the Indian name for the Grand River) Club built this clubhouse on Reeds Lake in 1886. After the clubhouse was destroyed by fire, the club eventually disbanded. Courtesy, Grand Rapids Public Library

Facing page, left: The Masonic Temple on Fulton Street, considered one of the finest in the country when it was built in 1915, was home to thirty-two Masonic lodges and affiliated bodies. Courtesy, Grand Rapids Public Library

Facing page, right: The late U.S. Senator Arthur Vandenberg, pictured, former President Gerald R. Ford, and former Fifth District Congressman Harold Sawyer are among the distinguished political figures who have served on the Grand Rapids Chamber of Commerce's board of directors. Courtesy, Grand Rapids Public Library

"handicapped in the race for commercial supremacy by one great drawback. In the transportation sense, it was a city on a sidetrack." Moreover, other Michigan towns that owed their early existence to lumbering, as did Grand Rapids, were "waning in importance" as depletion of Michigan forests stripped away their economic base. Van Asmus feared the same thing might happen to Grand Rapids because:

unlike Detroit and Jackson, the former the first city in the state and the latter the third, Grand Rapids was not located on the main trunklines of the railroads running through Michigan. Detroit and Jackson grew because of favorable location. Grand Rapids has maintained its proud position in spite of a handicap.

The fact that the city was not located at the center or even on the periphery of a transportation hub was a costly problem for manufacturers shipping their goods to buyers throughout the country. By the 1880s the primary means of transporting goods in and out of the city was by railroad, and the freight charges from Grand Rapids to the Atlantic seaboard were higher than for other Michigan cities.

The 1880s were the heyday of the railroad barons, and the exploitation of shippers was rampant. The railroads charged what the traffic would bear—exorbitant prices in one case, next to nothing in the next, depending on competition from other roads. Short-haul rates were often much higher than long-haul rates, and most shippers had no recourse but to pay. The situation was a national outrage, and shippers and organized groups such as boards of trade were clamoring for relief.

Besides wanting equitable freight rates, many Grand Rapids businessmen, including Van Asmus, thought that making the Grand River navigable from Grand Haven to Grand Rapids for large lake-going ships would give the city direct access to Lake Michigan, and would provide another economical means of shipping Grand Rapids' goods, particularly to western markets.

Determined to avert the threat of economic derailment because of the city's transportation problems, and believing that a formally organized group could affect and even guide the economic fortunes of the city, Van Asmus set about organizing local businessmen into a Grand Rapids Board of Trade, the original

name for today's Chamber of Commerce. The idea of establishing a Board of Trade did not originate in Grand Rapids, but was part of a national movement in which similar groups were being founded throughout the country.

The first meeting of the Grand Rapids Board of Trade was October 18, 1887; the organization received its charter from the state three weeks later, on November 8. One hundred forty-seven members signed the charter. Officers were elected, and Van Asmus was named secretary, the only paid position.

Except for an interim in the mid-1890s, Van Asmus was secretary for seventeen of the Board's first twenty-four years. One early account states, "For the first few months . . . Mr. Van Asmus gave only part of his time to his duties as secretary. But by the end of the first year, activities had increased to such an extent that it was necessary for him to devote full time to the work." The job paid $1,200 a year and, according to the minutes of February 1887, the secretary was allowed thirteen dollars for the services of an office boy.

Businesses that joined the Board paid a fifteen-dollar initiation fee and annual dues of ten dollars.

During the "Van Asmus years," the dedication, foresight, and ambitions of the secretary and Board of Trade members laid the cornerstone of the organization—commitment: commitment to progress and economic prosperity, commitment to members' interests, commitment to Grand Rapids and its future.

Just as today's Chamber of Commerce committees reflect the primary interests of Chamber members, so did the committees of the Board of Trade. Committees established by that first Board were appeals, arbitration, transportation, grain and produce, lumber, provisions, printing, statistics, legislation, auditing, public improvements, and municipal affairs.

Committee members served in a voluntary capacity, another tradition that has continued for 100 years. On the occasion of the organization's fiftieth anniversary, E.A. Stowe, editor of the *Tradesman* and a charter member and past president of the Board, remarked, "It was wonderful what men in those days would do without being paid for it. . . . Grand Rapids is forever indebted for the great deal of voluntary service it received in the past."

Stowe also recounted some of the difficulties that the Board of Trade confronted in getting the railroads to lower their freight rates from Grand Rapids. The freight rates were computed on a percentage based on mileage. Kalamazoo and other Michigan cities paid a lower rate than Grand Rapids because they were on the main trunklines. While Kalamazoo paid 93 percent, according to Stowe, Grand Rapids paid 96 percent. And so the Board of Trade petitioned the railroads to grant Grand Rapids shippers the same rate as Kalamazoo. The negotiations were a long, drawn-out process fraught with many setbacks and frustrations. At last, recalled Stowe, the committee received a telegram, "Your request granted. Kalamazoo raised to Grand Rapids basis." That wasn't quite the solution the Board of Trade had in mind, and negotiations with the railroads continued.

Although the government had created the Interstate Commerce Commission (ICC) in 1887 and attempted to regulate railroad rates, the power of the railroads was so great as to render the ICC virtually impotent, and rate charges still depended largely on the deals individual shippers were able to negotiate with their carrier roads.

The Grand Rapids episode took three long years of concerted effort, but in the end the negotiators finally did get a reduced freight rate. Years later, furniture manufacturer John Widdicomb told Van Asmus that the reduced rate saved the Grand Rapids furniture industry hundreds of thousands of dollars.

Van Asmus and committee members that first year spent innumerable hours compiling statistics for a booklet called "Grand Rapids As It Is," which listed facts and figures about the area and extolled the advantages of living and doing business in Grand Rapids. Several thousand copies of the booklet were mailed to colleges and universities, banks, publications, libraries, potential investors, and other appropriate parties and business interests in towns and cities in the East, in an effort to persuade manufacturers and entrepreneurs to locate their businesses and industries in Grand Rapids.

The Board of Trade that year also embarked on what proved to be a long-term but futile campaign for a federal dredging project that would make the Grand River navigable for good-sized cargo ships. Hope, however vain, kept the issue alive until 1917 when the Board's Grand River Improvement Committee reported that the U.S. Army Corps of Engineers recommended abandoning the project. Only a few years later the issue was moot as the automobile entered the transportation scene and trucking gave manufacturers cost-efficient access to all national markets.

In the Board's second year, the federal government invited seventeen Central and South American countries to a conference to foster better trade relations between the United States and Latin America, and to induce the Latin Americans to channel to the United States trade dollars then going to Europe. The conference also included trips to several prominent trade and manufacturing centers in the country.

"It became the ambition of our Board," stated Secretary Van Asmus' annual report, "to have Grand Rapids known at home and abroad as one of these prominent cities." A telegram was dispatched to Washington inviting the Latin Americans to Grand Rapids. Through the influence of such prominent local business and political figures as Edwin Uhl, and on the strength of Grand Rapids' reputation as a furniture manufacturing center, the invitation was accepted by U.S. Secretary of State Charles Blaine. It was a "Red Letter Day," reported the secretary, and ". . . there is no question but that the result of their visit will divert a large share of the trade now controlled by our competitors across the Atlantic to our own home market."

From the first, the Board concentrated much effort on promoting Grand Rapids as a convention city, a task it has never relinquished. In the April 1889 minutes, it is noted that the convention committee had made arrangements to "escort" delegates of the National Woman Suffrage Association on a visit through some of the furniture factories.

Over the years the Board of Trade worked with city government and other civic leaders to promote the city, bring new businesses and manufacturers to the area, retain existing businesses, and always to formulate and implement plans to enhance the Grand Rapids business climate and the city as a whole.

In 1898 the Board's industrial committee was instrumental in bringing to the city two canning factories, a manufacturer of "cheap piano stools," and a manufacturer of a patented cabinet clamp. In 1900 the Board raised $2,500 and bought land to entice Keeler Brass of Middleville to move its facilities to Grand Rapids. The Pere Marquette Railroad shops were located in the city in 1909 after a five-year-long campaign by the Board's industrial committee. The Wolverine Button Company, the Van-L-Commercial Car Company, Grand Rapids Hosiery, and the Decatur Car Company were all manufacturing concerns brought to Grand Rapids through the efforts of the Board of Trade.

In 1913 the Hot Blast Feather Company, a name later changed to the Grand Rapids Bedding Company, located in the city. Blackmer Rotary Pump of Petoskey moved its operations to Grand Rapids in 1923. And, in a decided coup for West Michigan, General Motors came to town in 1936. The establishment of that first plant eventually led to three more, making the auto manufacturer for many years the city's largest employer.

Other committees were just as active as the industrial committee. Good roads was responsible for developing the East Beltline in 1927 and applying pressure

for a north/south expressway. Construction on the latter was begun in 1954, and continued into the mid-1960s, with the completion of an east/west, north/south interstate freeway system.

It was through the efforts of the aeronautics committee, working with the city and county, that the Kent County airport was built (1926), airmail service instituted (1933), and the airport named an international airport and port of entry with a U.S. customs office (1976).

Annual outings were a Board of Trade tradition. This one, in 1904, had U.S. Congressman T.E. Burton on board to impress upon him the importance of a government dredging project to make the Grand River navigable for larger vessels. Courtesy, Grand Rapids Public Library

Right: **Downtown Grand Rapids was photographed in 1920 from Crescent Park on Bostwick Avenue. Courtesy, Grand Rapids Public Museum**

Facing page: **This parade along Division Avenue marked the kick-off of Cleanup Week, an annual event sponsored by the Chamber of Commerce in the 1950s. Courtesy, Grand Rapids Public Library**

The "healthier city" subcommittee of the municipal affairs committee started investigating in 1905 the possibility of getting Lake Michigan water to Grand Rapids; this plan was finally realized in 1939-1940 under Mayor George Welsh. Another municipal affairs subcommittee, the "city of conveniences committee," under Samuel Ranck of the Grand Rapids Public Library, developed and implemented a plan to renumber houses and businesses on the block system. Up to that time, address numbers had been assigned according to an inadequate system held over from village days. Citizens were averse to giving up the familiar and it took Ranck and the board five years to persuade the city to adopt the rational and orderly plan; finally, in 1911, the big change came. Division Avenue was deemed the east/west dividing line, Fulton Street the north/south dividing line and numbers advanced out from those starting points.

The Board's interests and programs were many and diverse. To keep Calvin College from moving to another West Michigan city, the Board helped raise $10,000 to buy ten acres of land for the school. The Board also endorsed proposals for a new city charter in 1905, and formed the Kent County Farm Bureau and the Furniture Market Association. In 1922 it was a Board committee that established the Grand Rapids Foundation, an organization that has, in its sixty-four years, put back into the community many millions of dollars. Grand Rapids was the forty-sixth community in the nation to establish a community foundation.

The Chamber's own foundation, the Greater Grand Rapids Chamber Foundation, was established in 1972 for the explicit purpose of supporting the area's economic climate and business community. The non-profit organization underwrites economic and career education programs in area schools and colleges, an activity that has benefited more than 10,000 teachers and students.

The foundation also funds Leadership Grand Rapids and Silent Observer, a program which encourages individual and community involvement in combating and solving local crime.

In 1911 the Board of Trade reorganized and changed its name to the Association of Commerce. This name was retained until 1940 when it was again changed to the Chamber of Commerce; "Greater" was added to the name in 1958. One more change took place in 1975 when the chamber became the

Grand Rapids Area Chamber of Commerce.

But whatever the name, the goals have been the same. From public safety and health to an enhanced cultural life and economic growth, the chamber's constant concern has been for the good of its members and the community. There have been failures as well as successes, but the leadership of every decade has pointed with pride to the fact that the organization has always been in the forefront in recommending and supporting community development.

In the early 1940s the chamber helped secure World War II defense contracts for local manufacturers and in the latter part of the decade promoted expansion of the airport. The big issues in the late 1950s were relocation of the airport to its present site in Cascade Township and urban renewal, which continued on into the 1960s. Efforts to rebuild the downtown did not stop a gradual decline of the downtown business section. Since the 1970s, the chamber has focused on

joining forces with the city and other interested groups in revitalizing the downtown and preparing Grand Rapids, and West Michigan, for continued growth and prosperity on into the twenty-first century.

Always seeking innovative ways to meet new challenges, the chamber continues to add new services that are directly aimed at continued success for Grand Rapids and its environs. One such service is the Small Business Division, founded in 1981. More than 95 percent of all Grand Rapids chamber members are businesses of fifty or fewer employees, and the Small Business Division meets the specific needs of those businesses. Entrepreneurship has always been a strong element in American business, but during the last ten to fifteen years the number of small businesses nationwide has increased at an unprecedented rate and the trend seems destined to continue well into the next century. The Small Business Division and its volunteer arm, the Small Business Council, recognize that trend

and continue to add services and programs that address problems and concerns confronting small business owners.

The division's services and programs are available to non-members as well as to chamber members. Basically, its services fall into four categories: requests for information and preliminary assistance, which includes one-on-one counseling; seminars and workshops; small business promotional activities such as Minority Business Month; and advocacy.

The division has put particular effort into aiding and promoting minority business, and its Minority Business Month in the spring highlights the scope and achievements of local minority entrepreneurs.

The Right Place Program, begun in 1985, is one of the most ambitious and comprehensive enterprises of the chamber's career. The program works with GGREAT toward the goal of adding 15,000 new jobs, beyond the normal projected growth of 23,000 jobs, to the West Michigan economic base by 1989. The

Above: **Ronald Reagan was the keynote speaker at the Chamber of Commerce's annual meeting in 1960. Courtesy, Grand Rapids Public Library**

Right: **Minority-owned businesses are becoming an increasingly significant aspect of the local economic scene. Tim Turner, former Ford Motor Company executive, owns and operates Plainfield Lincoln-Mercury, one of two Lincoln-Mercury dealerships in Grand Rapids. Photo by William Hebert**

Facing page: **Alex and Alice Lin, originally from Taiwan, recently opened their second Chinatown Restaurant, located on 28th Street S.E. Photo by William Hebert**

program is funded by investments from the private sector and local governments, and it is guided by a volunteer committee of business and government leaders, all of whom are convinced, and committed to prove, that Grand Rapids is indeed "the right place."

Leadership Grand Rapids, instituted in 1985, is a year-long program which identifies new, emerging, and potential leaders, bringing them together in monthly seminar settings to learn about their community and its particular needs, and strengthening individual leadership abilities. By creating a never-ending pool of leadership talent, this program assures the community of high-quality leadership necessary for the growth and development of the metropolitan area for years to come.

And that growth and development shows every promise of continuing unabated into the future. The commitment of the founders of the old Board of Trade has held steady over the last 100 years. There is no reason to think it should not hold for another century.

A statement in the chamber's seventy-fifth anniversary *Bulletin* is as true today as it was twenty-five years ago:

The Chamber . . . does not claim in any sense that it has been solely responsible for the industrial, commercial and civic progress of Greater Grand Rapids. It does assert, in all due modesty, that it has played a large part in shaping the city's destinies—thanks to the efforts of many dedicated citizens. . . .

With the Chamber for 100 Years

Twenty-five of the Grand Rapids firms that joined the Board of Trade in 1887 are still Chamber members today.

American Seating Company
Barclay, Ayers & Bertsch
Bissell, Inc.
Bixby Office Supply Company
Consumers Power Company
Coye's, Inc.
Crosby and Henry
Davenport College
Dun & Bradstreet
Groskopf's, Inc.
Herkner Jewelry Company
Herpolsheimer's
Leitelt Iron Works
May's of Michigan
MichCon
Michigan Bell Telephone Company
S.A. Mormon Company
Old Kent Bank & Trust Company
Preusser Jewelers
F. Rainiville Company
Siegel Jewelry Company
Steketee's
Stow & Davis
Waddell Manufacturing Company
West Michigan Printing Company

5 Government by the People

Government is a contrivance of human wisdom to provide for human wants. —Edmund Burke, Reflections on the Revolution in France

In the 1820s, "government" in the Grand River valley meant that far distant entity, the United States federal government, for Michigan was not yet even a state, but part of the Territory of Michigan. The federal government's presence was most evident in its relation with area Indians, but beyond that, neither it nor the territorial government intruded to any noticeable degree into life in the tiny settlement on the Grand River.

Beginning in the 1830s, townships and counties were established according to long-standing precepts. Settlers and land developers acquired land from the federal government (land offices were in White Pigeon, Ionia, and Kalamazoo), and for most of them, such transactions just about took care of any brush they might have with formalized government.

The handful of settlers were self-sufficient in their daily lives, and the minimal government-provided services and improvements of the times were not readily available on the outer reaches of the frontier. The Grand River valley pioneers relied on the sweat of their own brows and the good offices of their neighbors to provide whatever rudiments of civilization they were able to achieve.

This cityscape captures the grandeur and clear skies of Grand Rapids. Photo by John D. Strauss

73

Right: The landmark Kent County building did not survive the urban renewal of the 1960s. Courtesy, Grand Rapids Public Library

Facing page: Designed and engraved by City Clerk Aaron Turner, the Grand Rapids City Seal was officially adopted by the City Council on June 25, 1850. The motto, *Motu Viget,* means "strength in activity." Courtesy, Grand Rapids Public Library

By 1834, however, circumstances overtook the settlement and local government by necessity reared its authoritative head.

Kent County was established by federal survey (and named for James Kent, a well-known New York state jurist of the period) in 1831. The settlement on the east bank of the river was known variously as Kent or Grand Rapids, depending on whether a resident lived in Louis Campau's plat (Grand Rapids) or Lucius Lyon's plat (Kent). With the survey, the village was officially recognized as Kent and designated the county seat. The township of Kent was not established until three years later and encompassed all of the county which lay to the south of the Grand River. The township of Walker, organized in 1837, was comprised of that portion of the county which lay to the north of the river. From these two townships, the village, and subsequently the city of Grand Rapids, was

carved. The names of both the village and the township of Kent were officially changed to Grand Rapids in 1842.

The township board was the primary local governing unit, although the village also had a village board with seven trustees. Township officials paid bounties of varying amounts, from two dollars to five dollars each, depending, presumably, on the state of the township coffers and the degree of the scourge, for every "wolf scalp" brought in. They also issued marriage licenses and formulated and passed such regulations as were needed to deal with the issues which affected both village and township life. The village board's jurisdiction was confined to strictly village matters, such as appropriating property for streets, levying and collecting taxes for village use, and passing laws prohibiting horse racing, discharging firearms, or maintaining gaming houses within the village limits.

Revenues were small, and so, by necessity, were expenditures. The township collected assessments and called for commute money from residents to pay for maintenance of public "highways" and roads. Residents unable to pay in cash paid instead in work days on the roads. Even so, roads were crude affairs scrabbled from the wilderness, often by the farmers, homesteaders, or businessmen past whose property they ran.

There are no accurate census figures for the valley for the years before 1845. Letters and other documents indicate that fewer than fifty lived in the village in the early 1830s, but the population increased steadily each year as new families moved into the area.

Between 1833 and 1836, years historian Albert Baxter calls "the years of occupation," cheap, rich land, abundant water, and other bountiful resources brought both settlers and land speculators to the area in a rush. A year later, the nation was brought to its knees by the Panic of 1837, a financial crisis that sent banks and businesses crashing down and left the common man poor or poorer. The crash broke the land speculation fever in the Grand River valley and settlement slowed for a few years. But the financial crisis seemed to have created a permanent indigent class, for township records indicate that each year thereafter, funds were voted for support of the poor.

In 1838, the village incorporated. By 1845, the year of the first census, there were 1,510 residents in the township, and Grand Rapids published a small brochure to send back East to entice settlers to this new land of plenty.

The village was now a proper village indeed, with a thriving community which boasted among its commercial enterprises fifteen stores, three flour mills, pail factories, tanneries, a woolen mill, a sash and door factory, a salt works, a plaster mill, saddlers, shoe cobblers, tailors, hatters, tin-, copper-, and blacksmiths, two printing offices, three public houses, plus four churches, three physicians and about a dozen lawyers.

In 1850, the village of Grand Rapids, under a new charter, became the city of Grand Rapids. The governing body was called the Common Council, and elected officials were one alderman from each of the city's five wards, and the mayor.

For the next forty years, city government played catch-up, a mighty struggle to provide adequate services for a population that doubled every ten years.

Streets, water, lighting, public transportation, police and fire protection, public health and all the other issues and problems of a growing municipality were dealt with as the times dictated. The charter was amended or revised on several occasions, the first as early as 1851, and each time the boundaries of the city were extended, east and west, north and south.

It was not until 1888 that the city fathers got around to building a city hall. In the very early days, there was no central location for village offices. The Board of Trustees met wherever it happened to be convenient—a hotel, a trustee's home or place of business, or at the clerk's office, which was also his place of business.

After the first few years, offices were established in rented quarters and moved whenever the space got too small and inconvenient. Efforts to get a city hall began as early as 1854. Over the years, various sites were purchased for the building, but for one reason or another sold off, and then the process began again. Finally, in 1883, lots at the northeast corner of Ottawa and Lyon streets (now the site of Union Bank parking lot) were purchased, and in 1885 the cornerstone was

In 1865 the Kent Street Company of volunteer firemen put out fires with a hand pumper. Courtesy, Grand Rapids Public Library

In 1865 the Kent Street Company of volunteer firemen put out fires with a hand pumper. Courtesy, Grand Rapids Public Library

laid. The building was dedicated in 1888 and used continuously until it was razed during the urban renewal of the 1960s.

A similar history attends the building of the county courthouse. In 1833, two years after the village of Kent was named the county seat, stakes were set in what is now Fulton Street (Veterans Memorial Park) for a county courthouse. The courthouse, a two-story frame building, was built in 1838 and used until it burned in 1844. A second structure, this time a small, one-room, single-story building, replaced the original and served until 1852 as courthouse, meeting hall, and site of the county fairs. By 1852, the building was too small for county use, and county offices, like the city offices, were often at the home or place of business of the clerk, treasurer, or supervisor. The court and board of supervisors occupied rented quarters at half a dozen different locations between 1852 and 1889. A fire at one of the sites in 1860 destroyed most of the county records.

There was much contention over whether the courthouse should be located on the east or west side of the river. At one point, the question was put to the electorate, which voted for the west side, but even the voice of the people did not seem to settle the question for the supervisors.

Not until 1887 did they pick a location—about two blocks north and west of the city hall site—and proceed with plans to build. The cornerstone was laid July 4, 1889, the building dedicated July 4, 1892. Like City Hall, the courthouse served until it was swept away by the winds of urban renewal.

By 1890, Grand Rapids was a city of 64,000 people, with a growing national reputation as the home of quality, mass-produced residential furniture. Residents and officials took note that visitors found the city had not outgrown its "country village ways," perhaps an allusion to its valiant but not too successful struggle to provide services for a constantly growing population. Still, the city could boast of its affluent neighborhoods and gracious homes, and take pride in a growing sense of its destiny.

With the erection of their new government buildings, city and county government entered a period of orderly record keeping and responsibility. As the city's population increased and geographic boundaries extended ever outward, the number of wards likewise increased—from the original five to twelve by 1892. The

Left: Just as motor vehicles replaced the city's horse-drawn patrol wagons, also known as "Black Marias," a new police headquarters at Monroe and Michigan replaced the old brick and stone structure that once stood at the corner of Lyon and Campau. Courtesy, Grand Rapids Public Library

Below: The Grand Rapids police force posed for the camera in 1917. Courtesy, Grand Rapids Public Library

Right: The old City Hall building came down in the 1960s despite a last-ditch effort by some preservationists to save at least the clock tower. Courtesy, Grand Rapids Public Library

Facing page: Grand Rapids is not a major stop on the national campaign trail, but presidential hopefuls have spoken here from time to time. On January 23, 1920, General Leonard Wood, seeking the Republican presidential nomination, posed in front of Union Depot before speaking to 300 Republicans. Unsuccessful in his presidential quest, Wood was named governor general of the Philippine Islands in 1921. Courtesy, Grand Rapids Public Library

Common Council was becoming unwieldy, and mutterings of government reform rippled through the public and political consciousness for the next two decades, causing a moderate stir but never inciting overt action.

Charter revision commissions came and went. A couple of scandals rocked the government and dragged through the courts, one for six bitter years. But at last, in 1916, all the elements—public pressure, political awareness, official willingness, and dire need—were in place. The proposed charter reduced the number of wards from twelve to three, with all the commissioners elected at large. Although bitterly opposed by the working class, which rightly claimed that the provisions would destroy its power base, the charter did pass by a vote of 7,692 to 6,021. The new charter called for complete reorganization of the government.

A commission/manager form of city government was a popular notion in government circles across the

country in that second decade of the twentieth century. Grand Rapids was one of the first major cities in the United States to adopt such a form, and it has endured, with many modifications, to the present.

The 1916 charter provided that the city be divided into three wards, with seven commissioners elected at large, and the commissioners chose the mayor from among their own number.

The system was not always, or perhaps not often, serene. Almost immediately, the charter became subject to amendments, the first in 1923, which provided that two commissioners be elected from each ward rather than at large, and the mayor be elected at large. There were many vacillations between a strong-manager, figurehead-mayor concept or a strong mayor and limited powers for the manager, but there were never successful challenges to that form of government. Factions waxed and waned, party politics wove their usual tangled web, and political upheaval jolted the system from time to time.

The city survived the dark days of the Great Depression under the innovative leadership of George W.

Welsh. A controversial but memorable politician, Welsh served the city as alderman in 1914, city manager from 1929 to 1938, and mayor from 1938 to 1949, when he resigned, amidst a brouhaha between warring political factions.

As city manager, Welsh developed a welfare system that gave jobs to the city's jobless, shelter to the homeless, and food to the hungry. He persuaded the voters to pass a $1.5 million bond issue to build a civic auditorium, a project which put scores of men to work, and as mayor, he brought Lake Michigan water to Grand Rapids.

In the late 1950s, the city embarked on a massive downtown rebuilding program, leveling forty acres of bricks and mortar. The public and private sectors together re-created a major section of downtown Grand Rapids. Despite scattered opposition to the tearing down of such historic structures as City Hall and the County Building, urban renewal went forward: spanking new city and county, state, and federal office buildings as well as commercial buildings rose from the rubble of old Grand Rapids.

These Heartside buildings, located at One Ionia and Seven Ionia, have been restored and in use for nearly a decade. The rest of the block is scheduled for restoration in late 1987. Photo by Wes Morton, courtesy, Bruce J. Poppen

Thus was started a rejuvenation program that continues today and gives every indication of going strong for years to come. City government has vigorously promoted such enterprises and in many instances provided tax abatements and other incentives that induced private investors to bank on the future of downtown Grand Rapids.

While the downtown attracted a great deal of long overdue attention, neighborhoods throughout the city were becoming cantankerous about the lack of attention they seemed to get from City Hall. It was a restlessness that was endemic throughout the nation, and led, in the late 1960s, to the rise of neighborhood associations.

The flight to the suburbs left cities with a reduced

tax base which in turn led to reductions of city services. Borrowing from the political lessons learned in the 1960s during the civil rights movement, neighborhood groups realized that "clout," an ability to influence local government, could come only through organized effort.

In Grand Rapids, neighborhood groups formed around a variety of issues—increased crime, redlining, deteriorating housing, preservation of historic landmarks, and more equitable distribution of city resources. The first association to form was Ottawa Hills Neighbors Association in 1970, followed a year later by Heritage Hill Association, and a year after that, Eastown Community Association. Funding for the associations came in those early years from residents themselves, corporations and local foundations, and such federal programs as CETA and the Urban Corps, and later from community development block grants.

The movement eventually led to coalitions among associations to deal with issues that crossed neighborhood boundaries, such as relocation of fire stations, crime, and housing code enforcement. Out of those coalitions came CONA, the Council of Neighborhood Associations. The council, with a small paid staff, serves as a liaison agency between neighborhood groups and the city's community development department. The CONA board of directors is made up of members from the individual associations.

Today there are twenty-five neighborhood associations in the city, encompassing about 90 percent of the city's neighborhoods. The groups have had considerable success in exerting influence on city government, and in developing and maintaining control over events in their own districts. The associations have proven, too, to be a valuable training ground for members to move up into the political mainstream. Several city commissioners and at least one mayor, Gerald Helmholdt, got their political start in neighborhood associations.

If the city government process was often stormy, the city/county relationship was mostly, even bitterly, antagonistic. The city, with more than half the county's population but fewer than a third of the votes on the county board of supervisors, found itself grossly under-represented in county government. Aggrieved city officials constantly charged that the small-city and rural supervisors, who controlled a majority vote on the board, had no concept of the needs and trials of the larger urban area and unfailingly voted the out-county's interests on every issue. For their part, the out-county supervisors complained that the city imperialistically gobbled up land in huge chunks, obliterating the distinctive identities of small communities, and totally disregarded the wishes of county citizens and governmental units alike in any matter that was contrary to the city's ambitions and designs.

The situation was not resolved until 1968, when reapportionment was mandated by the state Supreme Court. The decision assured the city of representation proportionate to its population on the county board. At that time, the county adopted a commission form of government and shortly thereafter renamed the body the Kent County Board of Commissioners. Since that time, even though there are still sharp differences on certain issues, the spirit of cooperation between city and county governments is vastly improved.

Some of the discord and rivalry between the smaller cities and Grand Rapids has been eased by the founding of the Association of Grand Rapids Area Governments. A body without authority, AGRAG is, nevertheless, a forum in which mayors and other city officials from Grand Rapids and neighboring communities can air their differences and confront potential problems before they become divisive issues.

In addition to being the county seat, Grand Rapids is the regional hub of West Michigan; it was developed early on as the legal and governmental center for the west side of the state.

Before Muskegon County was established in 1859 and Ottawa County in 1837, these areas belonged to Kent County, and voters came to Grand Rapids from as far away as the villages of Muskegon and Grand Haven to cast their ballots in all but local elections. Judicial proceedings for the area commenced soon after Kent County was established in 1836, although there was no federal court here until 1860. Previously, the only federal court in the state was in Detroit, but in 1836 Congress divided the state into eastern and western federal judicial districts. Grand Rapids was the seat for the western half of the state until 1878,

STATE OF MICHIGAN

and the first judge, Solomon Withey, was appointed by President Abraham Lincoln. In 1878, judicial business for the Upper Peninsula became sufficient to establish a federal judicial district for that region. The Grand Rapids district was named the southern district, and Marquette was established as the northern district.

In addition to being a judicial and governmental center, the city is, and has always been, the legal center for West Michigan. There are approximately 1,300 attorneys in town offering expertise in specialties and sub-specialties across the spectrum of legal services. Several of the state's leading law firms are Grand Rapids-based, and a number of Detroit's largest firms have branch offices in Grand Rapids.

Nowadays, the cluster of official buildings—federal, state, county, city, police, and courts—concentrated on Monroe and Ottawa avenues, centralizes the governmental units in one geographic sphere. Begun in 1966 with the dedication of the Hall of Justice, the complex grew, building by building, until dedication of the state building in 1976.

The Gerald R. Ford Federal Building houses all the federal offices and courts for western Michigan. State courts and offices are in the handsome State Office Building across the street from the Federal Building on Ottawa. The city and county buildings on Calder Plaza just west of the Federal Building, and the police and courts in the Hall of Justice at 300 Monroe N.W., complete the complex.

Although the county office building is part of the downtown governmental complex, other county facilities are concentrated on the city's near northeast side. The jail and sheriff's department, juvenile court, and Child Haven, a shelter for neglected children, are in close proximity to Kent Oaks, a 56-bed mental hospital, and Kent Community Hospital for treatment of chronic disease and substance abuse.

In spite of the turmoil and sometimes tumultuous proceedings, area government on the whole has been relatively stable. Each new decade has brought its own crises, but the government always met the challenges, sometimes in ways surprisingly avant-garde for a city that has always had a national reputation for being arch-conservative.

One of the city's most important assets is the remarkable cooperation between government and business for the welfare of the community. Knowing that a healthy business community is the lifeblood of a healthy city, municipal government makes a concerted effort to accommodate the needs and interests of local business and industry. Business leaders in turn bring to the partnership a generous contribution of time, money, and leadership to help keep the city and region on a forward-moving course.

One of the more recent and significant ventures brought forth by this coalition is the Greater Grand Rapids Economic Area Team (GGREAT) under the auspices of the city, and The Right Place Program, established by the Grand Rapids Area Chamber of Commerce. From a recent study that indicates that the Grand Rapids area in the next two to three decades will be the most economically viable and the fastest-growing region in Michigan, this committee of government officials and civic and business leaders is developing an economic development master plan that will continue the region's pattern of growth into the twenty-first century.

Grand Rapids', and thus West Michigan's, bright future owes much to the quality of leadership it has enjoyed in present and past decades.

Facing page: **The State of Michigan Building is part of the downtown government complex that was built during the urban renewal project of the late 1960s. Photo by J. Phillip Haven**

Above: **The Grand Rapids City Building, part of the downtown civic center complex, overlooks Calder Plaza. Photo by David Jackson**

6 Getting Here, Going There

As the leading metropolis on the west side of the state, Grand Rapids is at the center of a transportation network that fans out over the Midwest, making the city easily accessible by air, rail, and highway to travelers and shippers.

It was not always so. The concept was that one didn't pass through Grand Rapids on the way to someplace else, and one didn't happen on the place by accident. If you ended up in Grand Rapids, it was by design, because it just was not on the way to any place else.

The first Europeans to come to the area, the trappers and traders, came by canoe or bateaux or on foot along the Indian trails. The early settlers simply widened those Indian footpaths to carry wagons and teams, arduously hacking away trees, shrubs, and undergrowth as they moved forward. Those crude highways were, says historian Albert Baxter, "devious, winding ways, hard roads to travel."

As more people moved into the area, roads, such as they were, were developed to link farm to farm and farms to villages. In the early days of the township, settlers were charged a commute tax on the roads running past their property. Most paid in labor, and that constituted the sum total of the work done on those early roads.

Delightful summer days and festive occasions such as the Fourth of July and Celebration on the Grand always bring out the hot air balloons. Photo by John D. Strauss

85

Right: Before the turn of the century, water was sprinkled from these carts to help keep the dust down on unpaved streets. Courtesy, Grand Rapids Public Library

Facing page: Built in 1871, the Fallasburg covered bridge crosses the Flat River east of Grand Rapids near Lowell, and is one of the few remaining preserved covered bridges in the state. Photo by Larry Heydenburg

Settlers began arriving in the early 1830s, but there was neither money nor plan for upkeep of public roads. The lack of public money for roads prompted the rise of private companies that built and maintained toll roads. One of the first and most important of such roads was the Kalamazoo-Grand Rapids plank road which was the primary route south for thirteen years.

The public objected to the tolls, but it was not until the 1890s that the Common Council began buying the roads within its jurisdiction and abolishing the tolls. A few of the private toll road companies managed to hold out for six or seven years into the twentieth century.

Even in the village of Grand Rapids, main roads were little more than well-defined ruts, hazardous to teamsters and pedestrians alike. Within the village, "for nearly twenty years," says Baxter, "the teamster chose his route over unfenced lands, through bushes and past the bad places, picking the best way." And nowhere within the village, he adds, was there a truly passable east and west wagon road.

Getting to the village might have been a hardship, but getting about once there was not an easy matter either. Muddy streets presented continuing difficul-

ties from the early days of the village, and attempts to resolve the problem occupied village trustees for many years. From the chronicles of one early resident comes this description:

In the late fall and early spring Monroe street, from Division to Canal street, became literally a river of mud. This mud was frequently from six to eight inches deep the whole width of the street, and thick like hasty pudding. From the summit at Luce's Block the descent was much more rapid than now, and in the early morning could be seen unmistakable evidences that, during the night, the whole viscous mass of mud to the depth indicated, had, like an immense Swiss glacier, moved bodily down the hill, ten, fifteen or twenty feet.

Despite the digging of drainage ditches and other abortive measures to alleviate the woeful condition of city roadways, nearly unpassable muddy streets in wet weather and dusty streets in dry weather were a persistent and unrelenting municipal problem. Not until 1856 were there serious and continuing efforts to begin to pave the streets, usually with cobblestone. Interestingly, Trowbridge Street and North Avenue still have sections of cobblestone street. In the 1870s, flat blocks of pine and later cedar replaced the stone. The wood proved to be a durable street material and certainly much less detrimental to sacroiliac, foot, and hoof.

Sidewalks were no less a problem than the streets. Business people and residents usually built wooden plank sidewalks outside their own establishments. As the city became more prosperous, and providing sidewalks became a municipal function, wooden sidewalks were built throughout the city and stone sidewalks appeared in the downtown business section and around government buildings. In the 1890s, a new building material, called cement or "artificial stone," was being experimented with countrywide as a possible answer to that age-old problem—how to protect the walking populace from the inconveniences of dust and mire underfoot. The walks, molded in blocks "on the spot," led builders and pedestrians alike to hope for walkways of durability, even permanence.

Long-distance travel was accomplished by horseback, wagon, and stagecoach. Stagecoach lines were operating east, west, and south by 1841. Not until the 1850s were there lines running north. The first coaches were rude affairs, fashioned from farm wagons. Passengers were accommodated by a board seat laid over springs; canvas, stretched over bent frames and painted to make it somewhat waterproof, offered some protection from the elements. The Concord, specifically designed as a stagecoach and truly luxurious in comparison to the wagons, was introduced in the 1850s. Travel by stagecoach was subject to the hazards of bad weather and bad roads, but it thrived until replaced by the iron horse.

If land travel was tedious at best, river travel was easy street in comparison. The Grand River had been the principal avenue through the region for the Indians as well as the white settlers, and it served as a major transportation artery into the 1860s.

Above: The Sixth Street Bridge was designated as a historic landmark in the late 1970s, and has been completely restored. Photo by Larry Heydenburg

Facing page: By the turn of the century, electric rail service connected Grand Rapids to such West Michigan cities as Grand Haven, Holland, and Muskegon. By 1915 an interurban line also linked Grand Rapids to Kalamazoo. The Great Depression spelled the end of the lines, and the bridge at the foot of Lyon Street, over which the Grand Rapids-Kalamazoo interurban once ran, is now a pedestrian walkway. Photo by William Hebert

Above: The Fulton Street Bridge, completed on August 29, 1928, replaced the iron bridge that had been built in 1885. Courtesy, Grand Rapids Public Library

The first river craft were the Indian canoes. The French traders brought with them the bateaux, and early settlers all along the river from Jackson to Grand Haven built for themselves little flat-bottomed skiffs which they poled along. But the settlers, too, often found the canoes practical and certainly swifter and easier to maneuver than the skiffs. "A good canoe, bought of an Indian, cost three dollars," wrote Franklin Everett, an early historian.

Passage from one side of the river to the other was accomplished by canoe, skiff, and pole boat until a foot bridge was built in 1842. Ferries of one sort and another existed even after the first bridge to carry heavier traffic, a free bridge, was built at Bridge Street in 1845. The Leonard and Pearl Street bridges were wooden toll bridges built by private companies in 1858. Public discontent with the tolls prompted the city to buy the bridges in the 1870s and abolish the tolls. The city replaced the wooden bridges with iron spans in 1883, and over the next quarter century built bridges across the river at Fulton Street, Sixth Street, Wealthy Street, and the last at Ann Street in 1908.

The river was navigable as far as the rapids, and river traffic increased with the population. During the navigable months, usually late March through October, supplies and goods for the village came from Detroit up Lake Huron through the Straits of Mackinac and down Lake Michigan, or across Lake Michigan from Chicago to Grand Haven and upriver to Grand Rapids. River travel in the early days was by scow or pole boat, later by steamboat.

Storms and shipwrecks on the big lake could mean the difference between dearth and abundance to the people of the Grand. During the nationwide financial crisis of 1837-38, according to one source, supplies became very short in the village, still called Kent at that time. A schooner carrying flour was bound for the Grand River but got caught in a storm while still out on Lake Michigan. The vessel leaked so badly that the flour cargo got soaked. When the flour finally got to the village, it had caked hard and had to be broken off in chunks with a hatchet. It was the color of lake water, but the people bought it and used it anyhow for it was the only flour to be had the whole winter.

The Grand really came into its own as the lifeline of the river communities with the advent of the steamboat. The *Governor Mason* initiated the steamboat era with a maiden voyage on July 4, 1837. A bugler was a member of the crew and signaled arrivals and departures at each of the landings along the river between Grand Haven and Grand Rapids. For the next twenty years, the steamboat was a principal purveyor of passengers and supplies in and out of the city.

In 1841 exports shipped from communities along the Grand included 5,426 barrels of flour, four million feet of pine lumber, more than 2.5 million shingles, 4,000 barrels of potash, and $25,000 worth of furs. Thousands of feet of logs were floated down the river every year to supply the sawmills that dotted the river banks and to be shipped across the lake to the Chicago and Milwaukee markets.

An event of great import to these isolated midwesterners occurred in 1842 when merchandise ordered from New York arrived in just fifteen days via the Erie Canal and the Great Lakes, and upriver

Right: The *William H. Barrett* was put into service on the Grand River in 1874 primarily to carry freight. When freight traffic declined, a second deck and passenger accommodations were added, and the *Barrett* continued to ply the river until it was destroyed by fire in 1894. Courtesy, Grand Rapids Public Library

Facing page: Although today's local producers depend more on rail and truck transportation for shipping their goods, the proximity of the Port of Grand Haven, only thirty miles away, affords ready access to Great Lakes shipping. Photo by J. Phillip Haven

from Grand Haven to Grand Rapids. Not too long after that, traffic had increased to four boats a day steaming between Grand Haven and Grand Rapids, carrying freight and passengers.

Because the river was essential to commerce and travel, improving navigation was imperative, and efforts to improve the harbor began early. A canal and locks system was begun on the east side of the river in 1835. Although the canal was completed in 1842, the locks were never finished. Other locks were contemplated but never materialized. In the 1860s, a west side canal and guard gate were built, primarily to provide power for a furniture manufactory.

River traffic reached its peak in 1858, the year the first train arrived in the developing small city on the Grand. Inevitably, shipping and travel shifted to the more convenient overland passage provided by the railroads, and the heyday of the steamboat drifted into

oblivion. Pleasure boats still plied the river, and some freight was still sent by water, but the volume diminished year by year. By 1899, only one steamboat was left on the Grand, though a steamer, the *May Graham,* made a final voyage in 1917.

Railroading, with horse-drawn cars, began in the United States in the early 1830s, but Grand Rapids had to wait nearly thirty years to get rail service. The first line, east to west, was the Detroit, Grand Haven and Milwaukee Railroad. In September 1858, two months after the "Emperor" had steamed into Grand Rapids from Detroit, amidst wild rejoicing by the citizenry, the last track was completed to Grand Haven and it was possible to travel by train across the state from Grand Haven to Detroit.

Traveling north and south by train would not be a reality for another fourteen years, when rail service between Grand Rapids and Kalamazoo was estab-

The stern-wheeler *May Graham* operated until 1917, carrying passengers on excursions and hauling freight between Grand Rapids and Grand Haven. Courtesy, Grand Rapids Public Library

lished. Up until 1869, the city's only link to rail service south was by plank road—wooden planks laid crosswise across the roadbed—to Kalamazoo, which had been served by the Central Michigan Railroad since 1847.

The Civil War slowed railroad building all over the United States, but by 1869 railroading was a boom industry and companies sprang up like crocuses in spring, establishing lines and extending tracks to every corner of the country. In Grand Rapids, between 1869 and 1872, five additional lines reached the city from various directions. By that time the east and west coasts were connected by a transcontinental railway.

The years between the Civil War and World War I—1865 to 1917—have been called the golden years of the railroads. Most of the country's freight and traveling public moved by rail. In Grand Rapids, at the peak of the railroad era, thirty trains a day steamed into Union Station. One source states that on a sunny weekend, upwards of 2,000 west-staters might arrive by train for shopping and holidaying. The furniture manufacturers depended on the trains to ship their products around the country, and to bring buyers and customers to the annual furniture shows.

But as the train displaced the steamboat, so the railroads gradually lost out to the automobile and airplane. Rail use decreased, as did the service. Freight trains dwindled to just a few trains a week. By 1971, Grand Rapids' passenger rail service had come full circle. Travelers drove to Kalamazoo to catch the train, east or west.

Left: The Parnell House was one of a cluster of hotels that grew up around the old Grand Trunk Depot on Plainfield Avenue. Courtesy, Grand Rapids Public Library

Below: This engine, owned by the Grand Rapids and Indiana Railroad, ran between Grand Rapids and Allegan during the 1870s. Courtesy, Grand Rapids Public Library

Above: Tracks in the railroad yards cut linear patterns in the dusting of snow. Photo by Jean Hoyle

Right: Although the coming of Amtrak in 1984 was not the momentous event that the arrival of Grand Rapids' first railroad was in 1858, residents nevertheless turned out to greet Amtrak's first Grand Rapids to Chicago train. Photo by Marian L. Carter

Facing page: The CSX and Amtrak stand side by side in the rail yards in this photograph. Photo by Pat Bulthuis

The city's first horse-car routes were built in the 1860s to take passengers to and from the train depot. The five horse-car lines that served the citizens of Grand Rapids were eventually replaced by electric trolleys. Courtesy, Grand Rapids Public Library

But in 1984, the nation's subsidized railway system, Amtrak, restored passenger service between Grand Rapids and Chicago. Today's passengers can board the sleekly modern Pere Marquette at a brand new depot at Market Avenue and Wealthy Street at 7:30 a.m., arrive at Chicago's Union Station four hours later, and return home again in the evening. Within a few years, officials expect the route to attract 57,000 to 67,000 passengers a year.

The railroad was not the only mode of transportation done in by the automobile. Public transportation was a continuing victim of technology. The city had several streetcar lines, beginning in 1863 with horse-drawn cars, followed soon by cable cars. But the horse-drawn cars and cable cars gave way to electric trolleys, the trolleys to motor buses. The trolley and streetcar companies were profitable for a relatively short period. Bedeviled by equipment failure, labor strikes and riots, dwindling passenger use and revenues, and finally the great American romance with the private automobile, the trolley and interurban systems finally succumbed to the gasoline engine. Grand Rapids in 1934 was the second city in the nation to completely change its public transportation system over to buses.

The municipally owned and operated transit sys-

tem of the 1980s, known as GRATA (Grand Rapids Area Transit Authority), offers area-wide service weekdays and Saturdays over thirteen routes. GRATA also operates GO!BUS, a door-to-door bus and taxi service for senior citizens and the handicapped, and GUS (Grand Rapids Urban Shuttle Service), which provides downtown office workers with shuttle service between their offices and parking lots on the periphery of the business district.

At the turn of the century, the automobile was still a novelty. There were only four auto owners in the city, and an electric car sold for $600 to $1,000. However, the internal combustion engine and Henry Ford's assembly line production made the automobile affordable to the average consumer—$290 for the Model-T in 1925. That same year, 79 percent of Kent County's population owned vehicles, and the cartage and freight business within the city had pretty much made the switch to motorized vehicles.

The private automobile precipitated a trend begun in the first two decades of the century by the electric trolley—the middle-class movement to the suburbs on the periphery of the city. This trend changed forever the American landscape and lifestyle.

As populations shifted from cities to suburbs, the

Left: Grand Rapids' streetcars did more than carry passengers. Cars such as this one—No. 323 purchased in 1912—were equipped with boxes to collect the mail. Courtesy, Grand Rapids Public Library

Below: For a brief time, the trolley buses provided service in the downtown business district and took visitors to cultural spots around town. Photo by Jack Standley

need for good roads became top priority for municipal, state, and federal governments. Beginning in the 1950s, the two-lane macadamized highways of the 1930s were replaced by four-lane concrete super-highways, and highway construction became the growth industry of the mid-century. The first freeway to go through Grand Rapids was U.S. 131, built in 1959 and running south and north from the Indiana state line to Petoskey. It intersects in the center of the city with I-96, built in 1964, which provides a direct route from Muskegon on the west side of the state to Detroit on the east. U.S. 94 from Chicago to St. Joseph/Benton Harbor meets I-196, which runs along the lakeshore to Holland, then veers northwest through Grand Rapids to connect with I-96. Within the city limits, I-196 is called the Gerald R. Ford Freeway for its native son, the thirty-eighth president of the United States.

The freeway system not only gives West Michigan residents easy access to major U.S. highways and

Facing page, top: An old London bus now rolls along Grand Rapids streets. Operated by Tootsie Van Kelly's nightspot, the bus can be rented for special occasions. Photo by Larry Heydenburg

Facing page, bottom: The Gerald R. Ford Freeway moves west through Grand Rapids. Photo by Pat Bulthuis

Right: On August 23, 1946, Grand Rapids celebrated the twentieth anniversary of the beginning of regular air service to the city. On hand for the occasion were Lieutenant Colonel James Colovin, who was in charge of the army exhibit that was part of the ground show; the "twentieth anniversary girl," Mary Webb; and Senator Arthur Vandenberg. Courtesy, Grand Rapids Public Library

Below: These military precision flying jets were photographed on a visit to the Kent County Airport. Photo by James Glessner

turnpikes, it makes travel within the city fast and convenient. About 25,000 people drive into jobs in the city each working day. Most can be in their offices within twenty minutes of leaving home. There are few traffic jams, even on congested 28th Street, billed by the state highway department as the second most traveled urban street in Michigan.

Developing concurrently but much more slowly than automobile travel was air travel. The city's first commercial airline, operated by Roseswift Airplane Company, began service in 1919 with a 12-person passenger plane. However, regularly scheduled passenger flights did not begin until seven years later, in 1926. By that time, there was sufficient air traffic to open an airport, maintained by the county, south of the city.

The jet age, marshaled in by Viscount turbojets in 1952, made the old airport, which had no room for expansion, obsolete. The county in 1963 opened a modern nine-million-dollar facility southeast of the city in Cascade Township.

In 1976, the airport was designated a port of entry, with incoming and outbound service by U.S. Customs agents. Reflecting its new status, the airport in 1977 was renamed Kent County International Airport. More than twelve million pounds of freight are moved in and out of the airport annually, and more than a million passengers a year use the terminal, the second busiest in the state, next to Detroit's Metro Airport. The city is served by nine airlines, including commuter feeder services, with more than 100 incoming and outgoing flights a day, connecting with every major city in the United States.

The Kent County Aeronautics Commission has maintained a continuing expansion and modernization program to keep the facility concurrent with the demands of air travel technology and ever-increasing freight and passenger use. The facility is one of the few airports in the country that is self-supporting, without the use of public funds. Revenues come from concessions such as gift shop and restaurants, from such tenants as the airlines, Hertz, and Avis, and from parking. All profits are automatically poured back into improving the facility. The airport recently completed a seven-million-dollar expansion that makes it one of the most modern and convenient in the country. One survey predicts that the Grand Rap-

Facing page: The advent of the freeway system in the 1950s and 1960s made Grand Rapids a remarkably easy town in which to get around. Photo by Larry Heydenburg

Left: Balloon rides are a great way to see Grand Rapids. Photo by James Glessner

Page 100: Night traffic makes ribbons of light along Grand Rapids' freeways. Photo by William Hebert

ids airport will develop as an important northeast hub.

On the ground, the city is a major distribution area for the more than 100 trucking firms that serve the area, and Greyhound and North Star bus lines still offer bus passenger service with connections to all points east, west, north, and south. Just as the private automobile became the favored means of transportation for the masses, so too did the truck take over the cartage business. Long before the advent of the super highways, transportation of goods by truck was flourishing, and trucks for private use in business and agri-culture soon replaced horse and wagon.

In today's economy, trucks and trucking are a primary means of transporting everything from the U.S. mail to products from the area's many manfacturers. The city is served by eighty-six truck lines, many with national affiliation and many with local terminals.

Far from being an isolated little pocket in the corner of West Michigan, Grand Rapids is well served by every major transportation mode except a navigable waterway. "You can't get there from here" has not been a valid lament for a very long time.

7

A Rich Mosaic

Many ethnic and racial groups call Grand Rapids home. Seeking the freedom to practice their religion, fleeing from war, famine, and political oppression, or pursuing the nearly universal dream of economic prosperity, people of diverse places and differing cultures have been making their way to Grand Rapids ever since Frenchman Louis Campau brought his little band of relatives and helpers to the frontier in the late 1820s to run a trading post beside the rapids of the Grand.

In the ensuing years, those who came to Grand Rapids brought their ethnic traditions and religious beliefs with them, and the values instilled by their various cultures and faiths remain a strong thread in the fabric of contemporary community life. Separated by the individual cultures, customs, and traditions that they have worked so hard to preserve and pass on, the city's ethnic groups are nevertheless united into an intricately patterned mosaic, formed from a richness and diversity that the community continues to appreciate and celebrate.

Throughout the nineteenth century, Europeans packed up their belongings and left their homelands in increasing numbers, seeking a better life on foreign shores. And as the American frontier moved further westward, so did they. The Irish claim the distinction of being the first group of immigrants to arrive in the Grand Rapids area. Hired by early entrepreneurs Lucius Lyon and Nathaniel Sargent to dig the East Side Canal, a crew of Irish laborers, along with two black men, made their grand entrance into town in 1835 to the accompaniment of a bugle fanfare

St. Adalbert's Catholic Church was built in 1881 by Polish settlers on Grand Rapids' west side. Photo by Jack Standley

105

played by one Alanson Crampton. More came in the 1840s, refugees from a homeland ravaged by famine. Attracted by farmland that was selling at $1.40 an acre, some settled in nearby Parnell, Cascade, and Marne. Others chose city life on Grand Rapids' west side and in the Creston area, finding work as police officers and firefighters and worshipping at St. Andrew's and St. James's Catholic parishes. By 1880, according to official records, the Irish-born population of Kent County numbered nearly as many as the area's Dutch.

Deeply religious and sternly moral, the faithful Dutch followers of the precepts of John Calvin have stamped their imprint on Grand Rapids almost since the time the first group of Dutch arrived in West Michigan in 1847. Traveling under the leadership of Dr. Albertus Van Raalte, the small group made its way to Black Lake near the Lake Michigan shore and established the colony of Holland. Later arrivals from the Netherlands founded their villages within a ten-mile radius of Holland and, like Van Raalte's group, named their own new communities—Zeeland, for example— in memory of the towns and cities they had

left behind. But once safely settled in the area they called *de Kolonie,* the Netherlanders had to cope with the problem of dwindling supplies. A shortage of wage work that would have enabled *de Kolonie's* teen-age children to supplement the meager incomes of their large farm families sent many of them—along with some adult colonists unable to afford farmland—to Grand Rapids, where they found employment as household servants, farm workers, or in small trades.

By 1850, about 200 Dutch immigrants had moved to Grand Rapids from *de Kolonie,* finding the city congenial for any number of reasons—ample employment opportunities; a Dutch-language worship service that had been organized in 1848 by Hendrick Van Driele; and a Dutch population large enough to offer a generous selection of suitable spouses for their children. The city's attractions drew even more Dutch newcomers, and the number of Grand Rapids Dutch quickly increased to more than 900 by 1860.

The flow of immigrants to the United States was temporarily halted by the Civil War. But the floodgates reopened in the 1870s to admit the great wave of immigrants from all over Europe who continued to

pour into the United States for the next four decades. After their cramped and uncomfortable journeys across the Atlantic, substantial numbers left New York, their port of entry, to venture to cities in the Midwest where many of their countrymen lived and prospered. Grand Rapids, with its expanding economy and newly minted reputation as the Furniture Capital of America, attracted its own share of immigrant new-comers. The years immediately following the end of the Civil War brought many more Netherlanders to Grand Rapids, swelling the city's Dutch-born population to 2,722 by 1870. Unlike earlier Dutch immigrants who moved to Grand Rapids from *de Kolonie,* these new arrivals came directly to the city. By 1900, persons of Dutch birth or ancestry made up 40 percent of the city's population, the largest proportion of Dutch in any American city with a population of more than 25,000.

Immigrants who headed for Grand Rapids in the decades following the Civil War were attracted to the city by the prospect of finding employment in the fur-niture factories. Skilled German woodworkers were welcomed into the furniture factory ranks as they ar-rived from the old country in the years between 1870

Above, left: Place names such as Holland and Zeeland, in addition to the windmills of West Michi-gan, are reminders of the area's rich Dutch heritage. Photo by J. Phillip Haven

Left: These children, dressed in Dutch costume, depict just one of the many ethnic groups that com-prise Grand Rapids' cultural mosaic. Photo by J. Phillip Haven

Facing page: Thousands of green balloons take to the air at the Federal Building in celebration of St. Patrick's Day. Photo by Pat Bulthuis

and 1890. Earlier German immigrants had found work in local breweries, and one of the city's first breweries, in fact, was founded by the German-born Christopher Kusterer. German immigrants had begun to arrive in Grand Rapids as early as the 1840s and prospered in an area whose mercantile and commercial opportunities were much to their liking. Until a wave of anti-German sentiment swept the city in the wake of World War I, the large German community had its own churches, fraternal organizations, bands, and even a German-language newspaper. The city's largest immigrant group in the 1850s, the Germans subsequently remained second only to the Dutch in number until they were surpassed after the turn of the century by the influx of Polish immigrants.

Joseph Jackoboice, generally acknowledged to be the first Polish settler in Grand Rapids (apart from the Reverend Andreas Viszoczky, who was appointed pastor of St. Andrew's parish in 1835), reached the city in 1854, the first of many who would flee to Grand Rapids from a country besieged by foreign invasions, beset by domestic insurrection, and beleaguered by economic privation. By the 1850s and 1860s, an exodus from German-occupied Poland brought growing numbers of Poles to Grand Rapids' west side, where they settled in the German community clustered around St. Mary's Church and where they found work as shoemakers, tailors, carpenters, blacksmiths, wagon makers, and cabinet makers. Other Polish immigrants of the time settled in the northeast section of Grand Rapids where large brickyards offered employment. The last wave of Polish immigrants reached Grand Rapids between 1890 and 1914. Largely farmers and laborers from the impoverished regions of Austrian and Russian Poland, these immigrants settled in the southwest section of Grand Rapids, near John Ball Park, and worked in the gypsum mines and furniture factories.

Like the Dutch and the Germans, the Poles tended to congregate in their own tight-knit community which safeguarded its traditions, staged its own entertainments, published a native-language newspaper, looked after its needy, and took its religion seriously. Then, as now, Catholicism and Reformed Christianity were the two dominant religions in the city.

Grand Rapids' earliest religious institutions were the Baptist mission founded by the Reverend Isaac McCoy in 1825 and the Catholic mission established by Father Frederic Baraga in 1833 to convert the local Ottawa Indians and minister to their spiritual needs. But by 1836, in the face of Indian land cessions and federal treaties, the Ottawa were being moved off their ancestral territories and onto government reservations. As Louis Campau succinctly put it: "A few white men came and there was a little trouble. A few more white men arrived and there was more trouble. Then a lot came and the Indians became bad. Finally, the Indians were relieved of their possessions." Inevi-

Facing page: **Built to serve the city's increasing German population, St. Mary's Catholic Church was consecrated in 1874. Photo by Marian L. Carter**

Above: **These dancers, dressed in traditional Polish costume, entertain at an annual Polish Heritage Days festival, which is sponsored by the city and the Polish Heritage Society. Photo by Pat Bulthuis**

tably, the missions outlived their usefulness; churches founded by and for the growing number of settlers quickly took their place.

The earliest Catholic settlers in Grand Rapids, Louis Campau and his family, were followed by the German and Irish immigrants who made their way west in the 1830s and 1840s. By 1850, the city had its first Catholic parish and first consecrated Catholic church, St. Andrew's, which served about 160 German and Irish families. The parish boundaries extended east to present Ionia, west to Grand Haven and Muskegon, south to Yankee Springs, and north to Ludington, and Father Viszoczky and his assistants covered the entire area by horseback. Within the next fifty years, Grand Rapids would have seven parishes, a number that has since grown to forty-two. St. Mary's parish was organized in 1857 to serve the growing number of German residents, St. James's parish was founded in 1869 for the west-side Irish population, and St. Alphonsus was established in 1909 for what was then the northern part of the city. Polish Catholic settlers, eager to celebrate their own rites in their own neighborhood, built St. Adalbert's in 1881, St. Isidore's in 1897, and Sacred Heart in 1903. In 1882, given the size of the city's Catholic population and its growing number of active parishes, a papal brief established Grand Rapids as the headquarters for a new West Michigan diocese encompassing Kent, Ottawa, Montcalm, Gratiot, and Saginaw counties.

Grand Rapids is also the headquarters of the Christian Reformed Church, a denomination which arose from the Old World pieties of the first Dutch settlers in West Michigan, who preferred their own Dutch-language brand of Calvinism to the more Americanized practices of the Reform Church in America. Established in New York (then the Dutch colony of New Netherlands) in 1628, the Reform Church in America founded its first Grand Rapids congregation in 1840. Although separated today by differences in their respective governmental organizations and variations in individual practices, the two denominations are united in their adherence to the same articles of faith, and their innate conservatism and unshakeable moral convictions have had a profound and lasting effect on the character of the West Michigan

109

region and the city of Grand Rapids.

Today, members of the Christian Reformed Church and the Reformed Church in America together make up about 40 percent of the city's population. Catholic citizens comprise another 40 percent. Although these two major groups have tended to live on opposite sides of the river and have often been staunch and vocal supporters of opposite sides of such public issues as Prohibition and Sunday closing laws, they, and the city's many other religious groups, have found Grand Rapids a comfortable haven in which to practice their faiths.

With 480 Protestant churches, forty-two Catholic parishes, and two Jewish congregations, Grand Rapids has often been labeled a city of churches; yet, other cities—Muskegon, for one—have more churches per capita than Grand Rapids. But while it may not accurately be awarded the title of city of churches, Grand Rapids is indisputably a city of churchgoers, its houses of worship regularly filled and firmly supported by devout congregants. Virtually every religious tradition and a vast assortment of denominations, from the highly conservative to the ultra liberal, are represented here, and the time-honored traditions of good works and strong faith, along with the willingness to work together toward common goals in such organizations as the Grand Rapids Area Council for Ecumenism (GRACE), continue to play a major role in city life.

Ethnic traditions and styles of worship are often closely intertwined, and the city's diversity of churches mirrors its rich array of ethnic groups. The stream of foreign immigrants to Grand Rapids has ebbed and flowed over the past century and a half, and while the countries of origin may have changed, the tide has never entirely been stemmed. Immigration changed the face of the city as each of the incoming groups settled in specific neighborhoods, forming their own cultural and religious pockets. While Germans, Poles, Swedes, and Danes settled on the west side of town, the Dutch immigrants, whose numbers swelled in the aftermath of World War I and World War II, made their homes in the southeast section of the city. In the 1890s, Armenians established a community along Front Street between First and Seventh streets.

Above and facing page: **St. Adalbert's Catholic Church is one of the forty-two Catholic parishes in Grand Rapids. Above, photo by Pat Bulthuis; facing page, photo by William Hebert**

Lithuanians, who arrived in 1875, lived in the West Grand area near Leonard and Turner. The Italians, who began arriving in significant numbers in the 1880s, settled in the South Division-Franklin area and later clustered near John Ball Park. Greeks, Lebanese, and Syrians likewise lived in their own neighborhoods, built their own churches, and preserved their distinctive traditions to pass on to succeeding generations.

The twentieth century has seen a substantial increase in the number of immigrants from Asia and Latin America and other third-world areas plagued

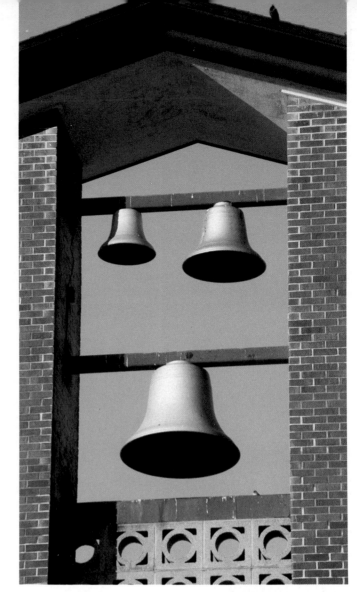

Above: The ultra-modern stone, concrete, and glass Trinity Lutheran Church, located at Fulton Street and Cascade Road, was built in 1950. Photo by J. Phillip Haven

Above right, right, and facing page: Although other cities may have more churches, Grand Rapids is indeed a city of churches, with as many architectural styles as denominations. Above, photo by Pat Bulthuis; right, photo by David Jackson; facing page, photo by William Hebert

Following pages: Once a Baptist congregation with roots that can be traced back to the Baptist Mission founded on the west bank of the Grand River in 1826, Fountain Street Church is today nondenominational. Photo by William Hebert

Above: Jewish residents of the area worship at Ahavas Israel Synagogue, shown here, or at Temple Emanuel or Chabad House. Photo by Boots Schmidt

Above, left: A spectacular Grand Rapids sunset silhouettes these church spires. Photo by William Hebert

Left: Saying mass at Monroe Mall Amphitheater during Polish Heritage Days, pictured here, one of many ethnic celebrations held annually in the city. Photo by Pat Bulthuis

Facing page: Immanuel Lutheran Church serves many of the Lutheran families in Grand Rapids. Photo by Marie Velting

Above, left: **Mexican Americans Mike (shown here) and Isabel Navarro are among the city's many successful minority entrepreneurs. Celery pickers when they first arrived in West Michigan in 1948, they started their El Matador tortilla factory on Stocking N.W. in 1977. Their corn and flour tortillas and tortilla chips are sold throughout the state. Photo by William Hebert**

Above: **Grand Rapids celebrates its ethnic diversity with gala ethnic festivals held on Monroe Mall and at Ah-Nab-Awen Bicentennial Park. Photo by Boots Schmidt**

Facing page: **Ottawa Indian Jerry Pigeon posed for this photo in full native dress. Photo by John D. Strauss**

by war, disease, and poverty. Many local church groups have sponsored the arrival of refugees from Vietnam, Cambodia, and Ethiopia, and the Jewish community has been instrumental in settling Soviet Jews in Grand Rapids.

Hispanics, as is true for the nation as a whole, now constitute the fastest-growing cultural and ethnic group in West Michigan. According to current estimates, Kent County's Hispanic community now numbers about 20,000 individuals. Of those, some 10,000 to 17,000 live in Grand Rapids, predominantly on the city's southwest side, which has become West Michigan's largest Spanish-speaking neighborhood.

Mexicans make up about 60 percent of the city's Hispanic population; Puerto Ricans, 16 percent; and Cubans, about 7 percent. These newcomers to Grand Rapids have had to deal with many of the same problems that have faced all other immigrant groups—poverty, inadequate housing, the language barrier, lack of education, the erosion of native culture, and prejudice. By dint of their own hard work and the assistance of their own and other local organizations es-

tablished to help them, many Hispanic families have been able to surmount these difficulties, but unemployment for Hispanics is more than twice that for the overall population, and 20 percent of Kent County's Latin American families live below the poverty line.

Unemployment, poverty, and discrimination are problems common to the area's Native American community as well. Once the sole inhabitants of the

Right: Members of the Ottawa, Potawatomi, and Ojibway tribes gather at the Three Fires Indian Pow-Wow held annually in Ah-Nab-Awen Bicentennial Park to perform the dances and ceremonies that have been passed down since ancient times. Photo by Larry Heydenburg

Facing page: The Juneteenth Festival is a very special annual celebration in the black community. It is one of the Grand Rapids Parks Department's ethnic festival series. Courtesy, City of Grand Rapids Parks Department

territory on which modern Michigan has been built, members of the Ottawa, Potawatomi, and Ojibway tribes were moved off their ancestral lands and onto reservations by a series of treaties negotiated by the federal government in the nineteenth century. By the 1930s and 1940s, however, the growing need for employment began to move Native Americans off the reservations and out of rural areas into the cities.

According to the most recent census figures, Grand Rapids is home to about 2,000 Native Americans. Victimized by discrimination, many have difficulty finding jobs. High school dropout rates are high, employment skills are low, and the rate of alcohol abuse among Native Americans is higher than for any other group.

Working to provide services to the Native American community is the Grand Rapids Inter-Tribal Council, founded in 1972 as a social organization and incorporated two years later as a human services agency which receives funding from a variety of sources, including the county, state, and federal governments. Among the Inter-Tribal Council's many services are mental health programs, a large community education program operated in cooperation with the Grand Rapids Public Schools for individuals over the age of seventeen, and skills training. "We've helped more than 200 students earn their high school diplomas," says J. Wagner (Wag) Wheeler, the council's executive director, "and we do a great deal in the way of employment training. We've found many members of the community jobs with the city's larger industries, and our work with families has helped many people get their lives straight."

The city's black population, now estimated at about 40,000, has faced the same problems that have confronted other minority groups. The first blacks to

live in Grand Rapids were two men who arrived in the 1830s and a third, named Scott, who came in the 1840s. The 1850s saw the Hardy, Huntley, and Minisee families leave the state of New York to settle in Gaines Township on the outskirts of Grand Rapids. Like many of the city's other Yankee settlers of the time, the men came first to buy land and sent for their families later. The Hardy, Huntley, and Minisee names remain closely associated with Gaines Township. Not only do the descendants of those first families still live in the area, but William Hardy, who became township supervisor in the 1870s, enjoyed the distinction of being the first elected black official in Michigan.

The Grand Rapids black population grew slowly, numbering about a thousand in 1920. In a pattern common to all the other ethnic groups who settled in the city, members of the black community tended to worship in their own churches, belong to their own mutual aid societies, form their own social and cultural organizations, and live in their own neighborhoods. As early as the 1870s, a distinctive black neighborhood of homes, churches, and small businesses grew up alongside Heritage Hill, whose affluent residents provided a source of domestic employment for their black neighbors.

The years following World War II saw a significant increase in the local black population as southern blacks moved north in search of economic opportunity. In Grand Rapids as in other American cities, discrimination has been an integral part of the black experience. Nevertheless, great strides have been made. Blacks have seized the social and economic opportunities that have become more available and have risen to prominence in such aspects of city life as the professions, education, and social service organizations. Although Grand Rapids elected a black mayor, Lyman Parks, in 1971, blacks have had only limited success in local politics, and greater political influence remains a goal of the city's black leadership.

The combined efforts of black leaders and citizens, civil rights groups, government regulations, and a more enlightened citizenry have accomplished a great deal in eliminating the more blatant forms of racism in Grand Rapids. But there is no doubt in the

Above and facing page: **These Dutch children celebrate their cultural heritage in traditional costume at an annual Grand Rapids cultural event. Photos by Boots Schmidt**

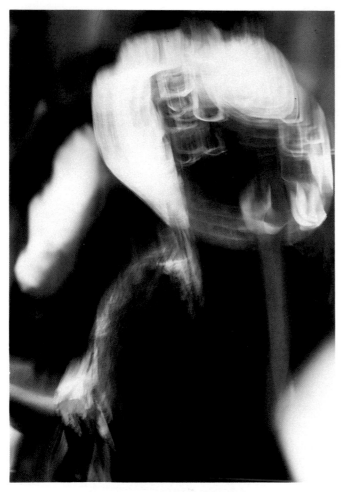

minds of many citizens—black and white—that much more needs to be done. According to a 1985 study commissioned by the Michigan State University Urban Affairs program and the Council of Michigan Urban League Executives, Grand Rapids, Michigan's second largest city, remains the state's fifth most segregated area. Walter Brame, president of the Grand Rapids Urban League, contends that opportunities for blacks to live outside central Grand Rapids are limited. Some black businessmen, for their part, see a general reluctance by the local marketplace to accept goods and services purveyed by minority entrepreneurs, and they point out that the lack of financing for minority-owned businesses continues to be a serious concern.

Although such problems have yet to be solved, changing times have brought about a change in attitudes, and where once such complaints by minority groups might have been given short shrift, today they are being addressed. The Chamber of Commerce, for example, recently instituted a new program to help minority business owners obtain financing from local lending institutions, and Grand Rapids government officials have gone on record as saying that their goal is to make sure that "all people have accessibility throughout the community."

Access to opportunities is what attracted so many people from so many places to Grand Rapids to begin with, and the dream of creating a better life for their children is what kept them in the city. For some, the dream has been slowed by obstacles; for others, it has been achieved beyond all expectations. For most, there have been problems to solve and choices to make; and for all, there has been the desire to acknowledge their roots and remember where they and their ancestors came from. A great resurgence of ethnic pride has been a national phenomenon, and Grand Rapids ethnic groups have exemplified the trend.

Recognizing that ethnic and religious diversity have played a significant role in shaping the character of Grand Rapids and enriching the quality of community life, the city and its cultural institutions have also taken steps to provide opportunities for ethnic groups to highlight their cultures and traditions, display their talents and contributions, and promote community-wide appreciation of their heritages. The Grand Rapids Public Museum stages a major ethnic exhibit every year, and groups recently in the spotlight have included the city's Armenian, Jewish, black, and Greek communities. The Grand Rapids Parks Department helps mount gala ethnic festivals throughout the summer for the entertainment—and edification—of the community at large. Ah-Nab-Awen Park was the scene in 1986 for separate Dutch, Mexican, and Hispanic Festivals, as well as for the Three Fires Indian Pow-wow that recalls the traditions of the Ottawa, Potawatomi, and Ojibway tribes who lived in Michigan before the European settlers came. Monroe Amphitheater featured an Oktoberfest and a Festa Italiana.

On July 4, 1986, Americans everywhere celebrated the 100th birthday of the Statue of Liberty, symbol of the nation's diversity and promise of new opportunity. In Grand Rapids, that same diversity has given color and texture to community life, and opportunity still beckons.

Above and facing page: **Proud of its rich cultural heritage, Grand Rapids enjoys many ethnic festivals throughout the year. Above, courtesy, City of Grand Rapids Parks Department; facing page, top left, photo by William Hebert; top right and bottom, photos by Boots Schmidt**

8
Furniture City

For more than 100 years, furniture has been Grand Rapids' fame—and its fortune. The residential furniture produced in the city in the second half of the nineteenth century earned Grand Rapids its enduring reputation as the Furniture Capital of America. And the business and institutional contract furniture manufactured today represents a multibillion-dollar industry that has kept Grand Rapids' place secure as the nation's Furniture City.

The earliest pieces of furniture made in Grand Rapids were nothing to write home about. Crude and functional, they were produced by hand in small, one-man shops just for the local trade. William "Deacon" Haldane, generally credited as the city's first cabinet maker, moved to Michigan from Ohio in 1836 to set up shop in what is now downtown Grand Rapids, selling his chairs for three dollars apiece, bedsteads for five dollars, and coffins from $2.50 to seven dollars. It wasn't long before competitors arrived from the East, trusting that their own cabinet-making skills would offer them a similar opportunity to prosper in the growing frontier town.

Originally used as a warehouse, the Exhibitors Building on Lyon Street was redesigned in 1925 expressly for furniture exhibitions. Photo by John D. Strauss

By the late 1840s the fledgling furniture industry began moving beyond the cabinet-maker stage to a new, machine-propelled era. The Industrial Revolution introduced machinery to the manufacturing process, and local furniture makers were quick to adopt the power lathes and saws that enabled one to do the work of many. With the completion of the East Side Canal in 1842, Grand Rapids furniture makers had a power source to operate their machinery. William Haldane soon moved his shop to the

127

George Jr., Harry, and John—set up shop in 1859. The Berkey brothers, William and Julius, started out modestly enough by making tables in William's sash, door, and blind factory. Within two decades, they were numbered among the industry's leading lights. Julius became a partner in Berkey and Gay, while William was long associated with the Phoenix Furniture Company.

In 1857 C.C. Comstock, originally the owner of a tub factory, bought out the Winchester Brothers Furniture Company, a firm in which William Haldane had earlier been involved. Six years later, Comstock formed a partnership with James and Ezra Nelson, who had previously been in the logging and sawmill business and had, in fact, rafted the first shipment of lumber down the Grand River in 1838. Out of that partnership eventually evolved Nelson, Matter and Company, which, like the Phoenix Company and Berkey and Gay, became one of the largest and best-known furniture manufacturers of its day.

The period after the Civil War inaugurated an era of tremendous growth in the United States. The immigrants who streamed into the country from abroad and the settlers who pushed further and further west created a vast new market for household furnishings. At the same time, the expansion of the nation's railroad network and the coming of the railroad to Grand Rapids enabled local producers to sell their expanded output—made possible by the factory system—to new and more distant markets. Railroads became the furniture industry's lifeline, connecting producers to their customers and giving manufacturers a new way to market their goods.

By the 1870s, with their proximity to the power supplied by the Grand River, their access to nearby forests rich in pine, oak, walnut, maple, cherry, and ash, their skilled artisans and designers, and the four railroad lines that connected Grand Rapids to major midwestern cities and thus to the expanding markets of the West, the city's furniture producers were well positioned to make a significant impact on the national furniture trade.

Their opportunity came in 1876 when three of the largest and best-known producers—Nelson, Matter and Company, the Phoenix Company, and Berkey and Gay—all sent elaborate and costly examples of their work to the nation's Centennial Exposition in Philadelphia. The Nelson, Matter entry, winner of a $10,000 prize for excellence, was a magnificent three-piece bedroom suite carved with the figures of American heroes and crowned with eagles, their wings outstretched. The furniture was literally an overnight sensation, garnering widespread critical acclaim and capturing national publicity. Grand Rapids emerged from the centennial claiming to be America's undisputed Furniture City.

Just as they took advantage of new technology to transform what had originally been small, one-man cabinet shops into full-scale, modern furniture factories, the Grand Rapids furniture entrepreneurs in the 1870s adopted innovative marketing strategies to attract growing numbers of customers. They sent their salesmen from town to town by train, not only to show catalogs, photographs, and miniatures to prospective buyers, but also to set up displays of sample pieces in hotels or in railroad cars diverted to railroad sidings. Julius Berkey, who also pioneered new machinery and production methods, was among the first to see the advantages of selling wholesale and was the first to advertise his company's wares nationally.

By 1880, Grand Rapids, with eighteen major producers and countless support industries supplying them with hardware, veneer, mirrors, springs, and other related products, had become the nation's seventh largest furniture manufacturing center. Four years later, thirty-two companies were producing $5.5 million worth of goods a year. Furniture dominated the city's economy, and Grand Rapids was well on its way to becoming the nation's third largest producer, surpassed only by Chicago and New York. What allowed a city so much smaller than its two major competitors to rise so high in the national rankings was the size of its factories and the enormous volume of their production. Unlike the New York and Chicago

Left: More than 6,000 pieces were used in the construction of the Nelson, Matter Furniture Company's bedroom suite that won a $10,000 prize for excellence at the 1876 Philadelphia Exposition. The bed and dresser shown here were so tall that only a room with an eighteen-foot ceiling could accommodate them. Courtesy, Grand Rapids Public Museum

Facing page: Immigrant labor was the mainstay of Grand Rapids' furniture factories. Here, foreign-born workers attend a citizenship English class at the Grand Rapids Chair Company in the 1890s. Courtesy, Grand Rapids Public Library

furniture industries, which depended for their output on many small factories, the Grand Rapids industry boasted some of the largest furniture factories in the world.

Like business owners in any industry, the Grand Rapids furniture makers had a heavy stake in keeping wages and overhead costs down, freight rates low, and prices at profitable levels. To that end, in 1881, they formed the Grand Rapids Furniture Manufacturers Association (FMA) and elected Elias Matter of Nelson, Matter and Company as its first president. In 1901 the FMA designed a registered trademark identifying its members' products in order to protect Grand Rapids furniture from imitators trying to cash in on the Grand Rapids name. The FMA's registered "made in Grand Rapids" trademark was assurance

Left: Furniture buyers' and manufacturers' representatives flocked twice a year to the Grand Rapids furniture market. Here they are gathered in the lobby of the Pantlind Hotel for the 1917 mid-winter exposition. Courtesy, Grand Rapids Public Museum

Facing page, top: Fine hand decorating was one of the attributes of Grand Rapids-made furniture. Courtesy, Grand Rapids Public Museum

Facing page, bottom: The "Made in Grand Rapids" trademark distinguished the famous Grand Rapids product from that of its competitors. Courtesy, Grand Rapids Public Museum

to growing numbers of eager and name-conscious customers that they were indeed purchasing the real thing.

One of the factors that made Grand Rapids furniture so appealing to so many was the price. As they built their new factories, Grand Rapids furniture makers developed and applied the latest organizational methods and technological advances to speed production and cut costs. Every invention designed to improve quality was seized upon; every machine that would increase output and improve efficiencies was installed. Between 1860 and 1890, machines, many of them developed by local manufacturers, took over much of the work of rough carving, finishing, toning, boring, shaping, planing, gluing, and dovetailing. After machines roughed out the pieces, the job of sanding was often parceled out to women and children working at home. Back at the factory, skilled artisans and fine cabinet makers did the detailed carving, painting, inlay and marquetry work, and other decoration by hand. Although aimed at the mass market, Grand Rapids furniture was nevertheless distinguished by its unmistakable craftsmanship and design. Talented designers, as many as 200 working at the same time during the early years of the twentieth century, created

the high styles—some of them new and others reproduced from the past—that placed expensive-looking furniture within reach of the average home. While machine production kept costs within reasonable limits and enabled manufacturers to produce in volume, hand finishing and close attention to detail gave Grand Rapids furniture the look of handcrafted quality that resulted in its widespread appeal.

Between 1880 and 1890, the number of Grand Rapids furniture factories doubled, and by 1897, the city's thirty-four companies and 6,000 workers had captured 10 percent of the national furniture market share.

In 1878 the city staged its first furniture market, a trade show designed to give buyers, manufacturers, and dealers from all over the nation an opportunity to compare products, examine new lines, and place their orders for the coming season. Only eleven buyers came that year, but as the city's reputation spread, the markets continued to grow.

In the earliest years of the furniture markets, held every January and June or July, exhibitors displayed their wares in hotel lobbies, mezzanines, and even storefronts. Before long, new exhibit space became a priority. Between 1889 and 1916, as many as eleven

Furniture company showrooms, such as this one set up by the Davies-Putnam Company in 1914, displayed an impressive variety of each manufacturer's wares. Courtesy, Grand Rapids Public Museum

downtown buildings, some new and others converted to furniture use, were jammed to capacity during the semi-annual markets. At one time, during the heyday of the residential furniture industry, the city had over one million square feet of exhibit space, as well as forty hotels and 1,500 hotel rooms to accommodate the hordes of buyers and exhibitors who made their twice-yearly pilgrimage to the furniture industry's mecca.

The turn of the century saw a continuing increase in the number and size of Grand Rapids furniture factories and in the array of products being sold to national and international markets. But trouble was looming on the horizon. For one thing, the local supply of hardwoods had been thoroughly depleted by 1900, and the need to import raw materials was beginning to raise production costs. Increased railroad rates, warehousing fees, and marketing costs were likewise sending overhead skyward. At the same time, the furniture workers were beginning to press for their own share of the industry's prosperity. In 1911, wages averaged $1.91 for a ten-hour day, and workers were expected to put in a six-day week. Workers in other industries and other localities had made significant gains as the nation's growing labor union movement picked up steam in the 1890s. Now the Grand Rapids furniture workers were ready to push for their own de-

mands—a 10 percent pay increase, a reduction in their workday from ten to nine hours, an end to a piecework system they considered iniquitous, and the right to bargain collectively.

Manufacturers countered with claims of rising costs and refused to recognize the Finishers Union and the Brotherhood of Carpenters and Joiners as the workers' bargaining agents. On April 11, 1911, more than 7,000 workers walked off the job. While the strikers marched in parades and carried banners expressing their solidarity, the manufacturers held fast to their resolve not to negotiate with the unions and began importing strikebreakers to keep the factories running. Violence erupted on May 15 at the Harry Widdicomb factory when someone threw a stone at a car filled with strikebreakers driven by the owner himself.

Although the strike officially lasted seventeen weeks, not all the participants held out that long. Some individual owners eager to resume production negotiated settlements with workers anxious to return to their jobs. Solidarity within the ranks weakened, and by August 17, the strike was ended.

By the time the United States entered World War I in 1917, such advances as electric motor-driven machinery, multiple carving machines, and automatic

The terra cotta facade of the Exhibitors Building, redesigned in 1925 as a salute to the furniture industry, is embellished with representations of T-squares, compasses, palettes, brushes, and other tools of the furniture maker's art. Photo by John D. Strauss

lathes were making it possible for manufacturers to produce an even greater supply of their product than before. But as other consumer goods—automobiles, radios, and electrical appliances, for example—began vying for customers' dollars, the furniture producers discovered that there were limits to the number of items that could be sold. At the same time, overhead costs continued to rise, and the South, with an abundant supply of raw materials and cheap labor, began to emerge as a major producer, cutting into the Grand Rapids companies' traditional market. The industry was becoming much more competitive, and once the skyrocketing demand of the post-World War I period fizzled, some local companies began seeing a drop in sales. Even before the war had ended, the venerable Nelson, Matter and Company was forced by financial difficulties to shut down. Other well-known producers,

including the Macey and Widdicomb companies, also suffered business reverses.

Despite these early signs of trouble, a mood of optimism prevailed. New producers did not hesitate to set up operations. To combat a chronic shortage of skilled and semi-skilled labor in the local furniture factories, and in keeping with the national trend toward vocational education that preceded World War I, the Grand Rapids Public Schools offered

Above: At the turn of the century, furniture workers in Grand Rapids put in a ten-hour day, and a six-day week. Courtesy, Grand Rapids Public Library

Facing page: A Grand Rapids police "riot squad" was called to action during the 1911 furniture strike. Courtesy, Grand Rapids Public Library

courses in furniture manufacture and design. In 1928 the Kendall School of Design was founded in order to train and keep a steady supply of designers flowing to the local furniture industry. Some manufacturers, in an effort to boost sales and cut costs, introduced cheaper, mass-production methods; others began pruning their product lines, moving out of low-end, low-priced production and into more expensive "high-end" goods. Berkey and Gay took another tack by teaching its retail salesmen how to convince prospective customers that furniture, rather than an automobile, should be the top item on their shopping lists.

The plant closings and reorganizations of the post-World War I era were symptoms of an ailing industry. Nevertheless, the picture that appeared to the outside world was one of prosperity as local furniture makers burnished the city's reputation to a high gloss with such carefully placed reports as the following, which appeared in a 1924 *Ladies Home Journal:*

There is being made, right here in the United States, furniture of such beauty and fine style, reproductions of antique museum pieces . . . no one need be lured across the seas to acquire the finest furniture in the world. [The Grand Rapids furniture market] is the biggest factor in determining the sort of furniture we shall be able to buy in the future.

Small wonder, then, that the number of out-of-town buyers flocking to the city for the semi-annual furniture markets swelled from more than 2,500 in 1914 to more than 6,000 in 1928. Besides seeing the styles and placing their orders, the out-of-towners had a sig-

nificant impact on the city's economy, spending about two million dollars a year during the 1920s on accommodations, meals, and entertainment.

In 1924 the January market enjoyed its greatest turnout ever, with 561 exhibitors displaying their wares. Five years later the stock market crashed, ushering in an era of hard times. The Great Depression brought the Grand Rapids residential furniture industry to a virtual standstill. Sales plummeted, unemployment soared, and many companies folded or sold out to larger operations. Berkey and Gay, perhaps the most famous company of its era and virtually bankrupt at the time, was bought out by Simmons in 1929; Luce, another well-known name in the city's furniture annals, was taken over by Kroehler. Neither Grand Rapids company survived the change in ownership. By 1932 furniture production in Grand Rapids had fallen by 75 percent. The factories still in business ran at only 25 to 50 percent capacity.

To combat the hard times, Depression-era manufacturers continued to promote their products by staging a centennial celebration in 1936 and opening a furniture museum, the first of its kind in the world. In 1931 the Furniture Makers Guild, a group of ten local manufacturers, sought to increase sales by awarding franchises which entitled selected dealers to display a special guild insignia identifying them as the purveyors of quality merchandise.

By the time the Depression ended and the country's attention was fixed on winning World War II, the Grand Rapids residential furniture industry had endured two decades of financial difficulties that had brought about plant closures, mergers, consolidations, and other retrenchments. By 1940 only forty-seven companies remained out of the seventy-two producers that had thrived in earlier days, and many of the best-known names were gone. Nevertheless, Grand Rapids' reputation as the nation's furniture capital remained

Above: **This sumptuously painted and decorated Sheraton armchair is part of the Baker Furniture Stately Homes Collection. Courtesy, Baker Furniture**

Facing page: **The Irwin Seating Company manufactured the seats for the Grand Rapids DeVos Hall. Courtesy, Irwin Seating Company**

to purchase the luxuries—and necessities—that had to be deferred during hard times and wartime. Once the surging postwar demand receded, however, the local mass-market furniture manufacturers continued to lose ground to the factories of the South.

In keeping with a trend that had begun several decades earlier, local companies, in order to survive, moved into high-end production, turning out small lines of fine, hand-crafted furniture in a wide range of classic and contemporary styles. The high-volume, mass-market, low-end production that had been the key to the industry's forty-year run of success gave way to a more limited production focused on the demands of a smaller, more affluent, and highly selective market.

The customers who make up that market continue to furnish their homes with the beautifully crafted pieces turned out by the 106-year-old Baker Furniture Company, the ninety-year-old John Widdicomb Company, Forslund's, and the many other local producers whose names are synonymous with fine-quality residential furniture. Testimony to the continued prospects for profitability represented by these companies is the fact that Baker, Knapp and Tubbs, which owns Baker Furniture, was recently purchased by the Kohler Company of Wisconsin, and five Grand Rapids investors recently returned the John Widdicomb Company to local ownership by purchasing the firm from the Hickory Furniture Company of Hickory, North Carolina.

While the city's residential furniture manufacturers were coping with their industry's woes in the late 1940s, the local manufacturers of business and office furniture were poised to ride the crest of an enormous wave of demand that was about to sweep the country. Actually a separate industry, distinct from the manufacture of residential furniture, the production of institutional seating and contract furniture for offices, factories, schools, public buildings, and businesses grew up alongside the residential furniture industry.

During most of the nineteenth century, when virtually all furniture was made out of wood, few differences existed between household chairs, tables, and desks and those produced for the institutional and business markets. Even so, right from the very begin-

intact, and the "made in Grand Rapids" trademark affixed to locally produced furniture still carried such a distinct cachet that some out-of-town manufacturers found it hard to resist the temptation to capitalize on the city's name. In 1942 the Seventh Circuit Court of Appeals enjoined a Chicago firm from attempting to pass its goods off as Grand Rapids-made, ruling that

the words "Grand Rapids furniture" have acquired in the trade a special significance; and furniture made in that city is held by a large part of the purchasing public to be superior in design, workmanship and value.

The end of World War II revitalized the local residential furniture industry—temporarily, at least—as consumers embarked on a nationwide shopping spree

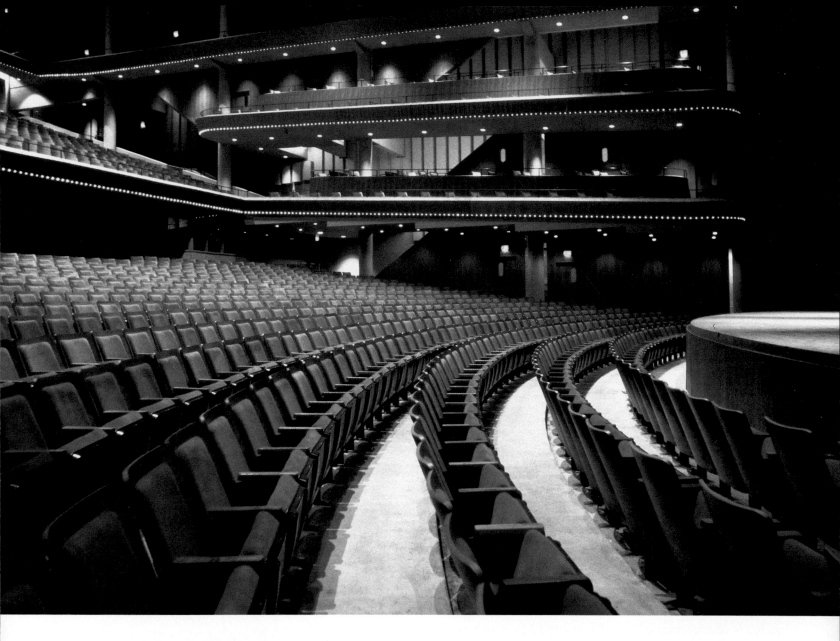

ning, there were a few local companies which recognized the potential of institutional production.

While such residential furniture firms as the Phoenix Company and Berkey and Gay were turning out the parlor sets, mirrored coat racks, bedroom suites, hall stands, rocking chairs, commodes, and cabinets that were so popular among Victorian-age homeowners, the Grand Rapids School Furniture Company, later incorporated as American Seating, was producing the wood and cast iron "combination" desk and seat that would become familiar to generations of schoolchildren across the nation. Within two years of its founding, the company expanded its workforce and diversified its product line into self-folding seats for auditoriums, opera houses, and meeting halls.

Ever responsive to the needs of the marketplace, American Seating, still one of the city's largest employers, moved into the manufacture of grandstand seating when baseball became the nation's favorite pastime, and has since branched out into office chairs, transportation seating, and, most recently, office

systems and furniture for hospitals and laboratories. Ironically, the school furniture line which gave the company its start in 1886 was purchased in 1986 by Irwin Seating, a fast-growing, family-owned, Walker-based company which was founded in 1907 and in the past two years has captured a growing share of the theater and auditorium seating market, the result of a five-year-long boom in movie theater construction.

Another old-line company which moved early into the office furniture market was Stow/Davis, now a subsidiary of Steelcase. Founded in 1880 as Stow and Haight, the company originally specialized in the manufacture of dining room tables. A decade later, with George Davis as its president and operating under a new name, Stow and Davis, the company began manufacturing tables for office use. So successful was this venture that by 1917 Stow and Davis discontinued its residential production entirely.

While many of the city's residential furniture manufacturers found the going rough during World War II and the postwar era, Grand Rapids' business

Right: **The Grand Rapids School Furniture Company, today's American Seating, began producing the famous "combination" desk and seat in 1886. Courtesy, Grand Rapids Public Museum**

Below, right: **This folding opera house chair was one of American Seating Company's many fine products in the 1890s. Courtesy, American Seating**

and institutional furniture producers were entering a period of unprecedented growth, propelled by wartime needs and fueled by a postwar economic upswing. Wars may be fought on the battlefield, but they are run from government offices, and the welter of offices that emerged to oversee the war effort provided a steady market for desks and chairs and files. When the war ended, citizens by and large regarded victory as a reaffirmation of the American way of life. Long deprived of the opportunity to buy luxury and necessity items, Americans went on a spending spree. The postwar demand for consumer goods soared and industry boomed, accelerating the need for office and institutional furnishings and fixtures of all kinds.

Along with industrialization came a postwar surge in construction. The age of the skyscraper had arrived, and the new contruction methods called for fire-retardant furniture in place of the wooden products of old. At the same time, the new metal and plastic technologies and product changes that had arisen from efforts to speed wartime production were readily applicable to postwar furniture manufacturing. Just as their residential counterparts had been quick to apply the latest technology to their operations, so too did the city's business and institutional furniture producers adopt new and innovative materials and methods to supply the needs of business and industry nationwide.

As the American economy shifted its emphasis from industry to service during the late 1960s and to a computer-based information economy within the past ten years, the white collar workforce expanded significantly, creating an increased demand for office space and a growing need for specialized office furniture of all kinds, including the office systems that have revolutionized the contract furniture industry.

At one time, business furniture was simply a matter of desks, chairs, and filing cabinets. By contrast, today's highly flexible, open-office systems, which make use of the latest in metal and plastic technologies, feature free-standing partitions, movable storage walls, and semi-enclosed work stations which instantly transform empty space into fully functioning, multi-staffed offices. Offering workers the benefits of efficiency, privacy, and sound control, office systems carry the additional advantage of ease of rearrangement, enabling businesses, educational facilities, hospitals, and public buildings to reconfigure the work environment as needs change without having to embark on costly construction or remodeling projects.

Among the nation's largest manufacturers of office systems are four West Michigan producers—Steelcase, a privately held company founded in 1912 as the Metal Office Furniture Company; Herman Miller, established in 1923 as a producer of antique reproduction residential furniture; Haworth, Inc., a privately held corporation begun in 1947 to produce store display fixtures, room dividers, and cabinets; and Westinghouse Furniture Systems Division, originally founded as a locally owned and operated firm specializing in floor-to-ceiling office-divider partitions and purchased by Westinghouse in 1961.

The history of each of these companies has been characterized by a willingness to adapt new technologies and innovations to the demands of the marketplace and to identify the special needs of previously untapped markets. Steelcase, founded by Peter Wege, Sr., and Walter Idema, got its start when Wege discovered that he could use sheet steel to make office safes that were as strong as iron, but far less costly. The combination of Wege's technical skills, Idema's financial expertise, and the sales know-how of David D. Hunting, Sr., who joined the company in 1914 and built its dealer network, set the company on the course that would see it become the world's largest producer of office furniture.

Herman Miller shifted from residential to institutional production as a result of the Depression. Long famed for innovative design and such ubiquitous products as the Eames chair, Herman Miller claims to have introduced the world's first open office system with the launching in 1968 of its Action Office. Haworth was the first to develop an open-plan system using panels prewired for electrical power, while Westinghouse captured a growing share of the market by housing electrical and telephone cables beneath raised-access flooring.

Just as 100 years ago the city's residential furniture producers set the standards for the American home, today's business and institutional furniture manufacturers set industry-wide standards for safety and design. And the contract industry continues to grow. In 1947 the total value of all furniture made in Grand Rapids, residential and institutional combined, was sixty-three million dollars. Today, 35 percent of the nation's office furniture industry is concentrated in West Michigan. Business and institutional furniture manufacturing accounts for more than 90 percent of all furniture made in Grand Rapids, and the total value of office furniture shipments in 1986 amounted to somewhere between $6.8 and $6.9 billion, a figure which has risen steadily from $1.1 billion in 1975.

The furniture industry accounts for a substantial portion of the area's employment. One out of every five manufacturing employees in Kent and Ottawa counties works in the furniture business, and of those 18,300 workers, two-thirds are employed in the office furniture segment. Not only have industry employment figures held steady, but wages are comparatively high. Grand Rapids area furniture workers in 1985 drew an average hourly wage of $9.76, slightly higher than the rate for furniture workers statewide and 10 percent lower than the $10.61-an-hour average for all

manufacturing workers in the state, including those in the automobile industry.

Despite some slowdowns after the unprecedented 41 percent sales increase enjoyed industry-wide between 1983 and 1985, local manufacturers anticipate continued growth that, while not spectacular, will be steady. Although metal furniture has long been an industry mainstay, styles and fashions do change, and the greatest growth is expected to occur in the wood furniture lines: 9 percent a year for wood seating, storage, and desks, and 14.3 percent for wood office

systems.

Although tax reform and foreign competition may have an effect on sales and profits, the Grand Rapids area office furniture industry continues to invest in its future. Steelcase recently completed a forty-eight million-dollar computer furniture plant in Kentwood and began construction in 1986 on a multimillion-dollar research and development center in Gaines Township that will double the company's workforce to 16,000 by the year 2000. Herman Miller has announced plans for its own research and development

Left: The growth enjoyed by the West Michigan office furniture industry over the past three decades is reflected in the strikingly designed headquarters of Westinghouse Furniture Systems, located on 36th Street in Kentwood. Photo by William Hebert

Facing page: Steelcase's corporate headquarters is shown in this photo by David Jackson.

facility near Holland, and Haworth, Inc., recently expanded its main plant near Holland. New companies continue to enter the industry, while established producers develop and introduce new products to increase their market share.

Furniture, in the form of two separate but related industries—residential and contract—has played a major role in Grand Rapids' economy and its history virtually since the days of the city's founding. Once the country's best-known producer of furniture for the home and still renowned for the quality and styling of its residential products, Grand Rapids today enjoys a position as one of the largest office furniture producers in the world. Companies have come and gone; markets, products, materials, and styles have changed; but Grand Rapids continues to be, in fact as well as in reputation, the nation's acknowledged "Furniture City."

9

The Good Life

There's never a shortage of things to do in and around Grand Rapids. Blessed by its location at the gateway to a peerless recreational wonderland, the city and its environs offer area visitors and residents a full panoply of recreational and cultural activities for every age, taste, and season.

West Michigan has long been a magnet for tourists, and tourism, in fact, is the region's second leading industry. Summer brings an armada of boaters, many from Milwaukee and Indianapolis. They anchor their power cruisers and sailboats at the many marinas that dot the Lake Michigan shoreline, and they ply the big lake's waters, putting in at a string of colorful and welcoming resort towns from South Haven and Saugatuck in the south to Charlevoix, Harbor Springs, and Petoskey further north. Wind surfers, water skiers, jet skiers, sun worshippers, and swimmers also flock to the white sand beaches of Lake Michigan and to the area's countless inland lakes for their full measure of summer fun.

Windsurfing is fast and exciting on Lake Michigan. Photo by John D. Strauss

Sightseers and festival fanciers can keep busy from May through October, partaking in the diverse pleasures of such events as the Holland Tulip Festival, the South Haven Blueberry Festival, the Grand Haven Coast Guard Festival, the Ionia Free Fair, the Wyoming Rodeo, the Cedar Springs Red Flannel Festival, the Rockford Harvest Festival, and a lot more besides.

Winter draws the skiers to the snow-covered slopes

145

Above: Jet skiing is a favorite sport on Lake Michigan at Holland State Park. Photo by John D. Strauss

Above right: Grand Rapids residents are shown enjoying the beach at Stearns Park, Ludington. Photo by John D. Strauss

Facing page: West Michigan's beaches and sand dunes are a major recreational asset. Photo by William Hebert

just a few hour's drive north of Grand Rapids, while hunting enthusiasts and fishermen have their own seasons of abundance in which to pursue their avocations. Sports fans—whether participants or onlookers—can enjoy the Old Kent River Bank Run, one of the country's best 25-K races and an event that attracts upwards of 3,500 runners, some of them world class, and 35,000 spectators; the Gus Macker Three-on-Three Basketball Tournament in nearby Lowell, now the largest event of its kind in the nation; auto racing at nearby tracks; and the Queen's Cup Regatta, which pits some of the area's top sailors against one another in the all-night race between Milwaukee and Grand Haven. There are also bike races, three adult baseball summer leagues, "iron man" contests, and, of course, golf, either for players at one of the area's forty-five courses, or for onlookers at the Greater Grand Rapids Open, played for the first time, but certainly not the last, in 1986 by big-name golfers on the PGA Senior Tour.

Grand Rapids area residents enjoy a distinct advantage over the tourists. Not only are they close

Facing page: **Holland State Park is a popular destination for many Grand Rapids residents. Photo by John D. Strauss**

Above: **The Old Kent River Bank Run was photographed by David Jackson.**

enough to avail themselves readily and regularly of all that West Michigan has to offer, but they live in a city which itself boasts a splendid array of recreational and cultural charms, not the least of which are its parks.

Generous citizens and a progressive city government have long understood the value of green spaces in which urban dwellers can come together to enjoy the outdoors in each other's company. Parks not only offer a respite from the hubbub of city life, they foster a sense of community.

Many parks and playgrounds have been donated to the city over the years by private individuals. Garfield Park is not only named for its donor, Charles W. Garfield, who devoted much of his life to city park and playground development, but is also his final resting place. Richmond Park, which boasts Grand Rapids' largest swimming pool, built during the Depression as a city public works project, was donated in stages by Rebecca L. Richmond over a seven-year period beginning in 1915. In 1884 prominent local attorney John Ball contributed forty acres to found the park which today bears his name and is home to the state's second largest zoo.

A favorite spot for visitors all year long, the John

Right and facing page: John Ball Zoo is a treat for visitors of all ages. Right and facing page, bottom, photos by Pat Bulthuis; facing page, top left, photo by David Jackson; facing page, top right, photo by William Hebert

Above, left: Dedicated on September 17, 1885, to the men and women who fought for the Union cause, Grand Rapids' Civil War monument stands at the south end of Monroe Mall. Photo by Pat Bulthuis

Above: The swans at John Ball Zoo gracefully swim around their pond. Photo by Pat Bulthuis

Facing page: The waterfall at John Ball Zoo adds quiet beauty and serenity to the park's atmosphere. Photo by William Hebert

Ball Zoo had its beginnings as a simple menagerie of domestic wildlife. Today an ambitious long-range master plan has started the transformation of old-style, caged-animal displays into exhibits whose natural and spacious environments embody the latest concepts in zoo design.

Long a regional tourist attraction, the zoo is heavily used by county residents living outside Grand Rapids city limits. That fact, combined with the rising costs of maintenance and operation, prompted both the city and the county in 1986 to examine the need for a change in jurisdiction and to consider transferring ownership and financial responsibility from Grand Rapids to Kent County. In May 1986, Kent County voters were asked to approve a millage proposal that would have consolidated the zoo, Grand Rapids Public Museum, and Grand Rapids Public Library under county control. Although the proposal was soundly defeated, county officials came forth sev-

eral months later with an offer to buy the zoo from the city, and in March 1987, the concept of such a transaction was approved.

While citizen generosity has helped bring many Grand Rapids parks to life, the city, for its part, has enlarged donated parks through additional purchases, has created new parks and, for more than a century, has undertaken the responsiblity of park operation and maintenance. By 1926, in fact, on the occasion of Grand Rapids' centennial anniversary, historian

William Etten was able to point with some pride to the fact that "Grand Rapids has all but achieved its ambition to have a park or playground within ten minutes' walk of every home."

With the passage of time and a renewed focus on the Grand River as a vital and integral part of community life, a new ambition gradually emerged. On July 7, 1981, the City of Grand Rapids adopted a Grand River Edges plan, calling for uninterrupted and interconnected green spaces on either side of the river, from county border to county border. Thirteen parks—three in the Kent County system, one administered by Plainfield Township, and nine in Grand Rapids, including the 170-acre Butterworth Park which rose from the refuse of a one-time garbage dump—now border the river, and efforts continue to acquire, develop, and link riverfront properties into a green and unbroken chain.

Developing additional park land is not a new idea in Grand Rapids. Sixty years ago, the city owned 902 acres of park and boulevard lands in or contiguous to Grand Rapids. Of that total, 337 park acres had already been improved, and 165 acres were in the process. Annual maintenance costs at the time amounted to $1.35 per person, with thirty cents of that going for permanent improvements.

Today, area residents have some eighty city parks and thirty county parks to choose from, with facilities ranging from baseball diamonds and picnic areas to swimming pools, exercise trails, bike paths, soccer fields, nature walks, and fishing and boating access. The city budgets some three million dollars a year to maintain more than 2,000 park acres, while the county park system, comprising more than 3,000 acres, costs well over a million dollars a year to operate and maintain.

At one time, parks were geared specifically to children's activities. Today, city and county park officials pride themselves on their responsiveness to the needs of citizens of all ages, and the enormous variety of activities taking place year-round in city and county parks reflects the attention paid by government officials to recreation as an important feature of community life. As early as 1926, centennial historian William Etten reminded his readers that:

supervised recreation has become a recognized factor in the physical, moral, and mental well-being of all

154

Left: Natural beauty abounds at Comstock Riverside Park, located just north of downtown Grand Rapids. Photo by Pat Bulthuis

Far left: Autumn comes alive in a burst of yellow and orange in this photo of Pinery Park. Photo by Jean Hoyle

Below: These children enjoy a moment of splashing while cooling their feet in the fountain at Veterans Memorial Park. Photo by Pat Bulthuis

classes and ages. As a force for the building of character, teaching the lessons of teamwork and responsibility to one's fellows, it is practically indispensable.

Above: **Winter brings a host of recreational activities to the West Michigan area. Photo by Pat Bulthuis**

Facing page: **Tobogganing is cold and fun at Echo Valley, south of Grand Rapids near Kalamazoo. Photo by John D. Strauss**

In light of the prevailing philosophy at the time, the city's Welfare Department and the Board of Education embarked on a cooperative venture to develop school playgrounds that would not only be accessible to schoolchildren and neighborhood adults, but would offer year-round recreational programs as well. By 1926 the city was operating seventeen playgrounds and eleven municipal swimming pools, all under the jurisdiction of a single administrator responsible to the Welfare Department and the Board of Education. School gyms were open to adults, skating and coasting were offered in the winter, and programs such as crafts, basket weaving, rug making, and reed work were made available to all who were interested.

Today, that philosophy remains essentially unchanged. The Board of Education makes a contribution of one million dollars a year, half in cash and half in in-kind services, and the city, through its Parks and Recreation departments, continues to finance, spon-

sor, and supervise a year-round recreational program, with activities for the entire family—from sports and crafts in the summer to tobogganing, ice skating, and cross-country skiing in the winter.

Besides providing its residents with places to play, the city has also come to embrace the concept of cultural enrichment through the establishment of its Community Enrichment Group. An umbrella organization with an assistant city manager at its head, the Community Enrichment Group was formed to coordinate the activities of the city's museums, recreation department, library, zoo, and Grand Center. The Community Enrichment Services Office, previously part of the Parks Department, was established in 1982 as a separate entity under the Community Enrichment umbrella to sponsor a variety of free or low-cost activities for children and adults at parks, playgrounds, and downtown. The Community Enrichment Office stages

ethnic festivals, concerts, story-telling hours, hands-on art experiences for children, zoo- and theater-in-the-parks days, and entertainment, fashion shows, carnivals, and market days downtown on Monroe Mall. The fact that these events take place under city auspices and with the cooperation of leading cultural institutions, the Downtown Management Board, businesses, and local civic and ethnic organizations—is yet another indication of how seriously both the public and the private sector view the quality of life in Grand Rapids.

Although quality of life may be a complex term to define, Grand Rapids residents, when asked, have little difficulty in enumerating its components. Ranking high on many lists are the city's fine cultural institutions, which offer a depth and breadth of programming perhaps unequaled in other cities of similar size in the United States.

Like so many other local endeavors past and present, Grand Rapids' cultural institutions have their roots in the volunteer efforts of involved citizens who recognized particular needs and set about satisfying them. The origins of the Grand Rapids Public Library, for example, date back to the formation in 1858 of the

Grand Rapids Library Association. Short of funds three years later, the association transferred its volumes to the Board of Education, which placed the collection in Grand Rapids Central High School. Some years later, the Ladies Reading Club established the City Library Association which eventually merged with the Board of Education and YMCA libraries to form the Public Library. In 1901 Martin Ryerson donated funds for the construction of an appropriate downtown building to store the growing collection, and in 1903 came the establishment of the Library Commission, an independent governing body appointed by the City Commission. A modern addition to the Ryerson Building was put up in 1966.

Today, the Grand Rapids Public Library and its five branches supply patrons not only with books and periodicals, but lend films, videocassettes, and phonograph records as well. County residents are also served by the Kent County Library System, which celebrated its fiftieth anniversary in 1986 and enjoys the largest circulation rate in the state.

The Grand Rapids Public Museum traces its beginnings back to 1854 and the founding of the Grand Rapids Lyceum of Natural History, an organization

Face painting is a favorite activity at Kids' Day, which is held at Monroe Mall under the sponsorship of the Community Enrichment Office. Photo by Jack Standley

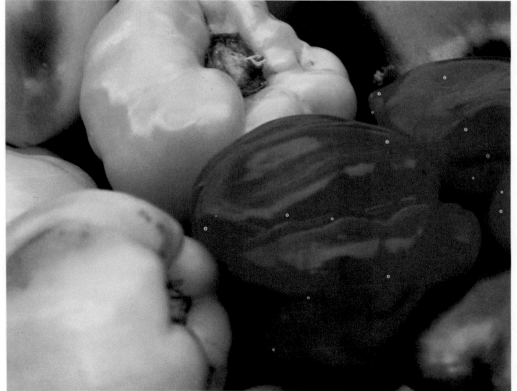

Above: A great way to see Lake Michigan's Sturgeon Bay is on horseback. Photo by John D. Strauss

Following pages: The Monroe Mall Amphitheater is the perfect setting for many of the programs offered by the Community Enrichment Department. Photo by William Hebert

Left: The Fulton Farmers Market, operated by the Grand Rapids Parks Department, gives area growers the opportunity to market their fresh produce and flowers to city dwellers. Photo by Jack Standley

Left: The Public Museum and volunteers from the Kent County Council for Historic Preservation maintain Voigt House, its furnishings, and the family's personal belongings exactly as they were when the Voigt family lived there at the turn of the century. Photo by J. Phillip Haven

Facing page, top: The room that today houses the Grand Rapids Public Library's collection of microfilmed newspapers was the lobby of the original Ryerson Public Library. Courtesy, Grand Rapids Public Library

Facing page, bottom: This building, a car dealership in the 1920s, became the Grand Rapids Public Museum's East Building in 1958. Courtesy, Grand Rapids Public Library

of scholars and hobbyists whose intent was to preserve the natural history of West Michigan. In 1868 the Grand Rapids Lyceum merged with another like-minded organization, the Kent Institute, and adopted a new name, the Kent Scientific Institute. In 1903 ownership of the institute's collection, displayed for many years at Grand Rapids Central High School, was transferred to the Board of Education, which wasted no time in purchasing the museum's first real home, the Nelson-Howlett property on the corner of Jefferson and State streets. Three years later, the city assumed jurisdiction over the new museum, and in 1916, a new city charter created the Art and Museum Commission, whose job was to govern the museum and whose members were appointed by the City Commission.

From its meager beginnings in 1854, the museum has expanded its holdings to include the Stilwill Horse-

shoe Shop; the Calkins Law Office, oldest surviving frame building in Grand Rapids; Blandford Nature Center; Voigt House, a turn-of-the-century Victorian mansion turned museum; Engine House Number 6, which will eventually become a firehouse museum; the Gerald R. Ford boyhood home; and the Norton Indian Mounds, among the best preserved Hopewell burial mounds in the nation.

Renowned for its furniture collection and ranked as one of the country's finest regional museums, the Grand Rapids Public Museum has long been a major attraction for tourists and residents alike. But budget cuts, expanding community needs, and the deterioration of its main buildings—one built in 1942 and the other remodeled for museum use in 1958—have brought the institution to a period of hard times.

In response to its current problems, the Public Museum is focusing on plans for the future. Despite

163

Above: The schoolhouse at Blandford Nature Center, built in 1853, is just one of the attractions at the center of a 108-acre parcel of the small working farm, natural woodlands, ponds, open fields, and nature trails on the west side of town. The nature center is a property of the Grand Rapids Public Museum. Photo by David Jackson

Facing page: The Public Museum's Gaslight Village is a re-creation of a turn-of-the-century Grand Rapids gaslit street. Photo by William Hebert

a major setback in May 1986, when Kent County voters overwhelmingly rejected a millage which would have increased museum funding and consolidated the museum, John Ball Zoo, and the Grand Rapids Public Library under county authority, Public Museum officials have announced their intention to continue seeking the means for constructing and financing a new facility, complete with a state-of-the-art planetarium theater and a working carousel, worthy of its outstanding and irreplaceable collection.

The newest jewel in the city's museum crown, the Gerald R. Ford Presidential Museum, was built entirely with private funds to honor the hometown boy who served for twenty-five years as the city's Fifth District congressman, became House Minority Leader

and vice president, and on August 9, 1974, took the oath of office as the thirty-eighth president of the United States.

Since its dedication on September 18, 1981, amidst much fanfare and in the presence of former President and Mrs. Ford, President and Mrs. Ronald Reagan, and many foreign heads of state, the museum, distinguished by its striking design and full-scale replica of the White House Oval Office, has attracted a total of nearly one million visitors.

The Ford Museum dedication was preceded two days earlier by another gala event—the dedication of the Grand Rapids Art Museum, newly installed in a historic Beaux Arts-style downtown building that had once housed the city's post office. Organized in 1911

as the Grand Rapids Art Association, the museum first saw the light of day through the efforts of volunteers who raised funds to acquire and exhibit works of art in a rented downtown building. A disastrous fire in 1919 destroyed the nascent collection but not the association's hopes and determination. In 1924 a suitable home finally materialized thanks to Mrs. Emily J. Clark's donation of the Pike House on Fulton Street and a fund drive which raised $25,000 to start the new museum on its way.

Today the Grand Rapids Art Museum continues to expand its holdings and its exhibit space. Noted for its collection of prints and the quality of its German Expressionist and nineteenth- and early-twentieth-century paintings, the Art Museum also boasts an ex-

Above: The Gerald R. Ford Presidential Museum welcomes visitors with this lovely fountain. Photo by William Hebert

Left: This Oval Office replica is a favorite attraction at the Gerald R. Ford Presidential Museum. Photo by James Glessner

Facing page: Since its opening in 1981, the Gerald R. Ford Presidential Museum has attracted more than one million visitors. Photo by Pat Bulthuis

Right: The Women's City Club of Grand Rapids, founded in 1924, has occupied its beautifully appointed clubhouse, once the home of Grand Rapids banker, hotel owner, and one-term mayor Martin L. Sweet, since 1927. Photo by Doug Diekman

Facing page, top: The west wall of Bixby's Office Supply Company, located at 45 Ottawa N.W. in the heart of downtown, was permanently brightened in 1976 with a delightful mural commissioned by company president Roger Mayo and designed and executed by artist Roger Bruinekool. Photo by Boots Schmidt

Facing page, bottom: The butterfly mural that brightens the facade of the Water Building took flight on the wings of the efforts of Steketee's youth advisory board. For the past fifteen years, the downtown retailer has chosen eighteen outstanding teenagers annually to serve on the board, which devotes 75 percent of its time to community projects and the rest to in-store programs. The butterfly, which became part of the cityscape in 1979-1980, was designed by a Swedish foreign exchange student serving on the board at the time. Photo by J. Phillip Haven

tensive decorative arts department and will soon be opening a new photographic images gallery. Untold numbers of Grand Rapids schoolchildren have developed a love of art thanks to the museum's educational programming, and the Women's Committee, one of the institution's premier support groups, has been instrumental in introducing an artistically conservative population to the excitement—and the controversies—of contemporary, avant-garde sculpture.

Not all the art in Grand Rapids is confined behind museum walls. Here and there throughout the city, colorful murals brighten formerly blank walls and pieces of sculpture are exposed to the elements and the scrutiny of passersby. Grand Rapids, in fact, boasts one of the largest and most impressive outdoor sculpture collections of any city of its size in the United States. Although few area residents would describe Grand Rapids as an artists' colony, the city has certainly become increasingly art conscious in recent years. Hundreds of talented Grand Rapids area artists exhibit in local museums and galleries, and collectors number not only private individuals but area busi-

Above: **This gallery at the Grand Rapids Art Museum beckons visitors to explore and open themselves up to art. Courtesy, Grand Rapids Art Museum**

Facing page: **This metal sculpture welcomes visitors to Ah-Nab-Awen Bicentennial Park. Photo by Larry Heydenburg**

nesses and governments as well.

Neither the musical nor the dramatic segments of the lively arts have been neglected in the city. Grand Rapids has had a symphony orchestra since 1921, when Ottokar Malek and the St. Cecilia Society organized the Grand Rapids Civic Orchestra, which changed its name two years later to the Grand Rapids Symphony. Incorporated in 1929 and made up solely of unpaid community players for many years, the orchestra took a giant step toward professionalism under the baton of Theo Alcantara, who was appointed conductor and music director in 1974. That year, thanks to a generous grant from the Richard and Helen DeVos Foundation, the symphony hired its first six artists-in-residence, a number that has now risen to more than thirty-five. Today ranked as one of the nation's finest regional orchestras, its principal and assistant principal chairs endowed by local corporations and foundations, the Grand Rapids Symphony Orchestra attracts first-rate international soloists and plays its ten-concert classical series and six-concert pops series to packed houses each season. The 1986-87 season brought to the podium Catherine Comet, the first woman ever hired as music director and conductor of an orchestra of the Grand Rapids Symphony's size and stature.

Sharing the DeVos Hall stage with the orchestra are Opera Grand Rapids and the Grand Rapids Civic Ballet, both homegrown organizations which have come a long way in their pursuit of excellence. Founded in 1967 as the West Michigan Opera Association, Opera Grand Rapids weathered the lean, under-funded, under-attended years to emerge by 1980 as a top-flight, professionally managed company able to at-

tract supremely talented soloists and increasingly re-
ceptive audiences. The Civic Ballet, organized in
1971, has had a similarly successful tale to tell and
an ever-expanding repertoire of beautifully performed
programs.

The curtain also rises regularly at the St. Cecilia
Music Society, which has been an important fixture
of the city's cultural life since its inception. Founded
by local women in 1883, the society occupies a landmark building, completed in 1894 and extensively renovated in 1986, which was the first such structure of
its kind in the country to be built, financed, and operated entirely by women.

For those whose tastes run to legitimate theater,
Grand Rapids has a reservoir of talented players and
a roster of productions in abundance. Area houselights
are lit virtually all year long—at Junior College's
Spectrum Theater, home of the Robeson Players and
Actors' Theater; at Community Circle Theater, in its
recently refurbished summer playhouse in the pavilion
at John Ball Park; at the many summer theaters that
are within easy driving distance of the city; and at
Grand Rapids Civic Theatre, the oldest community
theater in Michigan and one of the oldest in the United
States.

Founded in 1926, the Civic Players, as the group
was originally called, performed throughout the trying
years of the Depression and remained a fixture of the

Facing page: The Grand Rapids Symphony Orchestra presents thirty-two subscription concerts at DeVos Hall each season and numerous chamber orchestra, ensemble, and recital performances throughout Michigan. Photo by Tim Bie er, courtesy, Grand Rapids Symphony Orchestra

Above: Founded in 1883, the Schubert Club all-male chorus is the oldest organization of its kind in the country and is still going strong. Courtesy, Grand Rapids Public Library

community cultural scene despite the lack of a permanent home. That situation was finally remedied in 1979 with the move into the completely renovated Majestic Theater, the only downtown moviehouse to survive the urban renewal of the 1960s. Season after season of increasingly ambitious productions—running the gamut from low comedy to high drama—have attracted a faithful and growing audience. In addition to the six main-stage productions featured each season, Civic Theatre offers two children's productions, adult and young people's acting classes, workshops, open houses, tours, and special events.

Civic Theatre is truly a community organization: over 1,500 area residents are directly involved each year as actors and technical staff for the productions, while hundreds more serve as season ticket campaign workers, ushers, ticket takers, box office personnel, and guild members.

Just as theater audiences are seldom aware of the backstage activities essential in mounting a polished production, so, too, do they tend to forget that ticket sales alone generally account for less than half the money needed to keep the houselights lit and the curtain up. Like arts and cultural institutions everywhere in the United States, those in Grand Rapids rely for their funding on a variety of sources, public as well as private.

The Michigan legislature allocates money every year for arts and cultural institutions. Although the vast bulk of the appropriation is earmarked for Detroit and the eastern side of the state, West Michigan does receive a modest share of the funds through the outstate equity package, established several years ago to

Right: **Civic Theatre's 1985 production of** *A Chorus Line* **played to more than 23,000 people in thirty-one performances. Courtesy, Grand Rapids Civic Theater**

Facing page: **A quiet walk along the shores of Lake Michigan is always a nice way to end the day. Photo by William Hebert**

fund projects involving tourism, civic centers, historic parks, libraries, and zoos. In 1987 Grand Rapids was set to receive more than $500,000 in outstate equity funding through seventeen state grants. Grant recipients included the Grand Center, the Grand Rapids Art and Public museums, the Community Enrichment Office, Ladies Literary Club, and the St. Cecilia Music Society.

The Arts Council of Greater Grand Rapids, incorporated in 1968, also extends financial support to area arts and cultural institutions. One of the largest arts councils in the country, the umbrella organization raises funds for its member institutions, which include most of the city's major performing arts groups, through its sponsorship of the city's annual festival of the arts and the yearly Combined Arts Campaign.

Community efforts also play a significant role in preserving the liveliness of the local cultural scene. Every arts and cultural institution in Grand Rapids has its own dedicated volunteers who raise funds, serve

tirelessly on committees and boards of directors, and devote enormous amounts of time and energy to a variety of unheralded but entirely necessary tasks. Private benefactors, local businesses, corporations, and foundations can always be relied upon for financial and in-kind assistance, and the general public has been more than generous in donating prized possessions to local museum collections and contributing money to arts and cultural organization fund drives.

Although certain corporate and personal names recur constantly on the lists of major donors to the city's cultural institutions, these organizations and individuals have no monopoly on service and giving. Grand Rapids, above all, values personal commitment, and those who choose to become involved are welcomed for their talents, their enthusiasm, and the diversity of their contributions. Whole-hearted citizen support greatly enriches the organizations that contribute so much to the quality of life in Grand Rapids, and the entire city reaps the rewards.

PART

2

Partners in Progress

From Old-Line Business to High-Tech Industries

The Grand Rapids Area Chamber of Commerce celebrates its 100th anniversary this year—1987. But it is not just the longevity of the Chamber that we celebrate. It is the strength, the support, and the dedication of our "Partners in Progress" that has brought us to this 100-year mark; we are grateful for that dedication and support and we salute the many businesses and corporations, and the individuals who represent them, that have helped us to shape and guide our economic destiny.

In our long history, Grand Rapids has grown from a small industrial city to a large metropolitan area, the second city in the state, and the business, financial, legal, and medical center of western Michigan. The area has weathered economic downswings and periods of calm. Today West Michigan is on the threshold of unprecedented growth, and the Chamber, through its membership, is pledged to participate in that growth.

The Grand Rapids Area Chamber of Commerce serves more than 2,800 firms, professional offices, and individuals. Its mission is to promote business and commerce for the Grand Rapids area through leadership in economic, political, and social development, and its programs are carried out through a strong committee system.

It is this committee system that is the lifeblood of the Chamber—a core of hardworking volunteers who give of their talent, their expertise, and countless hours to further the work of the Chamber.

The Chamber is governed by a volunteer board of directors, which includes the chairman of the board; chairman of The Right Place Program executive committee; the president of the Chamber Foundation; the Long-Range Planning Committee; and the vice-chairpersons of each division. Many more volunteers (approximately 800) labor devotedly in the ranks as committee members. Staff people, including the Chamber president, support the entire organization.

It is to the volunteers that we pay tribute. The forebear of today's Chamber was the Board of Trade, organized in 1887. That first group established the tradition of dedicated volunteerism that has prevailed for 100 years.

Grand Rapids is singularly blessed with the spirit of volunteerism, and nowhere does that spirit shine more brightly than in the business community.

It goes without saying that the industrial and entrepreneurial communities contribute, even determine, the economic health of West Michigan business. But as corporate and business citizens of the community, they also make enormous contributions to the cultural, educational, and social welfare of the area.

As organizations, they give many dollars, and other resources, to a variety of community endeavors. They encourage employees to participate in civic activities, and make sure they have the time to chair committees, attend functions, and contribute time and energy. Without the blessing of employers, where would volunteer organizations be?

But it is not just the organizations that benefit from the activities of their volunteers. Volunteers themselves derive many rewards from their association with the organizations.

Volunteers learn new skills, make new friends, exploit hidden talents, and reap the rewards of helping to make their community grow in the many intangible attributes that improve the quality of life and make a community unique. Volunteerism is the coin with which citizens invest in their communities, an investment that pays significant and long-term dividends.

The Grand Rapids Area Chamber of Commerce is proud of its volunteers and grateful for their efforts—over the past 100 years and into the next. are detailed on the following pages have chosen to support this important literary and civic event. They are a mixture of the recently founded juxtaposed against the old-line, of the small enterprise beside the orporate giant, of the locally owned contrasted with the subsidiary of an international organization, of the service oriented, of the educational institution beside the business that needs its graduate; but more important, these are the stories of enterprising individuals within a particular time and place.

The Amway Grand Plaza Hotel lights up in tones of orange in downtown Grand Rapids. Photo by William Hebert

179

X-RITE, INC.

The story of X-Rite, Inc., is the classic entrepreneurial story, says company president D. "Ted" Thompson—from a moonlighting basement operation to a gleaming 127,000-square-foot, $4-million corporate headquarters and $14 million in annual sales in less than 30 years.

X-Rite manufactures quality-control products for the graphic arts, photographic, packaging, microfilm, X-ray, and nondestructive testing industries. The firm markets its products across the United States and to more than 40 foreign countries, and is one of the few companies in the United States to sell computerized photographic products in Japan.

X-Rite was founded in 1958. Five of its founders, including Thompson, were aerospace engineers working for Lear Siegler, Inc., in Grand Rapids. The two remaining founders had backgrounds in manufacturing and television advertising. The group had one objective—to own their own business. They incorporated as Foresight Enterprises, and, without giving up the security of their daytime jobs, set about looking for a product—one that would not require much capital to produce.

The group toyed with a whole series of products, but none proved successful until, putting into practice an axiom of entrepreneurship, the partners found a need and filled it. At the time the only way to provide permanent identification on X-rays was with small lead letters that were stored in much the same way as printers' type and had to be laboriously applied one by one. Why couldn't Foresight Enterprises develop an adhesive radiopaque tape that could be attached to the X-ray film cassette, written on, and processed with the X-ray?

It took the little band of engineers two years to develop a successful product, including the machinery to manufacture the tape. "Fortunately," recalls Thompson, "it didn't take a lot of money, just a lot of time." The tape was named X-Rite, and the company was on its way.

By 1968 sales were strong enough that the partners believed the firm could support one full-time person. Thompson was elected. "I swept the floors, made the product, packaged the product, and answered customers' questions," he recalls.

But a one-product company was not the prototype of Foresight Enterprises' dream of a high-flying business. As a result, the corporation developed a silver-recovery system to reclaim the silver from photographic fixer solutions. Now the firm had two products, and sales were sufficient to support two full-time people. Another of the founders, Quinten "Jack" Ward, came aboard as president and general manager, and Thompson took over engineering.

After being housed in member basements and then in a series of rented buildings, most of them uncomfortable and inadequate but with low rent, the company finally had enough capital to think about more spacious and practical quarters. The firm leased a building at 4500 Roger B. Chaffee Drive, and a third partner, Leonard Blanding, left

The computerized machine shop at X-Rite.

X-Rite, Inc., moved into its new $4-million facility in early 1987.

The more than 200 instruments
in the company's product line are
assembled in this area.

his full-time job at Lear and came into the business as shop manager. In 1974 Foresight Enterprises built a new facility at 4101 Roger B. Chaffee Drive.

From that time on the company experienced slow but steady growth. In 1976, with sales approaching one million dollars, Thompson took over as president and chief executive officer. One of his first acts was to put together a management team that has been a major factor in the firm's growth.

The core of the team included Edward Hamilton as operations manager, Bernard Berg as director of engineering, and Beverly Ingle as controller and financial director. All vice-presidents today, these people are still with the corporation. Later Robert Jernstadt was added to the team as information manager, and Phillip Wolf became vice-president of marketing.

It was also in 1976 that the firm began a shrink-wrapping operation and decided it had the resources to manufacture electronic instrument-type products. "That was our turning point," says Thompson.

The first such product was a photo optical instrument to control the processing of X-ray film. A companion instrument for the hospital laboratory darkroom came along soon after. With the introduction of the electronic instrument products, the company has, since 1976, experienced an average 30-percent annual growth.

In the spring of 1986 Foresight Enterprises changed its name to X-Rite, Inc., and went public, issuing 835,000 shares to raise capital for many projects, including the construction of a new manufacturing facility. In the spring of 1987 the firm, with a work force of 170 people, moved into its new corporate headquarters at 3100 44th Street SW.

In addition to Thompson, Blanding, and Ward, the original founding partners were Larry Fleming, Dave Hoyle, Rufus Teesdale, and Chuck Van Namen. When the company went public, Dr. Marvin DeVries, an economist

and dean of the F.E. Seidman School of Business at Grand Valley State College, and Glenn M. Walters, a local business consultant, were elected to the board of directors. Hoyle is currently chairman of the board.

Today more than 75 percent of X-Rite's business is in electronic photographic instrument products, with more than 200 instruments in the X-Rite line. The company recently signed a multimillion-dollar, long-term contract to manufacture densitometers for Eastman Kodak Company, and it supplies sensitometers and densitometers to all the world's major film manufacturing companies. The graphic arts industry represents another vast market that X-Rite officials say they have barely tapped.

Grand Rapids has been an ideal location for X-Rite, Inc. Area resources, such as transportation, shipping, and special professional services, are excellent. But the area's greatest resource is its people—upstanding, hardworking people—the kind who make the best employees.

X-Rite's employees are X-Rite's success.

The new X-Rite quality-control
densitometer made for photofin-
ishing mini-labs.

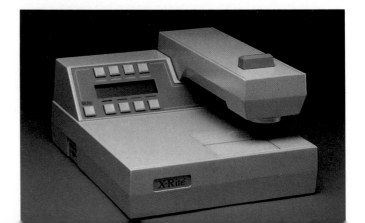

FISHBECK, THOMPSON, CARR & HUBER

When the complex demands of our modern society waste energy or pose a threat to the environment, engineers on the staff of Fishbeck, Thompson, Carr & Huber (FTC&H) employ a wide range of engineering and scientific skills to avoid or correct environmental damage and conserve energy resources. The emphasis on innovative, effective, affordable design has earned the firm national recognition.

FTC&H was founded in Lansing more than 30 years ago as a civil engineering practice. In the ensuing years further capabilities were added in response to the increasing complexity of clients' problems. Headquartered in Ada, Michigan, since 1984, the company employs civil, chemical, mechanical, electrical, structural, and environmental engineers, as well as geologists, hydrogeologists, geophysicists, microbiologists, chemists, and support staff.

The firm serves more than 100 industrial clients and more than 50 municipalities in Michigan and throughout the United States. Municipal clients in West Michigan include Grand Rapids, Kalamazoo, Grand Haven, Lowell, Big Rapids, Cadillac, and Fremont. Private-sector clients in the area include Steelcase, Inc., Amway Corporation, Wolverine World Wide, Inc., Mazda Corporation, Keebler Company, St. Mary's Hospital, Hackley Hospital, Blodgett Memorial Medical Center, WZZM Television, Shaw-Walker, Lear Siegler, and General Motors Corporation. FTC&H was also recently retained by the World Bank and the U.S. State Department as a consultant on projects in Tunisia.

Staff members design municipal and industrial wastewater treatment facilities; hazardous waste identification and control methods; water treatment, storage, and distribution systems; and energy-saving HVAC and lighting systems. For its work, the company has received major design awards, including the Consulting Engineers Council/

Innovative treatment of metal-finishing waste at the Murray-Ohio Manufacturing Company in Tennessee received a major engineering award.

Michigan Eminent Conceptor Award for the innovative treatment of metal-finishing waste at the Murray-Ohio Manufacturing Company plant in Lawrenceburg, Tennessee; the *Specifying Engineer Magazine* Engineering Achievement Award for the fan coil induction system designed for one of the buildings in the Amway Corporation complex in Ada; and the Joint Engineering Council of Western Michigan's Outstanding Engineering Achievement Award for the Wolverine World Wide waste treatment and materials recovery project.

Other innovative concepts developed by FTC&H include the extraction of volatile materials from groundwater, which significantly reduces clean-up costs; a direct-filtration water treatment plant in Michigan; a thermal storage system for interior environmental control; specific treatment for specific wastes; and the treatment of hazardous waste on the site of the incident.

The past growth and development of Fishbeck, Thompson, Carr & Huber has been directed to meeting clients' needs. In the future, capabilities will be further expanded to enable the company to continue to respond to clients' requirements with the latest technology and innovative solutions.

Northwest Ottawa Water Treatment Plant—the first direct-filtration system in Michigan.

MAZDA DISTRIBUTORS GREAT LAKES

The gleaming, pyramidal building at 618 Kenmoor SE that houses Mazda Distributors Great Lakes is symbolic of the company—contemporary, innovative, forthright, enduring.

Mazda Distributors Great Lakes is a Mazda automobile distributorship for five midwestern states—Michigan, Illinois, Indiana, Ohio, and Wisconsin. Representing one of the top-quality foreign-manufactured cars in the country, Mazda Great Lakes is a 10-year-old organization that was founded on the happy circumstance of being in the right place at the right time.

The company was formed in 1977 by Peter Cook, Robert Hooker, and Max Boersma at a time when the Japanese automaker, Toyo Kogyo, was seeking a more secure niche in the American auto market for its Mazda automobiles. Mazda then ranked among the top three in sales in auto markets in other countries, but only 17th in the United States. The firm was revamping its U.S. marketing strategy and looking for new, enthusiastic, aggressive distributors to handle its product.

Cook had owned a European-import auto distributorship for 22 years, but eventually, the parent company would be taking over the distributorship. Cook wanted to keep his own organization intact and was looking for a new business opportunity. Taking Hooker and Boersma into partnership, Cook formed an alliance with Mazda that has proven sound and rewarding for both.

In 1977 there were 65 Mazda dealers in the five-state region that Mazda Great Lakes serves; today there are 125.

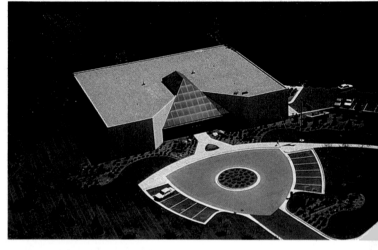

Mazda's high-performance rotary engine is unique in the automotive industry. The driveway in front of the Mazda Great Lakes offices was designed to resemble the engine's triangular-shape rotor.

Mazda Great Lakes has developed a comprehensive support organization to serve those dealers.

In addition to supplying cars and parts, Mazda Great Lakes maintains a training facility in Grand Rapids to train Mazda mechanics and technicians. The firm also has on-site training programs in parts department management, business management, and sales. Mazda dealers can count on the company to be fair and straightforward. "We make no private deals with any individual dealer," says president Bob Hooker. "The arrangements we make are applicable to all, and our records are open to any of our dealers to show how we allocate cars."

Openness, in fact, is a key word in the Mazda Great Lakes business philosophy. "Our building makes a statement about how we operate—the open look and feel of the building reflect our approach to business and to our management style," says Hooker.

The same attitude that prevails toward the firm's dealers extends to employees. The loosely structured, informal organization, with easy access to management, makes for pleasant working conditions and little turnover among staff members. Innovative employee benefit programs add incentive to stay with the company.

The service philosophy also extends to the community at large. Mazda Distributors Great Lakes executives and staff members donate much time and energy and money to community activities and causes.

The central atrium in Mazda Great Lakes' office building blends an exterior-type garden with an elegant reception area, and brings natural light deep into the center of the building.

S.J. WISINSKI AND COMPANY

Just nine months after its founding in January 1986, S.J. Wisinski and Company ranked as one of Grand Rapids' largest commercial, industrial, and investment real estate firms. The business has grown very fast, "but it has been controlled growth," says company owner and president Stanley J. Wisinski III. "We are taking one step at a time, weighing each move carefully."

Wisinski, former president of Westdale Commercial Investment Company and active in the commercial real estate business for more than 25 years, attributes his firm's rapid growth to "a very good following in the business" and to a "competent, experienced sales force, also with very good client followings." Complementing the sales staff and contributing to the company's success is an efficient and capable office staff. Says Wisinski, "We believe our success is a result of providing excellent service and a complete job regardless of the size of the task to be performed."

Further evidence of the firm's commitment to excellence is the number of professional real estate designations—including Certified Commercial Investment Member (CCIM), Certified Property Manager (CPM), and Society of Industrial and Office Realtors (SIOR)—held by its sales personnel. Wisinski himself holds the SIOR and CCIM designations, and was selected Realtor of the Year in 1985 by the Grand Rapids Real Estate Board.

Currently headquartered at 3940 Peninsular Drive SE in Grand Rapids, the firm will be breaking ground for a new corporate office at Cascade Road and East Paris Road in Grand Rapids Township.

S.J. Wisinski and Company specializes in sales and leasing of commercial, industrial, and office properties in western and Central Michigan, and also offers a complete property management service. Property profiles include existing structures, conversions, new construction, and build to suit.

While not a development company, the firm works closely with commercial and industrial developers, handling site selection and acquisition, leasing and marketing, and management. S.J. Wisinski and Company represents giant corporations as well as individuals with small holdings, buyers and sellers, and tenants and landlords.

Wisinski began his real estate career with the Westdale Company in 1960, the same year he got his Michigan real estate license. In 1973 he organized Westdale Commercial Investment Company and remained its president until 1985, when, feeling the time had come "for a change," he formed his own business. A prominent member of the business community and active in civic affairs, Wisinski is a past director of the board of the Friends of Marywood Foundation and a past member of the Marywood Academy Board of Education. He has also served on the board of directors of the Greater Grand Rapids Chamber Foundation and is currently senior vice-chairman of the board of directors of the Grand Rapids Area Chamber of Commerce.

Members of the staff of S.J. Wisinski and Company. Seated (left to right) are Barb Dunstan, Sue Molhoek, Nancy Fraser, and Pia White, corporate vice-president. Standing (left to right) are Robin O'Connor; Mose Hattem; Norris Brookens; Jim Badaluco, corporate vice-president; Stanley J. Wisinski III, president; Gary Steinhoff; Denny Anastor; and Charlie Boylen. Not pictured, Stuart Cok and Bill Taminga.

AUTODIE CORPORATION

Founded in 1963 as a small tool and die shop, Autodie Corporation has risen to become the largest and most modern die-making operation in North America and the only one capable of producing complete sets of dies for an automobile's entire outerbody shell. What has moved the firm into its position as a leading manufacturer of the large-scale, complex dies used by the automobile industry to stamp out car bodies is a 25-year history of innovation and the vision of its founder and president, Joseph N. Spruit.

Insisting from the beginning on high-quality products, on-time delivery, fair pricing, and the ability to produce out-of-the-ordinary tooling, Spruit has consistently planned for and sought out opportunities for growth. Over the years he has had the foresight to invest in state-of-the-art equipment, no matter how costly, and to apply the most advanced technology to the company's operation.

In 1982-1983, when other tool and die manufacturers were just considering the idea, Spruit had already made the decision to expand into CAD/CAM (computer-aided design/computer-aided manufacturing). That decision not only gave Autodie the jump on its competitors, but the new technology dramatically increased both the firm's efficiency and its ability to respond to significant changes in automobile manufacturing practices.

In an attempt to reduce labor costs the Big Three automakers have begun simplifying assembly procedures by combining small parts into larger components. With its state-of-the-art equipment, Autodie was already geared up to meet the new demands and is now under contract to General Motors and Chrysler Corporation to produce complete sets of dies for three upcoming car models. The firm also manufactures the large-scale injection and compression molds used to form plastic parts such as car and truck bodies, and supplies tooling to the aerospace, home furnishings,

The largest and most modern die-making operation in North America, Autodie Corporation is capable of producing complete sets of dies for an automobile's entire outerbody shell.

communications, and farm implements industries.

Craftsmanship and quality are paramount at Autodie. Employees' skills are constantly being honed, and a rigorous four-year apprenticeship program is currently training 40 metalworkers in the exacting tool and die craft.

The tremendous growth of Autodie in recent years has led to an issue of publicly traded stock and an enormous plant expansion. The company's facilities, headquartered at 44 Coldbrook NW, now extend over a four-block area. The recently purchased Wolverine Building on Ottawa NW will house Autodie's newly formed subsidiary, Autobond Corp., which will manufacture automatic welding and bonding tooling for the automotive industry. Another wholly owned subsidiary, Autocam, makes high-precision parts used primarily in fuel-injection systems.

The spirit of innovation and an unswerving commitment to quality have taken Autodie to the top. And no matter where continuing growth leads the company and its subsidiaries in the years to come, Autodie Corporation will continue to take the utmost pride in the quality of its work and the caliber of its people.

Autodie Corporation is headquartered at 44 Coldbrook NW, Grand Rapids.

SUSPA INCORPORATED

Suspa Incorporated, a daughter company of the German-based Suspa Federungstechnik GmbH, was established in Grand Rapids in 1974 to manufacture a pneumatic gas lift cylinder for the U.S. automotive industry.

In 1974, because of the gasoline crisis and the soaring price of automobiles, the small, economical, energy-efficient hatchback was becoming a popular car among American automobile buyers. Suspa of Germany was a leading supplier of the gas cylinder used to raise and hold open the hatchback lid, and, because the demand for U.S.-made hatchback cars was on the increase, the company decided to open an American manufacturing facility to directly supply the U.S. market.

Grand Rapids was chosen as the site for a variety of reasons but primarily because of its close proximity to Detroit and the major U.S. auto manufacturers. Still the only Suspa U.S. facility, the Grand Rapids plant is both a manufacturing operation and the firm's sales office for the United States market.

Suspa gas cylinders in all sizes are used the world over in hundreds of different applications. The small Type 16 cylinder, found on hatchback car lids, is currently the only product made in the Grand Rapids plant, but other products will be added to its manufacturing operation in the future.

Suspa has, in addition to the Grand Rapids plant, three manufacturing facilities in Germany and one in Switzerland. The company also has sales offices throughout Europe, the Far East, and Australia.

Suspa was founded in 1950 as a manufacturer of mechanical and hydraulic suspension elements for bicycles, mopeds, and motorcycles. Faced with a need to diversify, the company, under the direction of Fritz Bauer, sought other applications for suspension parts. The immediate answer was SUSPAMAT, a suspension system for automatic washing machines.

Although it might seem like an implausible leap from motorcycles to washing machines, in truth, the similarity between the action of motorcycle wheels and the horizontal axis action of the European automatic washer was such that the Suspa suspension system could be easily adapted to the washer. Today more than 90 percent of the washing machines built in Europe still use the SUSPAMAT suspension system.

Erina Hanka (standing), vice-president and general manager of Suspa Incorporated, with Gary A. Babcock (left), director of engineering, and Michael A. Dunlap, director of marketing.

Currently the product manufactured by Suspa Incorporated is the Type 16 gas lift cylinder for hatchback automobile lids.

The success of that product led to further diversification. Volvo, the Swedish auto manufacturer, asked Suspa to help develop a pneumatic spring. Such a spring had been invented in 1875 by a Frenchman living in the United States, but the invention had never been perfected to the point where it could be mass produced. Suspa solved the problems inherent in the original design and put itself on the road to becoming a multinational corporation.

Next the firm turned to the office seating industry. It recognized that by adding a simple locking valve to the gas spring, it could be used as a mechanism that makes office chairs adjustable—both for height and for the angle of the chair back.

That concept also proved successful, and the European office seating industry became a major Suspa customer. It has only been in recent years, says Suspa Incorporated vice-president and general manager Erina Hanka, that U.S. office seating manufacturers have begun to use the gas cylinder in swivel office chairs. The versatility of the Suspa-designed gas cylinder makes an office chair adjustable to any individual, regardless of height or weight.

Because Suspa Incorporated made only the gas cylinder for the hatchback car, its first years in Grand Rapids were difficult. "We had only automotive customers," says Hanka. "When they worked overtime, we worked overtime, and when they laid off employees, we laid off employees."

It was obvious that the company needed to find other uses for its product. Through an innovative sales and marketing program, Suspa Incorporated developed more than 1,000 additional applications for the Type 16 gas cylinder, which can now be found in office electronic equipment such as printers and copiers, electronic test equipment, hospital equipment, industrial machinery, trucks, catering trucks, boats, and buses.

Within four years of its founding Suspa Incorporated was producing double its 1974 production rate, and demand for the Type 16 products continued to double every year. Today the plant manufactures 50,000 units per week. Six years after it opened the company had outgrown its original quarters and moved to a new 54,000-square-foot facility at 3970 Roger B. Chaffee Boulevard SE. By 1986 even that space had become inadequate, and the firm began a remodeling and expansion project to add another 10,000 square feet to the facility. In 1983 *Inc.* magazine listed Suspa Incorporated as number 177 among its 500 "fastest growing, privately held businesses in the United States."

The remarkable growth of the company owes much to its personnel, says Hanka. "The quality of the people in Grand Rapids is extraordinary. And without the people in the plant, we wouldn't be here. The worker/management relationship is excellent. We employ the team approach in every department, and it has been enormously successful for us."

Suspa Incorporated is a stellar member of a small but important group of manufacturers in the Grand Rapids area—firms with parent companies outside the United States. The corporation has grown and prospered in the Grand Rapids business climate, and its success has led it to persuade other foreign companies to share in the Grand Rapids experience.

KENDALL COLLEGE OF ART AND DESIGN

Kendall College of Art and Design is heading into the future on the crest of an exciting wave of growth. During the past 10 years, under the dynamic leadership of president Phyllis I. Danielson, the school has increased its enrollment 100 percent, launched its first Capital Fund Campaign, moved into downtown Grand Rapids, added five new majors, offered two new degree programs including the four-year bachelor of fine arts, which was instituted in 1979, and gained a national reputation for excellence.

Founded as the David Wolcott Kendall Memorial School in 1928 by the famous furniture designer's widow, Helen, the institution opened its doors in 1931 to 35 students. Over the next 30 years, in response to the changing needs of students, the business community, and society at large, the David Wolcott Kendall Memorial School evolved into the Kendall School of Design, and now the Kendall College of Art and Design.

In 1962, with student enrollment climbing, the college moved out of its original quarters in the Kendall home and into a facility at 1110 College Avenue NE. Within two decades Kendall was ready to move again—this time into a building acquired in 1981 from Grand Rapids Junior College. Centrally located in the heart of downtown, close to the business and design communities and the city's cultural center, the carefully renovated building at 111 Division North was ready for occupancy in 1984.

In addition to superb studio facilities, a permanent exhibit gallery, and five floors of classroom space, Kendall's new location boasts a Learning Resource Center whose 11,000 volumes, 35,000 slides, and fine collection of master furniture drawings represent an invaluable source of art and design information.

Kendall College of Art and Design is made up of three major divisions—Design Studies, for furniture, industrial, environmental, and interior design; Visual Communications, for advertising, graphic, and broadcast/video design; and Visual Arts, for fine art and illustration. No matter what division they choose, all Kendall students spend their first year in a foundation program to develop artistic and verbal skills.

Kendall is the only area college to offer professional degrees in art and design. Three degree options are available, but more than 90 percent of the students opt for the four-year bachelor of fine arts degree, and over 90 percent of the college's graduates find employment in their chosen fields. Kendall students and faculty members are consistently among the winners of prestigious art and design competitions nationwide, and the interiors of countless area buildings are graced by their works.

Dedicated to graduating highly qualified professionals, the institution is equally committed to serving the community. Not only does Kendall offer educational programs to area residents and creative design services to businesses and nonprofit organizations throughout the region, but Dr. Danielson also plays an active community leadership role. Under her energetic and capable direction, Kendall College of Art and Design is well on its way to becoming one of the finest design schools in the nation.

The colorful mural on the north wall of the Kendall College of Art and Design was done by faculty member Ron Riksen, associate professor of visual communications and coordinator of graphic design.

Portrait of a ballet dancer by Kendall illustration graduate Vicki Van Ameyden.

MICHIGAN NATIONAL BANK

Michigan National Bank has consolidated for growth. Known for its tradition of innovations and service, the statewide banking corporation, which is one of the largest bank holding companies in Michigan, recently restructured its organization to create a more service-oriented, cost-effective branch banking system.

Today serving individual and commercial banking needs in major population centers throughout the state, Michigan National Bank was founded in 1941 by Howard J. Stoddard through the purchase of six Michigan institutions. One of those initial acquisitions was the National Bank of Grand Rapids, which became a branch of Michigan National's Lansing bank. Later acquired as affiliates were two other area institutions: Central Bank, N.A., in Grand Rapids and First National Bank of Wyoming.

The history of Michigan National has been marked by innovation. A state pioneer in branch banking, Saturday banking, and in extending credit for mobile homes, Michigan National introduced the nation's first drive-in banking window in 1948, installed the state's first computerized bank operations center in 1959, started one of the country's first credit card operations in 1966, and established the largest automatic teller machine network in the United States in 1982.

The Grand Rapids market, like all of the institution's local markets, is important to Michigan National and to its many community-minded employees. Not only is there an extensive network of branch offices and Michigan

Money automatic teller machines throughout the Grand Rapids area, but the corporation also has had long-standing ties with the city and a tradition of community involvement that goes beyond serving financial needs.

The Michigan National Bank Building at 77 Monroe Center is a Grand Rapids landmark. The structure's architectural embellishments, depicting rapids, pine forests, and canoes, pay tribute to the city's past.

Until the reorganization, which was announced in December 1986, Michigan National Corporation operated a system of 21 banks, each with its own charter, board of directors, and branch system. Under the new structure, made possible by a change in Michigan's banking laws, 15 of Michigan National's banks have been merged into one corporate entity—a single-chartered statewide bank operating under the name Michigan National Banks.

The institution's nine former geographic regions have been consolidated into three: the Southeast Region, headquartered in Detroit; the Central Region, based in Lansing; and the Western Region, headquartered in Grand Rapids. Alden G. Walters, a West Michigan native who began his career with Michigan National Bank in Grand Rapids in 1958, is the Western Region chairman.

With assets of $7.7 billion and earnings that continue to show a steady annual rise, Michigan National Bank intends to expand its West Michigan presence by providing exemplary service to its customers.

Michigan National Bank's Grand Plaza office. The magnificent ceiling, dating from 1915, has been carefully restored to its original splendor.

C-TEC, INC.

C-Tec, a top U.S. manufacturer of access flooring, is one of Grand Rapids' newer companies, although the product it manufactures has been produced in the city for 20 years.

Access flooring is a system of removable floor panels installed in office buildings and computer rooms that provides easy access to the miles of electronic cable that are the lifelines of computer systems. Like the computer industry it serves, access flooring has come a long way in 20 years.

The manufacturer's origins date back to 1957, when G. Jack Cooper, a Grand Rapids building contractor, started a business called Move-A-Wall Corporation, which manufactured and installed office partitions. The partitions were the forerunner of today's modular office systems. Most were eight to 10 feet high with wood paneling three-quarters of the way up and a top section of glass or wood to the ceiling. The panels could be put together in many different configurations to create partially open but private work areas, or even enclosed offices with glass windows.

Easy to assemble, the panels were the answer to creating practical and efficient office space at a reasonable cost. In 1959 Cooper changed the corporate name to Architectural Systems, Inc. Three years later he sold the business to Westinghouse Electric Corporation and joined that company himself. Over the next 20 years Cooper was involved in developing a large division of Westinghouse, manufacturing systems furniture, office seating, and access flooring, which was introduced in 1965.

In 1981 Cooper organized C-Tec and bought the access flooring division from Westinghouse. The purchase included the complete product line, the manufacturing equipment, and the dealer organization.

Access flooring was developed to solve the problem of getting electrical power, other cables, and air conditioning to the computers. Today office electronic work stations have created the need for access flooring in the general office area. At first the raised flooring was thoroughly practical but utilitarian in appearance, offering limited choices in standard vinyl floor-covering materials, and was hollow sounding and cold underfoot.

C-Tec has taken the original concept and improved upon it. In 1985 the company introduced a new type of access flooring called Tec-Crete. The new product combines the tensile strength of steel and the compressive strength of concrete to create a safe, durable, exceptionally strong, uniform, and quiet floor panel. Best of all, the panels come in a choice of surfaces, from high-pressure plastic laminate to plush carpeting in several colors and patterns.

C-Tec sells to a worldwide market, with its largest foreign markets in Japan and Israel. C-Tec flooring can be found in practically every *Fortune* 500 company in the United States—Lockheed, Boeing, Hughes Aircraft, IBM, and GTE, to name a few. "Two of our most interesting installations," says Cooper, "have been 20 stories in the World Trade Center in New York and at the Cape Canaveral Space Center in Florida."

C-Tec is not just innovative in the product it manufactures. The firm practices progressive, innovative management as well. "We are technology-oriented—we use welding robots, for instance—but we are people-oriented, too," explains Cooper.

The company has instituted the three-day work week for production employees. The plant operates six days a week, and people work 12-hour shifts, day or night. Every eight weeks the shifts rotate. In that way employees get an extra paid week off every 16 weeks in addition to their regular vacation time. The system not only gives the production employees freedom to pursue other interests, it provides C-Tec with excellent facility utilization.

In addition, all employees, production and administrative, are salaried. "Production and office people are treated alike and are expected to assume responsibilities in a like degree. Our people have responded very well. We have far less absenteeism and similar problems, and our people bring to the job a greater degree of respect and sense of responsibility to their work," says Cooper.

G. Jack Cooper, founder and president.

Corporate offices and the original manufacturing facility are located at 3433 Lousma Drive SE, Grand Rapids.

A local television control room is enhanced with access flooring produced by C-Tec, which is not only utilitarian but attractive as well.

As a member of the business community, C-Tec has added significantly to the community as a whole. The firm, which started with 50 employees in 1981, now has 140, and company officials point out that if Cooper had not purchased the access flooring division from Westinghouse, the entire operation would have been moved out of the area. In 1984 C-Tec built a 40,000-square-foot manufacturing facility at 3700 32nd Street for the production of its new Tec-Crete line, and has an additional 25 acres for expansion. Corporate offices and the original manufacturing facility are located at 3433 Lousma Drive SE.

Company personnel also have a commitment to the community and make a point of becoming involved in community activities. Cooper, long active with the Grand Rapids Area Chamber of Commerce, is its 1987 chairman of the board.

C-Tec represents the very best in Grand Rapids business and industry—a company on the cutting edge of new technology, committed to its product, its people, and its community.

GERBER PRODUCTS COMPANY

Babies are Gerber's business, but mothers are the company's mainstay. And whatever a mother buys for her child, quality is the most important consideration.

Gerber Products Company has been built on quality because mothers are the most quality-conscious, best-informed consumer group in the world. In fact, it was one such mother who helped set the firm on the road to the preeminent position it occupies today.

In 1927 Frank Gerber and his son Dan were running the family canning factory in Fremont, Michigan, and Dan's wife, tired of straining peas for their seven-month-old daughter, wanted to know why the Fremont Canning Company couldn't market a product that would relieve her of the chore. Dan approached his father, who liked the idea, and the following year a line of five Gerber Strained Baby Foods made its debut. The rest, as someone once remarked, is history.

In 1943, two years after the Fremont Canning Company became Gerber Products Company, the adult food line was discontinued entirely, and baby products became what Gerber began calling in 1948 its *only* business. In 1956 the firm went public, but the family connection remained in the person of Daniel F. Gerber, Jr., who served as chairman of the board until he stepped down shortly before his death in 1974.

Today mothers in 60 countries around the world have 177 Gerber baby food products to choose from, and the famous Gerber baby, sketched in 1928 by Dorothy Hope Smith, is a grandmother herself. During the 1980s Gerber began to diversify. Acquisitions of such companies as Bates Childrenswear, Buster Brown Apparel, Weather Tamer,

The state-of-the-art juice-filling operation at Gerber's Fremont baby food manufacturing facility handles 800 eight-ounce jars per minute.

and Century expanded the firm's product line into a broad selection of children's merchandise—much of it sold worldwide—that currently includes furniture, mattresses and accessories, strollers, clothing, car seats, pacifiers, squeeze toys, and diaper pins. The company also markets low-cost life insurance to growing families, provides quality preschool education through its network of Gerber Children's Centers, and most recently the company organized Soft Care Apparel, Inc., which manufactures and markets Curity®-brand children's wear, bedding, and cloth diapers under an exclusive trademark license with The Kendall Company.

Baby food remains the foundation on which the corporation rests, and food products continue to account for two-thirds of its profits. And what accounts for the Gerber brand's consistent position as a top seller in all categories is a 60-year tradition of excellence.

As chairman of the board and chief executive officer William L. McKinley pointed out to stockholders in the company's 1986 annual report, "Dan and Frank Gerber understood and reiterated to all the fact that only the best would do in serving a parent's most precious possession. Quality was never to be compromised, advertising would be truthful and helpful, and we would use input from nutrition experts in every offering. . . . This heritage persists today. . . ." and will continue to guide Gerber Products Company through the years to come.

The Gerber Products Company corporate headquarters in Fremont, Michigan. Tours of the baby food manufacturing plant, also located in Fremont, attract approximately 15,000 people each year. Tourists are greeted at the Visitor Center, which includes a museum and gift shop.

RYDER TRUCK RENTAL, INC.

The yellow Ryder truck is a familiar sight on West Michigan highways, and most people think of Ryder as a one-way or local truck rental company. In fact, Ryder Truck Rental, Inc., is the largest truck rental firm in the world, and the consumer truck rental business is only half the story.

The company is also the world's largest provider of long-term, full-service commercial truck leasing and truck rental. Many of the major corporations in America do not own their truck fleets but rather lease them from Ryder.

Ryder has two options for commercial customers—renting equipment (from a week to a year) or leasing (from one to five years) from Ryder, or using customer-owned, Ryder-maintained equipment. Available vehicles range from small vans to 18-wheel tractor-trailer combinations. Ryder will provide full maintenance service for the life of each vehicle, and will even provide drivers.

The West Michigan Ryder story began in 1973, when the Miami-based firm moved into this market with no facility and only one employee—the newly appointed executive district manager, Richard Goodrich. The company purchased four acres at 651 A.I.S. Drive SW, and Goodrich supervised the building of a new Ryder-designed "shop." Business started with 10 trucks and one customer—Weyerhaeuser Company. Revenues at the end of the first full year, 1974, were $275,000. At the close of 1986 revenues for Ryder Truck Rental, Inc., of West Michigan were $34 million. And Weyerhaeuser is still a customer.

The Grand Rapids district is the parent of a second West Michigan district—Grand Haven—and includes 16 Ryder facilities, from Lansing and Jackson on the eastern edge, to Grand Haven and Muskegon on the west side, and as far north as Traverse City and south to White Pigeon. Among Ryder's commercial customers are Amway Corporation, Herman Miller, Yoplait USA, and Squirt Pak. The firm also has 44 dealers in the Grand Rapids district alone offering one-way or local consumer truck rentals.

Service and safety are the cornerstones of Ryder's success. The nationwide network of Ryder company-owned facilities guarantees that any customer driving a Ryder truck anywhere in the United States has access to emergency services as well as routine maintenance.

Safety is of paramount importance to the company. Ryder maintenance crews are carefully trained, and Ryder equipment, leased or rented, is maintained to meet strict corporate standards.

Ryder Truck Rental, Inc., is very proud of its West Michigan connection. "We came here on a shoestring—strictly on the strength of a marketing study," says executive manager Richard Goodrich. "West Michigan is a great place to do business. It has been an excellent market for us, and the labor force is phenomenal. We are pleased to be a part of the West Michigan business community."

Ryder Truck Rental, Inc., at 651 A.I.S. Drive SW, has more than 2,000 units operating from its West Michigan facility.

AQUINAS COLLEGE

Caring and service are key words at Aquinas College, a private institution with a strong liberal arts orientation and a Catholic Christian heritage. At Aquinas the doors are open to students of all faiths, and the programs are designed for students of all ages.

Founded as a traditional undergraduate liberal arts institution, Aquinas College has gone out of its way over the past two decades to attract growing numbers of nontraditional students. By creating and tailoring new programs to meet a wide range of educational needs, the institution has significantly—and deliberately—broadened its base. Today Aquinas serves several major constituencies—traditional full-time, college-age students; older working adults whose education has been interrupted; and individuals ages 55 and over.

Aquinas College's 1,300 traditional full-time students enjoy the benefits of a strong liberal arts curriculum, with more than 40 majors from which to choose. Combined with the traditional academic coursework is an innovative, nationally recognized career-preparation program, complete with counseling, seminars, workshops, and optional field experience, that helps students to define their personal and professional goals and readies them for entry into the world of work. One indication of the program's success is the fact that within six months of receiving their degrees, more than 95 percent of the school's graduates are either working in their chosen fields, attending professional schools, or enrolled in master's or doctoral degree programs.

Another 1,800 Aquinas students are adults beyond college age who are working toward their undergraduate degrees, primarily in business fields, through the school's continuing education degree program, launched in 1969 and offered at night and on weekends. Also available exclusively in the evening is a graduate management program, which focuses on human behavior within organizations, leads to a master of management degree, and was developed in response not only to student needs but also to those of area employers. Ever attuned to the needs and expectations of its student population, Aquinas College continues to be a leader in providing opportunities for working adults to pursue an education.

Equally at home on the Aquinas campus are the many students in the 55-and-older age range who enroll in a wealth of noncredit liberal arts courses offered through the college's Emeritus Center. Founded in 1974 and serving more than 2,200 senior scholars per year, the center is testimony to the institution's belief that learning is a lifelong adventure.

All students at Aquinas receive personal attention from a faculty, administration, and staff deeply committed to their academic, spiritual, and emotional well-being. Readily accessible to their students, faculty members are dedicated to quality instruction. Aquinas employs no graduate assistants, and department heads regularly teach freshman classes.

The same philosophy of caring and concern that ex-

The **Academic Building** recently underwent major renovation.

Holmdene, the manor house of the Lowe estate, now houses administrative and faculty offices.

tends to students also embraces the college's Eastown neighborhood. Troubled by the deterioration that had begun to afflict the neighborhood during the 1960s, the institution sought and received a Kellogg Foundation grant to address the problem through the establishment and support of an Eastown Neighborhood Association. Not only was this pioneering effort instrumental in revitalizing Eastown, but also it helped spark an active citywide neighborhood association movement. Aquinas and Eastown continue to maintain their close and mutually beneficial relationship, and the college remains dedicated to the neighborhood's welfare.

Aquinas also retains its close ties with the Dominican Sisters of Grand Rapids, whose Marywood motherhouse is opposite the college on Fulton Street and whose predecessors a century ago founded a novitiate normal school for the purpose of training candidates to the order. In 1922 the normal school merged with Marywood College for laywomen, also founded by the Dominican Sisters. Known as Marywood College of the Sacred Heart, the new institution moved downtown in 1931 and was reorganized as the two-year Catholic Junior College, the first coeducational Catholic college in America. Nine years later the school adopted the name Aquinas, in honor of the medieval theologian and philosopher, St. Thomas Aquinas, and began operating as a four-year institution.

In 1945 Aquinas College purchased the Lowe estate on Robinson Road, site of its present campus, and used the existing buildings for offices and classrooms. Increasing enrollments and changing needs prompted much new construction, including the recently built art and music center, but the beautiful Lowe gardens, with all their flora indigenous to Michigan, have been carefully and lovingly preserved.

Aquinas has had just three presidents in its 47-year history as a four-year institution. First was Monsignor Arthur E. Bukowski, who began serving as dean of Catholic Junior College in 1934 and oversaw that institution's successful transition into the four-year Aquinas College. In 1969 Dr. Norbert Hruby succeeded to the presidency. Under his leadership, Aquinas undertook an intensive 15-month self-study that resulted in its transformation from a traditional liberal arts college to a forward-looking institution whose innovative programs continue to reach out to a broad spectrum of ages and needs. A dynamic and effective leader, Dr. Norbert Hruby was recently cited by a George Mason University study as one of the 100 most effective college presidents in the United States.

In July 1986 Dr. Peter D. O'Connor assumed the presidency of Aquinas College and has pledged to move the school in new directions. One goal is to expand services to the minority community and to the area's various minority groups.

Throughout its history the institution has reached out in many ways to serve its community. And no matter what the future holds, Aquinas College will preserve its liberal arts foundation and continue its commitment to community service.

Ken Marin, economics professor.

Sister Rosemary O'Donnell leads a group discussion in a Graduate Management Program course.

AMERICAN SEATING

American Seating has 100 years of manufacturing success behind it, but the company is as new as the times. Redefining itself in markets where it has established a foothold and reaching out to new markets, the firm is entering its second century with a new philosophy, new products, and an absolute confidence in a bright future.

Founded in 1886 as the Grand Rapids School Furniture Company, American Seating is establishing itself in the marketplace as a manufacturer of premium quality open office systems and seating for the transportation, auditorium and arena, and office furniture markets.

American Seating has three marketing groups—Transportation Products, Architectural Products, and Interior Systems.

The Transportation Products Group, which makes seating for public transportation and school buses, dominates its market and has a long list of firsts in the industry. The first fiberglass transit seat, the first fiberglass school bus seat, the first spring suspension cushion construction, and the first handicap seat systems to accommodate wheelchairs are just a few of the innovations introduced by American Seating. In 1986 the company brought out its extra-wide recliner seats for intercity buses, and in 1987, in partnership with the Grammer Company of Amberg, West Germany, American Seating introduced an "air ride" driver's seat for the trucking industry.

Called the American Seating/Grammer truck seat, the seat rests on an air-filled base that remains stable, no matter what the road conditions. The driver is protected from being bounced against the top of the truck cab or bottoming out on rough roads. The seat also features an air lumbar control and independent cushion length adjustment, as well as height and back angle adjustments.

TEChair, the newest line from the Interior Systems Group, is comfort designed for use in any office situation, and so easily adjusted that it is particularly useful for multishift and shared-use work stations.

"One System Does It All—By Design" is the slogan for System R ("R" for responsive), an open-office panel frame modular system so versatile and flexible that it can be used in offices, factories, and laboratories with equal efficiency. The panels can be put together in a multitude of configurations to create office, computer, technical, lab, and factory work stations.

The firm is also known for its premium-quality auditorium and stadium seating, produced by the Architectural Products Group. From its earliest days American Seating has been in the forefront in designing and manufacturing seating for lecture and concert halls and theaters. The company is concentrating its efforts on high-end installations and can boast that its seating is the choice of most of the major league baseball and football stadiums in the country—plus sports arenas in Canada, Puerto Rico, Saudi Arabia, and Japan.

Many of the nation's leading performing arts and civic centers have American Seating chairs, including Madison Square Garden, Meadowlands Arena in New Jersey, the John F. Kennedy Performing Arts Center in Washington,

American Seating's System R panel frames and other components can be adapted to meet the requirements of countless work situations in factory, laboratory, and office. Shown here is a System R open office (below left) and a research laboratory station (below).

D.C., the Lincoln Center complex in New York City, and the Welsh Auditorium in Grand Rapids.

The Centrum 3 is the Architectural Products Group's current shining star—an innovative auditorium chair that is long on aesthetics, comfort, and practicality. Such notable corporate clients as Coca-Cola, Equitable Insurance, Steelcase, and Disneyland in Anaheim, California, have installed the Centrum 3 in their facilities.

Comfort and practicality are the foundation of American Seating's design philosophy and have been since the company was founded. Back in 1886 ergonomics—designing the environment for human comfort—was not an everyday word. Nevertheless, it was ergonomics that spurred the president of the Grand Rapids school board and two associates to found the Grand Rapids School Furniture Company. School board president Gaius Perkins determined that schoolchildren sat for 15,000 hours from kindergarten through college. The desks at which the children sat were shaping their bodies, he contended, and he was not impressed with the results. Perkins, William Peregrin, and Seymour Hess were convinced that poorly designed classroom furniture was impeding the children's productivity and physical development.

The men developed the school desk unit that included the now-familiar lift-top desk with bookbox attached to the seat and back of the unit in front. A totally new concept in school furniture, the design was an immediate success. A year later the firm branched into theater seating, producing the first noiseless, automatic, self-folding seat for opera and concert halls, and a few years after that the wood-slat folding chair became a part of the company line. By 1892 the company was the largest seating manufacturer in the world.

Just before the turn of the century the firm merged with 18 of the largest public seating companies in the United States to form the American School Furniture Company. By 1920 the enterprise was also making church furniture,

and the corporate name was changed to American Seating. At the end of that decade American Seating was a $10-million-per-year enterprise.

In the 1940s the company developed its line of seating for buses and light rail cars. The next major diversification came in 1977, when the Office Systems Group was added.

Throughout its century of producing public seating for a variety of uses, American Seating has adhered to a commitment to high quality, and has consistently introduced products that have redefined the state of the art for the seating industry. With the introduction of the Office Systems Group and the divestment of school furniture, American Seating has positioned itself for growth and prosperity in the twenty-first century.

"We want our customers to know that we are an easy company to do business with," says president Ed Clark. "We have built our company not just on quality products, but on service as well. We have always provided products and services that respond to customers' needs."

Interior of a General Motors coach with American Seating's exclusive cantilevered seats.

Among the outstanding performing arts centers equipped with American Seating chairs is the Orange County Performing Arts Center in Costa Mesa, California.

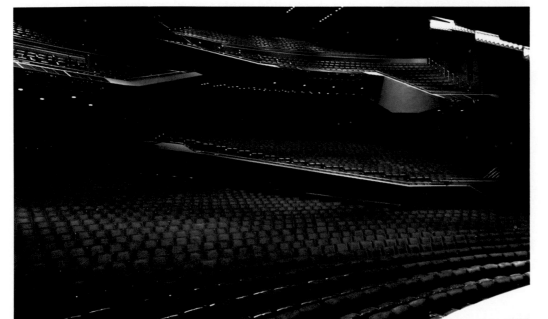

FERRIS STATE COLLEGE

Innovative, high-quality technical and professional career-oriented education is the hallmark of Ferris State College's academic programming.

Since its founding in 1884, Ferris State College has met the educational needs of students and citizens of the state by offering a broad range of academic programs, now totaling more than 120, which combine state-of-the-art technical education with a solid liberal arts component. Testimony to the institution's fine educational programming is a graduate placement rate that exceeds 90 percent.

FSC's ongoing quest for relevance has been based on a strategic vision and the flexibility to respond to Michigan's needs where it is uniquely able to do so. One indication of this flexibility is the effort to make programs available to part-time and adult students in locations beyond the Big Rapids campus, 54 miles north of Grand Rapids.

Current program offerings in Grand Rapids include occupational teacher education, health systems management, environmental health, and manufacturing technology. The college's Southwest Michigan Regional Center, located at Two Fountain Place in Grand Rapids, coordinates Ferris activities in a 16-county area.

Ferris also is involved in the seven-member College Consortium to Assist Business and Industry. The consortium is a network clearinghouse that responds to Grand Rapids area business and industrial needs for problem-solving assistance and training.

The continuing commitment to provide Michigan with technically oriented professional personnel, all with "hands-on" experience and a "can-do" attitude, has led to the proposed Technology and Training Center in Grand

A Ferris faculty member works with an architectural drafting student in the computer-aided design and computer-aided manufacturing (CAD/CAM) laboratory.

A statue of the college's founder, Woodbridge N. Ferris, former Michigan governor and U.S. senator, is a prominent landmark on the Ferris campus.

Rapids, a joint effort between Ferris State College and Grand Rapids Junior College.

Cited by Governor James Blanchard as a "model for expanding higher education opportunities while limiting taxpayer expense by sharing resources," the $22.3-million, 150,000-square-foot Technology and Training Center is expected to open by fall 1989 on the JC campus. Owned by Grand Rapids Junior College but jointly operated by both institutions, the center will house JC's occupational programs along with laboratories and classrooms for FSC technical baccalaureate degree programs and students who live in the Grand Rapids area.

Technical assistance and training for industry will be a major focus of the JC/FSC Technology Center, which will link the applied research and development capabilities of Ferris' Manufacturing Resource and Productivity Center and its Technology Transfer Network with JC's Economic Development Program.

The Technology and Training Center also will provide the applied technology component for the Center for Research and Technology now being planned by the Greater Grand Rapids Economic Area Team (GGREAT) and The Right Place Program.

In this era of rapid technological and societal change, individuals and institutions are challenged to adapt and respond with new ideas and techniques. Ferris State College's continued program revision and expansion reflects its historical mission of providing a broad range of career-oriented and professional programs and public services to the people of the state.

GRAND RAPIDS JUNIOR COLLEGE

For nearly 75 years Grand Rapids Junior College, located in the heart of downtown Grand Rapids, has met the educational needs of a diverse population. Over 20,000 individuals avail themselves of the college's programs and services each year.

JC enjoys a wide reputation for academic excellence. In addition to a strong curriculum in the arts and sciences, the institution offers more than 50 Occupational Education programs for students who want to enter the work force directly.

Continuing education is available for the increasing number of adult students who enroll in credit courses offered evenings, weekends, or via television. Also available are noncredit programs for personal fulfillment or career enhancement.

JC provides several services to the community at large. The college's Heritage Restaurant, for example, operated by the Hospitality Education Division, is open to the public for lunch and dinner. Job placement services can be used by anyone in the community, including high school students. Three resident acting groups perform year round in the school's Spectrum Theater, and the Grand Rapids Junior College Dental Clinic, a training ground for dental auxiliary students, provides low-cost services to many area residents.

Working with local agencies and other educational institutions, JC is active in communitywide efforts to further economic development by helping business and industry upgrade employees' technical skills. Services include designing customized management and employee training and retraining programs, helping industry implement programmable automation and flexible manufacturing systems, and training workers in the use of small computers as well as the techniques of statistical process control (SPC) and CAD/CAM.

The college is a member of the Greater Grand Rapids Economic Area Team (GGREAT) and operates the Small Business Assistance Network (SBAN). SBAN helps small businesses obtain start-up funds, secure loans, and locate venture capital. SBAN also offers assistance with federal and state procurement procedures, site identification, licensing, and tax abatements.

Continuing the spirit of community service, Grand Rapids Junior College and Ferris State College have begun joint planning for the construction of a 150,000-square-foot Technology and Training Center. Owned by JC and operated by both institutions, the center, scheduled to be completed in 1989, will house occupational and technical programs and provide facilities for technical assistance and training for industry.

Since 1914 many thousands of students have benefited from JC's tradition of quality instruction provided by an outstanding faculty in small classes at low tuition rates.

In its continuing efforts to serve the community, Grand Rapids Junior College has changed with the times. But its mission remains constant: to serve as a community-centered resource fostering learning, wisdom, and skill in the arts, sciences, and practical pursuits.

Grand Rapids Junior College keeps its commitment to excellence in both arts and sciences curriculums and occupational programs.

Through its economic development program Grand Rapids Junior College helps business and industry upgrade employees' technical skills.

INDUSTRIAL BELTING AND SUPPLY, INC.

The one thing that sets Industrial Belting and Supply, Inc., apart from its competitors can be summed up in a single word—service. Says owner and president Charles Yob, "We are open any time anyone needs us. We are on call seven days a week; if a customer needs us, we are there."

IBS is an industrial distributor for power transmission equipment, bearings, and industrial hose, and is a distributor and fabricator of conveyor belting products. One of the reasons that IBS is always on call for its customers is that, in addition to being used in new installations, many of the products the company handles are used in equipment repair and replacement, which means maintenance work. And industrial maintenance work is often done at night and on weekends.

Being available and willing to ship supplies at all hours, every day of the week, to customers in need has made IBS a major supplier, particularly in belting products, in the Michigan, Indiana, and western Ohio area. The company maintains its own trucks so it can guarantee immediate delivery, and it also can provide installation and repair crews on short notice. Always modernizing and extending its services, IBS also can offer customers computer-to-computer ordering capabilities.

Among the many products IBS handles are bearings, clutches and clutch parts, electric motors and controls, engineering chain and drive and conveyor chain, gears and rack, shaft collars, sealants and adhesives for testing, speed reducers, and ducting and fitting and clamps for metal and rubber industrial hose. The company represents the top manufacturers in all the products it carries.

One of the few large, independently owned distributors in the business, IBS has stocking and distribution branches in Grand Rapids, where the home offices are located, and in Saginaw, Muskegon, and Detroit, Michigan, and South

From left: Peter J. Lamberts, controller; Charles W. Yob, president; and (standing) David W. Goudy, vice-president/sales; and Charles W. Yob, Jr., assistant to the president.

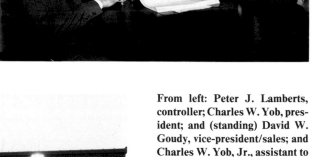

Industrial Belting and Supply Company's corporate headquarters and Grand Rapids warehouse building number one.

Bend and Indianapolis, Indiana.

Belting fabrication is the backbone of IBS' business, and the firm sells custom-fabricated belting to many *Fortune* 500 companies, be they end consumers, original equipment manufacturers, or distributors for resale. IBS will ship any of its products directly to a distributor's customers, using the distributor's packing slips and labels. The company also sells accessories such as belting lacings.

Most of the belting fabrication is done in Grand Rapids, but all the branches have belt-slitting capability and do some fabrication on site. IBS buys industrial belting in huge rolls similar to carpet rolls and cuts the belting to order. The firm can produce belts up to 30,000 pounds and 72 inches wide down to a half-inch wide. IBS also vulcanizes endless belts in thicknesses from paper thin to two inches.

IBS had its origins as an industrial hardware store in Stevensville, Michigan. Yob, a native of Hesperia, Michigan, bought the store with a partner in 1967, and soon began specializing as a supplier of industrial parts to large manufacturers, including the Big Three automakers. The partners opened a second store in Saginaw, closer to the automotive manufacturing center, and Yob moved his family there. Another move followed when the company opened an operation in Indianapolis.

Within three years after its establishment, it was apparent to the partners that the business could not survive if it depended too heavily on the automotive market, so they added other product lines and adopted a new name—Industrial Belting and Supply, Inc. By 1977 the firm had three more branches—in Grand Rapids, Muskegon, and South Bend.

By that time the partnership had dissolved, and Yob was owner with several stockholders. In 1985 he became sole owner of the company when he bought out the last stockholder.

Because of the nature of the business, location was not a factor in where the company's headquarters was estab-

From left: Charles W. Yob, Jr., Charles W. Yob, and Charles S. Steensma, customer service manager.

lished, and Yob decided to move his family once again. "I put it to a vote. I would establish the home office in any city where we had an operation, and the family could choose the location. They picked Grand Rapids." So in 1977 Grand Rapids became home for both IBS and the Yob family.

Yob and his wife, Jackie, have five sons and one daughter. Chuck Jr. is assistant to the president and in charge of all company operations. The third son, Randy, oversees warehouse operations. The second son, Rick, is a student at New Mexico State University. Ron is a pilot, currently attending Western Michigan University, and daughter Gina and the youngest son, John, are still in school.

Chuck Yob is high on Grand Rapids. "I'm proud to tell people I'm from Grand Rapids," he says. "We moved here because it is a good place to live, a good place to raise a family, a good place to put down roots."

And—a good place to do business. "There are independent business thinkers here, and the small business people are as important as the big corporations," says Yob. "Everyone pulls together—the chamber of commerce, the banks, the businesses, the service clubs, they all help to pull the business community together for the good of the whole community."

Yob's personal philosophy is inextricably bound up with his business philosophy, and the key to both is politics. A political activist all his business life, Yob has been Republican committee finance chairman in every county he's lived in. Since coming to Grand Rapids, he's served as chairman of the Kent County Republican Party and as fifth district committee chairman. He also is budget committee chairman for the Michigan Republican Party. States Yob, "We control our own economic destinies, and politics is important to that. Politics is an insurance policy for my business and my family. I keep fighting for a better place to do business and, ultimately, to raise my family."

From left: Randy Yob, warehouse supervisor; Charles W. Yob, and Charles W. Yob, Jr.

CALVIN COLLEGE

Faith and learning are the watchwords at Calvin College, a Christian liberal arts college founded in 1876. Calvin encourages students to grow in every way—mentally, physically, and spiritually—and campus life is a blend of serious work, fellowship, and fun. Students come from diverse backgrounds, bringing to campus the richness of their special experiences.

Calvin's size, approximately 4,000 students, enables it to offer a diverse academic program. At Calvin, students have options as extensive as those offered by many universities, but with the added advantage of small class sizes and low student-faculty ratios. For students who need assistance, the Academic Support Program provides individual tutoring and attention.

Outstanding campus facilities range from an electron microscope, to an acoustically excellent, 1,000-seat concert hall, to well over 100 computer terminals available for students to use outside the classroom. Among the many other features of Calvin's modern campus are sophisticated language labs, a 16-inch telescope, and a 500,000-volume library.

The academic year is arranged on a "4-1-4" calendar, with two four-month semesters separated by a monthlong interim. During the interim students choose special classes or participate in internships or practicums designed to expand their horizons.

At the heart of Calvin's academic program is an outstanding faculty. Many have distinguished themselves through publications and research, and more than 70 percent have earned the highest academic degree in their fields.

Rapport between students and professors is important at Calvin. These students are talking to Dr. Henry Holstege, professor of sociology.

All of the faculty members are dedicated Christians, whose faith is an important part of their approach to teaching.

Life at Calvin is a total learning experience, and the diversity of campus life is part of what attracts students to the college. Dozens of clubs and organizations, as well as plays, concerts, lectures, films, recitals, dances, and sports events keep students busy throughout the year.

Residence halls are well-maintained, comfortably furnished, and designed to encourage friendships and study. Resident assistants living on each floor help students with a variety of problems and also encourage such activities as pizza parties, retreats, and outreach programs.

Faith, learning, and living are all integrated at Calvin in a community that encourages spiritual maturity and responsibility. The college has more expectations than rules for its students; the major expectation is that students come to Calvin as serious seekers interested in knowing God's will for their lives.

Many opportunities exist for spiritual growth through chapels, Bible studies, and volunteer programs. But at Calvin students' spiritual growth is just as important in the classroom, in the dorm, and in campus activities.

Calvin College is a place to search, to question, and to grow as a Christian. Says *New York Times* education editor Edward Fiske in his *Selective Guide to Colleges*, "No other religious college is quite so sincere about putting Christianity in the classroom as Calvin."

ROSPATCH CORPORATION

RoSPATCH Corporation is three diverse business groups united under one umbrella—the Technical Products Group, the Identification Products Group, and the Wood Products Group. The diversity of the three groups gives RoSPATCH a remarkable product depth and range in a wide variety of industries and for worldwide markets.

The Technical Products Group develops and manufactures electronic avionics subsystems and related products. Among its divisions are RoSPATCH Electronic Systems, a producer of airborne sonobuoy receivers and airborne electronic equipment, and Guidance Technology, Inc. (GTI), a leader in the design and manufacture of gyroscopes and related electromechanical devices and instrumentation utilized in aircraft, missiles, torpedos, and artillery fire control systems. Custom optics and infrared detectors are manufactured and marketed by another Technical Products division that was recently acquired.

The Wood Products Group manufactures speaker systems and ready-to-assemble furniture for wholesale and consumer markets, and applies wood-grain finishes to particleboard for the consumer electronics, furniture, and housing industries.

The third group, the Identification Products Group, is the founding organization of the company. It produces woven and printed labels and decorative trims and ribbons for the garment industry, as well as in-plant labeling machines and laundry marking and sealing systems for the textile/apparel and industrial laundry/linen supply industries.

RoSPATCH was founded in 1910 as the Rose Machine Company to manufacture and market a cloth label sewing machine that had been developed by Arthur Rosenthal and his brothers. The garment industry at that time used patches as reinforcements for buttons on knit underwear and as labels for laundry identification. The Rose machine streamlined the application of patches and labels to garments by sewing all four sides of a label or patch without turning the garment.

A few years later the Rosenthals developed a second machine to produce accurately finished sizes of cut and folded woven labels. Shortly thereafter, the sewing machine manufacturing and marketing rights were sold to a Cincinnati firm, and a new company was formed to manufacture and sell machines, attachments, patches, and labels. Called Rose Patch and Label Company, the new operation continued to bring innovative concepts and production methods to the cloth label industry. In 1924 Rose Patch developed a vat dye process for printing cloth labels—a revolutionary development in cloth label manufacture.

Each decade brought growth and expansion in new directions for the company. With diversification came the need for a new identity, and in 1967 the firm's name was changed to RoSPATCH Corporation.

Today RoSPATCH has 1,400 employees in manufacturing plants throughout the United States. It has over 2,000 stockholders and more than two million shares outstanding. Its customers range from the textile mills of the South to the U.S. military to foreign governments. Still the firm retains its Grand Rapids identity. As an integral part of the Grand Rapids business community for 77 years, RoSPATCH Corporation and its employees have from the company's earliest days been active participants in the community, contributing to the health, education, and welfare of the West Michigan area.

RoSPATCH Corporation has been part of the manufacturing community since it was founded in 1910 as the Rose Machine Company. Today, with manufacturing plants throughout the United States, its headquarters is still in Grand Rapids. Shown is RoSPATCH's operation at Rochester, New York.

THE KOEZE COMPANY

Long before there was Jif or Skippy or Peter Pan there was Koeze's, a family-owned and -operated company that manufactures 12 to 20 million pounds of peanut butter per year and is today the only surviving peanut butter plant in Michigan.

Koeze's was founded in 1919, when Albert Koeze, then in his early twenties, gave up his butter, egg, and cheese delivery route to buy out the Bel-Car-Mo Nut Butter Company. Koeze moved the business from its downtown Grand Rapids site to a building on Godfrey SW that he enlarged by adding a second story. Half the building he rented out to the Nehi Bottling Company, and in the other half he ran his peanut butter-manufacturing operation and did a little vinegar and mayonnaise making on the side.

By the late 1920s Koeze was doing well enough to buy a piece of nearby property at 1263 Burton SW. Swampland then, the property turned out to be one of the firm's best assets, and sometime in the late 1930s or early 1940s it became the site of today's company headquarters. When it was first put up, the new building housed the Nehi Bottling Company, which had moved with Koeze from the old building to occupy about three-quarters of the facility. The Wyoming Police Department rented space at the front of the building for a time, and Koeze maintained a modest peanut butter-manufacturing operation in the back.

In 1966 Albert Koeze died and left the business to his wife, who in turn sold it to their son, Scott, the one child

The Koeze Company headquarters, which also encompasses 60,000 square feet of peanut butter and confectionery manufacturing space.

of the five Koeze offspring who "seemed destined from early childhood to be the 'peanut man.'" Although the new proprietor had a business degree and extensive experience in the manufacturing end of the business, he was brand new to the office side of things and, he says, in need of money.

The first order of business was to increase sales in order to generate enough money to continue manufacturing. Koeze's began marketing fancy tree nuts, such as pecans and cashews, in an assortment of jars hand painted by Scott's wife, Ruth, to disguise their origins, to charitable organizations for use in fund-raising sales, still an important part of the business today. When Nehi moved out of the plant, Scott took over the space and, in addition to expanding the manufacturing operation, opened a retail shop. Over the years he continued to diversify.

Today Koeze's produces an extensive assortment of roasted nuts of all kinds, caramel nut corn, caramel apples, nut brittles, peanut clusters, chocolates, and chocolate nut candies, including the famous nut puddles—pecans, cashews, or peanuts lavished with caramel and swathed in chocolate. All of the products are sold by mail order nationwide, and the Koeze-designed decanters and imaginative packaging they arrive in are additional evidence of the company's painstaking attention to quality and detail. Koeze is also putting in a shell-molding plant to shape chocolates into distinctive designs.

Peanut butter remains the enterprise's mainstay. In addition to manufacturing peanut butter for retail customers, The Koeze Company is a private-label packer and markets this primary product, produced in 40 different formulas, to the retail, bakery, ice cream, and candy industries nation-

The Koeze product line started with peanut butter but has since diversified and broadened to include fancy oil-roasted nuts and gourmet confectionery products.

wide. Among the firm's customers are such well-known names as Spartan Stores, Meijer's, Amway, and Quaker Oats.

In 1980 the business opened a second retail store on East Paris Road SE. Originally an old farmhouse, the building was "transformed by a labor of love" and a collection of antiques into a charming Victorian shop. The property is now undergoing another transformation with a large addition that will preserve its old-world flavor while embracing a fully up-to-date mini-mall concept. The separate shops in the new mini-mall will include a bakery, deli, gift shop, coffee bar, and, of course, a considerable space devoted to the full line of Koeze's nuts and candies. As in the corporate offices and the retail stores, antiques collected over the years by Scott and Ruth, who is the company's retailing director, will play a major part in the decor. Among the treasures to be seen at corporate headquarters are the exquisitely detailed walls, drawers, shelves, and mirrors that once graced a local jewelry shop, and a handmade player piano in the shop that supplies music for customer contributions, which are in turn donated by the Koezes to the American Cancer Society.

Although neither retail operation is in a major shopping district, customers don't seem to mind. "Even when we didn't advertise," says Scott Koeze, "people came. If you have a good product, customers will beat a path to your door."

The company has grown considerably since Albert Koeze's day, and a sophisticated array of machinery has replaced the coffee roasters and deep fryers that were once

used to process the peanuts. The Burton plant has expanded to 60,000 square feet; a second plant, on Burlingame SW, was opened in 1984 to house the mail order and fancy mixed nut divisions; and the number of employees has increased from six to 75.

What has not changed in the 68 years since The Koeze Company's founding is Albert Koeze's commitment to quality—an essential ingredient in the nut and candy business. As his son explains, "One peanut butter plant in the United States goes out of business every year. In 1966 there were about 180 plants in operation throughout the country. Today there are fewer than 40. But we've been here a long time, and we should be here a long time more."

The peanut butter jar line used to fill millions of jars every year under labels such as Spartan and IGA.

The East Paris retail outlet showing the new addition of a mini-mall while maintaining its Victorian charm.

GRAND VALLEY STATE COLLEGE

Founded in response to the need for a four-year public college in West Michigan, Grand Valley State College has proven its worth many times over.

The institution, chartered by the Michigan legislature in 1960, became a reality in large part because a group of prominent area citizens, led by L. William Seidman, believed that Michigan's second-largest population center should be served by a public, baccalaureate institution. In addition to acquiring a beautiful 897-acre site for the main campus in Allendale, west of Grand Rapids, the founders raised more than one million dollars in private funds to give the institution its start.

Private funds, in fact, have continued to play a vital role in the college's growth. The Loutit Hall of Science, Seidman House, the WGVC/WGVK public television station, the Lubbers Stadium track complex, the engineering programs, the D.J. Angus aquatic science program and Water Resources Institute, the four-year physical therapy degree, the residence halls, and a number of other fine programs and facilities have all been made possible through private contributions.

The property for the college's new Downtown Grand Rapids Center, located on the west bank of the Grand River, was purchased through private gifts; the State of Michigan is providing the $20.9 million needed for actual construc-

GVSC's premedical and predental graduates have a much higher than average rate of acceptance into medical and dental schools.

tion, and a $6.1-million capital fund drive is raising the money to equip the facility and fund a number of its programs.

Grand Valley State has had a substantial downtown student base since 1973, and the new facility will consolidate services and classrooms formerly provided at various rented locations. When completed in early 1988, the Grand Rapids Center will be a nine-story, state-of-the-art educational facility with 43 classrooms and superbly equipped and maintained laboratories, conference and teleconference rooms, and seminar and workshop facilities. The Grand Rapids Center will relieve the growing pressure on the main Allendale campus and will also serve to strengthen the college's traditional partnerships with business, industry, government, and human services organizations.

The center will be home to Grand Valley's Office for Economic Expansion, which provides applied research, economic database and development, financial resource planning, customized training, and other needed services to area businesses. The joint Grand Valley/Michigan State University graduate engineering degree program in Grand Rapids will be headquartered in the new facility as will the Regional Center for Research and Technology, established through the efforts of the Right Place Program of the Grand Rapids Area Chamber of Commerce and the Greater Grand Rapids Economic Area Team.

In addition, Grand Valley State's Grand Rapids Center will house the Institute for Office Productivity. By bringing

Grand Valley State's Great Lakes research vessel, the *D.J. Angus*, docked at Grand Haven. Used by students and researchers alike, the *Angus* plays an important role in the college's highly regarded aquatic sciences degree program and Water Resources Institute at Grand Haven.

West Michigan's major manufacturers of office furniture systems together in a practical, collaborative effort with users of office systems technology and faculty and student assistants in Grand Valley's facilities management degree program, the institute will function as an international resource for research, training, and consultation in work place productivity.

WGVC/WGVK-TV—West Michigan's public broadcasting facility, licensed to Grand Valley State College—will also be moving to the Grand Rapids Center. The station is a nationally recognized leader in public television, each week bringing the best in artistic, educational, cultural, public affairs, business, and children's programming to a regional audience of more than 2.7 million viewers. Its quality programming regularly attracts one of the highest average gifts per member of any public television station in the country.

Educational offerings at the Grand Rapids Center will stress programs in high demand among working adults, including business, communications, computer science, education, engineering, industrial technology, nursing, office systems and facilities management, public administration, and social work. As part of an agreement with Grand Rapids Junior College, GVSC's downtown offerings are primarily third- and fourth-year and graduate degree programs to benefit those JC graduates who want and need further education but can't afford to quit their jobs or leave the city.

This cooperation with other institutions is characteristic of Grand Valley State's unique relationship to the community. More than 70 percent of GVSC students are residents of the local area. And more than 75 percent of GVSC alumni remain in Michigan after graduation—more than half living and working right in West Michigan.

The expansion of GVSC's services to working adult students in downtown Grand Rapids is only one reflection of the college's growth. Between 1982 and 1986 enrollment of the traditional student population on the main Allendale campus increased more than 31 percent to an all-time high of 8,361. While a large portion of GVSC students are commuters, increasing student demand for on-campus housing prompted construction of four unique community house residential units in 1986-1987. About 2,500 students live in college-owned housing, nearby private housing, or in various college-affiliated, privately owned, student apartment complexes that the institution continues to develop within close walking distance of campus facilities.

In addition to master's degree programs in business administration, education, health sciences, nursing, public administration, social work, and taxation, GVSC offers 75 baccalaureate degree programs. Classes are relatively small—the student/faculty ratio is 22 to one—and are offered days and evenings, on campus and off, both through Grand Rapids Center and the Lakeshore Center on the campus of Muskegon Community College. Students come to Grand Valley from nearly every county in Michigan, from other states, and from many foreign countries. Grand Valley belongs to the Great Lakes Intercollegiate Athletic Conference and is a five-time winner of the GLIAC all-sports trophy. The college fields seven varsity teams for men and six for women, and offers 30 intramural sports for men and 28 for women.

In the 27 years since its founding, Grand Valley State College has quickly established itself as a major community asset. The accredited, state-supported institution continues to perform an essential role in preparing citizens for the productive careers and lives that are vital to the economic and social strength of the region, the state, and the nation.

Architect's rendering of Grand Valley State College's Downtown Grand Rapids Center on the west bank of the Grand River.

Grand Valley's graduating classes reflect the college's balance between traditional, full-time students and the older, working adults who earn their degrees by attending part time.

207

SPARTAN STORES, INC.

Seventy years ago growing competition from national chain stores threatened to put local grocers out of business. As a plan for survival, 100 independent food retailers held a meeting in Grand Rapids on December 27, 1917, and decided to form the cooperative wholesale organization that eventually became Spartan Stores, Inc. Originally called the Grand Rapids Wholesale Grocery Company, the organization would enable its members to buy commodities at lower prices and pass the savings along to their customers. Twenty-seven retailers actually bought the required three shares of stock in the new cooperative.

widespread acceptance of the Spartan brand. Spartan is a name customers have grown to trust.

Today Spartan Stores, Inc., is a retailer-owned food wholesaler that serves 475 member stores in Michigan, northern Indiana, and Ohio. The firm also has three subsidiaries—United Wholesale Grocery Company, Shield Insurance, and 25 Spartan-owned supermarkets. With reported annual sales of $1.4 billion in 1986, Spartan Stores is ranked 12th in size nationwide among food wholesalers, and sales accounted for 70 percent of the Grand Rapids food market and 20 percent of Michigan's total grocery market.

The Grand Rapids Wholesale Grocery Company's first undertaking was the purchase of a carload of sugar. In 1986 member Spartan stores bought more than 36 million pounds of sugar, proof that the original venture was a success.

But success didn't come easily for the Grand Rapids Wholesale Grocery Company. In an era of tough times, the collapse of the sugar market was followed first by the Great Depression and then by the rationing, food stamps, and grocery shortages of World War II. Despite the economic gloom the firm fought back and continued to grow. Sales figures continued to climb, and by 1937, 175 retailers had joined the cooperative.

In 1954 the cooperative adopted the Spartan warrior as the symbol for all of its stores, but it wasn't until three years later that the company name was changed to Spartan Stores, Inc. Also introduced that year was the private-label line of Spartan-brand products. Grown to nearly 800 products today, the Spartan line is regarded as one of the highest quality private-label brands in the country. Strict quality-control standards are the key to customer loyalty and the

Ronald A. DeYoung, chairman of the board of Spartan Stores, Inc., and owner of Great Day Foods.

Spartan Stores serves its retailers from two warehouses. The main warehouse facility is located on 76th Street in Grand Rapids. In 1962 Spartan branched into the Detroit area by building a warehouse in Plymouth, Michigan. Employees number approximately 1,400 at the Grand Rapids headquarters and 370 in Plymouth.

In addition to supplying member stores with food and merchandise, Spartan Stores, Inc., offers many support services including research, merchandising, advertising, printing, coupon redemption, accounting, store development, insurance, and data information systems.

All Spartan stores proudly display the Spartan logo on their doors. Another readily recognizable symbol of this vast organization is the distinctive green Spartan truck. The company has one of the largest private fleets in the state, with 154 tractors and 300 trailers. Its 290 drivers traveled more than 10 million miles in 1986, making 1,200 deliveries per week to retail members. Spartan boasts one of the best safety records in Michigan and has been cited as a "model" trucking entity.

All departments of the Spartan corporation, from transportation to the warehouses and offices, continually strive to meet their ultimate responsibility—satisfying retail members. This commitment to service is expressed in the Spartan philosophy, "Together We Serve," created in behalf of all Spartan associates by current president and chief executive officer Patrick M. Quinn.

The corporate philosophy also states that Spartan Stores is "guided by a strong sense of social responsibility to the communities where we work and live." This commitment to community service is evidenced by Spartan Stores' exclusive sponsorship of the Michigan Special Olympics Summer Games held each year in Mount Pleasant. Not only do Spartan associates support the Special Olympics through countless hours of service as they prepare for and work during the event, but the corporation makes a healthy financial contribution as well.

Although Michigan Special Olympics is the company's major commitment, Spartan's community efforts reach much further. For the past several years Spartan has co-sponsored the Walter Hagen Golf Classic. This event benefits the Kent County Unit of the American Cancer Society and has been one of the top-ranked Walter Hagen tournaments in the United States each year.

Another link to community involvement is the annual United Way campaign. In addition to Spartan Stores' large corporate contribution, president Quinn chaired the B Division of this year's fund drive. In 1987 the United Way of Kent County experienced the largest single increase of any United Way campaign in the country.

As Spartan Stores, Inc., celebrates its 70th anniversary, members can reflect on seven decades of progress. Spartan salutes Grand Rapids for affording the company the opportunity to grow in a community that has encouraged so many businesses to thrive throughout the years. Thanks to the support of the city, Spartan turned a hopeful beginning into a bright future. In 1987 the company expects greater sales as existing store members and new affiliates increase their own sales.

Another significant factor in Spartan's success is the many contributions made by the firm's independent retailers to both the Spartan organization and their individual communities. Spartan's achievements are also the result of a progressive company that keeps pace with changing market conditions and responds to the needs of today's consumer.

Just as it all started in 1917, with a group of determined and committed retailers believing there was strength in numbers, so it stands today for this major wholesaler that prospers by serving "Together."

METROPOLITAN HOSPITAL

Combining modern medical technology with compassionate patient care, Metropolitan Hospital is known for interpreting its mission broadly. At Metropolitan Hospital emphasis is placed on the prevention of illness as well as on its treatment. This balanced approach to health is built on a heritage of excellence and leadership in traditional hospital services.

Founded in the late 1930s and located at 1919 Boston Street since 1955, Metropolitan is a hospital that offers sophisticated medical care in a comfortable setting. Over the years it has grown to a modern, superbly equipped, 248-bed facility. While primarily osteopathic in philosophy and commitment, its staff of 223 medical professionals includes doctors of medicine (M.D.s) and doctors of osteopathic medicine (D.O.s).

Always in the forefront of innovative medical techniques, the hospital has an enviable list of area firsts to its credit—the first in West Michigan to offer birthing room and short-stay delivery; the first in arthroscopic orthopedic surgery, urologic laser surgery, and streptokinase therapy; the first to establish a ventilator dependency unit; and the first general acute care hospital to offer alcohol and substance abuse rehabilitation.

Over the years the hospital has made a significant commitment to preventive services. The Wellness Center offers a broad range of programs that promote good health by changing unhealthy life-styles. Smokers, for example, learn to kick the habit at Smoke Stoppers. Overweight individuals discover how to lose excess pounds and adopt sensible eating habits through Be Trim. Personal stress management and personalized health improvement programs to increase cardiovascular fitness and lower blood pressure and cholesterol levels are also designed to help participants lead longer and healthier lives.

Deeply committed to the health and well-being of the community that it serves, Metropolitan reaches out to individuals of all ages with free and low-cost programs geared to meeting their special health and wellness needs. Children are the focus of such offerings as free babysitting classes, sibling preparation classes, and the healthy family parenting series, which explores topics ranging from infant care and appropriate toys to constructive discipline and summer safety. Of particular interest to women are prenatal care and childbirth classes, osteoporosis screening, and a premenstrual syndrome (PMS) support group. Prostate screening and an impotence help program, sponsored jointly by Metropolitan and Butterworth hospitals, address special male health concerns, and a yearly forum on aging was instituted with senior citizens in mind.

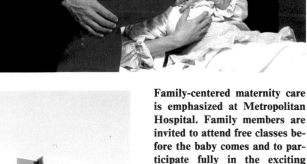

Family-centered maternity care is emphasized at Metropolitan Hospital. Family members are invited to attend free classes before the baby comes and to participate fully in the exciting childbirth process.

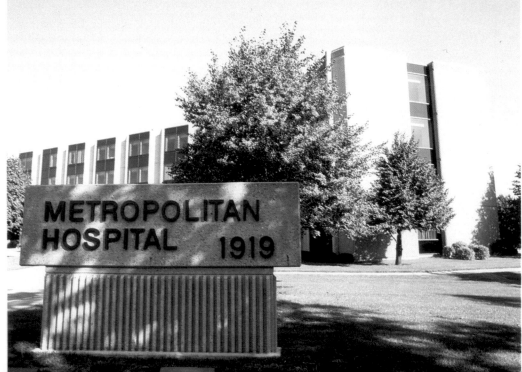

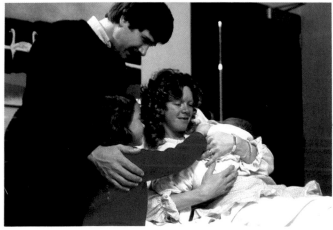

Metropolitan Hospital, 1919 Boston Street SE, is located in an easily accessible neighborhood setting where free parking is available for all patients and visitors.

Metropolitan Hospital has extended the wellness concept into the work place with a full range of wellness and fitness offerings geared to individual and company needs. In addition to presenting programs that promote better health among employees, Metropolitan Hospital stresses injury prevention on the job. Because back problems, for example, are a common and pervasive occupational hazard, Metropolitan offers the Back School, an employee education program designed to prevent back problems or to minimize their recurrence. Work Hardening, a program aimed at employees who have been disabled by injury or illness, is based on a systematic plan of exercise and work stimulation to promote rehabilitation and a return to the work force.

Rehabilitation, in fact, figures prominently in the hospital's overall philosophy. Central to Metropolitan's rehabilitative services is a team approach that focuses on the patient's emotional as well as physical state and frequently results in a significant reduction of the length of hospital stays. Patients under treatment for diabetes, cardiac problems, cancer, and strokes all benefit from the hospital's team approach, which involves not only physicians but nurses, social workers, dietitians, home care coordinators, occupational and physical therapists, and speech pathologists in their care.

The neuro team, for example, goes to work on the day a stroke patient enters the hospital, developing an intensive rehabilitation plan and then meeting regularly to monitor the patient's progress. Once the acute stage of illness has

The team of health care professionals at Metropolitan Hospital includes many employees who work behind the scenes, like this lab worker.

passed, the patient is moved to the rehab unit where the rehab team takes over and physical therapy begins.

Metropolitan is the area's only general acute care hospital to have its own physical rehabilitation unit. Staffed by therapists from Mary Free Bed, the 10-bed unit serves patients who have been neurologically or orthopedically disabled by such events as strokes and other illnesses, hip fractures, and amputations. Patients generally remain in the unit for two to six weeks, undergoing intensive therapy for at least three hours per day in preparation for their return home. Families are encouraged to take an active part in the rehabilitation process and are kept informed of the patient's progress every step of the way.

Quality medical care means much more than the treatment of illness. At Metropolitan, care is synonymous with caring, and one key element of that attitude is the emphasis on keeping patients and their loved ones informed. At the hospital's emergency treatment center, for example, a nurse, who functions as a patient advocate, greets each patient within moments of arrival and returns periodically to answer questions and ease concerns.

Because of its commitment to a very personal style of medical treatment, Metropolitan attaches great importance to the role of the family physician in health education, health maintenance, disease prevention, and the treatment of illness. Not only does Metropolitan operate a physician referral service to help patients find just the right doctor for their everyday health needs, but hospital officials stand firm on the concept that continuity of care requires the family physician to be actively involved in all phases of patient care, including hospitalization. The primary care physicians on Metropolitan Hospital's staff draw upon the expertise of a full roster of practitioners in every medical and surgical specialty and subspecialty to provide their patients with the best-possible care.

Modern medical technology plays an important role in patient care at Metropolitan, a hospital that has an enviable list of area firsts to its credit.

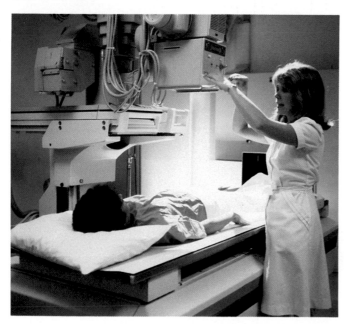

THORN APPLE VALLEY, INC.

Baseball and hot dogs—an American tradition. And the best all-beef hot dog in the country is made in Grand Rapids. It is the only brand of hot dog sold at Yankee Stadium, the Chicago White Sox's Comiskey Park, and Kansas City Royals Stadium.

But baseball parks don't have a steal on exclusive rights to the Thorn Apple Valley all-beef hot dog. That all-American classic, rated tops by a consumer reporting magazine, is also hawked at the home games of the Pittsburgh Steelers, the Pittsburgh Penguins, the New York Islanders, and the Detroit Red Wings, to say nothing of being equally at home in restaurants, consumer kitchens, and at neighborhood picnics.

The highly touted beef hot dog is only one of the many specialty meats produced by Thorn Apple Valley, Inc. The Grand Rapids Division of the company has been marketing high-quality meats since 1917 and shifted exclusively into the manufacture of specialty meats—hot dogs, luncheon meats, and sausages—in the 1950s.

The firm originated as a small retail butcher shop. The butcher-owner, Andrew Herrud, was a Norwegian by birth. He developed the business from a neighborhood meat market into a manufacturer of specialty meats, which he delivered in his own trucks to retail stores throughout the state. In 1969 the Herrud family sold the operation to its major supplier of pork, Frederick Packing Company of Southfield, Michigan.

The corporation, which operated as Frederick & Herrud Company, went public in 1971 and since that time has continued to grow and expand its product line, in part through acquisition of other specialty meat manufacturers. By the mid-1970s Frederick & Herrud Company was marketing its products nationwide. Thorn Apple Valley, originally the name of the meat manufacturer's premium-brand products, was adopted as the corporate name in 1984.

In addition to luncheon meats and 50 varieties of hot dogs, Thorn Apple Valley makes sausage and hams, and is the largest sliced bacon producer in the world. In response to the current national emphasis on fitness, the company has introduced new products, such as various chicken and turkey items, Lean 'N Trim boneless pork, and Lower Salt-No Sugar Added specialty meats, to satisfy changing consumer tastes. Another national trend, gourmet dining, has led the firm to introduce a new top-quality line, Epicure, which is drawing enthusiastic consumer response.

In addition to manufacturing and marketing its own brands throughout the United States and many foreign markets, most notably Canada and Japan, Thorn Apple Valley is the nation's largest private-label specialty meat manufacturer. With annual sales of $500 million, Thorn Apple Valley is rated 18th among U.S. meat manufacturers and is ranked on the *Fortune* 500 list.

Thorn Apple Valley, Inc., has spent the past few years adjusting to a changing market. Through restructuring, research and development, and careful market analysis, the company has emerged as a modern, efficient manufacturer with an eye on a productive future.

Some of the many Thorn Apple Valley products.

Home of Thorn Apple Valley's Grand Rapids Division, the nation's largest private-label specialty meat manufacturer.

KEEBLER COMPANY

One of the most famous product symbols in America is Ernie the Elf, who, with his elfin cohorts, bakes uncommonly good cookies in a factory housed in a hollow tree. Ernie is the Keebler elf, and he has represented the Keebler Company, beaming forth from America's magazine pages, billboards, and television screens, since 1969.

Keebler Company is the second-largest maker of cookies, crackers, and snacks in the United States. The firm traces its history back to 1853, when Godfrey Keebler opened a bake shop in Philadelphia.

Keebler in Grand Rapids began as Hekman Biscuit Company, established in 1893 by Edsko Hekman, a baker who came from the Netherlands to find a new career in the Grand Rapids furniture industry.

But 1893 was a year of depression in the United States, and Hekman's plans for a job in a furniture factory did not materialize. He had to fall back on his skills as a baker. He and his wife, Hendrikje, baked cookies in their southwest Grand Rapids home, and their five children helped sell the cookies door to door in the neighborhood. The business prospered, and within two years Hekman was able to move the baking operation into its own small building. By the 1920s the company had a proper three-story factory and was distributing cookies and crackers throughout the city.

In 1928 Hekman, along with 16 other local and regional bakeries, including the Keebler Company of Philadelphia, joined to form the United Biscuit Company of America. Each firm, however, retained its own identity and operated independently. Hekman's operation became Hekman Supreme Bakery and began to distribute its products throughout Michigan.

Over the years many of the bakeries in the United Biscuit Company were consolidated, leaving only six separate entities by the 1960s. In 1961 the firm undertook a unification program in order to centralize management, improve cost control and product consistency and quality, and to effect more efficient utilization of facilities. Five years later the operation changed its name to Keebler Company. In 1974 Keebler was acquired by United Biscuit (Holdings) Ltd., one of the largest food manufacturers in the United Kingdom. U.S. corporate headquarters are in Elmhurst, Illinois, with line bakeries in Grand Rapids, Michigan; Denver, Colorado; Cincinnati, Ohio; Atlanta and Macon, Georgia; and Van Nuys, California, and specialty bakeries in Chicago, Illinois; Bluffton, Indiana; and Raleigh, North Carolina.

Today the Keebler Company, with yearly sales of more than one billion dollars, serves the retail consumer market and food service institutions and restaurants with crackers, cookies, snacks, and specialty foods such as pretzels, ready-made pie crusts, and ice cream cones.

And just as Ernie is readily identified with one of America's favorite foods—the cookie—the Keebler name is recognized as a symbol of quality on America's supermarket shelves.

Ernie the Elf poses with his namesake outside the Keebler Company's Grand Rapids plant at 310 28th Street SE. Ernie was created for Keebler in 1969 by the Leo Burnett advertising agency.

Keebler's Ernie the Elf is the third-most-recognizable image in advertising, behind McDonald's Golden Arches and the Coca-Cola bottle.

213

AMWAY GRAND PLAZA HOTEL

The Amway Grand Plaza Hotel is an artful union of the old and the new, and more than any other structure in Grand Rapids, it symbolizes the stability and prosperity of the city's past and the confidence and vitality of a promising future.

A thoroughly contemporary gleaming glass tower grafted to the carefully restored early 1900s Pantlind Hotel makes the facility not only the focal point of a new downtown Grand Rapids, but also an architectural showpiece. And as a luxury hotel offering every amenity to its guests, the Grand Plaza has restored the city's reputation of yesterday as a great place to visit.

The Grand Plaza is headquarters for dozens of conventions during the year, and it plays host to occasional celebrities who come to town for various events. But the Grand Plaza is not just for out-of-towners. The hotel is becoming a mecca for West Michigan residents—for a weekend getaway, a special dinner in the fabulous Cygnus or gracious Victorian-era 1913 Room, or a casual lunch in the Monroe Cafe. Visitors from the city and around the state are learning that the elegant Grand Plaza is affordable elegance.

There are 11 restaurants and five bars in the hotel, each with a different theme. Plaza restaurants range from the sophisticated Cygnus at the top of the Grand Plaza West tower to the casual Splashes in the glass-enclosed pool deck next to the racquetball and tennis courts. The newest restaurant, opened in the fall of 1986, is Restauranté Europa, a cheerful room where diners can feast on the cuisines of Europe—adventures in dining at moderate prices.

The decor of the Lumber Baron Bar in the Plaza East harks back to the early days of Grand Rapids, when fortunes were made from Michigan's forests. In contrast, the

The Grand Staircase in the Amway Grand Plaza Hotel.

Inner Circle Bar in the registration lobby is as contemporary as tomorrow, with bright colors, lots of greenery, and a magnificent brass samovar. Tootsie Van Kelley's, an Irish pub in a Dutch town, has become one of Grand Rapids' favorite night spots.

The Grand Plaza features all the services of a truly first-class hotel—24-hour food and beverage service to all guest rooms and suites, complimentary parking for registered guests and valet parking for a small fee, free shuttle service to and from Kent County International Airport, laundry and dry cleaning, nonsmoking floors for the guest rooms, and turn-down service in each guest room. Hotel personnel are unfailingly pleasant, courteous, and efficient.

A concierge service makes arrangements for a wide range of services, from baby sitters and tickets to local events to interpreters for foreign guests. The hotel also has a fitness center that includes an exercise and workout room, a glass-enclosed 40-foot by 20-foot swimming pool, outdoor tennis courts, and a racquetball court.

The Tower Club, located on the tower's upper floors, offers special accommodations and services to guests who wish the ultimate in luxury and privacy. There are 29 banquet and meeting rooms in the hotel, including the beautifully restored Pantlind Ballroom. The Grand Plaza has been awarded the AAA Four Diamond Award and Mobil's Four Stars.

The hotel is owned and operated by Amway Hotel Corporation, a subsidiary of Amway Corporation, a direct-sales company located in Ada, just 10 miles east of Grand Rapids. At the end of the 1970s Grand Rapids embarked on a major revamping of the downtown area in order to recapture the retail and corporate business that had fled to the suburbs and shopping malls. The Pantlind Hotel, which opened in 1913 and had once been the city's most elegant hostelry, was a tired and shabby relic. Amway bought the facility—and $24 million and three years later, the hotel, reconstructed and renamed, opened during a weeklong gala that also saw the opening of the Grand Rapids Art Museum, which was housed in the renovated old Federal Building, and the Gerald R. Ford Presidential Museum.

By the time the building and renovation program was completed in 1983, at a total cost of $130 million, the Grand Plaza, with 682 guest rooms, encompassed two square blocks and included the original hotel, called the Grand Plaza East; a 29-story, glass-enclosed tower with 287 rooms and suites, known as Grand Plaza West; and Grand Plaza Place, the eight-story Renaissance-style Exhibitors Building, which was built in 1926 to house furniture showrooms for local furniture manufacturers. The first three floors of Grand Plaza Place are incorporated into the hotel complex and include a variety of shops and businesses. The other five

The Pantlind Lobby (left) and Ballroom (below left).

Guests enjoy dining in the gracious surroundings of the Victorian-era 1913 Room.

floors have business tenants.

The hotel registration desk is located in the main concourse, a modern two-story structure that connects Plaza East, Plaza West, and Plaza Place. The hotel is also interconnected by enclosed pedestrian skywalks on the north to the Grand Center for conventions, performing arts, and exhibitions, and on the south to the PrimeBank Building and the multilevel parking garage. Within a six-block radius of the hotel are most ot the city's legal, financial, governmental, and cultural attractions, as well as shopping and entertainment.

But the sparkling, modernistic atmosphere of Plaza West played off against the gracious and nostalgic luxury of Plaza East are only the visible symbols of the hotel management's dedication to excellence. At the Grand Plaza, the comfort and convenience of the guests come first, and the hotel makes every effort to meet the needs and desires of its guests.

TWOHEY, MAGGINI, MULDOON, MUDIE & SULLIVAN

To its clients and friends, this law firm is known simply as "Twohey, Maggini." Located for many years on the second floor of the Waters Building in downtown Grand Rapids, Twohey, Maggini presently has seven attorneys and practices in all areas of civil and criminal law. Members of the firm are Edward L. Twohey, Patrick M. Muldoon, Kent W. Mudie, Paul J. Sullivan, David Schoolenberg, LeRoy Kramer III, and Louis E. Maggini, of counsel.

Twohey, senior partner and founder of the firm, came to Grand Rapids in 1953, fresh out of the Navy and Notre Dame Law School. During the early years he attracted several partners and became proficient first as a general practitioner and later as a specialist in corporate law. Twohey is proud to say that his firm has been somewhat of a training ground for distinguished legal careers; several of his former partners have served in the judiciary or accepted appointment to important governmental positions.

The present members of the firm, with law degrees from major schools throughout the country, are a diverse and talented group. Providing services in all aspects of law, the attorneys nevertheless find sufficient time to engage actively in charitable, civic, professional, and political enterprises. Members of Twohey, Maggini have served as officers, directors, and trustees for such organizations as the Grand Rapids Bar Association, Grand Rapids Legal Aid Society, Grand Rapids Area Chamber of Commerce, Lions Club, Jaycees, YMCA, and a host of others. Three of the attorneys have also served as legal instructors at such local colleges as Aquinas, Seidman Graduate School, and the University of Detroit.

By design, Twohey, Maggini is large enough to provide a full range of legal services, and small enough to do so in a highly personal way. The firm's clients include large national and local corporations, as well as individuals who require personal or family legal services.

At Twohey, Maggini it is not unusual to see several attorneys huddled together in the conference room or library discussing a particular legal problem, because each attorney brings a different quality to the firm, and the blending of these qualities means better service for the client.

Twohey, Maggini, Muldoon, Mudie & Sullivan is also proud of the fact that its members are friends as well as business partners and associates, and the firm tries to extend that philosophy to its clients as well.

Seated (left to right): Edward Twohey, Kent W. Mudie, and Patrick M. Muldoon. Standing (left to right): David Schoolenberg and Paul J. Sullivan.

FIRST MICHIGAN BANK CORPORATION

The vitality of metropolitan Grand Rapids was a key factor in First Michigan Bank Corporation's decision to establish a presence in the area in 1975. That was the year that the Zeeland-based, multibank holding company brought its brand of personalized, community-oriented service to metro Grand Rapids by establishing a bank in Walker. Today FMB branch offices serve Walker and Plainfield Township, with the corporation's expanded area banking operation centered in downtown Grand Rapids in the Waters Building.

FMB-First Michigan Bank, Grand Rapids, n.a., may be relatively new, but its holding company's flagship institution, FMB-First Michigan Bank, Zeeland, is more than 100 years old. In the fall of 1878 Jacob Den Herder opened FMB-First Michigan Bank in the back of a Zeeland store. By 1908 he had laid the cornerstone at 101 East Main Street for the building that today serves as headquarters for the First Michigan Bank Corporation.

As part of the First Michigan Bank Corporation, FMB-First Michigan Bank, Grand Rapids, receives such centralized corporate support services as marketing, accounting, and operations. At the same time FMB-First Michigan Bank, Grand Rapids, retains local decision-making authority. As with all other affiliate institutions in the corporation, FMB-First Michigan Bank, Grand Rapids, operates under the supervision of its own board of directors and loan committees, thus providing faster, individualized service. Within the structure of the corporation, FMB-Grand Rapids is free to develop localized programs designed to meet the distinct and personalized needs of its corporate, retail, and trust customers.

The FMB-First Michigan Bank, Grand Rapids, philosophy of doing business centers on being involved with the communities it serves. On one level, that involvement means providing customers with full-service banking. FMB-Grand Rapids offers, among its range of convenient services, checking and saving accounts, loans, IRAs, trust and brokerage services, money market investment accounts, ATMs, and customer safe deposit boxes.

Community involvement also means striving to understand and meet community needs. FMB-Grand Rapids continually uses focus groups of customers and other individuals as a sounding board to gather information about what services are required and how existing services are being performed.

On a third level, community involvement means being active in local civic endeavors, community projects, and charitable organizations. The employees of FMB-Grand Rapids exemplify that philosophy through personal involvement in community affairs, helping to make their community a better place to live.

The efforts of each employee are rooted in the corporate mission. FMB-First Michigan Bank, Grand Rapids, n.a., strives to be recognized as a leading, community-oriented, progressive financial institution. In order to fulfill that mission, the bank offers a selected range of financial services, with a unique emphasis on quality and growth, for the benefit of its community, customers, shareholders, and employees.

FMB-First Michigan Bank, Grand Rapids, n.a., is located in the Waters Building in the heart of downtown Grand Rapids.

FMB-First Michigan Bank, Grand Rapids, offers its customers a full range of banking services.

AMWAY CORPORATION

Amway Corporation is one of America's great entrepreneurial stories. At the company's 1986 national convention meeting, chairman of the board Jay Van Andel, co-founder with president Richard M. DeVos, told his audience of Amway distributors, "There are no secrets to success. Success is doing the things you know you should do. Success is discovering your best talents and skills and applying them where they will make the most effective contribution. Success is 99-percent attitude. Success is perpetual growth."

DeVos and Van Andel followed that precept. They be-

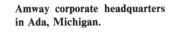

Amway corporate headquarters in Ada, Michigan.

came distributors for a health food supplement in 1949 and developed a large sales organization. Ten years later, in order to be in control of their own destinies, Van Andel and DeVos launched their own company, Amway.

Their first product—a household detergent known as L.O.C., Liquid Organic Cleaner. The rationale—everyone uses soap, so the product must be reordered on a regular basis. In 1960 Amway introduced S-A-8 Laundry Detergent, and entrepreneurial America had another legend in the making.

Van Andel and DeVos founded Amway as a direct sales business—individual, independent salespeople selling Amway products one on one, and developing their own sales networks. As the firm has grown and matured, and the consumer market changed, so Amway's concept has changed. Today the company's marketing plan is so broad it is called "network marketing." Products, still sold by independent distributors, are not limited to health and personal care items, but cover the spectrum of consumer goods and services.

Basically, Amway does business in eight product categories: home care, health and fitness, home-tech, personal care, commercial, knowledge and education, Personal Shoppers Catalog, and services.

Amway's venture into services has opened exciting new vistas for the company. Financial and legal services, communication, travel, real estate, automobiles, and education are areas in which the firm is developing new sales opportunities.

Amway is a multinational corporation with more than one million independent distributors and over 7,000 employees worldwide. The firm's products are sold in 40 countries. Manufacturing facilities are located at world headquarters in Ada, Michigan, and in London, Ontario. Amway also owns the Amway Grand Plaza Hotel in Grand Rapids; Nutrilite Products, Inc., in Buena Park, California; the Peter Island Resort in the British Virgin Islands; and Amway Communications, Washington, D.C.

The Amway Corporation of today is far different from Amway of 1959. But some things never change, and one of those things is the company's commitment to excellence. Another is Amway's dedication to its founders' original concept of presenting opportunity to individuals to become successful entrepreneurs in their own right and to share in the Amway success story.

As Rich DeVos states in his book, *BELIEVE!,* "I believe that one of the most powerful forces in the world is the will of the man who believes in himself, who dares to aim high, to go confidently after the things that he wants from life."

And that's the Amway story.

COUNTRY FRESH, INC.

World War II was over, but a new conflict was beginning in the nation's supermarkets. The upstart Pure Pak nonreturnable paper carton was ready to take on the traditional glass milk bottle for the milk-marketing championship of the world!

Local grocer L.V. Eberhard was so sold on the paper carton as a way to reduce the cost of marketing milk that he bought his own Pure Pak machine and joined forces with George Cope, a young Pure Pak salesman with a yearning to start his own dairy. This was a bold ambition, because there were already 40 milk processors operating in the Grand Rapids area at the time, and the competition was fierce. Retail competition was equally fierce, with A&P and Kroger tending to dominate the market by virtue of their national chain buying power.

That's why Eberhard suggested the proposed new dairy be established as a co-op. Not only would the grocers who joined the co-op provide a built-in market for the dairy's products, but the owner-members would also have a voice in the management of the enterprise. It was a mutually advantageous idea whose time had come.

In February 1946 the Grocers Cooperative Dairy was incorporated with 70 founding members, and the first quart of Country Fresh milk went on sale eight months later.

The history of the dairy is rich with innovation and marketing leadership. In January 1952 the first half-gallon paper milk carton was introduced, followed by the controversial gallon size a decade later. In 1964 Country Fresh was among the first dairies to use the revolutionary, time- and labor-saving Bossy System of wheeled carts for loading, moving, and stocking milk. The high-volume, gallon-size plastic containers were introduced in 1971, and half-gallon containers were added in 1982.

Over the years membership in the cooperative has grown to more than 400 retailers, and the dairy has expanded its services to other milk distributors and retail chains through the Embest subsidiary in Livonia, Michigan, acquired in 1982. Since then Country Fresh has also acquired the Thayer Dairy of Clare, Michigan, now a major supplier of ice cream novelties under the FROST-BITE brand name.

The dairy processes and distributes, under the Country Fresh name, a full line of dairy products, ranging from such standards as milk, ice cream, and cottage cheese to a wide variety of juices, dips, water, ice, and yogurt. The dairy also produces private brand products and distributes nationally advertised ice cream and milk specialties. All Country Fresh products are backed by an unconditional guarantee of quality that is printed on every package, along with a toll-free CAREline telephone number for direct customer communication.

The Country Fresh success has been built from the beginning on an unwavering commitment to quality, excellence, and customer service. In a highly price-sensitive industry, where customer loyalty often turns on a penny, the continued growth and prosperity of Country Fresh, Inc., stands as a testimony to the staying power of these basic virtues.

The headquarters of Country Fresh, Inc., is located at 2555 Buchanan SW.

DAVERMAN ASSOCIATES, INC.

Almost every person in West Michigan has been inside a Daverman-designed building. Many people attend a church, work in an office, or go to school in buildings designed by Daverman Associates, Inc.

Daverman has been designing West Michigan buildings since 1905, when the company was founded by Johannes Daverman and his son George. In the 1930s George's two sons and two nephews joined the firm. All the Davermans have now retired, but the traditions of quality and innovation that the family established still prevail.

In 1970 Daverman joined with Greiner Engineering, Inc., of Dallas, Texas. This alliance has made the company one of the largest architectural and engineering firms in the United States. Daverman has become a full-service architectural, engineering, and planning firm for clients in transportation, health care, education, commerce, industry, government, and corrections, both in West Michigan and throughout the country. There are Daverman offices in Grand Rapids and Petoskey, Michigan; Austin, Texas; Tucson, Arizona; and Berea, Ohio. Greiner Engineering maintains offices in 35 cities across the country.

Daverman is recognized not only for innovative design and engineering of new structures, but has a reputation for creative renovation as well. The company's skill and ingenu-

The exterior of the Furniture Building, at 82 Ionia NW, is headquarters for Daverman Associates, Inc. Formerly a retail furniture store, the structure was remodeled by Daverman.

The atrium of the Furniture Building is a dramatic example of adaptive reuse of historic structures.

ity in restoring existing buildings is evidenced by its own offices in Grand Rapids. Built first as an exhibitors' building for the Grand Rapids furniture industry, the structure at 82 Ionia NW, was most recently a retail furniture store. Daverman creativity and expertise was put to great use in remodeling the multilevel structure and designing a skylighted atrium—a showpiece in Grand Rapids' central business district.

Daverman has earned an outstanding reputation for its innovation in energy management. Through experience, the firm knows the unique problems involved in energy conservation retrofit. For example, Daverman's energy team has inspected more than 4,000 school buildings in 160 school systems and provided comprehensive energy management programs for industrial and educational clients nationwide.

Another Daverman success is its facilities management program, which provides advanced computer services for universities, governmental agencies, corporations, and hospitals across the country. Facilities management services involve diverse programming skills, including facilities inventory and evaluation, deferred maintenance programming, planned and preventive maintenance programs, facilities utilization studies, and space planning.

Daverman has played an important part in Grand Rapids' growth. "Innovation, adaptability to change, responsive service that puts the client's needs first, sound management, and the desire to create the best product possible are the reasons for our success," says president Neil A. Dick. Daverman Associates, Inc., has proven that ingenuity, hard work, and vision can meet the challenges of the present and secure prosperity for the future.

SYSCO/FROST-PACK FOOD SERVICES

SYSCO is an acronym for Systems and Services Company—a nationwide distributor of dry and frozen foods and foodservice supplies to restaurants, institutions, and industrial in-plant food systems.

SYSCO/Frost-Pack Food Services is a Grand Rapids success story that began in 1938, when Ed Hoekzema, with $6,000 capital, founded Frost-Pack as a distributor of frozen foods to the local retail and wholesale grocery market. That was less than 20 years after Clarence Birdseye had perfected quick freezing of fresh foods, and the frozen-food industry was very small and struggling.

Hoekzema also struggled in the early years, but frozen foods gradually came to be accepted by the public and became a staple in both the consumer retail and institutional food businesses. Responding always to market needs, Hoekzema increased his business to include West Michigan from Kalamazoo to the Straits and added dry groceries to the product line as well as additional frozen foods. Frost-Pack was the first company in West Michigan to market frozen foods, the first to use delivery trucks with refrigerated compartments, the first to have a refrigerated warehouse, the first to develop a wholesale cash-and-carry business for small restaurant accounts, and the first to sponsor an annual food show, bringing together vendors and customers during a two-day event at Grand Rapids' Civic Center (now the Grand Center).

The past 20 years have seen a dramatic change in the food industry as a whole. Known as the "dining-out revolution" in the trade, the trend among Americans of spending

SYSCO is the largest marketer of quality-assured foodservice products in the United States.

a significant portion of their income on restaurant and fast-food dining has changed the wholesale food supply business to a dynamic new industry known as foodservice. Recognizing the trend and aware that they must meet the new challenge, Frost-Pack and eight other food distribution companies around the country joined together in 1970 to form SYSCO. The merger has meant remarkable growth for each subsidiary operation and the parent company, which is headquartered in Houston, Texas.

At the formation of SYSCO, company executives decided to serve the foodservice industry exclusively; the corporation has not wavered from its original objective. As the largest marketer of quality-assured foodservice products in the country, SYSCO does an annual $3-billion-plus business and serves more than 125,000 restaurants, hotels, schools, hospitals, and other institutions in 139 of the 150 major metropolitan markets in the United States.

Frost-Pack built its business on a commitment to providing superior products and service to its customers and to anticipating market directions and needs. SYSCO/Frost-Pack continues that commitment to its customers, and it also maintains a commitment to Grand Rapids. Says company president David De Kock, "We take pride, as a corporate citizen, in taking part in community affairs, and we offer future employment opportunities—in sales, marketing, and transportation."

SYSCO/Frost-Pack Food Services, with headquarters at 3700 Sysco Court SE in Grand Rapids and branches in South Bend, Indiana, and Petosky, is growing with West Michigan.

From its Grand Rapids headquarters at 3700 Sysco Court SE, SYSCO/Frost-Pack Food Services distributes to an area from Kalamazoo to the Straits of Mackinac.

F.W. GROTENHUIS UNDERWRITERS, INC.

The life insurance business that Frank Grotenhuis started in 1958 with an investment of $145 has grown to be one of the largest regional insurance agencies in West Michigan.

After two years as strictly a life insurance agency, Grotenhuis, in 1960, offered a credit life insurance program to automobile dealers—a first in the insurance business. The agency has been in a steady growth cycle ever since, diversifying its insurance lines and acquiring other firms.

The company sold the credit insurance business in 1984 to concentrate on some of its newer lines, and today F.W. Grotenhuis Underwriters, Inc., is primarily a commercial agency handling property and casualty insurance enhanced by a broad range of specialized services. The firm has five departments—personal, commercial, financial institutions, association benefits, and employee benefits—and includes among it services capital needs analysis, estate planning, and incorporation feasibility studies.

The company's particular strengths lie in its commitment to providing comprehensive insurance programs to corporate customers. "Our goal," explains president Dana Sommers, "is to have specialists in each area of our business so we can offer a team approach to our corporate accounts. That is one of the reasons that we developed separate departments for the various types of insurance we handle."

Founder Frank W. Grotenhuis (seated), with president Dana Sommers (right) and executive vice-president Robert Topp.

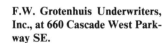

F.W. Grotenhuis Underwriters, Inc., at 660 Cascade West Parkway SE.

Another specialty the agency recently added for its corporate accounts is an aviation insurance subsidiary.

Grotenhuis anticipates considerable growth in its insurance coverage for the state's banking industry. The firm established its financial institutions department in 1985, and offered blanket bonds and D&O coverage to Michigan banks. It was a market with few underwriters and Grotenhuis stepped in to fill the void. According to company officials, the move has been successful and promises great potential.

Two other very successful programs have been group life, health, and workers' compensation for Grand Rapids Area Chamber of Commerce members. By belonging to the group, small businesses can buy insurance at more competitive prices than as individual buyers. More than 900 Grand Rapids companies subscribe to the group health plan. Grotenhuis is planning to extend the service to chambers throughout Michigan.

"The growth prospects for West Michigan are as great as for any region in the country," says Sommers. "We are positioning ourselves so that we'll have the depth to serve many markets as this area grows."

Officials of F.W. Grotenhuis Underwriters, Inc., like to point out that the firm's success is in direct proportion to the contribution and dedication of its people. "We're proud of our organization, our professionalism as an underwriter of insurance, and our commitment to our clients and to the community."

P.B. GAST & SONS COMPANY

The P.B. Gast & Sons Company of today traces its origins back to the P.B. Gast Soap Company, founded in 1894 by a 20-year-old soapmaker named Peter B. Gast.

Soap manufacture in the 1890s was more of an art than a science. Gast and the other soapmakers of his day liquefied beef tallow in large, cast-iron kettles of boiling water laced with caustic soda (lye), a highly alkaline substance. The mixture had to be just right: Too little alkali and the soap would turn rancid and spoil; too much alkali and the soap would be too "hot." Because even such simple chemical indicators as litmus paper were unknown at the time, soapmakers had to rely on their own senses of sight and taste to arrive at a mixture just slightly on the alkaline side.

The soapmaker's next step was to add salt to precipitate the soap, which was then skimmed from the kettle and poured onto a large metal-top table where it was dried and cut with piano wire into four-foot-long sticks. Gast marketed his soap sticks, packed in open-top barrels, to some 20 Grand Rapids steam laundries.

Like other housewives of the time, Emily Gast, Peter's wife, pared the soap sticks into small pieces that could be boiled with the family wash in a large copper tub. As the mother of seven children, Emily did lots of laundry and one day asked her husband why a machine couldn't chip the soap. He presented the problem to a machine shop in Syracuse, New York, and in 1908 began marketing P.B. Gast Soap Chips, a soap industry first, according to members of the Gast family.

By 1922 two of Peter's sons, Waldemar and Raymond, had joined him in the business, and the company name was changed to P.B. Gast & Sons. Four years later, faced with rising competition from such soap industry giants as Procter & Gamble, the firm stopped making soap entirely, devoting itself instead to the distribution of janitorial and sanitary supplies.

The Laundry Division of P.B. Gast & Sons was estab-

P.B. Gast and Sons Company has occupied this 82,000-square-foot headquarters building at 1515 Madison Avenue SE since 1950.

lished in 1949 by Frederick C. Gast, Sr., who is currently chairman of the board. This division distributes commercial laundry equipment throughout Michigan and northern Ohio. It provides complete laundry planning, engineering, installation, and implementation for all types of laundry processing, including schools, hospitals, nursing homes, and large commercial and industrial plants. This division is the exclusive representative of many major laundry equipment manufacturers and has installed some of the most energy- and labor-efficient laundry facilities in the Midwest.

A third generation of the Gast family is now active in the firm's management. Peter B. Gast, based in Detroit, is corporate president and general manager of the Laundry Division. Frederick C. Gast, Jr., is vice-president and chief operating officer. He heads up the Grand Rapids office with responsibilities for administration and sanitation sales.

They preside over a firm that has been transformed from their grandfather's small soapmaking operation into a large, diversified corporation dedicated to providing the most modern, innovative, and energy-efficient products and equipment to all its customers.

Today P.B. Gast & Sons Company is one of the largest distributors of its type in the Midwest. It provides janitorial supplies and equipment to a wide range of institutional, commercial, and industrial customers. It also maintains a retail outlet at the Grand Rapids headquarters for walk-in trade.

An integral part of the P.B. Gast & Sons Company's professional approach to business is to ensure customer satisfaction through quality service. This includes on-site analysis and staff training, specializing in the system approach to complete environmental sanitation.

Three generations of Gasts have been actively involved in the business founded by Peter B. Gast, whose portrait hangs on the far right and whose sons' portraits (from left: Waldemar B., Raymond A., and Frederick C. Sr.) are also represented in the family gallery at company headquarters. Active in today's management are (from left) Frederick C. Gast, Sr., chairman of the board; Peter B. Gast, corporate president; and Frederick C. Gast, Jr., vice-president and chief operating officer.

THE WBDC GROUP

"Good design is function and economy, in aesthetic form." For more than 27 years this concept has made The WBDC Group one of the top architectural firms in the Midwest. WBDC was recently named by *Michigan Business* magazine as the fastest-growing architectural and engineering firm in the state during the past five years.

After years of designing corporate office buildings for its clients, the firm moved into its own new corporate offices at 50 Monroe Place in downtown Grand Rapids in August 1986. The building, a medley of glass and chrome with a pristine, white metal "skin," stands out among the city's new downtown office structures and serves as a superb example of WBDC's renovation work. In a joint effort involving The WBDC Group, Fryling Development Company, and two other partners, two abandoned warehouse buildings were completely renovated and joined by a seven-story glass atrium. WBDC currently occupies the fourth and fifth floors of the seven-story building.

Paul D. Bowers, Jr., president and chairman of the

50 Monroe Place, Grand Rapids.

board of The WBDC Group, originally founded the company with a partner in 1960. Within two years three additional partners, Bud DeShane, Frank Covert, and Ray Gordon, were added, and the firm was incorporated. Shortly thereafter, Charles Gaskill, current executive vice-president, joined the organization.

Except for Bowers and Gaskill, all of the original partners are now retired. The new WBDC Group is stronger than ever, however. All company stock is owned by active employees, with no single partner holding a majority. Management is concentrated among 18 corporate officers and division managers, five of whom make up the board of directors.

In the beginning WBDC functioned like most small architectural firms, offering limited design services. Over the years, as clients became more sophisticated and needed a broader range of services, WBDC had the foresight to expand into new areas to meet the challenge.

Today the company provides not only architectural design, but also offers programming, engineering, space planning, interior design, signage and graphics, community development, site design, landscape architecture, and construction administration services. In addition, WBDC's staff includes a former city manager, several former city planners, and a former director of economic development, who can assist clients in obtaining financing and work with state and local governments to secure favorable tax treatment, zoning changes, and revenue bonding for building projects.

The Meijer, Inc., store no. 50 in Cascade, Michigan.

WBDC's organizational structure is somewhat unique. In 1975 a decision was made by Bowers to operate by divisions in order to encourage specialization among staff members. There are now five architectural divisions: Corporate Facilities, Commercial, Industrial, Health Care, and Education and Criminal Justice; and five support divisions: Engineering, Community Planning, Interiors and Visual Communication, Development, and Construction. Each professional staff member belongs to one of these divisions and works to become an expert in that project type or discipline.

One of WBDC's first projects was the design of the original Meijer Thrifty Acres Store in Grand Rapids. The association with Meijer, Inc., has continued to the present and has accounted for more than 18 million square feet of space and over $500 million worth of construction. In addition to most of the stores in the Meijer chain, WBDC has designed almost all of the company's offices and distribution centers.

Another corporate client that has played a key role in The WBDC Group's success is Steelcase, Inc. The design of Steelcase's $50-million corporate headquarters building in 1983 had a positive impact on WBDC's ability in the ensuing years to successfully attract major corporate building projects. Today The WBDC Group is involved in the construction of a new $75-million corporate development center for Steelcase and a new $75-million corporate headquarters building for Standard Federal Bank in Troy. In addition, the firm recently completed corporate facilities for Autodie Corporation and Meijer, Inc., in Grand Rapids, and Marion Laboratories, a national pharmaceutical firm in Kansas City.

"Such projects," according to Bill Bont, vice-president, "have already helped WBDC realize its goal of achieving a national market for its corporate facilities services." The unique thing about WBDC design, says Bont, is that there is no one "WBDC look." The firm designs buildings to "suit the function and needs of the client. We do not create buildings that force clients to adapt their needs to the building. Every project begins with a program that assesses the client's needs, goals, and objectives in relation to existing facilities, budget, and possible schedule constraints. Only after the program has been defined and solutions approved does the design process actually begin."

Paul Bowers believes that the "key to the firm's success has been our ability to get good clients and retain them through good performance and personal service. Solving client needs has always been more important than winning design awards at WBDC." As a result, more than 70 percent of The WBDC Group's work comes from repeat clients. That's an impressive record in any business.

An artist's rendering of Steelcase, Inc.'s, Corporate Development Center.

The corporate headquarters office of Steelcase, Inc.

Autodie Corporation's manufacturing facility.

IRWIN SEATING

In December 1986 the premier concert hall in the United States, Carnegie Hall in New York City, reopened with a star-studded concert that included Isaac Stern, Zubin Mehta, Marilyn Horne, and Frank Sinatra. The famed old, acoustically perfect Carnegie had just undergone a $50-million refurbishing that restored it to its original Victorian splendor. One account of that opening, describing the tattered condition of the hall before restoration, mentioned in particular the old seats that "squeaked and groaned" and took note of the new "squeakless seats."

Being squeakless is definitely a virtue in a theater seat, but the seats in Carnegie Hall are far more than that. Upholstered in a rich cardinal red mohair imported from the Netherlands, with backs and armrests of mahogany, the seats were specifically engineered for that hall by Irwin Seating Company of Grand Rapids. Both handsome and comfortable, they also are acoustically correct for that facility.

The contract was a plum for the Grand Rapids manufacturer, and a piece of cake, too, for Irwin Seating has been designing and manufacturing public seating since 1907. The company, which began as a manufacturer of school furniture, is the country's leading producer of theater and auditorium seating.

Irwin Seating has installed seating in many of the nation's leading theaters and auditoriums. Among them are the Louise M. Davies Symphony Hall (shown here) in San Francisco; the Boston Museum of Fine Arts auditorium, designed by I.M. Pei; the Crystal Cathedral in Garden Grove, California; the Portland, Oregon, Performing Arts Center; the Kansas City Music Hall; and Broadway's Portman-Marriott Theater.

School furniture is still a part of the Irwin operation, although demand has waxed and waned over the decades. Theater and auditorium seating has taken an upswing in recent years, and accounts for 83 percent of the firm's sales.

Part of the increase can be attributed to the building of new theaters and renovation of old facilities, but the big leap in theater seating demand has come from the building boom in new movie houses. Irwin sells to the Big Four—United Artists Communications, General Cinema, AMC Entertainment, and Cineplex Odeon—as well as to dozens of smaller chains. Of the 400,000 movie seats sold in 1986, 300,000 were Irwin seats.

The company gets involved in many restoration projects, such as the Carnegie and the Portland, Oregon, Performing Arts Center, which means working with architects and designers to create contemporarily comfortable seating that conforms to a particular period and style. Most of Irwin's sales, however, are from standard stock, with customers' choices limited to finish, fabric style, and color.

However, all seating must be specifically engineered for each installation. No two auditorium floors have the same degree of elevation, so seating standards are engineered to correspond to the slope of the floor. In 1986 Irwin installed seating in 700 auditoriums. That figure includes 50 in Canada and about 30 in other foreign countries.

Indoor stadium seating has long been an Irwin staple, but the firm recently made its first outdoor seating for an amphitheater in Nashville. Patrons in the Hoosier Dome in Indianapolis and the B.C. Place in Vancouver, British Columbia, watch sporting and entertainment events from Irwin seats.

The company also makes telescopic platform seating. The platforms fold, or telescope, for storage. Platforms are manufactured at the firm's wholly owned subsidiary, Irwin Telescopic Platform Company (ITP), in San Benito, Texas. A second subsidiary, Irwin Seating Canada Ltd., manufactures auditorium seating only.

Although Irwin started in the business as a manufacturer of school furniture, and during the 1950s and 1960s theater seating and school seating furniture each comprised about 50 percent of Irwin production, the demand for school furniture fell off in the 1970s because of decreases in school populations. At that time the company began concentrating on theater and arena seating.

But, as fate would have it, Irwin is back in school furniture manufacturing in a big way. In July 1986 the firm purchased American Seating's school furniture line. "We're very excited about it," say Earle "Win" Irwin, company president, and Paul Winchester, vice-president. "We have new lines, new sales force, new markets, and new emphasis. We expect sales to double in the next four years."

Between the addition of the school line and the increase in theater seating, Irwin's growth has already shown rapid gain. The company's sales jumped from $18 million in 1984 to $25 million in 1985 to $33 million in 1986. Employment went up from 175 to nearly 400, and the factory added a second shift to keep up with demand.

Irwin Seating was founded by Win Irwin's grandfather and namesake, Earle S. Irwin, and his brothers, and the company is still owned by the Irwin family. In 1984 Win Irwin took over as president, succeeding his father, William.

Some of the firm's rapid growth, says Irwin, can be attributed to both planning and fortuitous circumstance. "We recently completed an extensive formal strategic planning program, with an outside consultant, and plotted a five-year plan, which we update annually. We've never done that before, and it's been very helpful in coordinating what we're

Irwin Seating designed and manufactured 2,562 chairs for the recently renovated Carnegie Hall in New York City.

doing and the direction in which we want to go," he says.

Irwin Seating practices participatory management, and there are at least 15 quality circles in the Grand Rapids plant. Money saved through quality circle recommendations has been put into such projects as improvements to the company cafeteria. The firm also has several different employee profit-sharing plans and incentive programs.

Irwin Seating's plans for the future are "to continue as we have been, although perhaps to grow a little more slowly than in the last few years," says Irwin. "But we certainly plan to continue to dominate the public seating market."

Irwin Seating's Grand Rapids plant, at 3251 Fruit Ridge Road, NW, built in 1986 as an 80,000-square-foot facility, has gone through several expansions. The most recent, in 1986, brought the plant up to 275,000 square feet. The Canadian operation, which Irwin has owned since 1973, is building a new facility.

PRIMEBANK

The 1980s have been eventful years for PrimeBank.

In 1981 the firm, known for 93 years as Mutual Home Federal Savings & Loan, moved into a spectacular glass-and-concrete building, called the Mirror on the Mall, at Pearl and Monroe in downtown Grand Rapids.

In 1985, in response to changes in federal banking laws, Mutual Home converted from a mutual form of ownership to a stock corporation and became a federally chartered capital stock savings bank.

And in 1986, in a move entirely consistent with its recent history of changing its character to meet the demands of the times, Mutual Home discarded its nearly century-old name and identity to become PrimeBank.

But PrimeBank is not just a new name, a new logo, a new image. The name PrimeBank accurately reflects the corporation's new role in West Michigan's financial community. The second-largest locally owned bank in Grand Rapids, PrimeBank is no longer restricted to granting loans to home owners, but is a full-service banking and lending institution, serving both individual and commercial customers.

The "Mirror on the Mall," one of West Michigan's newest and largest office buildings, overlooks the many activities held year round at the Monroe Am-phitheater. It is the home office of PrimeBank's financial services network. Photo by Dan Watts

The institution may have been around for 98 years; nevertheless, it is an exciting newcomer to the commercial banking scene. PrimeBank is one of the relatively few savings and loan institutions in the country to successfully convert to a stock charter savings bank. Its dramatic changeover from S&L to full-service banking is almost a Cinderella banking story.

Mutual Home was founded in 1888 by William Sheppard as the Mutual Home and Savings Association, an organization established both as a savings institution and as a home mortgage lender, providing members with a means of financing home ownership. The institution fulfilled that role through many decades, and grew and prospered.

In 1966 the firm, which had always done business at one location in downtown Grand Rapids, opened its first branch office. Within the next 12 years eight other branch offices were built in different areas of the city, and there were 14 branch offices in all by 1981. The architecture of the branch offices, distinctive and thoroughly modern, in itself became a Mutual Home trademark and was incorporated into the logo—a roof-covered MH.

And then federal deregulation of the late 1970s hit, and S&Ls found themselves in a life-and-death struggle. The ceilings on deposit rates were lifted, but S&Ls were prohibited from expanding their market base and had to continue only as housing lenders, with no ability to increase yields on extremely large, fixed-rate home mortgages. By 1980 the nation's annual inflation rate had reached an astronomical 20 percent, and the prime interest rate climbed to 22 percent. The country was in its most severe recession in 35 years. S&Ls, unable to increase net revenues by reducing savings interest rates and not realizing adequate income

The Greg Meyer Jingle Bell Jaunt, named after Boston Marathon winner Greg Meyer of Grand Rapids, is cosponsored by PrimeBank and Westinghouse Furniture Systems. It is only one of the many community events the bank supports. Photo by Dan Watts

from their home mortgages, failed by the hundreds—more than 400 out of 4,000 between 1981 and 1983. Finally, in 1982, the federal government ruled that savings and loan institutions could offer full banking services.

Mutual Home chose to meet the challenges of the new financial environment by doing just that. Under the forceful and energetic leadership of a young, new president and chief executive officer, the institution entered into the complicated legal transactions that would change its charter from S&L to bank.

Charles Conville joined Mutual Home in 1983. With a young and aggressive management team, he formulated a strategy to make Mutual Home one of the leading banking institutions in West Michigan.

In the transition from a mutually owned to a stock corporation, Mutual Home sold 975,000 shares of stock to 1,778 stockholders. Among the shareholders are Prime-Bank directors, officers, and employees, who now own 20 percent of the stock. Explained Conville at the time of the stock sale, "Being an owner-employee is important to us. It's like driving a car you own versus driving a rental car.

You take better care of your own car. It's the same way in business. If you're an owner, you don't just work there." The company points with pride to the fact that 93 percent of the stock was sold to West Michigan investors, making the firm truly a locally owned institution.

In its new role as a full-service bank, PrimeBank is working to become a leader in making commercial loans to West Michigan medium-size and small business owners, and in making consumer loans for such purchases as boats and cars. The bank also offers lines of credit, checking accounts, charge cards, and recently installed automatic teller machines at six locations throughout the Grand Rapids area.

The transition period for PrimeBank was exciting for the staff, but it was a period of intense effort and long hours. That intensity served to forge a feeling of solidarity among staff that is an integral part of the PrimeBank persona. Making a successful transition was a common goal, and everyone had a hand in laying the foundation. Now they are all united in maintaining the momentum of creating a successful new business.

PrimeBank people are a part of the community they serve, and they take an active role in community affairs. The institution is built on the premise that its base of support is West Michigan. Its mission is to nurture that base; its goal is to be in every sense West Michigan's prime bank.

PrimeBank provides full commercial banking services, including financing for building projects. The Woodfield Apartment complex, shown here, is located at 60th Street and Eastern Avenue. Photo by Dan Watts

SEIDMAN & SEIDMAN

Seidman & Seidman has been a leading name in Grand Rapids since 1919. Like many Grand Rapids businesses, the accounting firm was established in the city in response to the needs of the furniture industry. From modest beginnings Seidman & Seidman has grown to a firm with a worldwide clientele and offices in more than 40 U.S. cities.

The first Seidman & Seidman office was opened in New York City in 1910 by Maximillian "M.L." Seidman, the oldest son of Russian immigrants. With optimistic foresight, he named the business Seidman & Seidman because he was certain at least one of his many brothers would join him in the accounting firm. Ultimately, three brothers joined M.L. in the business, as well as brothers-in-law and, in later years, nephews and sons of the founding partners.

Bright, ambitious, and energetic, all of the Seidman brothers were college graduates, most with at least one graduate degree. They earned a living during the day while pursuing an education at night.

Frank E. "F.E." Seidman first came to Grand Rapids in 1917 on business for the federal government. In those World War I days airplanes were made of wood and canvas, so the city's furniture manufacturers, with a skilled force of woodworkers, shifted part of their production over to aircraft parts for the United States Army. Young Seidman was a supervisory accountant for the U.S. Aircraft Produc-

tion Board, traveling between Grand Rapids and Detroit. He made many friends in the furniture industry and met a young Michigan woman, Esther Lubetsky, to whom he became engaged.

Seidman & Seidman's second office was opened in Grand Rapids in 1919 when F.E., who had just joined his brother's accounting firm as a partner, chose to move permanently to the area. He had a ready clientele among his friends in the furniture industry, and he soon established Seidman & Seidman as a valuable component of the local business community. F.E. and Esther were married in 1920, and the couple founded the Grand Rapids Seidman dynasty.

From the very beginning the Seidman brothers developed a business philosophy that is known within the firm today as "total involvement." Members of the firm oversaw, with genuine concern and watchfulness, the entire financial well-being of their clients, most of whom were small- to medium-size businesses and individuals of moderate means. Not only did the partners become involved with clients' business organizations, but they also dealt with individual financial matters, from estate and financial planning to conserving family resources.

Traditional areas of service were the cornerstone upon which Seidman & Seidman prospered. Excellence in ac-

counting and auditing was—and still is—a mainstay, while a special mastery of tax matters developed quite early in response to federal policy and regulations. An innovative and expanding scope of expertise positioned Seidman & Seidman as a leader in the profession.

The firm's national presence grew, with new offices opening across the United States until, in 1957, there were 15 practice offices from coast to coast. By that time younger members of the family had come into the business. The years took their toll on the founding partners, and in 1968 F.E.'s son, Bill, became chairman and chief executive partner. Under Bill Seidman's leadership, the firm enjoyed phenomenal growth through a complete restructuring, successfully making the transition from a family-held firm to a general partnership.

In the 1970s a formal philosophy was embraced, a philosophy that was based on six decades of service to clients. In essence, Seidman & Seidman's mission is to help clients succeed through outstanding services; dedication to the clients' welfare; a team approach to total involvement; an adherence to absolute integrity, quality, and high standards; and the willingness and flexibility to change in response to the ever-changing needs of clients.

From that willingness to meet the challenge of the times has emerged a vital new function—advisory services, an area that holds boundless possibilities for further expansion.

In its business advisory capacity, Seidman & Seidman helps clients obtain outside financing for expansion, acquisition, or other projects; reduce expenses, control costs, and increase profitability; select, design, and implement computerized networks; develop and implement strategic plans; and evaluate new business ventures. Clients also turn to the firm for aid in dealings with regulatory authorities; for assistance in the selection, organization, and management of personnel; and for guidance through the maze of going public or undertaking mergers or acquisitions.

In the late 1950s Seidman & Seidman developed an international clientele through an affiliation with foreign accounting firms. Over the next several decades firms from virtually every country in the Free World joined the loosely knit consortium, which united in 1983 to form a worldwide partnership under the name Binder Dijker Otte & Co. (BDO).

Seidman & Seidman/BDO offers clients the best of both worlds—the expertise of a worldwide network of financial professionals, coupled with the advantages of a decentralized management structure that assures clients of immediate, personalized attention.

Seidman & Seidman celebrated its 75th anniversary in 1985, and in that observance rededicated itself to the ideals that have sustained the firm over three-quarters of a century—integrity, objectivity, quality, continual striving for excellence and professionalism, and always, helping clients to succeed.

Both internationally and locally, Seidman & Seidman/BDO clients span a broad range of industries and professions.

FOREMOST CORPORATION OF AMERICA

Foremost Insurance Company began life 35 years ago, a new venture established to insure people pursuing a new life-style—mobile home ownership.

Carving its own unique niche in the insurance industry since its founding in 1952, FIC is the largest subsidiary of Foremost Corporation of America, the holding company for the Foremost Insurance Group of companies. Established in the late 1960s, FCOA is well on its way to becoming a billion-dollar corporation. FCOA has eight principal subsidiaries and has established a firm track record of financial stability.

The corporation's financial achievement is demonstrated in the independent ratings two of its subsidiaries have received from firms known nationally for rating corporate financial stability. Foremost Insurance Company, the

Foremost Insurance Company is the leading insurer of recreational vehicles.

largest subsidiary, is rated A + XV by A.M. Best and Company and has an AA rating from Standard and Poor, while Foremost Guaranty Corporation has earned Standard and Poor's AAA rating.

The corporate flagship, Foremost Insurance Company, was cofounded by Edward Frey of Union Bank and Richard E. Riebel, a Cincinnati insurance executive. Union Bank, itself an innovator in its field, began financing mobile homes, known in those days as "house trailers," as early as 1935. By the 1950s a much larger slice of the population had become attracted to mobile home living. The industry growth resulted in a corresponding need for property insurance. Foremost Insurance Company began as an answer to that need.

FIC and the mobile home industry grew up together, and the insurance company has been innovative and aggressive in creating new products and in developing new markets and meeting the challenges of changing markets.

The history of Foremost Insurance Company is one of many changes, but no era has seen greater changes than the mid-1980s, described by Foremost president and chief executive officer Richard L. Antonini as a "watershed point in our history." The changes of the 1980s, says Antonini, make the corporation and the insurance company "substantially different than we were in the past—in style, in nature, in focus."

One change has been a constant for both the corporation and the insurance company—the change necessitated by growth. In 35 years FIC has grown from a small Grand Rapids office certified to write insurance only in Michigan to a national company writing insurance in every state ex-

Richard L. Antonini, president and chief executive officer of Foremost Corporation of America.

cept Hawaii. Since 1985 operations have been consolidated in Grand Rapids, not in one small office as in the early 1950s, but in a large corporate complex in Cascade Township.

Most recently, Foremost Corporation of America has divested itself of its more diverse subsidiaries to focus on its "core" business—mobile homes, recreational vehicles, private mortgage, and credit life insurance.

Core subsidiaries of the corporation are the property/casualty company, Foremost Insurance Company; a mortgage insurance company, Foremost Guaranty Corporation; a financial service company, Foremost Financial Services; a life insurance company, Foremost Life Insurance Company; two preferred customer companies, American Federation Insurance Company and American Freedom Insurance Company; and specialty insurance providers such as American Signature Insurance Company.

Says Antonini, "We are developing each company as a specialty company. In almost every instance we are a leader in our market; we are, for instance, the largest property/casualty insurer in the mobile home and RV markets. We dominate those markets, and we intend to continue to dominate those markets. We are focusing on very narrow, very specific markets, markets where we have the competitive advantage. And we will expand where we feel we have strong market niches."

The restructuring has brought not only a new focus to the company but a new vitality as well. Antonini, who was FCOA's chief financial officer, became chief executive officer in mid-1986. The entire management team is highly experienced and knowledgeable about the business, ambitious, and imbued with the Foremost spirit—to move ahead and to be the best in the marketplace.

By centralizing the operations of the largest subsidiary at corporate headquarters, FCOA underscored its commitment to Grand Rapids. The restructuring necessitated a new, 50,000-square-foot building that has already been expanded. And the consolidation brought 500 additional jobs to the area. By the end of 1987 the corporation expects to have more than 1,600 employees in Grand Rapids.

FCOA's complex, Centennial Park, is a residential, recreational, and commercial area that the corporation began developing in the late 1960s and 1970s. It has set the tone for the development of Cascade Township as a business and industrial area.

The planned residential condominium development in Centennial Park features three distinct communities—Gatehouse, Meadows, and Heathmore—all high-end luxurious homes. Health and recreational facilities include the tennis courts and 18-hole golf course of the Meadowood Country Club, a private club, and the Charlevoix Club, which is a private athletic club.

Centennial Park is also the site of the Grand Rapids Marriott Hotel, which is 90-percent Foremost owned, and provides a prime business address for several major corporations, including IBM, Guardsman Chemical, and Witmark Corporation.

A company with a long-standing reputation for strength and stability, Foremost Corporation of America moves into the 1990s with clear goals for fulfilling its growth potential and a dedication to its traditional principles of excellence and service to customers, providers, and employees.

The Meadowood Club, part of the Centennial Park complex.

Foremost Corporation of America corporate headquarters.

AMERICAN ACQUEST, INC.

American Acquest, Inc., is a young aggressive company on the move. In five short years the organization has grown into a multiservice real estate corporation—one of the fastest-growing real estate developers in West Michigan. And it's still growing. "But," says company founder, president, and chief executive officer Frederick Riebel, "we are keeping our growth at a planned pace. We want to control our destiny, making sure it's done right, for the health of the corporation."

Riebel organized American Acquest, Inc., in 1982 as a traditional realty company. It soon expanded into a development firm, specializing in West Michigan waterfront condominiums in addition to conventional home marketing.

From that point management decided that other support services, such as commercial investment brokerage, mortgage lending, and property management services would broaden the company's base and enhance its capabil-

ities as a development firm. Today, through its five support subsidiaries, the multifaceted organization handles all types of real estate transactions, including the sale and marketing of residential and commercial properties, land development, arrangement of financing, and syndication of limited real estate partnerships. In addition, investment portfolio and property management services are offered during and after project completion. "We are truly a full-service corporation," says Riebel, "and with that quality comes an insatiable appetite to get the job done right—and right the first time."

American Acquest is an innovator in the real estate industry. Even its management style is unlike that of the average real estate company industrywide. Each corporate division is headed by a manager who is also an officer of the parent company, American Acquest, Inc. The parent corporation oversees and coordinates the activities of the five corporate divisions: American Acquest Realty Division, American Acquest Equity Partners, American Acquest Securities Corporation, American Acquest Mortgage

Frederick C. Riebel, president and chief executive officer of American Acquest, Inc.

Four members of the American Acquest team (from left): Allan Reider, manager of American Acquest Realty Division; Chuck Saur, registered representative, Securities Corporation; president and chief executive officer Frederick C. Riebel; and Deb DeGrote, office manager.

Corporation, and American Acquest Property Management Corporation.

"We don't have a large staff," says Riebel of his team of 35, "but the people we do have are upscale people. We want a first-string mentality here—first-string, first-rate people. We maintain a lean company, lots of muscle tone and very little fat. Our people have a track record of experience when they start here. They are well prepared, so they have better earning opportunities, and they're rewarded for continuing education and advanced certification."

American Acquest staff members participate in weekly general meetings and have access to a wide array of company resources and services to enhance their own abilities to serve clients and customers. The network of interrelated businesses contained within the corporation pulls together to create smooth business transactions and customer service.

American Acquest Realty Division is the marketing arm of the corporation, handling all real estate brokerage transactions, including residential, commercial, and leasing. It is also a member of the national relocation network, TRANSLO, which enables the firm to assist buyers transferring to or from Grand Rapids from all across the nation. American Acquest Realty Division is managed by company vice-president Allan S. Reider. Reider was the recipient of the 1987 Realtor Associate of the Year Award, given by the Grand Rapids Real Estate Board, which has a membership of 1,800.

Craig A. Black, CCIM, is executive vice-president of the parent company and is also managing general partner of American Acquest Equity Partners, which recently completed a 180-unit apartment project, Northwood Hills,

located on the city's northeast side. Equity Partners undertakes the formation of limited partnerships to finance development and acquisition of income properties.

American Acquest Securities Corporation is a full-service securities firm and an NASD broker/dealer registered with the Federal Securities and Exchange Commission and the State of Michigan. Headed by Timothy Kolkman, president, the firm offers a complete range of investment opportunities and has been the broker/dealer on the last two real estate limited partnerships of American Acquest Equity Partners.

American Acquest Mortgage Corporation is a broker company offering loans to commercial-investment property developers and owners for the acquisition or refinancing of existing properties, or the development of new properties. Loan placement and anticipated expansion to include mortgage banking services are coordinated by Thomas Reed, vice-president.

Riebel sums up his thriving company's services this way: "The subsidiaries of American Acquest, Inc., offer full-service investment opportunities to our valued customers and clients by coordinating the marketing, leasing, financing, and syndication of real estate within a full-service framework."

Northwood Hills Apartments of Devonwood Hills Drive, NE, Grand Rapids, an American Acquest Equity Partners development.

Peachtree Plaza, at the corner of Kalamazoo and 60th streets in Grand Rapids—a development of American Acquest, Inc.

235

GENERAL MOTORS

In 1935, in the midst of the Great Depression, General Motors invested seven million dollars in a new metal-stamping plant in Grand Rapids. In the 50-odd years since, General Motors has become an integral part of the Grand Rapids industrial community. With the construction in 1943 of the GM Diesel Equipment Plant, the company became the area's largest employer, and in the 1980s, with three plants in the metropolitan area (and a fourth in nearby Coopersville), GM remains a cornerstone of the area's economic base, channeling a half-billion dollars annually into the local economy.

Demonstrating continuing faith in the Grand Rapids business climate, the company's three area plants combined have, in 1985, 1986, and 1987, invested more than three-quarters of a billion dollars in plant modernization and expansions. The plants are among the most modern and technologically advanced facilities of their kind in the world.

The Chevrolet-Pontiac-Canada (CPC) Group Grand Rapids Metal Fabricating Plant, located at 300 36th Street SW, was the city's first GM plant, originally known as the Fisher Body Metal Fabricating Plant. A tooling and stamping facility, the plant currently makes tools, fixtures, and dies for other GM tooling and metal-stamping plants, and sheet-metal panels and parts for all of GM's passenger cars except the Corvette.

The Rochester Products Division, at 2100 Burlingame SW, was opened in 1943 as the diesel equipment division of General Motors, making gas turbine nozzles and military hardware such as gun barrels, trigger housings, and fuel injectors for military diesel engines. After World War II plant production concentrated on precision components for gas turbine, gasoline, and diesel engines. The plant's primary products today are hydraulic valve lifters and diesel unit fuel injectors. The division makes 400,000 valve lifters per day, which are sold mostly to General Motors' North American engine plants, but also to manufacturers in Germany, Japan, Australia, Brazil, and Great Britain. The diesel fuel injectors are for heavy-duty industrial and vehicle engines such as those used on semitrucks, oil drilling rigs, locomotives, and some marine equipment.

The Inland Division Group's trim plant, at 2150 Alpine Avenue NW, was established in 1952 as the Fisher Body Trim Fabrication Plant. For three years the facility made fuselages for the F-84 Thunderbird jet fighter plane used in the Korean War. In 1955 plant production was converted

A Rochester Products employee with one of the plant's products, a direct-acting hydraulic lifter.

A sewing operation in the PBS system, which is a totally computer-integrated manufacturing system at the Inland Division plant.

to interior trim for the 1955 Chevrolet. The present operation is the result of a marriage between two of General Motors' oldest divisions, Fisher Body trim operations and Inland. The plant manufactures seat covers for 7,800 automobiles per day, primarily for all General Motors' J-car line except Cadillac. The plant occupies 900,000 square feet, making it one of the largest soft-trim facilities in the world.

It is easy to get bogged down in superlatives when talking about local General Motors production. It is hardly surprising, given the size of the plants and the volume of output, that they use raw materials in prodigious quantity, and that they ship products out in quantities measurable in tons. The trim plant, one of six GM trim plants, foreign and domestic, uses the grand total of 160 million square yards of fabric per year. The metal-fabricating plant ships out several hundred thousand tons of parts per week, filling 250 railroad boxcars and 100 trucks each week.

Production at the Grand Rapids GM plants remains relatively stable and not critically affected by the ups and downs of the American auto industry as a whole. Nevertheless, the local plants reflect the changes that are taking place in American automobile manufacturing. The industry is in a period of tremendous change. Worldwide socioeconomic factors, including competition from foreign manufacturers, have forced the industry into reorganization from top to bottom. General Motors has been in the forefront in spearheading change, and the Grand Rapids plants and personnel are reaping many of the benefits of those changes.

Computerization and robotics have transformed the manufacturing process and dictated the expansion and modernization of the Grand Rapids plants to accommodate the new technology. With the commitment of capital funds has come a corresponding commitment to educate employees to meet the challenges of the new technology. For their part, employees continually demonstrate their willingness to accept new technology—a part of that famous Grand Rapids work ethic that is visible at every level, say GM executives.

The United Auto Workers and the three GM plants together built and equipped a training center to provide the technical training required by the new technology. The center, opened in 1985, is administered jointly by GM and UAW, and is just one example of the excellent working relationship the union and General Motors maintain in implementing new programs and preparing for future challenges.

In addition to educating employees in the new manufacturing techniques and use of equipment, the plants also offer courses in basic skills. Some retraining and basic education classes are conducted in-plant as well. GM employees have many opportunities to further their education—from completing requirements for a high school diploma to advanced schooling at area colleges.

General Motors is far more than a kingpin in the region's economy; the company is a good corporate neighbor. GM takes great pride in its consistently high-percentage employee participation in the annual Kent County United Way fund drive. As a corporation, it contributes generously to a variety of community activities and foundations, and works with area schools and colleges in supporting educational activities. Practically every major volunteer, human service, and philanthropic organization in the county boasts a GM employee on its board, and GM people are active in projects and causes throughout the community. Say company officials, "We're proud of our operations and the people who work here."

A CAD/CAM technician reviewing cutter scans at the CPC Metal Fabrication Plant.

A machinist copy milling on the Droop and Rein at the CPC Metal Fabrication Plant.

GUARDSMAN CHEMICALS, INC.

The Grand Rapids furniture industry spawned many support industries. One of the most durable and long-lived is Guardsman Chemicals, Inc.

Guardsman Chemicals produces finishes and coatings for all types of wood and metal products. The company also operates a custom-packaging aerosol plant for paint, household, and industrial products, and it has a consumer products line of polish, dust cloths, drain cleaners, spot removers, fabric protectors, and touch-up kits for wood furniture. Guardsman coatings are applied to furniture, golf balls, kitchen cabinets, household appliances, and space-orbiting vehicles. It would not be an exaggeration to assume that everyone in the country has a Guardsman finish of some kind in their home or car.

The company was founded in 1915 as Grand Rapids Varnish Corporation (GARVCO) and made varnish for the local wood furniture manufacturers. Always aggressive in its research and development of new markets and new products, the firm had, within 11 years, added metal finishes to its product line. The metal finishes, in fact, kept GARVCO alive during the Great Depression of the 1930s, when many of the wood furniture manufacturers failed.

One of Grand Rapids Varnish's first customers for the metal finishes was Terrell Equipment Company, a Grand Rapids manufacturer of metal office furniture. Terrell, known today as Steelcase, Inc., is still a major Guardsman customer.

In the post-World War II years the wood furniture industry became concentrated in the South, where low-cost labor and proximity to raw materials made production less expensive than in northern plants. In 1953 Grand Rapids Varnish, mindful of the shift, established its first non-Grand Rapids facility, a warehousing and studio operation in North Carolina. In 1960 the company added a manufacturing plant to that facility.

The firm added new product lines through acquisition of other manufacturers throughout the United States and Canada. Today Guardsman Chemicals has 10 other facilities in addition to its Grand Rapids plant and corporate headquarters at 2960 Lucerne SE.

Guardsman was a trade name the company adopted in the late 1930s for its top-of-the-line finishes. By 1960 only 3 percent of the firm's business was in varnishes, so it changed the corporate name to Guardsman Chemical Coatings, Inc. By 1975 even that name no longer was appli-

Guardsman Heritage furniture care products include furniture polish, fabric protection and cleaner, and dusting and polishing cloths.

cable, and Guardsman Chemicals, Inc., became the official name.

Part of the Guardsman corporate philosophy is being a good neighbor, and protecting the environment is an important element in the firm's good-neighbor policy. Guardsman not only adheres rigidly to federal regulations, but also maintains its own strict standards for the safety of its workers and the environment of the communities in which the company has plants.

Say Guardsman Chemicals, Inc., officials, "There is no room in the marketplace for a product that is just safe enough. Guardsman's success arises from our determination to manufacture products that improve the quality of life—without compromising the present or future environment."

Guardsman wood stains and finishes are used by most of the country's largest manufacturers of fine wood furniture.

MICHIGAN LITHO

The single most important feature of any label produced by Michigan Litho is invisible to the naked eye. That feature is the service that stands behind the product, the commitment to customer satisfaction that distinguishes this Grand Rapids company from its competition.

Michigan Litho got its start in 1901 manufacturing labels for a local brewery and soon branched into labels for local canneries and, as a sideline, commercial job printing—catalogs, brochures, business cards, letterhead stationery, and envelopes—for area businesses. By the mid-1960s the firm decided to phase out its commercial printing work and concentrate its efforts on the manufacture of food products labels for cans and bottles.

Today paper labels and metalized paper labels (resembling foil but more flexible than foil) for the food industry are Michigan Litho's prime product. The company has two distribution centers, one in Grand Rapids and one in Ceres, California, but all the labels that roll off its presses are manufactured in Grand Rapids. Michigan Litho's market is national and worldwide, and its customers include such companies as Vlassic, Gerber Products Company, Spartan, Gordon Food Service, and Faygo. The firm offers its customers a full range of services, including creative design, film work, press work, and binding. "Our clients know they can rely on us to make that extra effort," says Roger Martindill. "The quality of our labels speaks for itself, so what we sell is service."

Michigan Litho also continues to do some commercial printing work, supplying maps to the State of Michigan and tourist materials to the Eastern Michigan Tourist Association and the Upper Peninsula Tourist and Recreation Association.

Founded by the Mathieson family in 1901, Michigan Litho was owned by family members until 1959, when it was purchased by William Martindill, who sold it to a Canadian firm in 1978. In 1986 Michigan Litho's management bought the business back. Today Jim Owens is company president, Ron Rosencrans is secretary and vice-president/administration, and Roger Martindill, William's son, is vice-president/marketing.

As dedicated as they are to product quality and customer service, Michigan Litho's owners are equally committed to their community and their employees. Employee relations are important to the company—a union shop numbering 165 workers—and the owners take great pride in the fact that many of those employees are old-timers who have been at their jobs for years.

Michigan Litho places great value on the sense of continuity and permanence that characterizes the company. Founded 86 years ago by a Grand Rapids family, the firm has been at its Carlton SE location since 1905, and describes itself as a "well-established, old-line Grand Rapids company."

"We have grown with Grand Rapids from the beginning," says Roger Martindill, "and we're committed to remaining here for a long time to come."

EBERHARD FOODS

The Eberhard Foods chain, West Michigan's fifth-largest supermarket firm, bears the unmistakable stamp of its founder and guiding light, L.V. Eberhard, who, at the age of 84, is still pioneering in the business he established 68 years ago.

Eberhard was born into the food business. His father owned the Grand Rapids Home Dairy at the turn of the century and, when the senior Eberhard died in 1914, L.V., a teenager at the time, and his mother carried on. Four years later they expanded into the grocery business, with a starting inventory of $25 worth of groceries and 100 pounds of sugar.

Always a progressive retailer, Eberhard built his first supermarket in 1939 and had it equipped with the first self-opening doors in Grand Rapids. A second supermarket followed in 1941, along with such innovations as self-service meat counters and evening shopping hours. The Eberhard chain took another leadership role in 1951 with the introduction of S&H Green Stamps. In 1979 the company built its own warehouse facility and distribution center along with a headquarters building on the same site. Most recently, electronic scanning devices replaced traditional cash registers in all Eberhard's stores.

In addition to building a chain of 20 supermarkets throughout West Michigan, Eberhard was one of the founders of the highly successful Grocers Dairy Company (now known as Country Fresh), a grocer-owned enterprise that merchandised a full line of products. In 1945 Eberhard pioneered the packaging of milk in cardboard cartons through the use of what was then the new Excello packaging method.

In spite of his dairy-oriented beginnings, Eberhard is a self-proclaimed produce man at heart, believing that a store's reputation for freshness and value is most readily

L.V. Eberhard, founder of the Eberhard Foods chain.

made or broken in the produce department. His daily inspection tour of local stores always finds him checking out the produce and offering merchandising tips to his managers.

L.V. Eberhard's pioneering spirit is perhaps best exemplified in his attitude toward employees. In 1974 Eberhard's was one of the first 200 companies in the nation to establish an Employee Stock Ownership Plan (ESOP). Through the ESOP, employees are assuming ownership of the firm and are enjoying many of the incentives that accompany ownership. The Eberhard ESOP now owns 48 percent of the company stock, and plans are currently under way for L.V. to sell his personal holdings to the ESOP in a leveraged buyout that will make the plan and its employee-members full owners of the firm.

Ever since he began in the grocery business, L.V. Eberhard has made sure that his stores were distinguished by their variety, cleanliness, fine service, and competitive pricing. Known as a perfectionist, he will be remembered as an innovator. And as he looks back over his long and lustrous career, he says that he has remained young at heart by meeting the continuing challenge of change.

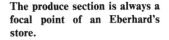

The produce section is always a focal point of an Eberhard's store.

HARTGER & WILLARD
COMMERCIAL MORTGAGE FINANCING

**Photo by Carle P. Turek of Real
Estate Photography**

Building an office complex, a shopping mall, or a retirement village requires the coordination and talents of many people—architects, designers, engineers, masons, and carpenters. But at a very early stage in any project, the one indispensable element is financing.

One firm that has supplied that essential ingredient and played a vital role in changing the face of the city over the past 40 years is Hartger & Willard. During the past decade loans in excess of $110 million have been arranged in the central city for various projects, many of which are pictured on this page.

Hartger & Willard is a mortgage banking firm. The company has brought millions of dollars into the community through residential and commercial mortgages. Over the years it has financed a wide variety of projects, including office buildings, shopping centers, apartment complexes, industrial properties, mobile home parks, hospitals, and elderly care facilities.

The firm represents more than 20 institutional lenders—major insurance companies, pension funds, commercial banks, and savings and loan associations—both local and in the nation's financial centers. In addition, the company has originated and placed a large volume of FHA-insured project loans through various private funding sources. Hartger & Willard now services in excess of $400 million in commercial loans, making it one of the largest independent commercial mortgage bankers in the country.

In response to the growing demand for professional real estate management and consulting services, Hartger & Willard, through its subsidiary, H&W Properties, entered the field and today manages a variety of commercial properties, including office buildings, shopping centers, apartments, and housing for the elderly.

The company, which is locally owned and managed, was founded in 1949 by Harold V. Hartger and Allan H. Willard to provide financing for single-family FHA and VA housing. The partners soon branched into commercial mortgage banking and eventually phased out the residential lending division.

Hartger & Willard takes pride in the part it has played in the economic development of Grand Rapids, West Michigan, and the state. With its experience in real estate financing, the firm will continue to be a valued participant in Michigan and Grand Rapids' growth and prosperity.

FRYLING CONSTRUCTION COMPANY

Founded in 1946, Grand Rapids-based Fryling Construction Company has grown to become one of the Midwest's leading general construction firms.

Fryling's experience in multiple-dwelling housing, hotels, warehouses, and office/commercial construction and renovation has given Fryling the expertise and scope to assure an owner of the highest quality results.

Working with a development team at project initiation, Fryling helps establish project objectives, budget considerations, research, feasibility studies, and site selection. Fryling's full-service staff also assists with regulatory and governmental consideration, and ultimately provides the most practical and cost-efficient type of construction to suit the owner's requirements. Fryling's "hands-on" management and field tradesmen assure the owner of labor to create high-quality structures on time and on budget.

Fryling Construction Company's skill at project coordination has been abundantly demonstrated by the conversion of the three-building, 70-year-old Helmer Complex into the

Robert E. Fryling, president. Photography by LeClaire Studio

Snowberry Heights housing for the elderly in Marquette, Michigan. Architect, Daverman Associates

242

striking seven-story office structure known as 50 Monroe Place. Initiated in 1984 by Fryling Development Company, the project became a $13-million enhancement to downtown Grand Rapids. With 165,000 square feet of prime office space, 50 Monroe Place includes among its tenants some of West Michigan's leading architectural, accounting, legal, and banking firms.

Prime examples of Fryling Construction's ability to renovate a building in strict accordance with historical accuracy are the Rood Building (Flanagan's Irish Pub) in downtown Grand Rapids and Paddock Place (Gibson's Restaurant) in the southeastern residential area. These restorations were closely monitored by the Grand Rapids Historical Society.

Through its involvement in Grand River 1990, a local development group, Fryling Construction has been active in the redevelopment of the west bank of the Grand River. A new eight-story Day's Inn hotel is the first result of these efforts.

Fryling Construction Company has built projects that serve many segments of the local community. These include Sentinel Pointe Retirement Community, an $8-million senior citizen facility, and a new $2.5-million dormitory facility for Grand Valley State College.

Now in its third generation of family ownership, Fryling Construction Company is headed by Robert E. Fryling. A subsidiary, Fryling Development Company, explores new construction opportunities to better the community and assists clients with complete coordination of new construction and renovation projects.

The Rood Building, Grand Rapids.

50 Monroe Place, Grand Rapids. Architect, WBDC Group. Photography by Dittmer & Co.

Millpoint Condominiums, Spring Lake, Michigan. Architect, J.D. Hess & Associates

VARNUM, RIDDERING, SCHMIDT AND HOWLETT

In 1988 the law firm of Varnum, Riddering, Schmidt and Howlett—Grand Rapids' largest law firm—will celebrate a proud tradition of 100 years of service to Grand Rapids.

Although its name is the product of a 1983 merger of the Grand Rapids law practices of Varnum, Riddering, Wierengo & Christenson and Schmidt, Howlett, Van't Hof, Snell & Vana, the firm traces its roots back to 1888. During that year Grand Rapids residents Robert Montgomery and McGeorge Bundy founded the law firm of Montgomery and Bundy, the nucleus for a succeeding organization that included Laurent Varnum and Carl Riddering as partners.

Predecessors of the Varnum, Riddering, Schmidt and Howlett law firm, as well as its present lawyers, have long served Grand Rapids residents and businesses in legal matters ranging from simple wills to complex litigation. They have also participated in 100 years of change in the legal system.

"There was a time when a Grand Rapids resident could reach our lawyers in the Michigan Trust Building by picking up the phone and dialing '83.' Keep in mind that our lawyers were in practice for more than 60 years before the electric typewriter came about," says Jack Wierengo, who began practice in 1937 and currently serves as counsel to the firm.

"In fact, I remember the 1950s when the electric typewriter came in, the joy of the labor lawyers—with onionskin paper and appropriate carbon paper, 12 copies of legal documents could be made at once!" states Wierengo. "Of course, when you did that, an inadvertent typographical er-ror had to be erased 12 times in order to make a correction."

Now carbon paper is a thing of the past, and even the electric typewriter is of diminishing importance at Varnum, Riddering, Schmidt and Howlett. The firm includes over 100 lawyers whose practices, extending from the Grand River to international waters, are aided by computer research terminals, laser printers, and a large bank of word processors.

"I guess I was a member of the last law school graduating class where lawyers knew everything," laughs Robert Howlett, who began practice in 1932. "The need for lawyer specialization began with the New Deal. That's when one government administrative agency after another was created. Next came administrative regulations. Since then individual lawyers have gradually had to concentrate on doing

The firm's offices overlook Grand Rapids' city skyline and the downtown Monroe Mall.

Varnum, Riddering's offices include three modern libraries in addition to computerized legal research facilities.

just a few things very well."

It was a commitment to a high degree of diversity in legal expertise that spurred the merger of the Varnum, Riddering and Schmidt, Howlett firms in 1983. The purpose and effect of the merger was to enhance the individual capabilities of the two predecessor organizations and to further strengthen their proficiencies in specialized areas.

The key to service at Varnum, Riddering is the firm's recognition that many areas of legal practice have become highly specialized and increasingly complex. Advice given in one area of the law regularly has ramifications that must be considered in other areas. Such situations are most effectively resolved by the firm's interdisciplinary concept. That is, while a greater number of lawyers may address an individual client concern than in years past, each lawyer will specialize in the matters addressed, thereby providing clients with cost-effective, specialized services.

The firm's size has further promoted the development of formal practice groups that form the backbone of Varnum, Riddering's interdisciplinary team approach. Formal practice groups include those specializing in general business and commercial matters, real estate, bankruptcy, environmental law, energy law, estate planning and probate, labor and employment relations, litigation, municipal and administrative law, pension planning, and patent, trademark, and copyright matters.

The core of Varnum, Riddering, Schmidt and Howlett's practice is its service to business and public institutions. The firm's Grand Rapids clients include banks, churches, colleges and universities, furniture manufacturers, governmental units, trade associations, utilities, manufacturers, and members of the media. Its lawyers, many of whom were born and raised in Grand Rapids, include graduates of virtually all of the nation's leading law schools.

Varnum, Riddering, Schmidt and Howlett attorneys have played a significant role in the government of the organized professional bar and in city and state government. Individual members of the practice have served as presidents or chairmen of the Grand Rapids, Muskegon, and Michigan State Bar associations; the Michigan Employment Relations Commission, Public Service Commission, and Natural Resources Commission; and the state bar's Municipal Utilities Committee; Patent, Trademark, and Copyright Council; Computer Law section; and Probate and Estate Planning section. The firm's attorneys have also served as professors and instructors at local and state universities and law schools.

Grand Rapids citizens who support local charitable, cultural, social, and community activities have been joined by Varnum, Riddering. Long active as a patron of the arts, the firm sponsors area music, theatrical, and artistic endeavors, while also funding causes such as National Public Radio.

Varnum, Riddering, Schmidt and Howlett maintains offices in Grand Rapids and Lansing, but all attorneys are headquartered on the fifth, sixth, seventh, eighth, and ninth

Varnum, Riddering's interdisciplinary team concept allows the firm to serve client needs with a combination of legal specialties.

floors of the PrimeBank Building on the corner of Pearl and Monroe in downtown Grand Rapids. The firm's modern offices include three libraries, 10 conference rooms, and views of both the Grand River and Monroe Mall. The offices are connected by a concourse to the Amway Grand Plaza complex.

The lawyers and support staff of Varnum, Riddering, Schmidt and Howlett look to the beginning of the second century of the firm's legal tradition in much the same way as Grand Rapids businesses and residents look to their own futures. The firm is intensely proud of its past, yet stands committed to the progress and innovation neccessary to assure excellence in legal services in the future.

Over 100 lawyers serve the needs of the firm's clients from the fifth, sixth, seventh, eighth, and ninth floors of the PrimeBank Building.

SACKNER PRODUCTS, INC.

Three very special flags fly from the flagpole outside the Sackner Products, Inc., corporate headquarters at 2700 Patterson Avenue SE—the SPEAR-1 (Supplier Performance Evaluation and Reporting Award) from General Motors, the Q-1 (Quality-1) from Ford Motor Company, and the QE (Quality Excellence Award) from Chrysler Motors. Only an elite handful of suppliers to the three giant automobile manufacturers has earned even one of the quality awards. Sackner has captured all three, plus quality citations from other major manufacturers such as Steelcase and Whirlpool.

Sackner Products, Inc., manufactures cordage and nonwoven padding fabrics for the automotive, furniture, and dielectric industries.

The firm, founded in 1916 as the Grand Rapids Fiber Cord Company, made welting and padding for the local furniture industry. By 1949 the manufacturer had so diversified its product line that the name was no longer applicable, and the company became Sackner Products, named for its founder, Wade Sackner. In 1966 Sackner became a wholly owned subsidiary of Bemis Company, Inc., of Minneapolis, a conglomerate that supplies a wide variety of products—from packaging materials and systems to machinery for the food, agricultural, chemical, paper products, automotive, furniture, pharmaceutical, and apparel industries.

Sackner Products, with corporate headquarters and manufacturing facilities in Grand Rapids, also operates plants in Albion, Indiana; Los Angeles, California; Statesville, North Carolina; Sterling Heights, Michigan; and

Verona, Mississippi. The corporation is structured with decentralized management and is committed to small plant operations of 50,000 to 150,000 square feet. Each plant is autonomous, with production capabilities, market, sales, and management, and, generally speaking, serves customers within its own geographic locale. Products from the Grand Rapids and Albion plants go primarily to Detroit automobile manufacturers and to midwestern furniture companies. The North Carolina, Mississippi, and California plants supply residential furniture manufacturers and industrial markets.

Sackner is changing the scope and nature of its role in the marketplace because the industries that it serves, such as automotive and upholstered furniture, are changing dramatically to meet the challenges of new technologies and foreign competition. The company is no longer strictly a manufacturer, but is evolving into a source of systems products and services for its customers.

To that end Sackner has become involved with automotive manufacturers at the beginning of the product design process. With the recent purchase of Integrated Trim Services in Sterling Heights, Michigan, a tooling and prototype business, Sackner not only supplies materials that go into the manufacture of General Motors cars, but the company also helps to design and make the tools necessary for GM's processing of those materials prior to final assembly.

Such versatility, say company officials, makes Sackner more attractive as a source to auto manufacturers as that industry moves to cut production costs and become more efficient and more competitive with foreign car makers. In

addition, being in on the design process from the beginning gives Sackner a critical edge in developing materials for new products. One company official describes the process as akin to "manufacturers going into partnership with their suppliers."

Being able to meet the highest quality standards of all of its customers is another factor that has put Sackner out front in its quest for new business. As American manufacturers lock horns with their foreign competitors for a fair share of the market, they have begun to emphasize quality of product with an intensity never before known in American industry, and they demand the same quality from their suppliers as from their own plants. Quality control has always been a Sackner virtue, but the firm intensified its own efforts to meet and maintain the highest industry standards. Sackner's winning efforts in quality control have assured it a niche in the marketplace.

The cordage made is of four different types—paper, either twisted or formed; synthetic fibers that are braided, much like cotton clothesline rope; and plastic cordage, formed by extrusion. Uses are as diverse as welting for automobile and furniture upholstery and lollipop sticks.

Nonwoven fiber products manufactured in Grand Rapids are made on machines that form a nonwoven fabric of synthetic fibers bonded together either chemically and/or mechanically. The resulting material is fabricated to the customer's needs by molding and die cutting. These products are used in a variety of padding applications in car door panels, seating, headliners, roof pads, and as sound insulation barriers in acoustical components for stereo systems and related products.

Sackner has patented products in its array of composites. Recently introduced is an automotive interior substrate material called Fibre Cor®. Fibre Cor is being touted as the next generation of substrate composites. The first use of this product will be for automobile headliners. Discussions with manufacturers in Europe and Japan will result in eventual licensing internationally. Fibre Cor is a result of Sackner's dedication to research and commitment to future technological requirements.

Sackner Products, Inc., is one of the dynamic companies in West Michigan, contributing much to the growth of the region, and to the growth of other companies in the area. Product development is becoming increasingly important in the firm's management and marketing strategies, positioning it for steady growth over the next decade.

JORDAN COLLEGE

Jordan College is dedicated to "resource" conservation. Not only has the college become deeply involved in energy conservation through the renowned Jordan Energy Institute, but it has also dedicated itself to fostering human potential by directing its programming toward those nontraditional and economically disadvantaged students who might not otherwise be served by an institution of higher learning.

Founded in 1967 in Cedar Springs, Michigan, as a church-affiliated Bible institute, the school was chartered as Jordan College five years later. At that time a conscious decision was made to broaden the educational scope of the institution beyond its original sectarian confines. The college has been building on that change in direction ever since.

Still committed to Christian values and still headquartered in Cedar Springs, Jordan College today operates seven campuses, serving 2,100 students throughout the state of Michigan with a diversity of programs designed to help them enhance their career opportunities and enrich their lives.

Jordan's growth arose out of need—its own need to conserve limited resources and that of students for whom economic, social, or cultural barriers stand in the way of pursuing higher education.

A combination of necessity and innovation pointed the way to a leadership role in energy conservation education. Needing to save money in any way it could, the school took aim at energy costs. Students and faculty, working together, designed and built an innovative solar-heating system for one campus building, using hundreds of thousands of aluminum soda pop and beer cans as solar reflectors and traps. That hands-on expertise, along with federal energy research funding made available in the wake of the Arab oil embargo of 1973, gave Jordan College the opportunity to offer an indispensable and highly sought after educational service.

In 1977 the federal Energy Research and Development Administration awarded Jordan College a $98,660 grant for the construction of a second solar-energy project (this one for demonstration purposes) on the Cedar Springs campus. In 1978 the college opened the Jordan Energy Institute (JEI).

Now located on a five-acre campus in Comstock Park, just north of Grand Rapids, JEI offers an extensive curriculum leading to certificates and two- and four-year degrees in a variety of energy management and renewable energy technology courses. Focusing on practical energy solutions to a multitude of individual, government, and corporate needs, JEI's unique renewable energy education program is one of the foremost in the world.

Energy was not the only field of education that Jordan College set out to address. Although the number of college extension programs, branch campuses, and community colleges had grown considerably by the late 1970s, not all Michigan communities had higher education opportuni-

Jordan College seeks to break the barriers that prevent some students from seeking a higher education. Photo by Studio Three Associates

The Jordan Energy Institute (JEI) is known throughout the world for its work in energy conservation and its unique educational program. Photo by Studio Three Associates

Jordan College's Grand Rapids campus. Photo by Allington Studios

ties, and not all prospective students enjoyed access to educational programming designed to meet their particular needs. Seeing its mission as one of providing educational services where the need was going unmet, Jordan College, in 1979, embarked on a period of rapid growth by opening a series of new campuses in Newaygo and Berrien counties, the Thumb area, Flint, Detroit, and Grand Rapids.

Opened in 1983, the Grand Rapids campus, located at the corner of Breton Road and Burton Street on the city's southeast side, is housed in a modern building equipped with 22 classrooms; computer, word-processing, and typing facilities; cosmetology and food-service labs; a library; physical fitness room; and fully licensed day-care center. The curriculum offers a broad range of one- and two-year applied science programs in such fields as accounting; child development; cosmetology; food service; executive, legal, and medical secretarial work; and a host of computer-related specialties.

Seeking to break down the personal, economic, social, or cultural barriers that continue to prevent a growing segment of the population from pursuing higher education goals, Jordan bases its admissions criteria not only on previous academic performance but also applies a broader "ability to benefit" standard to student enrollments. In keeping with that philosophy, Jordan has reached out specifically to the nontraditional student. The average age of today's Jordan College student is 29; minority students make up more than half of the school's total enrollment, and three-quarters of the students are women.

The Jordan College approach to education is a highly personalized one in which students are encouraged to realize their full potential. Small classes, individualized instruction, remedial education services, an extensive counseling program, "survival skills" workshops, career planning, and job placement programs are just some of the ways in which the college helps students to accomplish their academic, career, and life goals.

Jordan also makes every effort to remove the financial

obstacles to education by supplying textbooks free of charge and offering a strong program of financial aid counseling combined with liberal payment options. Jordan, in fact, is one of the few colleges that allows students to charge their tuition fees while they wait to receive their loans and grants.

Believing firmly in the value of developing human potential and in the worth of education as a "practical tool for coping with and rising above life's many challenges," Jordan College is committed to producing "educated men and women who are able to identify their individual strengths and weaknesses, articulate their life goals," and who will be able to "step out with a measure of confidence and skill into a complex society as informed and productive citizens."

Jordan College operates a state-wide network of campuses. Photo by Studio Three Associates

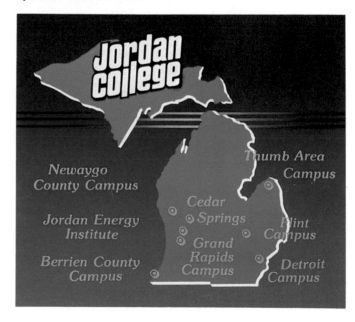

249

WEST MICHIGAN HEALTHCARE NETWORK (A BLUE CARE NETWORK HMO)

Spiraling health care costs have brought forth new alternatives to traditional health care delivery systems. One such alternative is the West Michigan HealthCare Network, a Health Maintenance Organization (HMO) of physicians, nurses, and other health care professionals whose mission is to provide comprehensive, high-quality medical services to enrolled members for a fixed and reasonable prepaid fee.

A nonprofit affiliate of Blue Cross and Blue Shield of Michigan (BCBSM) and a Blue Care Network HMO, West Michigan HealthCare Network began providing services in the Grand Rapids area on March 31, 1982. Preparations to open the new HMO were launched more than a year earlier, when executive director Hugh Hufnagel arrived in Grand Rapids to hold discussions with local physicians, employers, labor union representatives, hospital administrators, and health care planners in order to tailor a plan specifically designed to meet local needs.

By the end of 1982, 40 area employers had included the plan as a health benefit option to their workers, and 2,000 members were enrolled in the HMO. A year later Steelcase and General Motors were among 120 area employers offering the plan, and the number of members soared to 19,000. In 1984 came another milestone—the opening of the West Shore Area office in Muskegon.

Every year since the beginning has witnessed significant growth, and by the end of 1986 the West Michigan HealthCare Network, its staff grown from four to 130 employees, was serving more than 650 area employers and upwards of 87,500 members. More than 100,000 members are projected to be enrolled by the end of 1987.

Although most members are enrolled through employer participation in the plan, other options are available. Personal Plus offers services to individuals who do not have health care coverage through an employer, and Medicare Plus, a program for individuals ages 65 and over, has been offered since 1986 through a contract with the federal Medicare program.

Unlike traditional health insurance plans, which are essentially third-party payers for medical services rendered, HMOs function as direct health care providers and are responsible for the payment, quality, and appropriateness of care.

At West Michigan HealthCare Network, each member chooses his or her own personal physician (and one for every member of the family) from more than 200 participating internists, pediatricians, family practitioners, and general practitioners who are affiliated with the West Michigan HealthCare Network at more than 100 locations spread across a nine-county area. All of the member's health care needs—from routine physical examinations to hospital stays—are coordinated by the primary care physician, who serves as the member's health care manager, rendering care, ordering diagnostic tests, making specialist referrals, or arranging for hospital admission as each situation warrants. Over 400 consultants representing every medical specialty are available to see patients on a referral basis, and in-patient care is provided by all of the area's acute care hospitals.

One of the major differences between West Michigan HealthCare Network and the more traditional forms of health care coverage lies in the scope of the benefits provided. In return for their prepaid premium, HealthCare Network members are offered comprehensive benefits, which include coverage for office visits, emergency care, and all in-patient hospitalization services, including surgery, anesthesia, and intensive care. There are no deductibles or maximums, and no claim forms to fill out.

Cost control is the key to West Michigan HealthCare Network's ability to offer its members greater benefits at a competitive price. One element of keeping costs down is the emphasis on involving members in their own health care, because it is far less expensive to keep an individual healthy than to pay the costs of expensive medical care. Members have access to a wide range of preventive services and health education programs focusing on all aspects of wellness, from weight control and giving up cigarettes to stress management and the prevention of hypertension.

West Michigan HealthCare Network also works to control costs by eliminating unnecessary lab tests and carefully monitoring hospital stays to avoid overutilization. Moreover, because of the sheer volume of its membership, the West Michigan HealthCare Network can negotiate lower rates for laboratory and consultants' fees.

What all this means for the individual HMO member is comprehensive care at reasonable premium rates. Even in years when rates have risen, increases have averaged less than 5 percent, a rate far lower than the corresponding increase in the overall costs of care.

Lower costs in no way compromise the quality of care. Closely regulated by the state and federal governments, West Michigan HealthCare Network is required to have an aggressive quality assurance program that includes the continual monitoring of physicians' offices and medical records to see that services meet acceptable standards.

As an affiliate of Blue Cross and Blue Shield of Michigan, the West Michigan HealthCare Network is linked statewide with seven other BCBSM-affiliated HMOs and is also part of HMO-USA, a nationwide network of about 70 Blue Cross and Blue Shield HMOs. The advantages to members are obvious. Employees moving from one Michigan city to another may transfer their HMO memberships without losing coverage, and travelers may avail themselves of Blue Cross and Blue Shield HMO services nationwide.

Low premium costs combined with high-quality care and the Blue Cross and Blue Shield affiliation have made the West Michigan HealthCare Network increasingly attractive to growing numbers of health care consumers. Now the largest HMO in West Michigan and the one offering the widest array of benefits, the West Michigan Health-Care Network is committed to maintaining its leadership role in the area's health care marketplace.

West Michigan HealthCare Network's mission is to provide members with comprehensive, high-quality services.

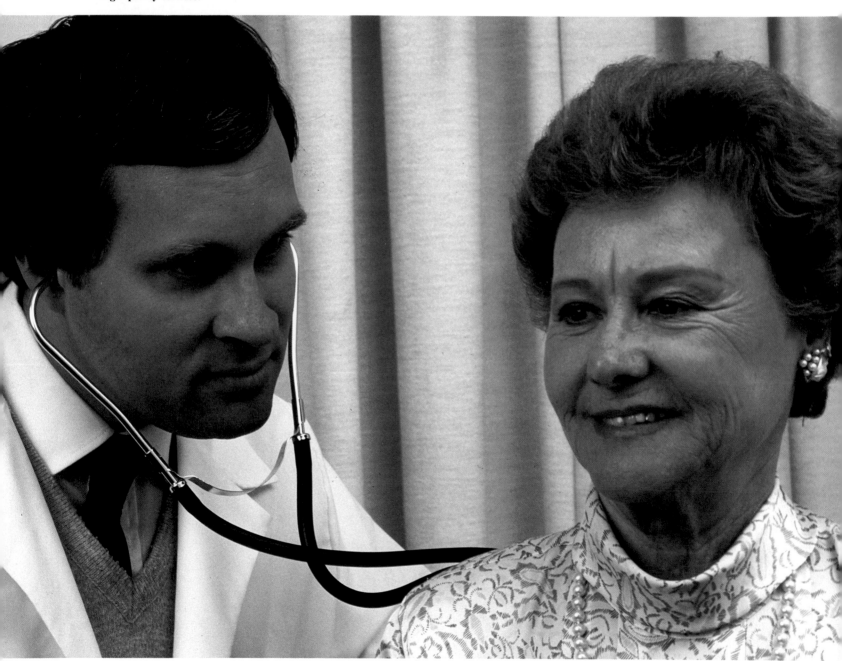

BISSELL INCORPORATED

BISSELL has been a household name since Melville R. Bissell brightened the lives and eased the burdens of housewives with the design of a carpet sweeper that really worked.

The year was 1876. Bissell, who with his wife, Anna, ran a crockery store in Grand Rapids, was looking for an efficient and easy way to sweep up the sawdust that spilled from the crockery packing cases. Bissell invented and patented an improved design of a contraption soon to become famous as the Bissell Carpet Sweeper. In less than 10 years the inventor and his wife had a product so successful they were selling not just throughout the United States, but in Europe as well.

BISSELL still makes manual carpet sweepers—and electric vacuum cleaners, steam cleaners, rug shampoo, and other related products—and still manufactures in Grand Rapids. But since the mid-1960s the corporation has been acquiring other manufacturers, and is now a family of companies providing home-care, health-care, and graphics products to American and European consumers. BISSELL companies operate 18 facilities in six states and five countries, with sales offices throughout the world. The firm's Grand Rapids plant and corporate headquarters is one of the most modern and efficient housewares-manufacturing facilities in the nation, and the BISSELL commitment to research and development and quality products is a constant throughout all of its divisions.

The manufacturer considers diversity one of its strengths, but president John Bissell, grandson of Melville and Anna, points out that the company and its subsidiaries stick to their own highly specialized niche in the marketplace.

Anna Bissell, who assumed leadership of the firm after the death of her husband in 1889, set the standard for creative sales, marketing, and management that a fourth generation of Bissells carries on to this day. As a female head of a corporation, she was light-years ahead of her time, and as a manager, she had a reputation for being firm but fair. As a wife and mother, Anna had a woman's sensitivity to the needs and concerns and hardships of raising a family, and her maternalistic management style fostered loyalty and dedication among BISSELL workers. BISSELL was perhaps the country's first corporation to have an employee benefits plan and an employee pension plan.

Although a much larger company than in Anna Bissell's day, the firm adheres to the principles of success established by the founders. BISSELL Incorporated describes its mission as the responsibility to make life easier for people. For more than a century the company has produced quality and innovative products to fulfill that mission. Its challenge for the future is to continue to make life

Anna Bissell

Melville R. Bissell

The current Bissell family executives are (foreground) John M. Bissell, grandson of the founders, and (in the background) Matthew R. Bissell, Mark J. Bissell, and Peter M. Sears, great-grandsons.

easier for people at home and at work. Says John Bissell, "We are an old company with a young outlook."

WARNER, NORCROSS AND JUDD

Warner, Norcross and Judd is committed to excellence. With more than 90 member attorneys, all of them graduates of the nation's major law schools, the firm provides diversified legal services to a statewide and regional roster of clients.

Established in 1931 by David A. Warner, George S. Norcross, and Siegel W. Judd, the firm drew the bulk of its clients during those dismal Depression years from the members of Grand Rapids' business and financial community. Not surprisingly, the founding partners spent a significant portion of their time handling bankruptcy proceedings, and they were pioneers in the newly created field of federal securities law. In the 56 years since its founding, Warner, Norcross and Judd has expanded its considerable expertise into a broad civil practice that includes virtually every area of the law—from real estate, labor, environmental, and tax law to the relatively new and rapidly expanding field of health law.

True to its business law origins, the firm still devotes more than one-third of its practice to general business and corporate law. Major area businesses have long turned to Warner, Norcross and Judd for legal advice and representation, and the firm numbers among its many clients such prestigious organizations as Steelcase, Inc., Stow-Davis, Haworth, and Wolverine World Wide. In addition to representing corporate clients, the firm provides cost-effective legal services to thousands of individuals and small businesses.

Litigation accounts for another one-third of the firm's practice. Member attorneys appear regularly before state and federal courts at the trial and appellate level to argue cases ranging from antitrust and labor actions to product liability and civil rights suits.

Banking has been an interest from the beginning. The firm currently represents a number of area banks, including

Old Kent, and serves as general counsel to the Michigan Bankers Association. Recent changes in state and federal banking regulations will mean additional growth in this important area of practice.

A half-century after its founding Warner, Norcross and Judd continues its commitment to the service of the community. The firm contributes money and time to the Grand Rapids Bar Association's pro bono legal services program for those who could not otherwise afford legal advice. In addition, members of the firm donate their own time and energies to a variety of community service organizations and endeavors. Among the Warner, Norcross and Judd attorneys who have entered public life are former Kent County prosecutor and Fifth District Congressman Harold Sawyer, who is once again practicing with the firm, and U.S. Congressman Guy Vanderjagt.

BLUE CROSS AND BLUE SHIELD OF MICHIGAN

In 1891 an enterprising insurance agent from Grand Rapids, Marinus Landman, suggested to Butterworth Hospital officials that they launch a group hospitalization plan that, for an annual five-dollar subscription fee, would admit "male clerks, factory and railroad employees, etc." to a hospital ward at any time during the year. "Chronic, contagious, and insanity cases" were to be excluded from coverage as were cases of "disease or injury arising from the use of intoxicating drink or drugs." Landman, unfortunately, was ahead of his time, and no action was taken on his visionary plan.

It wasn't until 47 years later, on October 3, 1938, that Butterworth, Blodgett, and St. Mary's hospitals joined with other community hospitals in the state to incorporate the Michigan Society for Group Hospitalization, which was subsequently renamed the Michigan Hospital Service and then later became Michigan Blue Cross.

In 1939 the three Grand Rapids hospitals were among the first in Michigan to adopt the society's group hospitalization plan, a plan that was very similar, in fact, to the one proposed nearly a half-century earlier by Landman. That same year doctors, under the auspices of the Michigan State Medical Society, incorporated the Michigan Medical Service, which later became Michigan Blue Shield. In 1975 the "Blues" consolidated into one corporation, Blue Cross and Blue Shield of Michigan (BCBSM).

From the beginning a strong connection existed between BCBSM and Grand Rapids, and that connection has grown even stronger in the half-century since. For five decades Grand Rapids physicians and hospital administrators have strengthened BCBSM's governing bodies, and they've seen the nonprofit corporation grow to become a leader in the field of health care coverage.

Back in 1939, 18 local professionals and businessmen, representing such companies as Bissell Carpet Sweeper, Old Kent Bank, American Seating, and Mueller Furniture, supported BCBSM by serving on the Grand Rapids sponsoring committee. That same year BCBSM opened one of its first district offices in the Grand Rapids National Bank Building. Today almost 60 men and women provide the citizens of West Michigan with BCBSM's array of products and services from its headquarters in a modern office building on 44th Street SW in Grandville.

Michigan's doctors and hospitals created BCBSM, and doctors, hospitals, and private citizens, including Ransom Olds, the founder of Oldsmobile, funded the new health plans; no state funding was involved. In the 1940s and 1950s the new health plans grew rapidly as employers and unions began offering group health benefits to employees and members.

Today almost half of Michigan's residents carry the blue-and-white BCBSM identification card. The company pays out more than three billion dollars annually for its members' health care. BCBSM also administers the federal government's Medicare program in Michigan.

Physicians once dominated the board of Blue Shield, and hospital representatives were in the majority at Blue Cross of Michigan. Each organization acted voluntarily—Blue Cross in 1964 and Blue Shield in 1971—to create a customer majority on its governing board.

The benefits received by today's Blue Cross and Blue Shield subscribers are substantially greater that those enjoyed by early customers. In addition to 365 days of hospital care, compared to the original 21 days, typical contracts now include dental services, vision and hearing benefits, outpatient psychiatric treatment, skilled nursing home care, and home-care programs.

BCBSM's market share peak was nearly 58 percent of the state's population in 1977. Since then alternatives to the traditional benefit packages have attracted many state residents. Health maintenance organizations have sprung up throughout the state and, in response, BCBSM organized a network of seven HMOs as subsidiaries. It's called the Blue Care Network.

West Michigan HealthCare Network in Grand Rapids is one of the subsidiaries. Located on Cascade West Parkway SE, this popular HMO now serves nearly 85,000 area residents. Employers currently offering West Michigan HealthCare Network to their employees include General Motors, Steelcase, Herman Miller, Aquinas College, Meijer, Inc., and the Grand Rapids Press. Many local branches of government, including the City of Grand Rapids and the County of Muskegon, also recognize the value of West Michigan HealthCare Network for their employees.

The Preferred Provider Organization is the newest health care alternative now being offered to cost-conscious employers. BCBSM established the first statewide PPO in 1985. Offered initially to the auto companies, it became available to other organizations in 1986.

In addition to its commitment to health care, BCBSM is committed to the community. BCBSM supports numerous civic events, such as the annual Health Expo in Grand Rapids that provides free health screening. BCBSM-sponsored fitness runs, cross-country ski meets, and the Walk Michigan program promote health and fitness among individuals of all ages.

Almost 85,000 Grand Rapids area residents belong to West Michigan HealthCare Network, an HMO affiliated with Blue Cross and Blue Shield of Michigan and part of a statewide network of seven HMOs called the Blue Care Network.

Students in Lakewood and Lake Odessa schools are benefiting from an important new program called Fitness for Youth. The program, cosponsored by BCBSM and the University of Michigan, includes exercise and nutrition education.

In October 1983 BCBSM and the Grand Rapids Area Chamber of Commerce cooperated to provide its members with high-quality BCBSM health care programs at reasonable group rates. In less than four months from the outset of the program, the chamber had enrolled more than 500 companies, approximately half of which were new chamber members. The plan combines Blue Traditional coverage, an

HMO option, and life/accident insurance from American Annuity, and is open to chamber members with as few as two employees.

Blue Cross and Blue Shield of Michigan is proud of its role in providing the people of Grand Rapids and West Michigan with top-quality health care coverage. Had Marinus Landman's group hospitalization plan been adopted back in 1891, Grand Rapids probably would have been home to the first such plan in the nation. It didn't happen that way, but others built the same excellent idea into Blue Cross and Blue Shield of Michigan, a company proud to have served Grand Rapids for almost a half-century.

KNAPE & VOGT MANUFACTURING COMPANY

Do-it-yourselfers have helped build Knape & Vogt Manufacturing Company into a home decor products industry leader. Today the nation's number one manufacturer of decorative wall-mounted shelving for the do-it-yourself market, Knape & Vogt distributes its vast array of shelving products and kitchen and closet storage aids to some 35,000 of the nation's 50,000 hardware and home improvement centers, serving twice as many retail outlets as its nearest competitor.

Always responsive to new opportunities, the firm has shifted gears several times since local machinist John Knape founded the business in 1898 to manufacture his newly invented chainless bicycle. Undaunted when the advent of the chain-driven coaster brake consigned his chainless model to the scrap heap, Knape turned his skills to the manufacture of specialty machinery and tools and dies. Knape's brother-in-law, Englebert J. Vogt, joined him in the business in 1902, and the partnership incorporated as the Knape & Vogt Manufacturing Company in 1908.

At the time Grand Rapids was basking in its stellar reputation as the nation's Furniture City, and Knape & Vogt, over the next several decades, shifted its emphasis from machinery to the manufacture of specialty hardware for the furniture industry. World War II ushered in another period of change as Knape & Vogt, like so many other local companies, discontinued civilian product lines to devote all of its resources to the production of glider wings, shell casings, and other products urgently needed by the miltary.

Knape & Vogt production methods make use of the latest in automated equipment.

Knape & Vogt corporate offices and production facility at 2700 Oak Industrial Drive NE, Grand Rapids.

With the end of the war came an unprecedented housing boom and a rapidly growing number of do-it-yourselfers eager to beautify their homes with retail products installed at the cost of their own labor. Recognizing an enormous potential for future growth, Knape & Vogt decided to concentrate its efforts on this newly burgeoning segment of the consumer marketplace.

Today the firm is a leader in home decor products for the do-it-yourself market. An estimated 90 of the nation's 100 largest home products retailers, including Ace and True Value, stock Knape & Vogt standards, shelves, and brackets. No other shelving products competitor comes close in terms of production volume, total sales, and the number of retail outlets carrying its line.

Most of those retailers also stock Knape & Vogt's specialty hardware products. The company's line of kitchen, closet, and storage aids includes closet rods, clothing carriers, cabinet and bookcase hardware, sliding towel bars, hooks for pegboards, and other commonly used household hardware items—more than 1,400 products in all.

Knape & Vogt also supplies specialty hardware to the original equipment manufacturer (OEM) market, and metal drawer slides—for kitchen and bathroom cabinet manufacturers and for the office furniture industry—have become an increasingly important product line.

The company's hardware products are manufactured at three Knape & Vogt facilities—the main plant in Grand Rapids and factories in La Mirada, California, and Rexdale, Ontario, near Toronto. A fourth plant, in Benton Harbor, Michigan, processes particle board for shelving. Products are shipped from warehouses at each of the plant sites through a highly efficient distribution and order-entry system designed to provide unparalleled customer service.

Strengths in product development, marketing, and production have combined with a long-standing reputation for quality products and outstanding service at competitive prices to build a solid foundation for growth. And to provide for that growth, the company has embarked on an ambitious long-range plan that centers around the expansion of production capabilities and the development and acquisition of new products.

Testimony to the firm's continuing commitment to state-of-the-art production efficiencies is an ongoing modernization program that has recently focused on the extensive use of computer technology and automation. Recognizing the importance of capital expenditures, the company has made a policy and a practice of reinvesting an average of three million to four million dollars per year in the upgrading of plant and equipment. In 1986 Knape & Vogt alloted $6.2 million to capital outlay, an investment that will pay considerable dividends, say company officials, in terms of reducing total manufacturing costs by lowering material costs, speeding production time and shipping schedules, and increasing overall productivity.

Innovative new products have already become instrumental in meeting the challenges of the future. Introduced in 1986, the bracketless Shelf Anchor, a new concept for the consumer market, and the heavy-duty precision drawer slide, for use in the manufacture of high-quality office furniture, represent the first salvo in Knape & Vogt's long-range strategy designed to sharpen its competitive edge in the consumer and OEM markets for years to come.

In 1986, in order to achieve its long-term growth objectives, Knape & Vogt completed a recapitalization plan that will enable it to take prompt advantage of future acquisition and expansion opportunities. Publicly traded since 1961, the company, through the new plan, has created an additional class of common stock with greater voting rights per share, and has authorized a three-for-one stock split. Not only does the recapitalization plan provide the financial underpinnings for the firm's strategic plan, but it also improves the marketability of Knape & Vogt stock, promotes long-term ownership of that stock, and assures that control of the company will remain in the hands of the Knape family. Today, as they have from the beginning, Knape family members continue to maintain a substantial interest in the firm as shareholders, board members, and in active management positions.

A retail display of shelving and hardware.

Guided by a spirit of innovation since its founding in 1898, Knape & Vogt Manufacturing Company heads toward a future that will see new accomplishments and further growth. At the same time the firm will hold fast to its stated commitment to provide "a stable investment return to shareholders, a secure work environment and quality of life for employees, and the resources to conduct its affairs as a conscientious corporate citizen."

Employees assembling and packaging drawer slides.

HAVILAND ENTERPRISES, INC.

For a wide variety of chemicals and related services, corporations across America look to Haviland Enterprises, Inc., of Grand Rapids.

From its beginnings as a research and testing laboratory, Haviland Enterprises has grown into one of the largest independent chemical distributors in the Midwest, shipping more than 200 million pounds of chemicals per year. A multimillion-dollar corporation, Haviland Enterprises serves industrial, agricultural, and consumer chemical markets and is a leader in the design and engineering of wastewater treatment systems.

Haviland Enterprises is comprised of five companies. Haviland Products Company, distributes industrial chemicals. Haviland Agricultural, Inc., is a leading supplier of chemicals to the farm market. Haviland Engineering, Inc., sells waste treatment systems designed to eliminate pollution in accordance with environmental protection regulations. Haviland Specialties, Inc., offers laboratory services and markets aluminum finishing processes and chemicals, and Haviland Consumer Products, Inc., markets a full line of swimming pool chemicals and accessories.

Headquartered at 421 Ann Street in Grand Rapids in a 400,000 square-foot office and warehouse complex, Haviland maintains warehouses, tank farms and compounding facilities throughout Michigan. Strict quality standards are assured by a superbly equipped on-site laboratory. The latest in computer technology speeds order processing and a "Just in Time" delivery system, using the corporation's own fleet of trucks and tankers, speeds products to customers when and where they are needed.

Haviland, which is owned and operated by the Haviland family, was founded more than fifty years ago by J.B. Haviland. Haviland graduated from the University of Detroit with a degree in chemical engineering and began his business career as a chemist for Ford Motor Company and Chrysler Corporation. In 1929 he left Detroit and moved to Grand Rapids and established a research and testing lab-

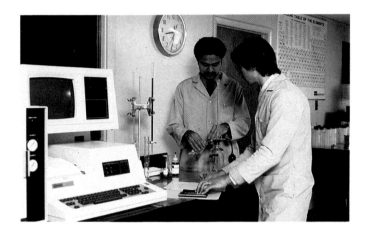

Haviland Engineering, Inc., is an affiliate, which specializes in the technology of wastewater treatment.

oratory for the Berkey and Gay Company, the world's largest furniture manufacturer at the time. By 1932 Haviland, chemist entrepreneur, left the furniture business and built his first laboratory with his wife's help and support. With Mrs. Haviland's active participation, the corporation has maintained strong profitability.

With great resourcefulness and foresight, Mr. Haviland was quick to respond to new opportunities in the marketplace. West Michigan's growing electroplating industry represented one such opportunity. Not only did Mr. Haviland pioneer new products and techniques for electroplaters, he also moved his company into the field of chemical distribution thus meeting the plating industry's growing needs for a reliable source of chemical supplies.

While Haviland Enterprises continues to be a major supplier to the plating industry, the company has expanded

Haviland's 400,000-square-foot office and warehouse complex is headquartered at 421 Ann Street, NW.

far beyond a single-industry market. Today, Haviland Enterprises serves almost every industry through Haviland Products Company, which supplies thousands of different chemicals and chemical compounds to companies spanning the entire spectrum of industrial production.

The largest of the corporation's affiliates, Haviland Products Company distributes chemicals manufactured by the world's leading producers. The company maintains a 3,000-item inventory of acids, alkalis, metals, solvents, plus liquid and dry chemicals to be formulated, compounded, repackaged, and shipped to meet specific customer needs. Industries that manufacture and process such diverse goods as automobiles, furniture, leather, foodstuffs, oil and petroleum products, and pharmaceuticals all turn to Haviland Products Company as their one-source supplier of high-quality chemicals and top-notch customer service.

A second Haviland Enterprises subsidiary, Haviland Agricultural, Inc., provides a full range of products and services to the farm community. Haviland Agricultural supplies the chemicals needed by fruit and vegetable growers to maximize crop productivity and ensure top quality, with sales representatives going directly into the field to analyze crop needs, diagnose problems, and prescribe the appropriate chemical solutions to assure a successful harvest.

Problem solving is also the focus of Haviland Engineering, Inc. A Haviland affiliate which specializes in the technology of wastewater treatment systems. Responding to environmental protection regulations, Haviland Engineering develops treatment processes, and technology to keep industrial processes ecologically safe. The company markets prefabricated modular treatment systems, upgrades existing systems, custom engineers new systems, and tailors each installation to meet specific applications and customer needs. Today Haviland Engineering has hundreds of successful wastewater-treatment systems in operation from

The company maintains 3,000 items in inventory, including acids, alkalis, metals, solvents, and specially formulated compounds.

coast to coast, each backed by the unwavering Haviland commitment to customer service and satisfaction.

Equally important to customers are Haviland's rigid quality standards and a tradition of technological leadership which centers on developing up-to-date products and processes essential in meeting the demands of modern industry. Haviland Specialities, Inc., for example, which markets aluminum finishing processes and chemicals, has developed a unique COLORMATCH system for anodizing aluminum. New to the United States, the highly advanced technology significantly expands the range of colors formerly available for anodized aluminum, a construction material widely favored by the architects and designers of fine buildings.

Haviland Consumer Products, Inc., another affiliate, is a key chemical repackager in the swimming pool chemical industry and continues to show steady growth as a pool chemical and spa equipment distributor. Supplies such as granular and tableted chlorine, algecides, PH chemicals and various specialty pool products are distributed locally as well as on a regional and national basis. In addition, the company has recently added a jetted baths and spa division that will offer a complete line of acrylic spa and acrylic jetted bath equipment and supplies. The pool and spa industry has been growing at a steady rate and Haviland Consumer Products, Inc., is proud to be a part of this dynamic leisure living industry.

Over the past half century, Haviland's diversity and expertise have enabled the corporation to attract an ever-increasing number of customers and to respond to an ever-expanding range of customer needs. As Michigan's economy continues to grow, those needs will grow, too, and Haviland will be there to meet them.

Strict quality standards are assured by a superbly equipped on-site laboratory.

RAPID ENGINEERING, INC.

When it comes to raising the roof, Rapid Engineering, Inc., has no peer. The roof is the 10-acre fabric roof of the world's largest domed stadium, the Silverdome, in Pontiac, Michigan, and it is an innovative Rapid Engineering air system that keeps the roof inflated.

The Grand Rapids firm is a leading manufacturer of high-efficiency heating and ventilating for a broad market—warehouses, aircraft hangars, sports facilities, factories, garages, and other large, open structures. When the Silverdome roof collapsed from an over accumulation of ice and snow in 1985, Rapid Engineering was called in to design a new air-handling system for the sports arena that eliminates the possibility of ice and snow buildup on the roof, maintains the temperature and air pressure of the building, and assures against a repeat of the 1985 debacle.

The company also designs and manufactures finishing systems for the automotive, appliance, and furniture industries. The equipment includes bake and drying ovens, multistage wash and phosphate systems, paint systems, thermal cleaning ovens, and parts washers. In fact, industrial ovens and parts washers were the first products manufactured by the organization that ultimately became Rapid Engineering.

In 1961 James Dirkes founded Rapid Sheet Metal, a company that contracted sheet-metal work for mechanical contractors. In the course of the sheet-metal work, the small operation was involved in fabricating economical, efficient gas-fired space heaters and ventilating systems, and paint-drying ovens and parts washers for industrial customers. By 1965 Dirkes decided there was sufficient market for such products to induce him to begin making that equipment on a full-time basis, so he founded a second firm, Vincent Manufacturing. In 1966 the sheet-metal company developed a pressurized space-heating system, an entirely new concept in industrial heating equipment. The system was so practical and so successful that Dirkes phased out the general sheet-metal work, and in 1969 merged Rapid Sheet Metal and Vincent Manufacturing under the name Rapid Engineering, Inc.

The new company was structured with two divisions—the heating and ventilating systems division and the finishing systems division. A service and field division has since been added to the corporate structure. Each division is autonomous, but all are housed in one manufacturing facility at 1100 Seven Mile NW in Comstock Park, Michigan.

Rapid Engineering got its first patent on the pressurized heating system in 1970, but it was the energy crisis of the mid-1970s that spurred sales and precipitated growth for the heating division. Industry, seeking energy-efficient, cost-cutting alternatives to the traditional and suddenly very expensive heating systems in current use, turned to the revolutionary pressurized systems introduced a decade earlier by Rapid Engineering.

To meet the new demand, Rapid Engineering devel-

Rapid Engineering designed the air-handling and heating systems at the Pontiac Silverdome, after snow and ice collapsed the roof.

To meet future business and employee growth, Rapid built a new 80,000-square-foot manufacturing facility.

oped the Rapid 3000, a direct-fired, natural gas heating and ventilation system that consumes a minimum of energy, responds instantly to changing temperatures, controls building cold air infiltration, and is both low cost and low maintenance.

The system pressurizes a building, eliminating heat loss around doors and windows, and recirculates air to keep it at a constant temperature. The heater's high-efficiency burner monitors itself and outputs only to the level of heat necessary to hold room temperature. The many customers who have installed the system since 1979 report energy savings of 20 to 50 percent.

Every Rapid 3000 system is engineered specifically for the building in which it is to be installed. Some of the biggest names in American industry are Rapid Engineering customers, among them, General Motors, Johnson & Johnson, Ford Motor Company, Steelcase, Inc., Bendix, and General Electric.

The company assures 100-percent efficiency for the life of the system, in contrast to the much lower efficiency of conventional systems using steam, forced air, electricity, gas, or infrared heating. Much of Rapid Engineering's business is in retrofitting conventional systems in existing facilities, although engineering systems for new facilities are on the increase as the firm gains in reputation.

The finishing systems are also engineered especially for each customer's particular production circumstances. Rapid Engineering designs and manufactures state-of-the-art paint-finishing systems, both batch and conveyorized for powder coating, high solids, and electrodeposition applications; high-temperature heat-recovery systems; thermal and catalytic incineration systems; metal-finishing systems; and specialty ovens and washers.

Rapid Engineering has experienced record sales and growth over the past five years, partly because the company is known in the industry for high-quality, high-performance products. It has just completed a $3-million expansion of its plant and increased its work force threefold over the past

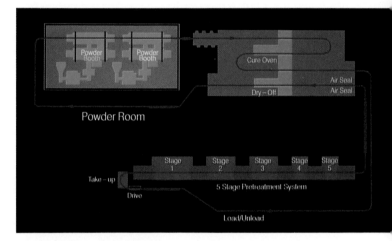

Rapid designs, manufactures, and installs complete paint finishing systems, including booths, multistage washers, and dry-off/cure ovens.

several years.

The firm employs a team approach to all its manufacturing; from design and engineering to fabrication, installation, sales, and service, each job gets the full attention of "Team Rapid." It is the people, say company officials, who have created an organization that is tops in its field in providing customers with unique and customized solutions to particular problems. The firm has 65 sales offices in the United States, and its products are manufactured in the United Kingdom by an English licensee.

As an innovator in the heating industry, Rapid Engineering was asked in 1982 to serve on the American National Standards Institute committee to write an industry standard for direct gas-fired door and space heaters.

Rapid Engineering, Inc., anticipates continued growth over the next 25 years, and its new facility represents its dedication to continuing research and development to provide customers with the most efficient, innovative, and cost-efficient equipment possible.

COMERICA BANK-GRAND RAPIDS

Innovation and responsiveness to customer needs are the hallmarks of Comerica Bank-Grand Rapids. A subsidiary of Comerica Incorporated, Comerica Bank-Grand Rapids brings to the metropolitan area the resources of a $10-billion bank holding company, whose constantly expanding network of banks and subsidiaries supplies financial products and services to customers and corporations worldwide.

Founded in 1849 with the establishment of its lead bank, Comerica Bank-Detroit, Comerica Incorporated serves corporate, consumer, and trust clients throughout Michigan with a branch network of 16 subsidiaries and 200 offices in the state's major cities. Comerica offices elsewhere serve other regions of the United States.

Comerica established its Grand Rapids subsidiary in 1977 through the purchase of Kentwood Bank, N.A. With its local presence secured, Comerica soon offered its full-service brand of banking through four offices—three in Kentwood and one in Grand Rapids. The main office and the Comerica Corporation Banking Center have been headquartered downtown on the 10th floor of the Campau Square Plaza Building since November 1985. In 1987 Comerica Bank-Grand Rapids significantly expanded its holdings through a merger with Metrobanc, a 125-year-old institution originally founded as Grand Rapids Mutual Home Federal Savings and Loan.

Comerica Corporate Banking Center in the Campau Square Plaza Building in downtown Grand Rapids.

Comerica's branch office in Grand Rapids, one of 16 subsidiaries and 200 offices throughout Michigan.

Enjoying a worldwide reputation for quality products, stability, experience, professional service, and innovation, Comerica is committed to providing each of its clients with specialized services for specialized needs. Corporate banking activities include corporate loans, cash management services, commercial finance, commercial real estate loans, corporate trust services, correspondent banking, equipment leasing and financing, auto dealer financing, international trade services, and transaction and investment accounts.

Products and services available to individual consumers include bankcards, discount brokerage, fixed- and adjustable-rate mortgages, fixed- and money-market-rate checking and savings accounts, individual retirement accounts, installment loans, revolving lines of credit, and private banking services.

The corporation also provides three principal types of trust services—investment management and personal trust services for individuals, settling estates and managing family assets for beneficiaries, and employee benefit trusts for corporations.

Comerica takes pride in its financial strength, leadership, and ingenuity in developing new financial products designed to meet ever-changing financial needs. Founded when the national economy was predominantly agrarian, Comerica has kept pace with the changes that have marked each subsequent stage of American economic development—the industrial age, the technological era, and the service-oriented system that promises to be the wave of the future.

For the past 138 years Comerica has met changing financial demands with progressive banking services. Although the primary functions of the banking industry are to provide secure investments and to extend credit to individuals and business entities, deposit and credit products are just the beginning of what Comerica regards as its responsibilities. In order to provide corporate customers with the ultimate in personalized service, Comerica assigns to each one a relationship manager to assess, analyze, and pinpoint financial needs. The Comerica relationship manager is well trained to recognize these needs and either personally or through specialized departments deliver state-of-the-art banking services. Not only do these services help clients accomplish credit and noncredit goals, but Comerica's relationship managers and departmental specialists play an important role in identifying and evaluating new financial opportunities and supplying the kind of information that will help customers prepare for a prosperous financial future.

Comerica's strategy for its own future is to build competitive superiority in four core business groups: consumer deposits gathering and service, primary commercial banking, personal trust/financial management, and consumer lending. Underlying Comerica's goals is a steadfast commitment to its shareholders, customers, employees, and the communities that it serves.

Quality is the key ingredient in carrying out that commitment. Comerica is dedicated to using state-of-the-art technology and intensive staff training to provide its customers with the best service possible. And because quality service depends on quality employees, Comerica stresses equal opportunity and high ethical standards, and maintains a work environment that motivates employees to increased productivity and greater job satisfaction by encouraging and rewarding hard work and personal initiative. Selectivity in products offered and markets served goes along with Comerica's commitment to careful risk management and the maintenance of strong asset quality, substantial liquidity, and an adequate capital base.

Comerica also strives to be a good corporate citizen by supporting and participating in projects designed to improve the quality of life and the economic climate in the communities where it does business. Comerica and its staff not only contribute substantially to the annual United Way campaign and other nonprofit organizations, but Comerica employees, as individuals, also make significant volunteer contributions by serving on local boards and committees and lending their time, talents, and expertise to a wide variety of cultural, educational, civic, and human service endeavors. Throughout its history Comerica Bank has applied its resources to providing the finest in customer service and to the refinement of traditional banking practices with new ideas, new products, and new solutions to financial needs. In the process, Comerica has established itself as more than just a bank; it is a financial partner whose relationship with customers and communities promotes mutual growth and prosperity.

STEKETEE'S

Steketee's downtown Grand Rapids store.

There has been a Steketee's store on Monroe Avenue in downtown Grand Rapids for more than a century and a quarter. The oldest name in Grand Rapids retailing, Steketee's has always been a family store, in every sense of the word. Five descendants of Paul Steketee, the founder, are active in the business today, and West Michigan families have always depended on Steketee's quality and value in clothing and furnishings for the home.

The original Steketee's was a dry goods store, the forerunner of modern department stores. Until the 1970s Steketee's continued that tradition, but, responding to changing consumer shopping habits, the store began a gradual phasing out of carpeting, occasional furniture, piece goods and sewing accessories, and finally its china, gifts, and housewares departments.

In the spring of 1987 Steketee's opened a new chapter in its long history with a gala celebration in its downtown store heralding the chain's new image as West Michigan's headquarters for family fashion. The company had just completed a $4.5-million renovation of its flagship store at 86 Monroe Center, the final step in shifting emphasis from a department store operation to featuring clothing and accessories. The other stores in the chain—Eastbrook Mall, Muskegon, Holland, Grand Haven, and Kalamazoo—had just completed similar renovations.

The top names in American fashion are represented in every Steketee's department—Liz Claiborne, Ellen Tracy, Pendleton, Esprit, London Fog, Lord Jeff, Gant, 9-West, Naturalizer, Nina, and Joyce, to name a few.

Though there has been a change in merchandising emphasis to career clothes and accessories for professional men and women, as well as clothing for their children, the Steketee philosophy still prevails—service, quality, and value, in the same friendly atmosphere that has always been a Steketee's hallmark.

Steketee's commitment to the downtown area is manifested in the total renovation of its downtown store, but the company has always exhibited a sense of obligation and responsibility to each community in which it maintains stores. One of the community events Steketee's offers is the annual thanksgiving to the communities it serves, called Church and Charity Days. On those days shoppers designate their favorite charity when they make a purchase, and 15 percent of their purchase is donated to that charity. As many as 400 different West Michigan churches and charitable organizations receive contributions from that event annually.

The recent period of renovation is just the start of an exciting new era of growth and merchandising leadership for Steketee's—Grand Rapids' oldest, yet newest, clothing store.

The men's department in Steketee's Eastbrook Mall store.

H.B. SHAINE & CO. INC.

Executives at H.B. Shaine & Co., Inc., like to say the firm provides one-stop shopping for the investor—a full range of investment opportunities and services precisely tailored to the needs and resources of each investor—individual, corporate, institutional, as well as municipal.

Just a few years ago an investment firm offered a client only stocks, bonds, and mutual funds. But computerization, changes in federal regulations, and investor needs have so changed the industry over the past decade that investment firms have added to their traditional brokerage functions a multitude of services, including retirement plans, financial plans, life insurance services, limited partnerships, and money management.

H.B. Shaine & Co. has changed with the industry. The firm is virtually a department store of financial services. "In the past four years," says Arthur Silverstein, executive vice-president, "we have developed products and financial services that hadn't even been thought of a dozen years ago."

Investors are so much more sophisticated and better informed than they have been in the past, says H.B. Shaine's chief operating officer, Ronald A. Lemmon, and they are looking for sophisticated, professional money management. "We are moving out of the era of simple financial planning into what we call asset management—a total management plan for the clients and their financial resources. That is what clients want today, and that is what H.B. Shaine offers."

Two wholly owned subsidiaries, Monitor Development, a real estate development and venture capital formation entity, and Monitor Capital Management, a registered investment adviser entity, were established by H.B. Shaine to round out the firm's abilities to develop its role as an asset

manager for clients.

H.B. Shaine & Co., Inc., was founded in 1957 by Hyman B. Shaine and Edward M. Silverstein. At the time Shaine was the only West Michigan broker to hold a seat on the New York Stock Exchange, and today the firm is still the only Michigan-based company outside of Detroit that is a member of the New York Stock Exchange.

H.B. Shaine has grown dramatically in recent years, but always with the needs of West Michigan in mind. The firm's effectiveness and uniqueness rests in its strong sense of community. All H.B. Shaine personnel are West Michigan people, attuned to the particular strengths, weaknesses, and preferences of the region and its investing public. The firm's offices are at 111 Pearl Street NW, in the Waters Building.

"H.B. Shaine has also grown with the investment market, from the infancy of investing to a totally computerized industry," says Silverstein. "And we are successful because we have developed our business to meet the needs of West Michigan. We have brought Wall Street to Grand Rapids."

NBD UNION BANK

Respected as one of the leading providers of financial services in the Grand Rapids area for nearly 70 years, NBD Union Bank is taking major steps to increase its presence throughout western Michigan and to ensure that it remains a banking force in the years ahead.

In a continuing effort to expand the bank's competitive position, Union Bancorp, Inc., parent of Union Bank and Trust Company, merged with NBD Bancorp, Inc., on July 1, 1986. This affiliation with the largest bank holding company in Michigan and one of the largest in the United States brings to the Grand Rapids market the resources of an industry leader that is consistently cited as one of the best managed financial institutions in the Midwest.

The new affiliation with NBD Bancorp not only enhances NBD Union Bank's already strong full-service capabilities in areas such as electronic banking; trust, investment, and brokerage services; real estate finance; international services; and consumer finance, but it also adds particular strength to NBD Union Bank's corporate banking presence in West Michigan. Immediately following the merger NBD Bancorp's successful corporate loan production office in Grand Rapids was integrated into NBD Union Bank. New facilities in NBD Union Bank's downtown

NBD Union Bank's Kent County International Airport banking office and electronic banking service makes banking in the airport convenient and easy.

Grand Rapids headquarters will house a larger Corporate Banking Department in order to provide greater efficiency and increased service to its customer base.

Increased customer convenience was also achieved when NBD Union Bank merged with the Grand Rapids-area-based NBD Grand Valley Bank. As a result, the bank has significantly expanded its current network of banking offices in Greater Grand Rapids.

NBD Union Bank, traditionally a market leader in consumer financial services, now offers its customers one of the most complete lines of products available in the marketplace; checking, money market savings, investment accounts, home equity and revolving credit lines, and installment loans all have been tailored to provide customers with the options necessary to meet their needs, both today and tomorrow.

The merger with NBD Bancorp has also resulted in new challenges for NBD Union Bank as an NBD Midwest re-

Since its construction in 1967, the Union Bank Building has served as the headquarters for NBD Union Bank, one of the leading financial institutions in West Michigan.

gional center. NBD Union Bank has assumed overall management responsibility for all NBD subsidiaries in western Michigan from Benton Harbor to Petoskey.

From its beginning as a Morris Plan Bank founded by John E. Frey in 1918, NBD Union Bank has continued to prosper through innovative banking practices and a tradition of service to its customers. NBD Union Bank has made many unique contributions to the financial services industry in West Michigan such as establishing the first collateralized mobile home credit plan in the country in the 1940s, developing West Michigan's first computerized bank data-processing system back in 1957, and was one of the first banks in the U.S. to offer a personal revolving credit line.

In the early 1960s, NBD Union Bank responded quickly when the Grand Rapids central business district was starting to show its age. The bank became involved in the city's renaissance as bank chairman, Edward J. Frey and other civic leaders raised funds for a planning study later named the Grand Rapids Urban Redevelopment Program. The Union Bank building, followed closely by its neighbor, the Frey Building, named for the bank's founder, became one of the first new urban-renewal structures to be constructed on Vandenberg Plaza.

Despite increased pressure to keep pace with the needs of its customers and meet the challenges of competing with nonbank financial service operations in a deregulated environment, NBD Union Bank is still dedicated and committed to addressing the needs of the community it serves. As

NBD Union Bank's Ottawa Square office provides an attractive environment for customers in downtown Grand Rapids.

one of the larger employers in Kent County, NBD Union Bank throughout its history has proudly supported numerous projects and organizations through corporate gifts and extensive volunteer efforts.

With a solid past behind it and a dynamic future ahead, NBD Union Bank is prepared to meet the exciting challenges ahead.

Alexander Calder's *La Grande Vitesse* and the Union Bank Building are both Vandenberg Plaza landmarks.

WOLVERINE WORLD WIDE

The Hush Puppies basset hound symbolizes one of the manufacturing, advertising, and marketing marvels of the footwear industry. Since 1958 this droopy-eyed dog has garnered 97-percent consumer brand-name recognition in the United States, making Hush Puppies shoes America's best-known footwear brand. Now marketed in 55 foreign countries, it could well be on its way to being one of the best-known shoe brands in the world.

Hush Puppies shoes, manufactured by Wolverine World Wide, Inc., first appeared on the market in 1958 and took America by storm in the 1960s, becoming the country's favorite leisure-time footwear. Made of "breathable" brushed pigskin and infinitely comfortable, Hush Puppies were good-looking enough to go from the clubhouse to city streets with aplomb. Today the Hush Puppies line features contemporary career styles in a variety of materials for men and women.

Still a major product line for Wolverine World Wide, Hush Puppies share popularity with other such notable brand names as Brooks athletic shoes, Town and Country women's shoes, Bates Floaters, Sioux-Mox, and the firm's original product—rugged, heavy-duty boots and shoes marketed under the Wolverine brand name.

Wolverine World Wide, a global complex of companies manufacturing and marketing shoes, apparel, and tanned leather, dates back to 1883, when G.A. Krause and an uncle founded a leather and shoe wholesaling company in Grand Rapids. Twenty years later Krause built his own shoe factory in Rockford, 30 miles north of Grand Rapids, on the Rogue River. Two sons, Otto and Victor, joined the business, and the family opened a tannery in 1909. The company's product, Wolverine boots and shoes, earned a reputation for comfort and long wear, and became one of rural and small-town America's most popular brands.

In 1921 the firm adopted the Wolverine name and became the Wolverine Shoe and Tanning Corporation. When the business was founded, it used cowhide for its products. Later horsehide became the principal material used in its footwear. To meet new market trends in the 1940s, Wolverine developed a pigskinning process that revolutionized its entire production methods and eventually launched the phenomenally successful Hush Puppies. The company today is the nation's largest tanner of pigskin leather, and it manufactures and markets a variety of pigskin leather products.

It was with Hush Puppies that Wolverine became an international company, opening retail stores overseas and licensing foreign manufacturers to produce Hush Puppies. In 1965 the firm went public, and the following year

The loveable basset hound has endeared itself and Hush Puppies shoes to consumers nationwide.

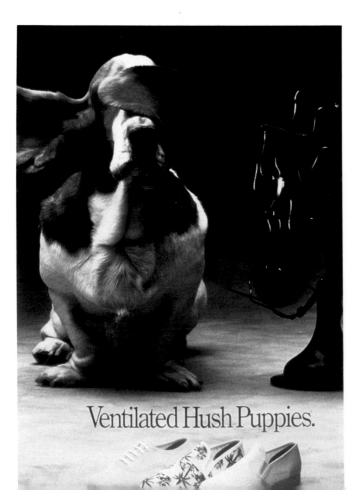

Ventilated Hush Puppies.

Comfortable Hush Puppies.

changed its name to Wolverine World Wide.

The company continued to diversify its product line and acquire new divisions to meet the changing tastes and needs of consumers, but in the late 1970s the world market began to change. Competition from foreign imports drastically cut sales for domestic shoe manufacturers.

Wolverine World Wide has met the challenge by restructuring the corporation. With nearly 80 percent of the footwear sold in the United States coming from abroad, Wolverine was forced to cut back its domestic production and is now organized to resource footwear and footwear components to all its divisions through strong overseas connections. It has embarked upon an aggressive licensing program with foreign manufacturers to produce and sell several of its lines overseas, including Brooks, Hush Puppies, and Wolverine. The tanning division supplies leather to both the domestic and foreign markets, and the firm also has a joint agreement with a Taiwan tannery to supply leather to footwear and leather goods manufacturers in the Orient. The result is that Wolverine product names have a wider popularity throughout the world than ever before.

The company also has modernized its domestic production methods, installing state-of-the-art equipment and implementing more efficient production methods. Always in the forefront in developing or responding to new trends in the footwear industry, Wolverine is currently adapting the latest advances in sports and human medicine to the manufacture of biomechanically correct athletic shoes.

The leader in this high-tech arena is Wolverine's Brooks division. Working with Michigan State University's biomechanical laboratories, which includes the department of human medicine and the athletic department, Brooks is developing shoes for running, basketball, aerobics, tennis, and related sports.

Through the use of computer technology, orthopedists and other doctors are learning the specifics of foot and body movement in various sports and other activities. Brooks technicians use that information to develop footwear designed to accommodate the effects of particular activities on the body and foot.

Shoes are designed from the inside out, explains a company spokesman. "We start with a concept and build the shoe around that concept rather than starting with a preconceived idea of what a shoe should be."

The sports shoe technology is also revolutionizing the conventional footwear industry. Carrying over the precepts of sports shoe design, the firm is engineering shoes for everyday wear that are comfortable, biomechanically correct, and don't look like sports shoes. According to company officials, this new technology gives Wolverine World Wide the capacity to create a superior product that will more than hold its own in the highly competitive footwear marketplace.

Wolverine World Wide, Inc., has overcome many challenges in its more than 100 years of manufacturing. The dedication to producing innovative, quality products and the ability to adapt and grow with the times that characterized the early years of the company are still Wolverine strengths. The company continues to grow and to be an industry leader.

Corporate Hush Puppies.

Sophisticated Hush Puppies.

PRANGLEY, MARKS & CO.

Prangley, Marks & Co., a locally owned certified public accounting firm, is committed to serving its clients' accounting, auditing, and tax compliance needs and to offering a full range of services that go far beyond those traditional needs.

By maintaining a close working relationship with its clients, PMC is able to understand the unique situations faced by each one and to provide pertinent and useful advice in today's ever-changing marketplace.

PMC serves a broad spectrum of clients—from individuals in locations from coast to coast, to sole proprietors throughout West Michigan, to multimillion-dollar/multistate corporations headquartered in the greater Grand Rapids metropolitan area. Construction, manufacturing, distribution, and retail companies, along with a multitude of support and personal service organizations, all turn to Prangley, Marks for accounting and financial services.

The diversity of its complex client base mirrors the array of talents and of technical and practical skills possessed by the firm's professional staff.

The principles upon which PMC operates are designed to provide the highest quality service in a timely manner. The firm's objective is to help clients maximize their profit potential and to preserve and nurture further growth.

The majority of PMC's business clients are closely held entrepreneurial operations. As entrepreneurs themselves, the PMC partners have experienced first hand many of the problems common to those who own their own businesses,

and as a result, are particularly sensitive to the needs and concerns of their clients.

PMC and its predecessors have been serving area clientele for more than 40 years. The firm has consistently adopted, monitored, and maintained the highest standards of performance for itself. Admittance to the firm is predicated on demonstrated technical abilities and performance based on established criteria that demand high levels of achievement. Firm partnerships are earned on the basis of client service, professional achievements, and high ethical standards. PMC was one of the first locally based firms to join the Private Companies Practice Section of the American Institute of Certified Public Accountants. In order to maintain membership, the firm has had to undergo outside, independent peer review of its accounting and auditing practice procedures. These reviews have demonstrated that PMC meets the highest standards of the profession.

As business operations have become more complex over the past 40 years, accounting practices and precepts have changed to keep pace with the needs of the business community. And when it comes to the services it offers to its clients, PMC has always strived to be on the leading edge. In the late 1960s, for example, PMC was one of the first CPA firms in the country to offer computerized accounting services to its clients. Today PMC is proud of the fact that it has one of the highest computer-to-personnel ratios in the industry.

Strategic management and tax and financial planning

Prangley, Marks & Co. partners (from left) Leslie N. Prangley III, Harold A. Marks, Thomas P. Jeakle, Kraig L. Klynstra, and John E. Mack.

for businesses and individuals have been an integral part of the PMC practice philosophy for many years. The firm's clients require, request, and receive assistance year round, not just at tax time. All year long the firm finds itself involved in providing expert guidance in such areas as information systems management, long-range financial planning, financial and tax strategies, organizational development, management succession, business expansion, acquisitions, mergers, and dispositions.

PMC's services extend to family financial planning as well. The firm works closely with its personal service clients to set individual goals, analyze resources, and develop tax and estate-planning objectives to assure the family's future financial well-being.

PMC's service capabilities are enhanced by its membership in CPA Associates, an organization of locally owned, independent, certified public accounting firms. Currently numbering 35 domestic and seven international members, CPAA not only avails associates of the resources and expertise of a very large international accounting firm, but also provides the highest level of professional development programs available. CPAA was the first major accounting organization to install a systemwide electronic mail network. Called LEANET (Leading Edge Accoun-

tancy Network), the system gives any member computer access to each or all of the members in the associated firms. PMC was a member of the initial LEANET task force, which tested the system, and has since continued in a leadership position for the program.

Prangley, Marks believes that the ability of its clients and professional staff to stay abreast of the latest trends and practices in the financial, tax, and accounting arenas is imperative in maintaining effectiveness. PMC staff members are constantly updating their skills and knowledge through professional associations, seminars, and training programs. The firm also offers clients its own seminars and training programs on subjects ranging from accounting and computers to financial planning, estate planning, and taxes. Regular and special-edition newsletters, brochures, and booklets on subjects of importance are also provided to clients and other interested parties.

The firm's philosophy also embraces a commitment to the communities in which it practices. Because the vitality of the West Michigan area and the stability of its economy have enabled the firm and its clients to grow, PMC views involvement in community affairs as a responsibility, an acknowledgement of the community's confidence in the firm. Over the years PMC members have participated in numerous community activities, often in leadership roles.

The necessary ingredient in any successful endeavor is the people involved. For Prangley, Marks & Co., the individual efforts of members of the community, clients, and the partners, managers, staff accountants, and administrative staff have combined to make the firm a success.

Prangley, Marks & Co. serves a broad spectrum of clients.

STEELCASE INC.

By the end of the 1880s Grand Rapids was well established as a center for the manufacture of fine wood furniture. Since 1914 it has also excelled in the production of office furniture. In that year the collective volume of eight Grand Rapids office furniture manufacturers exceeded $4 million. The Metal Office Furniture Company, founded just two years earlier and the forerunner of Steelcase Inc., was one of the eight.

Still owned by descendants of the founding families, Steelcase is today one of the leading privately held companies in the United States. The company has experienced steady growth since its founding, and in the past decade that growth has accelerated dramatically. In that time the corporation has more than doubled its manufacturing space and employees, moved into a new corporate headquarters building, and expanded its overseas manufacturing and marketing activities to include subsidiaries and joint ventures in both hemispheres.

With more than 8,000 employees in greater Grand Rapids, Steelcase is currently the city's second-largest employer. By 1992 the company plans to complete a 10-year, $350- $500-million expansion program that will add five new manufacturing facilities to the southeast side of suburban Grand Rapids and offer increased employment opportunities.

At the heart of the corporation's projected growth into the year 2000 is a $76-million Corporate Development Center under construction in nearby Gaines Township, expected to be completed in 1988. This seven-story, pyramid-shaped building, the most comprehensive research and development facility in the office furniture industry, will house 10 different research laboratories and provide Steelcase with on-site photometrics, acoustics, and ergonomics research capabilities. In addition, the building will serve to integrate the many disciplines and skills that must work together to successfully bring a product to market.

The Steelcase success story can be partially attributed

The production of quality office furniture systems at Steelcase Inc. includes the precise engineering delivered by a 500-ton transfer press that forms parts for assembly into furniture system components.

to socioeconomic factors. In the 1950s office workers made up 28 percent of the American work force. By 1990 that figure is expected to be 60 percent. But in 1912 the company that grew to be the largest office furniture manufacturer in the world began as a producer of steel office safes.

Peter Wege, a skilled sheet metal worker and plant manager for an office safe manufacturer, realized that sheet steel bent at right angles was as strong as iron and, properly insulated against fire, was suitable for the manufacture of safes. Less bulky and heavy than traditional iron safes, the steel safes were also less costly.

Wege, Walter Idema, son of a local banker, and several other investors founded the Metal Office Furniture Company to produce steel safes and filing cases. For two years

Since its founding in 1912, people have played an important role in the success of Steelcase. In this circa 1920 photo, a group of employees gathers before the company's Century Street ad-ministration building. Today the firm employs more than 8,000 local residents, making it Grand Rapids' second-largest employer.

the products were manufactured for and marketed by the Macey Company of Grand Rapids, but by 1914 the Metal Office Furniture Company was selling steel safes, lockers, filing cabinets, and wastebaskets under its own name.

The year 1914 also brought David Hunting to the firm as marketing manager. Hunting is credited with developing the strong dealership network that is today a Steelcase hallmark and a key component in the company's success.

The firm was launched into the manufacture of desks in 1915 by its first big order—200 desks for the Boston Customs House. Metal furniture was just becoming popular for office use, replacing flammable wood furniture which added fuel to the fires that often razed wooden factories and office buildings.

In 1917 the U.S. government bought a million dollars' worth of Metal Office Furniture Company furniture for government and military offices. The end of World War I brought a boom in office building construction and business, and a corresponding demand for furniture.

The Steelcase trademark was introduced in 1920 and business flourished in the following years as the firm added to its product line, developed new methods of manufacturing, and expanded its facilities.

A historic collaboration occurred when noted architect Frank Lloyd Wright was commissioned in 1936 to design the S.C. Johnson and Son, Inc. (Johnson Wax), Administration Building in Racine, Wisconsin. Wright also designed the furniture for the building and the following year se-

Sensor seating was introduced to the world market by Steelcase in 1986. Described by its designer as "a living chair," Sensor automatically adjusts to all body movements offering more postural comfort, dynamics, and adjustability than any other office chair.

Stow & Davis, manufacturer of fine wood furniture for over 100 years, continues the tradition of excellence today in partnership with Steelcase. The Stow & Davis product line reflects fine design, quality materials, and the most advanced manufacturing technology.

lected the Metal Office Furniture Company to engineer and assemble his designs for a variety of desks, tables, and chairs.

The Wright-designed furniture was constructed of cast aluminum and magnesite and, in appearance, echoed the streamlined curves and softer lines of the building. It was a radical departure from traditional office furniture and anticipated by two decades the modular systems and open office designs that are the foundation of the modern office furniture industry. Today, a half-century later, the Wright furniture is still in use in the Johnson Wax building.

By the end of the 1930s the Metal Office Furniture Company had acquired two other firms, Terrell Company of Grand Rapids, manufacturers of metal shelving, and Doehler Manufacturing Company of New York State, which made metal household furniture.

World War II brought new contracts from the U.S. government—including tables and chairs for the Navy. At the formal signing of Japan's surrender in 1945, aboard the U.S.S. *Missouri*, dignitaries sat at a Metal Office Furniture Company mess table as they affixed their signatures to the surrender documents.

The 1950s saw a number of significant milestones in the firm's history. The Metal Office Furniture Company had several factory locations on South Division Avenue, but in 1953 it purchased a 38-acre tract of land on 36th Street near Eastern Avenue. It was the modest beginning of the factory site that now totals 300 acres. In 1954 shareholders voted to adopt the Steelcase trademark as the corporate name, and the Metal Office Furniture Company became Steelcase Inc. With the building of a new plant near Toronto that same year, Steelcase became an international

273

corporation. In 1958 the company opened a California manufacturing facility, the first outside the local area.

Steelcase continued to adopt, adapt, experiment, innovate—and to grow.

By the end of the 1950s, the concept of the total office environment had begun to evolve. No longer were desks and chairs manufactured to a preconceived standard, but the entire work process was analyzed and furniture was designed to support specific work situations. Work productivity patterns were studied and the influence of light and color in the workplace came under scrutiny.

The single most significant factor influencing the office environment, and indeed the entire business world, has been the advent of office electronics. As entire corporations "computerized," furniture and work stations were developed to accommodate the revolution. "Furniture systems" is today the industry designation for the versatile, multipurpose, efficient furniture that meets the surface, storage, and privacy needs of the modern work place.

In keeping with the corporation's goal to produce the highest-quality, most efficient and comfortable office furniture, the Steelcase research and design departments are

Then and now. Steelcase trucks have long been a familiar sight in Grand Rapids. Today the company's modern fleet travels more than six million miles annually to make on-time deliveries throughout the United States and Canada.

dedicated to finding new solutions to office problems. Steelcase leads the industry in offering furniture for the total office environment—from completely integrated furniture systems to seating, lighting, and paper-handling components to elegant furniture for executive offices and reception areas.

The 1985 purchase of Stow & Davis, a local manufacturer of fine wood systems and office furniture, has significantly extended the Steelcase product offering. A major expansion of the Stow & Davis facility in suburban Grand Rapids, slated for completion in 1988, will increase production space from 100,000 to 800,000 square feet and offer additional employment.

In 1986 Steelcase introduced the Sensor line of seating. Designed by West German Wolfgang Muller-Deisig and developed at the Steelcase Grand Rapids plant, Sensor satisfies the office worker's need for a chair that provides support and comfort when performing a variety of office tasks for long periods of time.

Sensor is, says Muller-Deisig, ". . . an evolution from ergonomic chairs. It is a high-performance chair . . . a friendly chair. When you sit in it, it becomes one with you." As much as any other Steelcase product, Sensor symbolizes the Steelcase commitment to quality and fine design.

In its 75 years, Steelcase has progressed from a manufacturer of metal office furniture to become "Steelcase—The Office Environment Company." In this role, the firm serves as a resource for information about the ever-changing office environment and develops and markets products, programs, and services designed to meet the needs of the office worker.

The second generation of the founding families is active in the company today. They and other senior management members are building a solid foundation, implementing strategies for dealing with the continuing changes a new century will bring. The new Corporate Development Center is very much a part of their company's strategy, and is intended to give Steelcase the ability to respond quickly to customer needs and market trends.

Scheduled to open in 1988, the Steelcase Corporate Development Center will integrate the various disciplines that contribute to the development and commercialization of Steelcase products, programs, and services.

In 1937 Steelcase produced the furniture designed by Frank Lloyd Wright for the S.C. Johnson & Son Administration Building in Racine, Wisconsin. The furniture remains in active use today, a half-century later.

Vivid giant-size wall murals in the Steelcase panel plant create a visually stimulating environment for the employees. In a functional context, this enormous drill chuck and bit signifies the entrance to the plant's tool room.

But there are some basic management concepts that will never change. Steelcase's loyal work force is a reflection of the company's tradition of innovative management and fair wages and benefits.

Another tradition is one of strong corporate support of community events, activities, and institutions in areas where the company maintains manufacturing facilities. The Steelcase Foundation, founded in 1961, devotes its resources to projects targeted to improve the health, education, cultural, recreational, and environmental opportunities for community residents.

An example of the company's activities as a corporate citizen is its recent renewal of the Frank Lloyd Wright connection. Steelcase has been an active participant in the restoration of the Frank Lloyd Wright Home and Studio in suburban Chicago, and recently purchased a 1908 Wright house in Grand Rapids. The house is currently undergoing restoration and will open to the public in late 1987.

For Steelcase, the future is bright. Says Robert Pew, Steelcase chairman and chief executive officer: "Our research shows that the office furniture market will continue to grow and Steelcase will share in that growth."

"Steelcase's commitment to growth would not be possible without the support of greater Grand Rapids or without the support of the state of Michigan.

". . . I'm proud of our role in the growth of greater Grand Rapids. We intend to continue to try to be a good corporate citizen and the best neighbor possible."

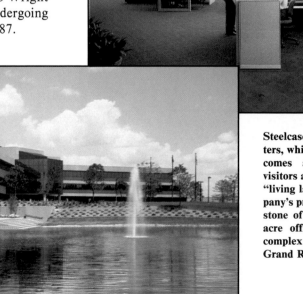

Steelcase corporate headquarters, which opened in 1983, welcomes an average of 8,500 visitors annually and serves as a "living laboratory" for the company's products. It is the cornerstone of the corporation's 300-acre office and manufacturing complex located in southeast Grand Rapids.

WZZM-TV CHANNEL 13

WZZM-TV, Channel 13, has been reporting the Grand Rapids scene for a quarter-century. Innovative, progressive, concerned, enquiring—many adjectives describe the station's dedication to interpreting and projecting to its television audience the special spirit of the West Michigan region.

An affiliate of the American Broadcasting Company since it went on the air in 1962, WZZM has become the news leader among West Michigan broadcast media. The station has been a winner for six consecutive years of United Press International's News Station of the Year Award (1981-1986), and has captured every other broadcast news award in the state, as well as national awards.

In honoring WZZM-TV with its Excellence in Journalism Award of 1986 for best newscast, the University Press Club of Michigan judged "Eyewitness News" to be "the best produced, best written, and had better pacing" than all other entries. Also in 1986 the station was honored with seven first place awards for newscast, investigative reporting, photography, editorials, and graphics. And the station is consistently cited for "a quality of news operation that should be the envy of many stations in larger markets."

National honors have included first place awards for investigative reporting from both UPI and Investigative Reporters and Editors, as well as the Station Emmy from the National Academy of Arts and Sciences and first place from the National Education Association for children's programming.

Such recognition has been hard earned for the station. As the newcomer to the area's television viewers, WZZM was faced, in 1962, with the challenge of breaking into a market that was already 14 years old and dominated by well-established and strong local stations. Veteran staffers occasionally like to reflect on the early days when they gave away free television antennas to potential viewers to persuade them to watch the fledgling station. They remember, too, that in those first years the station was sustained by revenues from early Sunday morning religion shows and compensation from the ABC network. Today 90 percent of WZZM-TV's revenue comes from the sale of commercials to local and national advertisers.

However, from the beginning, station management put the emphasis on news as a key element in developing WZZM-TV's own niche and capturing its share of the television audience. Launched was a progressive and aggressive approach to news to counter the more conservative and establishment approach of the competition. Investigative reporting, a sophisticated effort to project winners in elections, and a regular schedule of provocative editorials changed the face of local news.

From initial efforts of providing headline news service for morning viewers, a five-minute newscast at 7 p.m., and its major newscast—a whole 15 minutes—at 11 p.m., the station gradually developed comprehensive news programming. The 11 p.m. news became a half-hour broadcast, and other news programs throughout the day were expanded.

"Eyewitness News" became TV-13's number-one priority, but the station played two more cards in its bid for viewers—sports and weather.

As an ABC affiliate, the station was backed by a solid tradition of covering major sporting events. TV-13 followed suit and began broadcasting live coverage of the Michigan high school basketball finals, University of Michigan basketball, city amateur golf championships, and extensive news coverage of local sports.

In 1971 "Eyewitness News" introduced the West Michigan viewing area to radar weather reports. Within three years the aircraft radar system was replaced by a computerized color radar, and in 1983 WZZM-TV installed the area's first Doplar radar system. The finest in sophisticated weather technology combined with a team of three trained meteorologists set the trend in scientific weather reporting. The station continues to keep abreast of technology, always maintaining state-of-the-art equipment.

Purchased in January 1986 by Price Communications Corporation, TV-13 has evolved from just covering community events to becoming a part of community events. TV-13 is committed to helping maintain the quality and positive life-style in West Michigan. One way to honor that commitment is through involvement in community events, both by the corporation and by individual staff members.

In 1986 WZZM-TV became the first local television station in the country to broadcast live a senior PGA Tour event, and in 1987 the station originated a network hookup to the entire state of Michigan. TV-13 will continue to provide West Michigan residents with comprehensive coverage of local events and quality television entertainment. The station is looking forward to growing with West Michigan, one of only two television broadcast markets north of the Sunbelt that is in a growth pattern.

WZZM management has always maintained that the key to growth is quality and the key to quality is people. At TV-13, longevity of key people is far above average for the broadcast industry. Many staff members have been with the station for upwards of 25 years. That's because WZZM-TV, once the new kid on the block, has become, to the pride of its people and against the odds, a highly successful, competitive station with one of the finest broadcast facilities in the market. The progressive nature of the WZZM-TV family fits well into a pleasant and progressive region. Employees, like viewers, believe in the station, and TV-13 believes in West Michigan. It will continue to serve the region as an entertainment leader and a progressive, innovative, honest, and hardworking news organization and neighbor.

OLD KENT BANK AND TRUST COMPANY

Old Kent Bank and Trust Company embodies much of the unique spirit of Grand Rapids—progress based upon endeavor and a solid respect for people, customers, and employees.

Built upon a carefully crafted foundation of well-managed assets, exceptional customer service, emphasis on excellence, and community involvement, Old Kent is a corporate citizen that epitomizes the best in the West Michigan business community.

Founded in 1853, Old Kent Bank and Trust is now more than one-third of a century into its second 100 years. The bank's history is a compendium of the region's financial and business history, and its roster of officials over the decades is an elite list of the innovative, resourceful, dedicated individuals who wrote Grand Rapids', and West Michigan's, financial story.

Throughout its history the bank has been committed to the growth and welfare of the region it serves, and has endeavored, through good business management, to promote and maintain a healthy business climate in that region. At the time of urban renewal in downtown Grand

The Old Kent Bank River Run, a 25-kilometer race launched in 1978, has become one of the top road races in America, attracting approximately 4,000 runners a year—about 900 of them Old Kent Bank employees. A major event for bank and community, the race depends for its success on the many loyal volunteers who contribute their time and efforts year after year. The superbly organized event reflects the corporate commitment to excellence.

Rapids during the 1960s, Old Kent Bank was the city's first business to announce plans to build a new corporate office within the urban-renewal district. The renewal area had been dubbed Vandenberg Center after one of the city's favorite sons, Senator Arthur Vandenberg, and it is both fitting and symbolic that the OKB building, at the corner of Ottawa and Lyon streets, is Number One Vandenberg Center.

The first office structure to be built in Grand Rapids in 40 years, Old Kent Bank's main office is an agreeable combination of modern and traditional materials. Concrete, glass, and steel shape the bank's thoroughly contemporary facade rising 11 stories above Vandenberg Plaza. The lower Lyon Street entrance is faced with split fieldstone gathered from the farm fields surrounding Grand Rapids, and the

Old Kent Bank and Trust Company's headquarters building at One Vandenberg Center in downtown Grand Rapids.

plaza area above is topped by flags of the foreign countries with which Old Kent does business.

Many financial institutions since 1853 have joined, through merger and acquisition, to create today's Old Kent Bank Financial Corporation. The corporation, of which Kent Bank and Trust is a subsidiary is a bank holding company with 25 affiliate banks and 188 branch offices serving more than 97 Michigan communities.

Old Kent subsidiaries are full-service financial institutions offering a complete range of services from personal and commercial checking accounts and loans, automatic banking machines, bank credit cards, cash management, and computer services, to corporate and personal trust and investment services, international banking, security brokerage services, and credit life insurance.

The banking firm has seen much change in social and economic conditions in its many years in business, and its ability to meet change with resourcefulness and innovation has been the key to its success. Old Kent Bank and Trust is, as its literature claims, an old bank with young ideas—West Michigan's oldest—and newest—bank. But if adapting to new conditions has been a byword for the bank, service has always been the cornerstone of its business.

In the past two decades the banking industry has undergone phenomenal change, increasing by leaps and bounds the types and numbers of customer services. New banking laws and regulations have changed the industry, too. Old Kent's response has been renewed efforts to remain customer oriented.

Calling itself a "customer-driven" organization, Old Kent is committed to improving the financial well-being of its customers by delivering easily accessible, quality products and service, and at reasonable cost. Such programs as Advantage Fifty, designed to meet the needs and life-style of persons over 50 years of age; UltraLoan, a car financing plan that significantly reduces monthly car payments; and Prime Access, an unsecured line of credit, exemplify the variety and range of services the bank has introduced in recent

Old Kent's main branch located in downtown Grand Rapids.

Old Kent's personnel must meet the corporation's high standards of quality and must consistently demonstrate high-level performance.

years.

The Investor Center, another new service available at Old Kent's downtown headquarters, brings a broad range of investment services and information in one convenient location.

As important to the corporation as its commitment to customers is its commitment to its own people. Old Kent personnel must meet the corporation's high standards of quality and must consistently demonstrate high-level performance. In turn, the corporation offers them many opportunities to develop their own talents and to grow with the company.

If people, both customers and personnel, are Old Kent's bricks and mortar, so to speak, sound monetary practices are the bank's foundation. Quality assets and good management that enable the corporation to generate capital are essential to its health. Old Kent's emphasis on quality is nowhere more patently demonstrated than in its commitment to "common-sense procedures and controls that maintain quality assets in a 'no surprise' managerial environment." The corporation's business philosophy is firmly rooted in its belief in "a responsibility not only to Grand Rapids but to all of West Michigan to push for expansion and growth." Old Kent has invested more funds in local industry and construction than any other financial institution in the state, and it continues to concentrate much of its financial power behind the region it serves.

However, its strategy for continued growth is based on acquisition of other banking properties. Michigan's 1986 banking law allowing banking interstate acquisitions has prompted Old Kent Financial Corporation to evaluate acquisition opportunities in neighboring states.

Anticipated out-of-state growth, however, will not alter the corporation's commitment to western Michigan, and its unwavering objective to maintain a constant emphasis on quality service and a tradition of success.

CLIPPER BELT LACER COMPANY

Belting—leather, fabric, and later rubber—has been used in power-driven machinery since the dawn of the industrial revolution. And the one universal requirement of belting is that the ends must be laced together in a perfectly dovetailed, flat seam to make a continuous loop. Providing "lacing" and "lacers" for industrial belting is the business of Clipper Belt Lacer Company.

When the business was founded in 1905, industrial machinery was powered from a single source, usually steam, and run by pulleys attached to a single overhead shaft. The power transmission belts, made of leather and fastened together with leather lacing, often broke, causing expensive downtime while they were repaired.

In 1897 a New Jersey man perfected a metal ring fastener to replace the leather lacing. Two Englishmen, James and Frank Stone, further refined the lacing process by developing a lacing tool to install the metal ring lacings.

In the early years of the century the Stones immigrated to the United States and settled in Grand Rapids. They went into business as the J.B. Stone Company, repairing leather belting for industry. Shortly after founding the business, James Stone died. Frank continued alone and incorporated the venture in 1908 as the Clipper Belt Lacer Company. The name, so the story goes, was chosen because the clipper ship at the time was the symbol of the fastest mode of transportation, and, by association, Clipper products were the fastest method of lacing belts. One of the firm's lacers could lace a belt in three minutes, revolutionary for the times.

With the coming of electricity and the gasoline engine, machines were individually powered by their own motors, and the line shaft, turned by a single power source, quickly became a thing of the past. The belting fastener industry suffered a severe downturn, and many companies went out of business.

From the very beginning, Clipper Belt had been an aggressive and innovative organization. The firm's management, knowing it had a superior product, refused to succumb to the times and sought new markets for its lacers and flat material fasteners.

Turning to the conveyor, laundry, and textile industries, Clipper developed special hooks for different market segments. Round hay balers proved another source for sales. The company also worked with farm equipment manufacturers to devise fasteners for farm machinery.

Such resourcefulness is a hallmark of Clipper. The firm has continued to find new markets for its products and to work within various industries to develop products to meet the needs of manufacturers.

A manufacturer of light- and mediumweight fasteners, Clipper, in the early 1980s, formed an alliance with MATOCurt Matthaei of Offenbach, West Germany, a manufacturer of heavy-duty metal fasteners for conveyor belting used in the coal mining industry. The German product is marketed in the United States as Clipper Mato. Combining German engineering expertise with American sales and marketing techniques has broadened the market for both MATO and Clipper products.

Today nearly every industry in the world uses conveyor belting in one capacity or another. Clipper provides fastening systems for factory-installed new belts and for repair of old belts. The company's fasteners are used in conveyor belts in manufacturing, mining, food handling, photo pro-

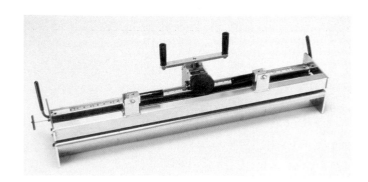

The Roller Lacer is the latest lacer technology for installing belt fasteners quickly, easily, and in one operation.

Clipper Mato belt fasteners used in heavy-duty applications such as coal mining.

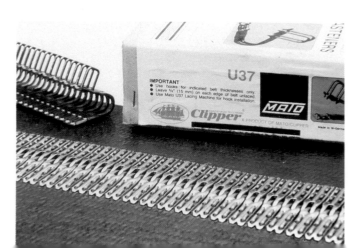

cessing, and parcel delivery services. There are even tiny Clipper fasteners for the delicate tapes and timing belts used in electronic equipment. The firm manufactures more than 4,000 different flat material fasteners in all sizes and all metals.

Clipper fasteners are only half the story. The company makes 25 different lacers, both manual and automatic, to install the fasteners. The lacers are simple and economical to use, guaranteeing that a user can make his own repairs without calling in expensive, highly skilled technicians.

Always a company that planned for the future, embraced new technology, and continually adapted to the demands of the market, Clipper also was a company that was innovative in its employee relations. Early in its history the firm gained national attention when it instituted a policy of wages for piece work—one of the first companies in the country to adopt the practice. It also was a pioneer in offering group insurance and profit sharing to employees.

The firm's commitment to quality embraces product and employees. "Our responsibility to our customers," say company officials, "is to understand their needs and be able to meet their quality and technical requirements and deadlines. Our responsibility to our employees is to make sure they know what we expect of them, and to help them meet our standards of performance. We take a team approach to manufacturing, and education is a key element in our program to help employees grow technically and professionally."

In keeping with its policy of long-range planning, Clipper, in 1984, changed from a publicly held company to private ownership and joined the MATO Group to provide

more funds for research and development.

The firm recently went into other conveyor belt line maintenance products, and is continuing to expand its product line, coming out with two or three new items each year. It also custom designs fastening systems for customers' specialized needs.

In its 80-plus-year history Clipper Belt Lacer Company has introduced many innovations in its own industry that have proven to be contributions to the industries it serves. Less than two decades away from its 100th anniversary, the firm's prospects for the future are exciting and challenging.

Clipper's light- and medium-weight fasteners are used in a variety of industrial, food-processing, and agricultural applications. Clipper products are sold through distributors in 59 countries and a network of 1,200 distributors in the United States, as well as eight agents who sell to the coal mining industry in the United States and Canada.

In 1981 Clipper Belt Lacer Company moved from manufacturing facilities it had built in 1911 to a new facility at 1995 Oak Industrial Drive NE. The new site has an additional 10 acres, plenty of room for future expansion.

PARAGON DIE & ENGINEERING & CASCADE ENGINEERING

An appropriate example of what makes the Grand Rapids area a dynamic industrial center is seen in two neighboring manufacturing firms—Paragon Die & Engineering, and Cascade Engineering. The common heritage of Paragon and Cascade blends quality leadership and family ties, altogether fitting in this West Michigan setting where traditions of respect for quality and family dominate everyday living.

The successes of these two companies are the result of a father and son, with each man dedicating his firm's energies to technological leadership within its field. According to customers and suppliers, those efforts have paid off in enviable reputations: Paragon, as a world-class supplier of large molds for the diecast and plastic-manufacturing industries; and Cascade, as a leader in the design, development, and manufacture of assemblies containing plastic injection-molded products.

By implementing the efficiencies of recent technologies and encouraging the development of employee talents, both firms have provided the products and services to develop loyal clienteles in the automotive and office furniture industries.

In 1963 Fred M. Keller took the helm of Paragon, moving the firm into a newly constructed facility on 36th Street in Grand Rapids within just five years. During the 1970s Paragon began placing an emphasis on the technology of fast, accurate metal removal to efficiently build molds. This emphasis led to a worldwide search for the finest equipment

A Cascade Engineering operator prepares to remove a part from the up-and-out robot.

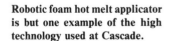

Robotic foam hot melt applicator is but one example of the high technology used at Cascade.

to meet this objective. This emphasis also led to several facilities additions.

Assuring customers of the highest quality products has remained foremost in the minds of Keller and his staff. In 1983 Paragon added an environmentally controlled room for a state-of-the-art coordinate measuring machine, for dimensional checks of incoming models and for layouts and checking of production projects. A CAD/CAM system, first installed in 1985, helped in the development and production of mold contours and components.

In 1987 Keller moved Paragon into facilities on 33rd Street, expanding into 72,900 square feet of manufacturing space and 19,600 square feet of office space. With the move came the acquisition of additional precision machining equipment and overhead cranes capable of handling larger tools and expediting material flow.

Quality, service, and technological leadership continue to be the focus of Paragon Die & Engineering's preparedness to meet customers' needs.

Cascade Engineering was founded in 1973 by Frederick P. Keller, son of Paragon's president. Cascade's initial work consisted primarily of tryout services for large molds, but soon expanded to include limited production runs for other custom injection molders. By 1976 the company had broadened its horizons, seeking out end-user customers through the efforts of Cascade Sales Associates, a sales and marketing affiliate.

Cascade took special pride in the success of its first opportunity to prove the "engineering" in its name by providing Herman Miller, Inc., with injection-molded chair arm pads. This success was just one example of a philosophy that would continue to focus on technical solutions to engineering challenges.

The success of Cascade is a credit to the people who work there. While Grand Rapids-area residents are widely recognized for their highly developed work ethic, Cascade employees carry that reputation a step further. Because of the company's philosophical and financial commitments to individual development, all employees are provided with the training and tools to become managers of their own jobs. As a result, every employee is ready and able to make on-the-spot decisions with positive impact on the finished product. And those employees regard themselves as members of a team whose ideas matter and whose mission is to provide the customer with excellence.

Cascade Engineering is recognized for its commitment to people programs such as quality circles, quality councils, Juran problem-solving teams, and "cost of quality"-based bonus programs. In fact, representatives of the firm have been invited to speak to colleagues and professional groups about the Cascade experience in those areas.

In order to provide technical support for the work of its employees, the company constantly monitors new technologies, updating its own manufacturing and communications equipment on a frequent basis. In molding equipment, quality assurance, and customer communications, sophisticated technology is put to work to consistently ensure the efficient manufacture of quality products for on-time delivery.

Today Cascade's South Plant, an expansion of the original manufacturing facility, is an assembly-intensive operation, producing a broad range of parts.

The North Plant was built in 1984 as a state-of-the-art manufacturing facility. The North Plant runs 24 hours a day, seven days a week, specializing in high-volume, large-part production and assembly operations.

In 1987 Cascade expanded into a third plant. The East Plant allows the firm to satisfy increasing customer requests for custom-molded, highly decorative products. The technological approach to production implemented in the East Plant makes extensive use of robotics. This plant also houses the expanded research and development, engineering, and quality assurance functions.

Individually and as a team, Paragon and Cascade have become world-class suppliers. State-of-the-art facilities, unique people programs, and a willingness to develop new ways of doing things, have led these firms to strong positions in their respective industries. The future is bright for these two companies as they continue to dedicate their efforts toward helping their customers achieve an unrivaled degree of excellence.

Paragon Die & Engineering has state-of-the-art precision mold-making capabilities.

A Paragon Die engineer checks the critical mold dimensions on the coordinate measuring machine.

BUTTERWORTH HOSPITAL

The huge red neon sign atop Butterworth Hospital is a familiar Grand Rapids landmark. The hospital, situated on a hill overlooking downtown Grand Rapids, is itself an enduring landmark—one that symbolizes for many the permanence and stability of the region, a beacon of steadfastness in an ever-changing environment.

But the red neon sign may be the only unchanging element in the hospital complex; Butterworth Hospital has been in a state of change for more than 100 years, always striving to keep abreast of the advances in medical knowledge and health care. The facility is West Michigan's largest and busiest general acute care hospital. In addition to providing primary medical care, Butterworth serves as a tertiary referral center for an 11-county area in seven specialties. It is as a tertiary hospital—a facility with highly specialized services—that Butterworth has experienced the most growth in the past decade and a half.

The health care industry itself has been undergoing tremendous change. The dizzying speed at which medical technology advances, relentlessly rising health care costs, and the increasing awareness and sophistication of consumers, are a few of the factors that have combined to create a continuing state of flux as the industry strives to deal with the changes.

To help contain rising health care costs, hospitals within a region are finding that it makes economic sense to concentrate in certain specialties rather than to each duplicate the services of the others. Grand Rapids' four acute care hospitals all offer primary care, but each has certain specialties for which it has become noted.

Butterworth is West Michigan's referral hospital for cardiology, cardiovascular surgery, high-risk obstetrics, microsurgery, neonatology, oncology, and trauma.

Many of Butterworth's specialties developed as an outgrowth of services already offered at the hospital. Butterworth recently acquired a lithotripter, a machine to dissolve kidney stones by the use of sound waves, a method more efficient, more cost effective, and easier for the patient than removal by surgery. Acquisition of the machine was a logical outgrowth considering Butterworth performs the highest number of kidney stone surgeries in the area.

The much-publicized helicopter patient transport service is an extension of the hospital's trauma unit, instituted in 1980. The unit is staffed by specially trained trauma teams, each consisting of surgeons, nurses, respiratory therapists, and radiology and medical technologists, and provides around-the-clock, seven-day-a-week care for the

Situated atop a hill overlooking downtown Grand Rapids, Butterworth Hospital has served as a pillar of West Michigan's medical community for more than a century.

Butterworth's 44-bed neonatal intensive care unit is staffed with five full-time neonatologists and provides a full array of services for critically ill newborns.

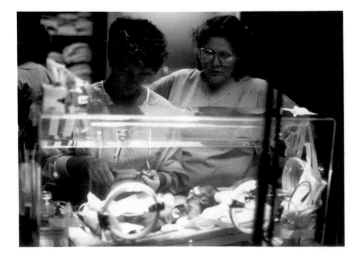

critically injured.

Teamwork, in fact, is at the basis of the Butterworth operation. All the departments of the hospital must, and do, work in concert to create an effective whole. From laboratories to nutritionists, the support services of the hospital are critical to the efficiency and success of individual functions.

To meet the demands of today's health care marketplace, Butterworth has taken a critical look at its role as a health care provider and is moving with the times. Even as it continues to update its facility and adopt the most advanced technology and techniques in the health care field, it remains cognizant of the fact that today's health care consumers are becoming more health conscious and more responsible for their own health needs. Health education and preventive medicine are popular concepts that will more and more dominate the philosophy of the health care field. Butterworth has developed many programs to support those concepts.

In a move to make medical services geographically accessible to all areas of the community, the hospital has established several med centers. It also operates a retail pharmacy and Grand Valley Nursing Center, which specializes in the care of closed head injury patients as well as services to geriatric and pediatric patients.

Butterworth has been a leader in the Grand Rapids medical community since its origin in 1873 as St. Mark's

Every Aero Med flight is staffed by a physician and nurse who are experienced in emergency medicine.

Butterworth was selected as the regional trauma specialty unit in 1980. Each year some 300 patients with life-threatening injuries are admitted to the trauma unit.

Church Home for the aged and sick. In 1887 local civic leader and St. Mark's member Richard Butterworth purchased and gave to the home property on Bostwick Avenue across the street from the present hospital. Butterworth died shortly thereafter, but left an endowment of $41,500, which was used to build and equip a hospital. Affiliation with St. Mark's Episcopal Church was severed in 1894, and the hospital was named Butterworth for its principal benefactor.

A new hospital was built on the present site in 1925. The structure has been remodeled and added on to many times in the intervening years. The present complex bears little resemblance to the original facility, but the concept remains the same—to provide patients with the best medical care available.

Butterworth in the 1980s is one of the most modern medical facilities in the state. It is a research hospital and a teaching hospital, and it provides the ultimate in health care.

But all the technology in the world does not supplant the human factor. It is the Butterworth people that make the difference. The medical, nursing, technical, administrative, and support staffs are united in their effort to be friendly and caring with patients and their families, treating not only the physical needs of the patient but the informational and emotional needs of the family.

Respect, compassion, and competence are the tenets by which the hospital operates. It goes out of its way to make every Butterworth experience the best possible for patients and other hospital guests.

DAVENPORT COLLEGE
THE W.A. LETTINGA
ENTREPRENEURIAL CENTER

For more than 100 years students interested in business careers have been coming to Davenport College to learn the basic skills of business, and then putting those skills to work in the business community.

Davenport has long had close ties with the Grand Rapids business community. Many Davenport faculty members work in local industry or own their own businesses. Local business people serve on the college's advisory boards, head volunteer projects, and appear as guest speakers in classes and at Davenport-sponsored seminars and workshops. And local businesses offer educational opportunities for Davenport students through co-op programs and internships.

Davenport, in turn, is a continuing resource to the business community. The college continues to revise and update its curriculum to provide its students with the most current business skills, and to provide business and industry with a ready source of well-trained graduates. Because of that special ongoing relationship with the business community, says Micki Benz, "business training was a natural outgrowth of our business education."

Business training is offered through Davenport's W.A. Lettinga Entrepreneurial Center, opened in mid-1986 and described by executive director Benz as an "organization that fills in the gaps for businesses." The center provides seminars and training programs on a wide range of business needs, and has worked individually with firms as diverse as D&W Food Stores, Gerber Products, Pine Rest Christian Hospital, Adams Plastics, Ernst and Whinney, the City of Grand Rapids, and the Grand Valley Health Care Plan. Center programs are individually designed and tailored to address the client company's needs—from improving managerial and communication skills to understanding business financing and updating computer literacy. Each case is handled individually; there are no "canned" materials or solutions for any set of circumstances. In addition, the center offers less formal assistance in such areas as developing marketing plans and writing personnel manuals. "We don't

help people do their business," says Benz. "We help them run their business."

One of the center's strengths is its focus on the needs of the small business. Large corporations have the resources to institute programs and to hire experts to solve problems. Small business owners lack the resources for such amenities and often cannot afford the luxury of a long-term academic program to help them learn business management skills. They need immediate professional advice and training that can help them identify and solve their problems. Providing that expertise through a full spectrum of services—from market analysis to office management—is the role of the Entrepreneurial Center.

The Entrepreneurial Center is only the latest innovation in Davenport's long tradition of providing specialized vocational training and general education for rewarding careers in business and related services. The school is an integral part of the business community, and contributes to and shares in West Michigan's economic stability, prosperity, and growth.

Top right: The W.A. Lettinga Entrepreneurial Center.

Right: Robert W. Sneden Academic Center of Davenport College.

FALCON MANUFACTURING

A new business, based on a new product and a new concept, was born in 1965, when James Allen and Robert Foster established Falcon Manufacturing in a small building in downtown Grand Rapids.

The product was EPS—expanded polystyrene, a foam plastic material. The new concept was that EPS was ideal for use in insulation and packing because of its mix of strength, insulating properties, and light weight.

First used in West Germany, the material made its appearance in the United States about 1960. Establishing itself as a manufacturer of EPS products, Falcon was obviously embarking on a voyage into virtually uncharted entrepreneurial seas. Today the company is considered a pioneer in the industry.

Growth came quickly to Falcon. The company moved in 1966 to larger quarters in Byron Center, where it now occupies a modern facility of 100,000 square feet and employs more than 100 persons.

Robert Foster left the business in 1982, but James Allen remained, with two new partners, Dirk Buth, named president, and Steve Buth, executive vice-president.

Approximately 80 percent of Falcon's sales volume is in insulating products; the remainder is in packaging. Its versatility, efficiency, economical cost, and ease of installation make EPS an attractive material for use in residential and commercial building. But many other industries also depend on EPS for insulation. Original equipment manufacturers in the RV industry, and the garage door, commercial, and residential door industries are making increasing use of the foam.

EPS packaging materials are used mostly for office furniture, appliances, and electronic products. Hot wires are used to cut the EPS sheet and blocks into countless shapes and configurations according to each customer's specifications.

Aggressive marketing as well as product has played a part in the company's success. Twenty years ago Falcon had one or two competitors; today it has more than a dozen. In the face of increasing competition, quality and service have become the focus of Falcon's marketing strategy. This emphasis on quality and service is made possible by Falcon's modern facility, state-of-the-art equipment, and fleet of truck-trailers that serve the company's marketing area—Michigan, Ohio, Indiana, and Illinois.

The key ingredient to Falcon's success, however, says president Dirk Buth, is its people. "It is teamwork, and team effort, that have made Falcon the outstanding company it is."

CLARY, NANTZ, WOOD, HOFFIUS, RANKIN & COOPER

Clary, Nantz, Wood, Hoffius, Rankin & Cooper is one of the largest and fastest growing law firms in western Michigan. This full-service Grand Rapids-based law firm provides legal services to a diversified client base and prides itself on finding effective, innovative solutions to client needs.

The firm was established in 1969 by Jack R. Clary, a labor relations attorney representing management, as the Law Offices of Jack R. Clary. He and Philip W. Nantz envisioned a law firm to represent management in labor relations matters. They were joined a few weeks later by Philip F. Wood. In 1970 the three attorneys formed a partnership under the name of Clary, Nantz & Wood.

In the early 1970s the firm decided to expand its range of legal services and become a full-service law firm. It did this by adding attorneys with established practices in various areas of business-related law. Leonard M. Hoffius and Richard Rankin brought to the firm a corporate, real estate, and business acquisition expertise in the mid-1970s. When Robert P. Cooper joined the firm in 1979, it became one of the select few Michigan law firms with a specialty in tax-exempt financing. That same year the firm adopted the name of Clary, Nantz, Wood, Hoffius, Rankin & Cooper.

Today this law firm is a professional corporation with approximately 50 attorneys, providing a wide range of legal services to a diverse business-oriented client base. Its client list reflects the diversification of specialties within the firm. Reading like a Who's Who of Michigan Business, the list includes manufacturing companies, service companies, investment companies, retailers and wholesalers, insurance companies, banks, restaurants, oil and gas developers, agricultural cooperatives, real estate developers, hospitals, and other health care facilities. The firm is also widely recognized for its representation of public entities, including cities, counties, school districts, road commissions, municipal health care facilities, and a variety of other governmental units. Although the bulk of its practice is in the West Michigan area, the firm also services clients throughout the State of Michigan and nationally.

The firm encourages its attorneys to be innovative and resourceful in dealing with client needs. Labor relations attorney Leo H. Litowich explains, "We enjoy the challenge of complicated legal matters and welcome the opportunity to solve problems. We don't like to say that something can't be done. We have found that innovative thought and hard work can produce solutions to even the toughest problems."

Jack R. Clary founded the firm in 1969.

Attorneys Philip W. Nantz and Pamela J. Kruse are shown here in the firm's pleasant lobby.

The firm's "can do" approach has attracted clients who welcome this sort of attitude.

It is also a law firm that prides itself on maintaining a high degree of professionalism, along with the accomplishment-oriented approach to solving legal problems. According to Richard A. Wendt, a business and municipal attorney, "We place the highest premium on excellence and professionalism in the practice of law." Other attorneys in the firm echo this approach.

The firm has experienced rapid growth in recent years. When asked about this growth, trial attorney Robert L. DeJong, stated, "It is true we have been growing. However, growth is not a goal in itself. It has been necessary to meet increasing client needs in various areas of law. However, we are quite insistent that the growth not be so rapid as to diminish the standards of excellence that we have established for ourselves."

Clary, Nantz, Wood, Hoffius, Rankin & Cooper is located in the prestigious Calder Plaza Building in downtown Grand Rapids. It maintains an extensive law library, including a large collection of resource material, computerized legal research, and numerous services providing up-to-date information on changes in the law. An interesting collection of artwork by West Michigan artists is displayed throughout the firm's hallways.

The firm's attorneys are also active outside the practice of law. The attorneys are encouraged to become involved in the community. They are active in various charitable and civic organizations, and a number of them have held offices in both local and state bar association organizations, while others have served under various public and private commissions and boards. The firm also maintains a speaker's bureau, which provides speakers to various local organizations without charge. Those speakers cover a wide range of legal topics.

Today Clary, Nantz, Wood, Hoffius, Rankin & Cooper is one of the major West Michigan law firms. Its rapid growth, commitment to excellence, and accomplishment-oriented approach to the practice of law have greatly enhanced its reputation in the community.

Attorneys Douglas W. Van Essen, Mark R. Smith, L. Allen Heneveld, Sheila A. Kinney, and John E. Anding meet in one of the firm's conference rooms.

Word processor Anna Sweetnam uses state-of-the-art technology to prepare a brief for attorney Charles F. Grzanka.

BLODGETT MEMORIAL MEDICAL CENTER

Blodgett Memorial Medical Center offers unsurpassed, comprehensive care for the entire family. Its tradition of excellence began in 1847 as a refuge for the sick and needy. Today Blodgett operates as a major medical center serving all of western Michigan. Blodgett is located on Wealthy Street in East Grand Rapids overlooking picturesque Fisk Lake.

With its 410-bed acute-care hospital, 14-operating-room surgical suite, and emergency care facilities that have earned Michigan's highest ranking, Blodgett cares for more than 16,500 patients and 26,000 emergency patients each year. More than 13,000 surgeries are performed annually.

At Blodgett patients are nothing new—but they're always something special.

Blodgett's seven medical and surgical patient care units offer a combination of private and semiprivate suites to accommodate adult patients of all ages. When patients need intensive treatment, the medical center's specially equipped Critical Care Units (Surgical, Medical, Transitional, Pediatric, Neonatal, and West Michigan Burn Unit) provide this vital nursing care.

Patients with cancer, nervous system disorders, heart conditions, and orthopedic problems know Blodgett's reputation for excellence in Oncology, Neurology, Cardiac Rehabilitation, and Orthopedic Services.

The major medical center that today serves patients from throughout the western side of Michigan began as a small organization in a home in Grand Rapids' present Heritage Hill.

Families have learned to trust and depend on Blodgett's Maternity Center for complete family-oriented services for prenatal, labor and delivery, and postpartum care. Since it opened in 1985 Blodgett's Special Care Nursery, staff, and neonatologist have helped 250 babies survive many life-threatening traumas and illnesses.

Blodgett's Rainy Day Care is also unique in West Michigan. The medical center's professionals care for children from one month to 16 years of age who are under the weather from a common, temporary illness. Parents can leave their child in our hands on the way to work and feel confident they will be given tender, loving care.

Not every illness requires hospitalization. Blodgett's Outpatient Clinics offer a variety of medical care services using the most advanced treatments while containing costs. The clinics provide comprehensive care for the entire family with routine as well as specialized treatment.

Health care providers know the value of early examinations in the detection of cancer. Blodgett's Cancer Screening Center assesses each patient's personal and family history while offering thorough clinical examinations and physician referrals.

Blodgett Wellness at East Hills Athletic Club offers a variety of programs aimed at keeping people healthy and physically fit.

Former cardiac patients participate in the final phase of Blodgett's three phases of Cardiac Rehabilitation through the Wellness Program.

Back pain is a nagging, irritating problem for millions of people. Others complain of tennis elbow, torn ligaments, and pulled muscles from athletic activities. The Back Pain Center and Sports Medicine Clinic at East Hills Athletic Club specialize in the evaluation and treatment of back and neck pain and sports injuries. The comprehensive programs include state-of-the-art testing, education, and therapy.

Nearby on East Paris is The Surgical Center, the first free-standing facility of its kind in this area. Its sole function is to perform outpatient surgery with convenience and efficiency.

Quality health care can be expensive, but there is an alternative health insurance plan to cover all your health care needs. Blodgett and Saint Mary's Hospital, in cooperation with doctors from both institutions, offer Care Choices. The aim of Care Choices is to encourage early and regular contact with physicians and to promote good health.

Blodgett staff have pioneered various procedures

for medical and surgical diagnosis and treatment. Innovations to their credit include techniques for cardiac catheterization, open-heart surgery, artificial joint implantation, and endoscopy.

Blodgett is a leader in the specialty of orthopedics. In 1933 Blodgett was the first hospital in Grand Rapids to establish an orthopedic residency program. West Michigan's first surgery to implant artificial finger joints made of silicone was performed at Blodgett in 1964. Now used by surgeons around the world, the prostheses and techniques used in this special surgery were invented by a Blodgett surgeon.

The teamwork of doctors, nurses, and technicians in Blodgett's Cardiac Study Group, begun in 1953, resulted in the first cardiac catheterization and the first open-heart surgery in West Michigan. Their skill and experience reflect one of the lowest mortality rates for bypass surgery in the state.

In 1985 Blodgett opened the city's most comprehensively equipped Cardiac Catheterization Laboratory, making available to heart patients the most up-to-date diagnostic and treatment procedures, such as cardiac catheterization, streptokinase infusion, and balloon angioplasty.

Blodgett's Neuroscience Team provides immediate and continuing care for strokes, encephalitis, multiple injuries, and other neurological disorders.

The West Michigan Burn Unit, a regional care facility designed to meet the special care needs of burn patients from a 12-county area in West Michigan, includes the most up-to-date medical equipment as well as specially trained staff.

The Blodgett Regional Poison Center, one of only 35 such facilities in the nation, provides 24-hour information and intervention services via toll-free telephone lines.

The major medical center that today serves patients from throughout the western side of Michigan began as a small organization. The Female Union Charitable Association was established in 1847 by a group of women whose goal was to care for the sick and needy of the pioneer village of Grand Rapids.

In 1916, following a charter revision that defined the association as an acute care hospital, John Wood Blodgett built and donated a hospital facility in memory of his mother, Jane Wood Blodgett. Originally called Blodgett Memorial Hospital, the building has been renovated several times and was renamed Blodgett Memorial Medical Center to reflect more accurately its comprehensive services and facilities.

A major teaching hospital, Blodgett is affiliated with the medical, technical, and nursing education programs of several universities and colleges. Medical education programs, begun in 1919, now include 70 resident physicians each year.

Although two different names and more than 100 years now separate Blodgett and its origins, its commitment to excellence in medical care and medical education provide an enduring bridge between past and present. By consistently keeping in step with—and often setting the pace for—advances in medical technology, treatment, and innovative services, Blodgett Memorial Medical Center has earned a reputation as an area leader in provision of up-to-date, high-quality, and personalized patient care.

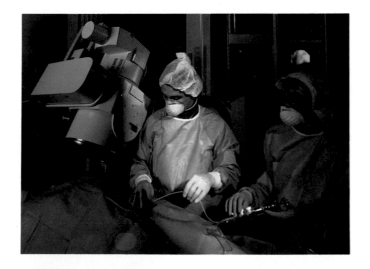

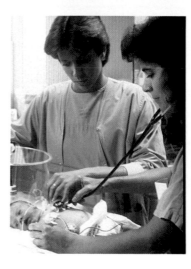

In 1985 Blodgett opened the city's most comprehensively equipped Cardiac Catheterization Laboratory, making available to heart patients the most up-to-date diagnostic and treatment procedures.

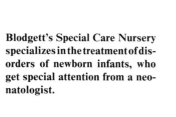

Blodgett's Special Care Nursery specializes in the treatment of disorders of newborn infants, who get special attention from a neonatologist.

HOPE REHABILITATION NETWORK

At Hope Rehabilitation Network, hope is more than just a name. It is a promise of opportunities for adults who are disabled and disadvantaged to lead dignified, productive, and independent lives.

Hope Rehabilitation Network looks for abilities in disability and seeks to honor and uphold the rights and dignity of every individual by helping the physically handicapped, developmentally disabled, emotionally and mentally impaired, traumatic brain injured, and spinal cord injured achieve their highest potential.

Formerly known as Pine Rest Christian Rehabilitation Services, Hope Rehabilitation Network, a community-based, Christian organization serving adults 18 years and older, is one of the largest private, nonprofit, rehabilitation programs of its kind in Michigan and in the United States. Funded by a combination of public and private dollars, Hope Network has been meeting the needs of the disabled for more than 25 years and currently serves over 1,400 clients a day.

Because Hope Network works in close cooperation with governmental units, the industrial sector, family welfare agencies, and other human services providers, it is able to offer its clients and their families a comprehensive, diversified, and innovative network of support systems, programs, and services. In addition to assessing individual abilities and recommending appropriate programs and services, Hope Network places great emphasis on the caring and on the commitment to fostering in each client the greatest-possible degree of self-sufficiency and self-respect. In 80 percent of the cases Hope Network sees that commitment to individual and family extends throughout the client's lifetime.

HRN's philosophy of rehabilitation centers on the goal of integration into the community. The Enclaves in Industry program, for example, designed in conjunction with Kent Community Mental Health and local businesses, carefully matches workers' skills to jobs and provides opportunities for clients to move out of sheltered work centers and into "real world" worksites. Today some 250 client/employees, working in groups ranging from four to 12 individuals, are successfully holding down positions at 10 worksites—including the Marriott Hotel, Steelcase, Inc., Meijer, Inc., and Guardsman Chemicals—throughout Kent County.

Skills training and sheltered work center employment are also available to HRN clients through Kent Community Industries (KCI). A member of the Hope Network, KCI is a major provider of subcontract manufacturing services to hundreds of area industries. Some 750 individuals with disabilities work in one of six work centers throughout Kent County at jobs that range from sorting, collating, and mailing to high-volume packaging of all kinds.

Closely supervised at their worksites by Hope Network

Instructor uses a computer to help client build memory and motor skills.

A Hope client practices independent living skills in CIL's model apartment.

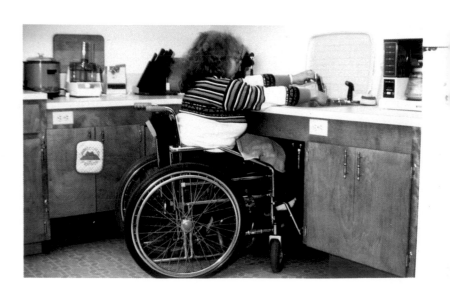

Clients busy preparing Easter
baskets for a local retailer in one
of HRN's six centers.

personnel and transported to and from their jobs by HRN's fleet of 50 radio-dispatched vehicles, these client/employees are able to use their abilities to the fullest, and to enjoy the considerable satisfaction that arises from being productive members of the community.

Businesses that hire HRN clients and subcontract for manufacturing services through KCI or one of the other six centers derive considerable benefits from the arrangement, too. Not only are employers assured of a prescreened, supervised, conscientious, and highly dependable work force, but Hope Network's vocational programming gives them access to a labor pool of unskilled and semiskilled workers willing and able to work at the kinds of jobs—janitorial, maintenance, and housekeeping positions, for example—that are otherwise becoming increasingly difficult to fill.

Businesses and industries may also avail themselves of HRN's consulting services. Hope Network will analyze the suitability of the work place for individuals with disabilities; test, evaluate, and retrain workers injured on the job; and assist in deciphering the many government regulations involving workers' compensation and other employment-related issues.

In fulfilling its role as an advocate for the disabled, Hope Rehabilitation Network works with more than 160 companies and businesses in West Michigan. Thanks to HRN's efforts, employment opportunities have become more available, and in 1986 Hope clients earned wages to-

taling more than $1.1 million, an increase of 11.4 percent over the previous year.

Approximately 60 percent of Hope Network's clients earn wages. But, as HRN officials point out, many individuals with impairments, particularly those with severe and profound disabilities, are unable to work for pay. To help those clients function in the community to the best of their ability, Hope Network operates a therapeutic day activities program that provides opportunities to develop independent living skills and social competence.

Residential programs, totaling 143 beds in over a dozen separate facilities, also focus on an improved quality of life through the strengthening of independent living and social skills. Hope Network's recently completed Sojourners Transitional Living Center is West Michigan's first non-profit residential facility designed specifically for individuals with traumatic brain injuries (TBI) and spinal cord injuries (SCI). Equipped for 16 TBI and 16 SCI residents, the center helps these individuals make the transition from hospital to community by providing the therapy and life skills training that will enable them to live as independently as they can. Nonresidential TBI and SCI programs also focus on independent skills and vocational development.

Despite its already broad range of vocational, residential, psychological, nursing, recreational, counseling, evaluative, therapeutic, pastoral, family support, and home modification services, Hope Rehabilitation Network is committed to further growth and to the development of new programs and services that address the needs of persons with disabilities and improve their ability to lead dignified and productive lives. As chief executive officer Herbert A. Start puts it, "Our staff has a passion for excellence—to make the good better and the better best."

A client with a brain injury finds
vocational placement through
Hope Network.

LACKS INDUSTRIES

Behind the remarkable growth of Lacks Industries—which has nearly doubled in the past four years—is its ability to be an integral source to customers, not just selling *to* them, but working *with* them. The manufacturer has achieved that role by consistently originating and developing programs dedicated to excellence—through new and better manufacturing techniques, the training and cultivating of employee skills, and cooperative product development with customers.

This commitment to excellence is more than a concept. The spirit of excellence is embodied in the daily activities of all employees, and is evident in the team approach to solving problems and generating new techniques in product manufacturing and design. While highly talented individuals exist in all areas of operations, there are no individual heroes. Lacks Industries' fundamental team spirit allows the organization collectively to reach greater levels of excellence than could be achieved by the individual talents within the company.

satisfy the diverse and changing needs of its customers.

From beginnings rooted in die-cast processing, Lacks Industries has evolved into a sophisticated, state-of-the-art plastic molding and finishing organization. Capabilities of the firm include molding, decorative and functional electroplating, and a range of painting techniques and assembly.

Electroless plating of computer enclosures and mineral-reinforced nylon are performed by Plastic Plate, Inc., a part of Lacks Industries. Add to these operations an ongoing program of developing methods to improve technologies—resulting in processes such as a fully automated plating system controlled simultaneously by a network of computers involving 30 microprocessors—and the commitment is endorsed by reality.

The automotive industry comprises the foundation of Lacks Industries' business. Products for this industry include injection-molded decorative grilles, headlamp bezels, intricate wheel covers, and complete front fascias. The products of other industries, however, also have benefited

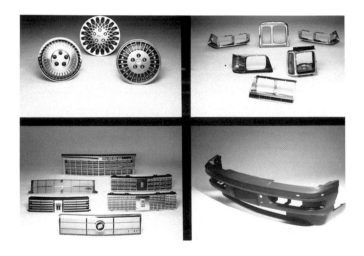

Products that set quality standards include automotive wheel covers, plated automobile grilles, reaction injection-molded automobile fascias, plated headlamp bezels, electroless shielded computer enclosures, and a power-operated rearview mirror.

Three generations of the Lacks family work together in managing an independent, multiplant manufacturing organization.

Ever since Richard Lacks, Sr., joined his father at REM Die Casting in 1959, the Lacks concept of working together has led to achievement. The early efforts of John and Richard Lacks at REM created the Metalac Corporation in 1961 to handle machining and specialized operations for the growing organization. Then Ace Plating was purchased to lessen the dependency of REM on outside sources for finishing requirements. By 1964 the owners of REM and its associated businesses sold their holdings to the two individuals who had been so instrumental in their growth, the Lackses. Personally guided by three generations of the Lacks family, the organization has evolved into Lacks Industries. It has become a multiplant corporation dedicated to producing acknowledged quality products efficiently to

A technologically current laboratory and testing facility evaluates conformity and tests durability and longevity characteristics of product samples.

An entire plant devoted to plating on plastic is controlled from a gondola populated with sophisticated computers that automatically control the locations of 10 crane/hoist positioning systems and five shuttles.

from the organization's expertise—appliances, plumbing and hardware fixtures, business machines, and computers. Now Lacks has its own product: a six-inch by nine-inch electric remote-control outside rearview mirror, called the Powermirror, used by van and RV manufacturers and consumers.

Quality is the fundamental approach to all activities at Lacks. The maintenance of a well-equipped laboratory and updated test equipment is instrumental, of course. But internal training and retraining is vital. And the creative ingenuity to find new ways, improve contemporary systems, and devise advanced methods of manufacturing is nurtured.

As one of the first such manufacturers to install Statistical Process Controls and apply Just-In-Time productivity methods, Lacks' teamwork has achieved a number one SPEAR rating (the highest "Quality" rating a supplier can receive—awarded to less than one percent of suppliers) from General Motors, a major customer. The award signifies Lacks' commitment to excellence in production and engineering, and employee involvement in workmanship and training.

From a network of nine plants around the Grand Rapids metropolitan area, as well as a 20,000-square-foot headquarters building, the 900 dedicated people of Lacks Industries apply their skills to reaction injection molding of urethane resins, selectively plating ABS plastic surfaces, painting intricate surfaces, and processing raw resin into complicated configurations. With four plants in Kentwood, two in Cascade Township, and one each in Wyoming, Grand Rapids, and Saranac, including three plants operated by Plastic Plate, the organization has placed roots deep within this West Michigan community. Because the Lacks family believes in the people of this area, Lacks Industries' entire growth has been confined to the local region. And this is where the company expects to continue to grow.

The headquarters building in Cascade Township acts as a nerve center for a pattern of nine specialized plants.

CONSUMERS POWER COMPANY

The story of Consumers Power Company can be summed up in a phrase—Powering Michigan's Progress. The utility, the nation's fourth-largest combination electric and gas utility, celebrated its 100th anniversary in December 1986.

Consumers Power Company has grown with the state. Conversely, the state's growth has been, and continues to be, dependent on the electricity and natural gas supplied by the utility. Over the past 100 years it has been this energy that powered Michigan's industry, made agriculture one of the state's top three revenue-producing enterprises, and kept pace with the energy demands of a constantly increasing population.

Consumers Power serves six million of the Lower Peninsula's nine million residents in all counties but Berrien. Named by *Forbes* magazine in January 1987 as the most improved utility in the country, Consumers Power is on the comeback trail after severe financial difficulties in the early 1980s caused by its inability to complete a nuclear power plant in Midland, Michigan.

The firm has completely reorganized its corporate structure, installed a new management team, and undertaken an aggressive campaign to contain operating costs. At the start of its second century CPCo has, according to company officials, "hit the ground running." Plans to convert the Midland plant to the nation's largest natural gas combined-cycle cogeneration plant, in partnership with Dow Chemical Company of Midland and others, are under way, and the firm has in place the strategy to meet projected energy demands over the next two decades.

CPCo's history parallels the state's history during the past 100 years, but the prologue is a part of the Grand Rapids story. In 1880 local industrialist William T. Powers founded the Grand Rapids Electric Light and Power Company. Fulfilling a contract to install electric lighting in the downtown business district, Powers mounted carbon arc lights on 100- and 200-foot-tall steel towers at strategic street corners. The lights lit up the sky, the treetops, and the rooftops, but left areas below swathed in darkness. Nevertheless, for the times, the lights were a success.

They were powered by a dynamo installed at Powers' sawmill at the lower end of the West Side Canal, in what is today's Ah-Nab-Awen Bicentennial Park. That central power station was probably the world's first commercial hydroelectric generating plant, preceding by two years the generally accepted birth date of commercial electricity— 1882.

But the real father of electric power in Michigan was W.A. Foote, who must surely have heard of the Powers venture. An entrepreneur and former miller from Adrian, Foote hitched his fortunes and his future to the new marvel, electricity. In 1886 he founded the Jackson Electric Light

Electric line construction and maintenance are prime responsibilities for linemen such as Ardell Carson (left) and John Bekker.

The company's James H. Campbell Complex, located west of Grand Rapids on Lake Michigan, can supply the electric needs of a community of about one million people.

Works, the company that through mergers and acquisitions over many years became Consumers Power Company. Among his acquisitions was Powers' Grand Rapids Electric Light and Power Company.

If energy is Consumers Power's business, service is its mission. Say CPCo officials, "Service is the only thing we have to give, and so it is the people on the line—the people who are in direct contact with the public, on a day-to-day basis—who are Consumers Power in the public mind. It is a credit to them that our difficulties of the past few years have not created a negative attitude about the company among our customers. In spite of severe budget restraints, our people still deliver service, whether it's restoring power after a storm, giving information about bills, or answering questions on the phone. Our people in the field are tremendous."

This concept of service does not encompass just customer service. CPCo is one of the foremost companies in the state in complying with federal environmental cleanup regulations. The utility has a close working relationship with the Michigan Department of Natural Resources (DNR), spending millions of dollars annually in achieving clean air and cleaner water at all of its facilities.

Consumers has always had a major role in providing recreation properties for the state. One example, announced in March 1987, was an erosion prevention project to protect the Manistee River embankment downstream of the company's Charles W. Tippy hydroelectric generating dam. The project called for installing more than 4,000 tons of heavy rock and constructing a pedestrian access to eventually stabilize the banks and prevent eroding riverbank sediment from covering downstream salmon and trout spawning grounds. It was the result of a two-and-one-half-year effort by the company, U.S. Forest Service, DNR, U.S. Department of Agriculture Soil Conservation Service,

Market Services representatives Steve Schouten (center) and Roger Cody share some economic development plans with Susan Roeder, Greater Grand Rapids Economic Area Team (GGREAT) executive director.

Jean McClure is part of a 47-person department that provides direct service to some 50,000 West Michigan customers each month.

and Steelhead Angler Society.

Education is another area in which the company shines. Since 1968 CPCo has offered its Educational Services Program (ESP) to state educators. Designed to help Michigan's elementary and high school students broaden their understanding of energy, ESP supplies teachers with thousands of curriculum aids annually—videotapes, booklets, posters, films, and multimedia kits, many of them award winners.

CPCo has an energy consulting service available to both commercial and residential customers to help them realize savings by using energy more wisely. The firm points out, too, that energy rates in Michigan remain competitive with the rest of the country, and that if rates had kept pace with inflation over the past 30 years, customers would be paying three times what they pay today.

The growth of electricity continues to accelerate, but Consumers Power Company will meet the requirements of its customers as it has for 100 years. Its future is pegged to Powering Michigan's Progress into the next century.

ADVANCE NEWSPAPERS

A one-of-a-kind West Michigan business venture has forged the largest weekly communications group in the state, and sights are set for expanding on the success of the media firm's newspaper and printing services.

Advance Newspapers, with more than two decades of growth and improvement in the market, is launching into a new era as a news and publishing organization of force statewide. The weekly newspaper chain of 11 editions serves the metropolitan areas of Grand Rapids and Kent and Ottawa counties. Through company tie-in with their adjacent publishing and printing firm, the owners of the *Advance* circulate news and advertising messages to more than 300,000 households.

A professional and full-service communications company has been formed from the joining of Advance Newspapers and the nearby Flashes Publishers, Inc., a printing and publications firm of Allegan and Kalamazoo counties. Of the 300,000 households contacted weekly with the products of this media force, more than 160,000 are receiving locally focused community newspapers that have built award-winning reputations in their towns. The other households receive shopping guides—increasingly with local news products, too—and plans call for continued expansion of the *Advance* and *Flashes* services in West Michigan communities.

A thrust of the Advance Newspapers' weekly communications business is shared-mail and insert business that marries the regular printed product with a myriad of pre-prints, coupons, and advertising messages that advertisers want to distribute in a timely and cost-effective way. Because the *Advance* and *Flashes* are such handy and inexpensive vehicles in which to deliver other printed messages, the joining and cooperative efforts of these two companies has

Printing facilities also are located in Jenison. The newspapers and commercial printing jobs roll off the presses and are shipped to readers and customers.

been a natural.

The purchase and reorganization of Advance Newspapers—which included a total redesign of the product, from broadsheet to the current tabloid-style newspaper—took place in the fall of 1986. The result of that total remake and retooling is a West Michigan business that ranks as one of the largest printers in the region, as the largest weekly mailer in the state, and as the largest weekly communica-

The Advance Newspapers building, located southwest of Grand Rapids, is headquarters for newspaper sales, editorial, and office staff.

tions group.

The owners of the *Advance*—Valley Media, Inc.—lead a management team that is young, enthusiastic, goal oriented, and ambitious. The president of both the *Advance* and *Flashes* is John P. Morgan, and the publisher is James A. Donnelly.

Both men come from strong publishing backgrounds. Morgan published and printed a large Central Michigan product in Alma, and Donnelly was publisher of one of the nation's leading weekly newspaper chains, in St. Louis, Missouri. Says Donnelly of plans for the two publishing companies, "We're creating a communications company that saturates southwest Michigan."

General manager Steven K. Haught said the Advance Newspapers were reorganized from the ground up when they were purchased, and the results are increased visibility for the company and its news product. He said that advertisers have responded with strong support for the new tabloids, which feature local news, opinion, columnists, features, and sports.

The newly introduced *Advance* reflects the progressive philosophy of the new management, and the papers emphasize local news of the communities in which each edition is circulated. Regular features such as gardening, food, arts and entertainment, and local events appear in each edition.

Advance senior editor Margaret DeRitter welcomes the new direction for the company. "We try to give people a sense of community, with emphasis on local news and sports. We get local names and faces, and try to do a consistent, top-notch job of reporting such local public affairs as the meetings of township boards, city councils, and boards of education. Our goal is to be a leader in each community."

That formula spells success for the company. Every newspaper editor understands that readers are most interested in people they know—friends, acquaintances, neighbors. Regional newspapers and broadcast media, committed to news of a larger geographical area, cannot devote the space or time to extensive neighborhood news coverage. And small retailers and service companies find it is often expensive and impractical to advertise regionally to markets they do not even serve. As community newspapers, however, the *Advance* can meet the needs of those local readers and advertisers.

Mark Lewison, managing editor of the *Advance*, is looking forward to the increasingly pivotal role the *Advance* will play in West Michigan publishing. "We're committed to this area's communities, and we're looking at a period of tremendous growth for the company."

The newspapers are only part of the story of Valley Me-

Editors help design and lay out the *Advance* weekly newspapers.

Hot off the press, the *Advance* is stacked on pallets to be transferred to circulation.

dia. The other major component is Jenison Printing Company, which also is in a period of growth. *Advance* editions are printed at the Jenison printing plant, in modern facilities located near the news building. The plant, managed by Kenneth Walski, provides a full-service printing house, with its own typesetting, layout and design, camera, plate-making, and bindery departments. It has six printing presses, including web presses—on which the newspapers are printed—and four-color capability.

Publisher Donnelly says the West Michigan market is more than ready for a media firm such as Advance Newspapers is forging. "We are developing high-quality, dynamic alternatives to the area's daily papers and other media, and we are creating high-profile publications that have real value and impact in their communities."

PINE REST CHRISTIAN HOSPITAL

Pine Rest Christian Hospital has completed more than 77 years of dedication to an unchanging ideal—providing Christian-oriented mental health services and care.

The concept took tangible form in 1910 with the purchase of the 173-acre Cutler farm, south of Grand Rapids. A small group of Reformed pastors and laypersons had formed an association to establish a Christian treatment center for the mentally ill. The group wanted an alternative to existing mental health systems, which provided only minimal and, in their view, substandard care. The group, calling itself the Association for the Mentally Ill in North America, had the desire and the vision to treat the mentally ill as human beings, created in God's image. The Cutler family farmhouse became the Christian Psychopathic Hospital, and the first patient was accepted in 1911.

Today's Pine Rest includes on its 340-acre campus at Cutlerville a 264-bed inpatient facility, a large outpatient center, buildings, and more than 600 employees. The hospital is in the midst of a multimillion-dollar modernization program. One of the largest private psychiatric hospitals in the United States, Pine Rest is still dedicated to providing quality, Christian mental health care.

Though the facility is Christian oriented in its philosophy, its approach to patient care is ecumenical. Pine Rest

Providing psychiatric services to children and adolescents is Pine Rest's largest inpatient program.

Pine Rest provides a caring and attractive environment for those who seek help.

believes in the sanctity of life, the need to improve the quality of life, and a holistic approach that includes spiritual as well as the physical support needed in mental health care. All services are provided in an environment in which every person who seeks help can grow and develop to the maximum of his or her potential, and the hospital accepts patients without regard to race, color, creed, or national origin.

This modern mental health care organization offers many services within three major areas of activity—inpatient service, outpatient counseling, and programs on education and prevention.

The inpatient facility is licensed for 264 beds, the largest inpatient facility of its kind in Michigan. More than half of the hospital's beds are occupied by children and adolescents. The facility is one of few area psychiatric hospitals offering long-term inpatient psychiatric care to children and adolescents. But, say hospital officials, Pine Rest cannot begin to keep up with the demand for children's services. With some 1,800 requests a year, Pine Rest does well to accommodate 600 children. Two-thirds of the requests must be referred elsewhere.

Another very successful program recently instituted at Pine Rest is partial hospitalization. Many patients do not need round-the-clock psychiatric care. For such people, Pine Rest provides a complete range of services on a daytime basis. The patients spend the day at the hospital and go home at night.

Historically Pine Rest has been an inpatient facility, but the hospital has been moving away from that concept as it establishes itself as a resource for the early intervention of mental and emotional problems ocurring in all age groups. An area of rapid growth for the facility over the past five years has been its satellite clinic system for outpatient counseling. Explains Charles Fridsma, director of community relations and development, "We are putting emphasis on accessibility and responding to needs where they exist out in the community, rather than requiring people to come to our main campus." The clinics, he adds, have been very successful in helping the hospital broaden its range of services and effectiveness.

Pine Rest's third major program, education and prevention, has several facets. Its objective is to offer the community programs that teach people how to cope with today's stresses—to recognize potential problems and prevent small problems from becoming big problems that need extensive counseling or hospitalization.

Pine Rest is one of the largest and most modern private mental health care facilities in the nation.

Through the speakers' bureau, Pine Rest professionals talk to area groups and organizations on topics as diverse as singles and divorce, personal growth and development, stress management, parenting, substance abuse, children of divorce, adolescence, and aging. Classes on such topics as creative family leisure, assertiveness training, managing marital differences, and weight control are held on the Pine Rest campus, and the Pine Rest Players offer dramatic presentations and role playing on a variety of subjects, including interpersonal communication skills.

The early years of the hospital were devoted to custodial care, because that was the only known method of caring for the mentally ill. As medical technology and knowledge have developed in the treatment of the mentally ill, so has Pine Rest developed. The hospital has always been in the forefront in mental health treatment.

Outpatient programs, early intervention, partial hospitalization, and many other services within Pine Rest's broad range of programs, are innovative, creative, and on the leading edge of treating mental disorders. The goal of the organization, says Fridsma, is to develop Pine Rest into a resource for "healthful living." Says Fridsma, "By the year 2000 we'd like Pine Rest to be thought of as a resource for all people—not just those who are experiencing conflict. We want to work with healthy families to ensure West Michigan residents of a richer, fuller life."

Pine Rest's modernization program will make the hospital one of the foremost such facilities in the world, but its mission to provide quality care for the mentally ill has not changed from the days of its founders. The Pine Rest difference is its deep commitment to Christian service.

REDCO MANUFACTURING DIVISION L.H.L. INCORPORATED

Tables for the contract and restaurant furniture industries have become a real success story for Redco Manufacturing Division, L.H.L. Incorporated, of Grand Rapids, which specializes in custom-made, top-of-the-line products for a selective market.

Redco manufactures tabletops, bases, and a variety of tables, including panel end, parsons, cube, and cylinder styles. The company's tabletops and bases are functional, versatile designs that can be adapted to any decor, design, or space requirements.

Working in fine woods, aluminum, stainless steel, laminates, and veneers, the firm turns out tabletops of all shapes and sizes along with chrome, wood, and bronze bases in cube, cylinder, and pedestal styles. Designs and finishes range from traditional to modern. Warm wood finishes in oak and mahogany are featured in plain, inlaid, and butcher block patterns. Colors run the spectrum from deep and vibrant greens and blues to muted and sophisticated pastels. Because of the vast array of choices, design possibilities are virtually endless.

Redco's roots reach back more than 40 years. In 1947 William N. "Red" Wilburn and his father, both veterans of the furniture industry and experienced in the installation of fixtures for restaurant supply houses, decided to establish their own business. With a $500 bankroll and one employee,

the pair started the Wilburn Company to manufacture furniture, bars, and backbars for the restaurant trade. In 1968, three years after the Wilburn Company was sold, Red and a member of the next Wilburn generation, his son Bill, founded Redco to serve the contract furniture market. Although the new company did about $800,000 in sales that first year, the Wilburns sold it a year later.

By the time father and son repurchased the business in 1979, sales had dwindled to about $500,000 a year, and times were rough. But Steelcase, Lumberman's, Inc., Victor S. Barnes, and other supportive suppliers were instrumental in keeping the company afloat. Today, with the Wilburns still at the helm—Red as chairman of the board and Bill as president and chief executive officer—Redco sales are close to six million dollars per year, with a projected increase to $10 million over the next few years. Grown to 110 employees, the firm now occupies spacious quarters in the former Dexter Lock plant at 1601 Madison SE, where there is still plenty of room to grow.

Seeking to remain very aggressive in marketing its products, Redco directs its advertising to national trade magazines. Manufacturers' representatives handle Redco products in all 50 states and some foreign markets, selling components to other manufacturers and proprietary products to dealers, designers, and end users.

With expanding markets across the country and reliable suppliers in Grand Rapids, Redco is on the move.

TNT HOLLAND MOTOR EXPRESS

TNT Holland Motor Express has been in the business of transporting Michigan products since 1929. The company has grown and prospered for nearly six decades in an industry characterized by challenge and change.

Company officials knew the business would have to expand to successfully meet the challenges of deregulation. It set out to develop from a moderately sized regional carrier to a major central United States carrier. The strategy adopted by the company, one of steady, controlled growth, more than doubled its revenue. Today TNT Holland is one of the fastest growing and most profitable LTL (less-than-truckload) trucking firms in the United States.

TNT Holland was founded in Holland, Michigan, by John and Katherine Cooper. It remained in the family until it was purchased in 1984 by TNT Ltd., a worldwide transportation group headquartered in Sydney, Australia.

The affiliation with TNT has opened new markets and worldwide shipping capabilities. TNT Holland's direct service area is concentrated in 12 states in the central United States—Michigan, Illinois, Indiana, Iowa, Kentucky, Missouri, Ohio, Pennsylvania, Wisconsin, Tennessee, Arkansas, and Mississippi.

In embarking on its expansion plans, the company believed that the one area in which it must distinguish itself from its competition was in providing fast, dependable, efficient service. An LTL specialist, TNT Holland provides consistent next-day delivery on shipments under 500 miles and second-day service over 500 miles.

To maintain that level of service, freight movement is controlled through a central dispatch operation in Holland. It is a unique system that adjusts to the daily variables in freight flow, providing a flexibility that results in efficient, faster service to customers.

Contributing to TNT Holland's reputation for first-rate service is the company's outstanding record in safety and claim-free delivery. TNT Holland has won numerous safety awards, and has been a perennial winner of the American Trucking Association National Freight Claim Council's First Place Award for its outstanding claim prevention program. In addition, the carrier was rated as the number one LTL service carrier in the United States by the readers of *Distribution Magazine*.

TNT Holland's goal is to be the leading carrier in the central United States, providing the best service value to all its customers.

A TNT Holland Motor Express truck on Monroe Avenue in downtown Grand Rapids. The West Michigan firm is one of TNT North America's 22 freight transportation companies serving the United States and Canada by truck, train, jet plane, and ship. TNT Limited, headquartered in Australia, operates freight transportation systems in more than 100 countries.

A TNT Holland Motor Express truck at Steelcase Inc., one of the trucking firm's many Grand Rapids customers.

303

GEMINI CORPORATION

As a brash young upstart on the Grand Rapids media scene, the *Grand Rapids Business Journal* sprang up in a business news desert and made it an oasis. The *Business Journal* and its sister publication, *Grand Rapids Magazine,* are the properties of Gemini Publications, a division of Gemini Corporation.

The *Business Journal* was launched in 1983 as a monthly magazine-format publication during its initial phase. It was immediately hailed by West Michigan business readers as a welcome newcomer, and its success has prompted other area print media to beef up their business news coverage or launch their own business publications.

Nine months after its initial appearance, the *Business Journal's* management ran a readership survey to determine the publication's future. "The survey confirmed our belief," says John Zwarensteyn, president of Gemini Corporation and publisher of Gemini Publications, "that there was a definite need for the *Business Journal.* So, based on our study, we altered the format to a monthly newspaper tabloid. Our original intention was to take the *Business Journal* from a monthly to a semimonthly and eventually a weekly. But the results of a second survey, taken one year after the first one, were so positive we decided to bite the bullet, scrap the semimonthly interval, and go immediately to a weekly. It was risky, but so far it has proven a wise decision." The survey also determined that a magazine format was unsatisfactory to readers, and so the *Journal* became a weekly tabloid.

Grand Rapids has always been a town with a strong newspaper tradition, but, inexplicably, no local news organization in the four or five decades before the appearance of the *Business Journal* had put much emphasis on news about and for the Grand Rapids area business community. To be sure, there were weekly stock reports and occasional stories of mergers, acquisitions, demises and defections, labor disputes, and other such articles that made headlines and good lead stories on the 6 p.m. news. News briefs about personnel changes also made the news pages, but there was a real dearth of good solid reporting of the day-to-day events and the issues, personalities, and other information pertinent to the local business community. The *Business Journal* filled that void.

The *Grand Rapids Business Journal* and *Grand Rapids Magazine* are Gemini Publications' two major products.

The production management team inspects *Grand Rapids Business Journal* page proofs at Grandville Printing.

Gemini chief executive officer and publisher John Zwarensteyn reviews plans with members of the business and circulation staff.

The magazine was the first publishing venture of the original company, Gemini Communications, established in 1979 by Zwarensteyn and three partners.

After college and a stint in the Army, Zwarensteyn returned to Grand Rapids as vice-president of communications for the Grand Rapids Area Chamber of Commerce, and edited its monthly magazine, *Grand Rapids.* He worked at the chamber for seven years, and developed the magazine from a publication devoted strictly to chamber news and issues to a general interest magazine, but still directed primarily to chamber members. Zwarensteyn envisioned the publication as a magazine with a broad community appeal, and so in 1979 he and three partners formed Gemini Communications and bought the magazine from the chamber.

"From a publication with a 2,000 circulation, we have grown to 12,000 circulation, with a readership of over 100,000," says Zwarensteyn, "which makes us one of the larger city magazines in the country, based on readership per capita for the size of the market. Our goal is to double our circulation by 1990, which will make us one of the largest city magazines in the nation again, based on per capita for the market."

From the outset the magazine chose to be both entertaining and to deal with significant community issues. By presenting opposing views, the magazine has, on several occasions, been pitted against the city's major news publication, the *Grand Rapids Press.* The confrontations have demonstrated, says Zwarensteyn, the need in the city "for a second opinion." The magazine made its mark with a commemorative issue for the opening of the Gerald R. Ford Presidential Museum in September 1981. That issue established *Grand Rapids Magazine* as the premier regional magazine, and it has continued to build on that image. A more recent issue, a newsstand sellout, dealt with AIDS, a subject that needed exploration from various local angles.

Perhaps the magazine's most popular regular feature is its restaurant reviews and annual dining guide. Both the columns and the guide present critical but fair appraisals of area restaurants written by informed columnists. The feature has on occasion angered local restaurateurs, but its honesty has earned the magazine the respect of diners and restaurateurs alike. And area restaurants covet the magazine's annual dining awards.

Like *Grand Rapids Magazine,* the *Business Journal* has tackled controversial issues, and has broken new ground in West Michigan journalistic circles. For the size of the market served, says Zwarensteyn, neither publication should exist, but because they strive to be fair and objective, they have developed loyal readerships and continue to increase their circulations and advertising revenues. "The staffs of our publications are ambitious, aggressive people determined to give the area first-rate publications that benefit the community as well as provide entertainment and information," notes Zwarensteyn.

In 1983 Zwarensteyn bought out his partners in Gemini

A *Grand Rapids Magazine* sales consultant discusses an ad layout with a client.

Communications and formed Gemini Corporation, a company comprised of three divisions.

Gemini Corporation is a multiservice organization devoted to publishing, public relations, media and project development, graphics, advertising, and consulting.

Gemini Publications publishes the *Grand Rapids Business Journal, Grand Rapids Magazine,* and special publications, *Guest Book, Lifestyles Guide,* and *Newcomers Guide.*

The third division, Gemini Ventures, an investment arm, is oriented toward small to medium-size investments and joint ventures, including real estate.

Each of the divisions, and the corporations as a whole, have experienced substantial growth since inception. "It is an exciting time for us," says Zwarensteyn. "Grand Rapids is growing into a major financial and business center, and as the area grows, we grow. It certainly is the right place for us."

An array of printed matter produced by Gemini Publications, one of Gemini Corporation's three divisions.

SQUARE REAL ESTATE, INC.

Square Real Estate, Inc., was founded in 1939 by R.R. Steed and today is one of the largest independent full-service real estate companies in western Michigan. Currently the Steed family's third generation is operating the company with Jim and John Steed, grandsons of the founder, at the helm.

The growth of the firm over the years from a small residential office of 250 square feet to the current corporate office of more than 6,000 square feet in impressive Square Centre has been due to the commitment of the family to the community and its real estate needs.

Square Real Estate has been active in more than 15 residential subdivisions over the years, in addition to several industrial and commercial parks in the Metro Grand Rapids area. Development plans for 1987 include two new residential subdivisions, a 120-acre industrial subdivision, and a 30-acre commercial subdivision.

Square Real Estate is a full-service real estate company that has distinct divisions, including Residential, Commercial/Industrial, Property Management, Construction, Architectural, Syndication, and Development.

The company has had considerable impact in the development of many areas of the city including recent downtown developments. Square has recently rehabilitated the downtown riverfront Forslund building, making the upper five stories into 20 luxurious condominiums.

Square Centre, a 33,000-square-foot downtown office retail center, was developed and owned by Square shortly after it leased the adjoining 110,000-square-foot Mutual Home (PrimeBank) building. These buildings were the key to the rapidly expanding skywalks now connecting several downtown projects.

Square Real Estate is currently expanding its Residential Division by opening an office on 44th Street in Kentwood, with plans for additional branch offices in other areas of the city.

Square's commitment to Grand Rapids is shown by its willingness to invest in many office, retail, industrial, and residential projects. Its professional staff of real estate marketing salespeople, architects, accountants, and attorneys is available to assist in the marketing, acquiring, and leasing of real estate in western Michigan.

Recently the firm undertook a two-year strategic planning program that provides Square Real Estate, Inc., with a blueprint for its future. The company has positioned itself for the growth and development that is projected for the West Michigan area during the next 20 years.

Square Centre, home of Square Real Estate, at 169 Monroe Avenue NW.

The homes of Heritage Hill, a 365-acre residential neighborhood adjacent to downtown, were built in the late eighteenth and nineteenth centuries by some of the city's wealthiest and prominent citizens. Rescued from proposed demolition in 1968 by the efforts of the newly formed Heritage Hill Association, the landmark neighborhood was placed on the National Register of Historic Places on March 11, 1971. Photo by J. Phillip Haven

PART

3

Energizing Community Progress

10
For the General Welfare

The true measure of any community, so it's been said, is the degree to which it cares for its unfortunates. By that yardstick, Grand Rapids stands tall. From the time of the city's first official appropriation of funds for the relief of the poor—$200 by Kent Township in 1838—Grand Rapids has taken care of its own. And today's vast network of human services agencies, volunteer groups, charitable organizations, medical facilities, and community foundations testifies convincingly to the longstanding efforts of a concerned citizenry and a compassionate government working to help those unable to help themselves.

The legacy of caring for others reaches back a century and a half to the period of hard times ushered in by the Panic of 1837. Beleaguered by the virtual financial collapse that had followed several heady years of wild land speculation in the small settlement on the banks of the Grand, the township government nevertheless managed to allocate $200 in 1838 for relief of the destitute and to come up with an additional $300 the following year. Some of the city's poor later found a haven of sorts in the county poorhouse on 32nd Street, which opened its doors in 1855 and, like most other institutions of its kind at the time, housed not only the indigent but the syphilitic, the elderly, the insane, and the mentally impaired.

The limited sums appropriated by government to aid the needy have seldom stretched far enough, and

The moon rising over Butterworth Hospital provides a lovely backdrop for this important medical institution. Photo by William Hebert

virtually from the beginning, members of the community have accepted much of the responsibility of caring for their fellows. As early as 1846 the need to provide for those who were poor, sick, and infirm led a group of local women to form the Female Union Charitable Association. This organization's board of managers also ran the Grand Rapids Orphan Asylum Association, which concentrated its efforts on the needs of children until the care of soldiers took precedence during the Civil War years. Later, the association shifted gears and, after incorporating in 1873 as the Union Benevolent Association (UBA), founded a home for the aged, infirm, sick, and needy.

Left: John Blodgett, who made his fortune in the lumber business, was a well-known community benefactor. Courtesy, Grand Rapids Public Library

Below: The Union Benevolent Association Hospital opened on February 23, 1886, with the backing of public funds. Courtesy, Grand Rapids Public Library

In those days, little distinction existed between the care extended to the infirm and that afforded to those who were ill. Medical science, still in its relative infancy, prescribed remedies—not all of them particularly efficacious—for some ailments; doctors also had the skill and training to set fractures, remove bullets, suture wounds, deliver babies, and extract teeth. But the treatment of disease was by and large a matter of letting nature take its course. Ambulatory patients generally sought treatment at the doctor's office, where fees in the 1850s ranged from twenty-five cents for a tooth extraction to twenty-five dollars for the amputation of an arm or a leg. Bedridden patients were seen and treated—even operated on—at home, and home was where they recovered, or died. Those individuals who had neither homes nor families to tend to their needs were relegated to the custody and care of such charitable institutions as the Union Benevolent Association home on Bostwick and Lyon.

By the 1880s, in the face of a rapidly growing population and advances in medicine which were beginning to increase the effectiveness of hospital care, the UBA home, more of a rest home than a hospital, was proving inadequate. Turning to the community in 1882 for public subscriptions and private donations, the UBA built a larger facility at Lyon and College. Opened in 1886, along with a separate school for nurses, the Union Benevolent Home and Hospital was converted nine years later to strictly hospital use. In 1916, thanks to a generous donation from John W. Blodgett, UBA president for more than twenty-five years, a new hospital was completed on Plymouth and Wealthy and renamed the Blodgett Memorial Hospital in honor of its benefactor's mother. Another handsome contribution by Blodgett in 1937 erased the hospital's $200,000 debt.

The city's other general hospitals followed a similar pattern in their development. Initially established by volunteers, these institutions owe much of their growth to the generosity of individual benefactors, the willingness of the community at large to reach into its own collective pocket for additional funding, and a continuing spirit of volunteerism among the many citizens who choose to devote their time and energies to fund raising, hospital guild activities, and other good works in support of these institutions.

Like Blodgett Hospital, Butterworth Hospital, the second oldest and today the largest of the city's four acute-care hospitals, had its origins as a home for the aged and indigent. Organized in 1872 by members of St. Mark's Episcopal Church, it was originally known as the St. Mark's Home. Four years later the home moved to larger quarters and incorporated as the St. Mark's Home and Hospital. Richard Butterworth bequeathed land at the corner of Bostwick and Michigan for a new St. Mark's Hospital, which was opened in 1890 and renamed Butterworth Hospital in 1894 when, at the church's request, it became a secular institution. In 1922, after a decade of generous personal contributions, Butterworth's grandson, Edward Lowe, and Lowe's wife, Susan, donated the land on which Butterworth stands today along with half a million dollars toward the construction of a new hospital. A city-wide fund drive raised another half-million dollars, and when the new hospital was completed in 1925, the original building was converted to a dormitory for the Butterworth Hospital School of Nursing, which had been established in 1890.

Stunning advances in medicine and surgery, coupled with the proliferation of private and federally funded hospital insurance plans during the Great Depression and World War II, created a significant need for more hospital beds and the latest in expensive, life-saving technology. In response to that need, citywide hospital building fund drives were launched in 1949 and 1952, and Grand Rapids citizens gave generously, contributing more than six million dollars to be shared by Butterworth, Blodgett, and St. Mary's hospitals.

Today owned and operated by the Sisters of Mercy Health Care Corporation, one of the country's leading nonprofit, multi-hospital systems, St. Mary's was established in 1893 when Mrs. Mary McNamara made a gift of her Lafayette Street home to the Sisters of Mercy. The facility was subsequently modernized and enlarged with a three-story addition built in 1898 and another expansion two years later. By 1911, a new five-story hospital was completed. Need sparked additional growth, and in 1914 a public subscription drive raised funds for a seven-story addition that was ready for occupancy in 1926.

Right: After nearly twenty years of struggling in a remodeled and expanded home, St. Mary's opened this five-story, sixty-five-bed hospital building in 1911. Courtesy, Grand Rapids Public Library

Facing page: Today, Blodgett Memorial Hospital is a fully accredited, nonprofit, 410-bed teaching hospital that offers comprehensive in-patient and out-patient medical and surgical care. Photo by William Hebert

Right: Grand Rapids hospitals have been quick to adopt the latest advances in medical technology. Here, members of the Butterworth Hospital staff prepare a patient for radiation therapy during the 1960s. Courtesy, Grand Rapids Public Library

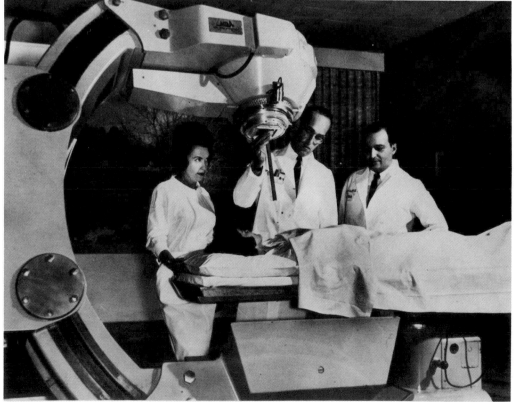

Donations from the community and from its staff physicians were likewise instrumental in the growth and development of Grand Rapids Osteopathic (now Metropolitan) Hospital. The fourth of the city's acute-care hospitals, Metropolitan started out in 1942 in a private home on Lake Drive and moved to its present Boston Street site thirteen years later.

Keeping up with major health-care developments over the past three decades has involved Grand Rapids' acute-care hospitals in a continuous cycle of improvement and growth. All four institutions have carried out major expansion projects in the 1970s and 1980s, increasing their combined capacity to more than 1,500 beds, and all are widely known for the quality of care they provide. Not only do the four hospitals serve as teaching hospitals for interns and residents, but they are all members of the Grand Rapids Medical Education Center (GRAMEC), a community-based organization founded in 1971 to provide clinical training for medical students attending the University of Michigan and Michigan State University.

Although each of the four institutions is a general-care hospital, the need to avoid duplication of services has brought about a degree of specialization. Blodgett Hospital, the state-designated emergency center, also houses the Blodgett Cardiac Rehab Unit, the West Michigan Burn Unit, and the Blodgett Regional Poison Center, which handles more than 20,000 calls and averts countless tragedies every year. St. Mary's, as the region's designated kidney treatment center, offers dialysis, hemodialysis, transplants, and organ procurements, and is also the site of the area's Breast Disease Detection and Education Center. Butterworth Hospital is home to one of West Michigan's two neonatal intensive care units. Established in 1971 with funds donated by Gerber Baby Foods, the unit serves tiny patients referred from eleven counties and twenty-two hospitals. A regional referral center for trauma victims, high-risk obstetrical cases, and the replantation of severed limbs, Butterworth boasts one of West Michigan's largest and best equipped oncology and radiology departments. Besides being one of the Midwest's major cardiac care centers, with more than 500 open-heart surgeries performed annually, Butterworth is now the site of the city's lithotripter (kidney stone crusher). Metropolitan Hospital, the smallest and newest of the city's acute-care hospitals, was the first to perform arthroscopic knee surgery, as well as the first to introduce a birthing room, and is the only area hospital to offer a ventilator dependency unit, the first of its kind in the state. Metropolitan is also the area pioneer in streptokinase therapy for coronary artery disease and in urological laser surgery.

Not only is the quality of medical care exceptionally high in Grand Rapids, but the cost of care is relatively low. A recent study by the Hospital Council of West Michigan indicates that area residents spend $230 less per person per year in hospital costs than the rest of the country, partly because they are not inclined to overuse hospital facilities. West Michigan, in fact, is the area of lowest hospital use in the state and one of the lowest in the nation.

According to statistics compiled by the West Michigan Health Systems Agency (WMHSA), a regional review organization serving twelve West Michigan counties, area patient admission rates are about 18 percent below the national average, and average hospital stays are two-thirds the national average. Hospital admission costs, moreover, are $1,000 less per patient than in the southeastern part of the state.

Rising hospital costs nevertheless remain a concern to area hospitals and to WMHSA. In operation since 1948, this voluntary, community-based, health care-planning organization is deeply involved in medical cost-containment efforts. As it analyzes community health needs and decides how those needs can best be met, WMHSA works to assure that West Michigan residents will continue to enjoy the same high-quality, lowest-possible-cost health care in the future that they are accustomed to today.

Local hospitals are also doing their part to respond to the pressing issues of today's health-care scene. As new methods of delivering health care continue to present consumers with a widening array of choices,

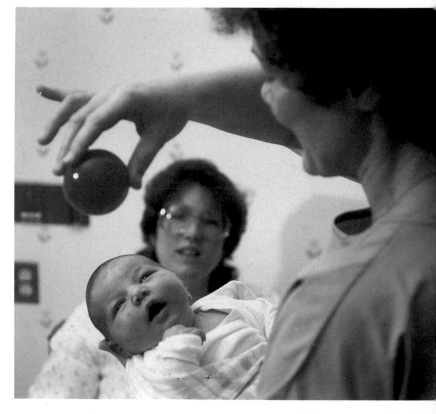

Right and facing page: **Excellent hospitals providing diverse, top-quality care have made Grand Rapids a regional medical center. Courtesy, Blodgett Memorial Medical Center**

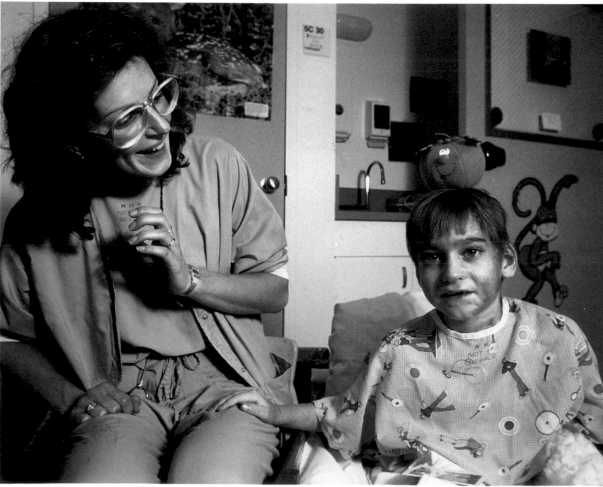

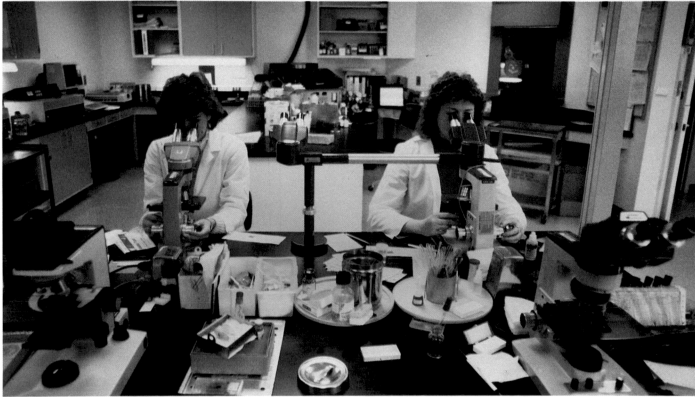

including privately operated HMOs and walk-in emergency clinics, hospital health-care providers are becoming more competitive in placing their services before the public and the many area businesses that offer their employees health-care benefit coverage plans. Blodgett, St. Mary's, and Metropolitan hospitals all market multi-faceted wellness programs aimed at disease prevention and health maintenance. Blodgett and St. Mary's have combined forces to form a joint HMO, and Butterworth and Metropolitan have done likewise.

All of the area hospitals are acknowledging in some way the trend toward increased outpatient services. St. Mary's has significantly expanded its Emergency Care Center, while Butterworth Hospital has invested $6.5 million in a major project to enlarge laboratory and pharmaceutical services and increase the number of outpatient surgical rooms. Butterworth is

also in the preliminary stages of another $6 million expansion that will focus on obstetrical, neonatal, and pediatric care.

Grand Rapids' position as a major medical center for West Michigan rests not only on the wealth of services provided by its acute-care hospitals, but also on its outstanding Emergency Medical Services program and on the special-care facilities which address a variety of other health needs. Ferguson (formerly Ferguson-Droste-Ferguson) Hospital, founded in 1929, has become world-famous for colon and rectal

Below: **Founded in 1908, the Santa Claus Girls, shown here with 1927 world heavyweight champion Gene Tunney, have been making certain ever since that no local child is ever without a gift on Christmas Day. Courtesy, Grand Rapids Public Library**

Facing page: **Financed by a highly successful Sunshine Bond drive that raised $600,000, Sunshine Hospital, the nation's first municipally owned tuberculosis sanitarium, opened its doors in 1923. Courtesy, Grand Rapids Public Library**

surgery and treatment, and is in the process of constructing a $2.5 million clinic and medical office building to expand its services. Mary Free Bed and Rehabilitation Center enjoys a similar international reputation for its rehabilitative work with stroke and accident victims and others who are physically impaired.

Like Blodgett Hospital, Mary Free Bed is an outgrowth of the Union Benevolent Association. In 1891 the UBA's hospital board established a committee to endow a free bed supported by contributions from those who had friends or relatives named Mary. Out of that committee's endeavors came the Mary Free Bed Guild, which turned over a substantial free-bed endowment to Blodgett Hospital in 1918 and then shifted its attention to the needs of crippled children. Beginning with the establishment in 1920 of the first

Crippled Children's Clinic in West Michigan, the guild has continually expanded its scope, reaching out to children and adults with physical problems and disabilities of all kinds.

Outstanding mental health facilities represent another component of the city's reputation as a first-rate medical center. Two psychiatric hospitals—Forest Hills and Pine Rest—offer a broad range of services to area residents. Pine Rest, financed and operated by the Christian Reformed Church and the Reformed Church of America, is the largest church-affiliated psychiatric hospital in America. Pine Rest also operates the Hope Rehabilitation Center for the developmentally disabled.

Kent Oaks, originally a city-owned institution, was opened in 1908 in response to the need to house mentally disturbed individuals somewhere other than

in the jail. Taken over by Kent County in 1918, the facility, the only such county-supported institution in the state, was replaced in 1963 after Kent County voters approved a special millage for a new and more modern structure. At one time simply a way station for those awaiting admission to state facilities, Kent Oaks today provides short-term intensive care and outpatient treatment to those in need.

Supplementing the care of the psychiatric hospitals is Kent Community Mental Health, a nonprofit agency which refers developmentally and emotionally disabled children, youth, and adults to appropriate mental health and human services agencies. A leader in community-based mental health care, Kent Community Health contracts with more than twenty local human services agencies for direct service to some

7,000 clients a year. Grand Rapids also has a full complement of support and self-help groups whose staffs and volunteers help others deal with a broad spectrum of problems, ranging from alcohol abuse and eating disorders to learning disabilities, coping with cancer, and spouse abuse.

The volunteer spirit which glows so brightly today was kindled in the last century by community leaders, church groups, women's clubs, civic groups, and fraternal organizations eager to address the multitude of problems that any growing city of that time inevitably faced. Charitable causes abounded, and citizens worked hard to ease the plight of orphaned and neglected children, reduce infant and maternal mortality rates, prevent blindness, build and finance the YMCA and the YWCA, offer free legal aid, collect

Facing page: **The United Fund campaign of 1968 raised a total of more than two million dollars. Courtesy, United Way of Kent County**

Above: **Linda Dykehouse, Miss United Fund of 1969, lights the torch on Monroe Avenue, downtown. Courtesy, United Way of Kent County**

effectively to the broadening array of community needs. In 1917, heeding the call of the Grand Rapids Association of Commerce (the Chamber's predecessor) for a "more systematic method of collection of funds; increased financial support for altruistic undertakings; greater efficiency and higher standards in welfare work with better service to the poor, [and], above all, planning for the welfare of the community as a whole," nine charitable groups formed a Federation of Social Agencies. Expanded to twenty agencies and reorganized in 1921 as the Grand Rapids Welfare Union, this umbrella organization, which became the Grand Rapids Community Chest in 1931, served as a clearinghouse for welfare information, studied the problems of charity and philanthropy, and raised funds—$388,110 in 1926 alone—through the efforts of its own dedicated volunteers, to support its member agencies. While the Grand Rapids Community Chest struggled to meet its annual fund-raising goals during the Depression, the Grand Rapids Council of Social Agencies, later called the Federation of Community Organizations and Services, was formed in 1938 to undertake community social welfare planning. In 1959 the two groups combined forces to become United Community Services, which in turn became United Community Fund, the forerunner of today's United Way.

Still relying on dedicated volunteers to raise funds through the generosity of the community at large, United Way currently funds more than 200 programs through sixty-four human services agencies. In addition to overseeing fund-raising activities, United Way's paid staff assesses total community needs, monitors services to reduce and prevent unnecessary duplication, conducts research, promotes and trains volunteer leaders, and develops and implements programs to meet changing community needs. United Way's First Call for Help, for example, provides troubled callers with initial assistance in seeking the right social service agency or support group. More than 450 organizations are listed with the program, and in the first six months of 1986, First Call for Help received 9,139 calls in behalf of 21,631 individuals.

The largest percentage of funds contributed to the annual United Way campaign comes from the

funds for the poor, provide shelter for the destitute, and raise money to combat such nationwide health problems as tuberculosis. In fact, the Grand Rapids Anti-Tuberculosis Society, established in 1905, was the first such organization of its kind in the state. The society's highly successful "Sunshine Bond" fund drive financed construction of Sunshine Hospital, which opened its doors in 1923 as the first municipally owned tuberculosis sanitarium in the nation. Thirty years later, with tuberculosis on the wane, the facility was deeded to Kent County and converted into Kent Community Hospital for the care of patients with chronic diseases.

With so many groups devoting their energies to so many causes, it became evident to community leaders early in the twentieth century that a greater measure of coordination was called for in order to respond

workplace, primarily from the workers themselves, and the rest is contributed by corporations and foundations. In 1985, more than 10,000 volunteers were responsible for collecting a record-breaking $7.2 million, a 14 percent increase over the previous year's contributions. Although the total fell short of United Way's $7.4 million goal, it earned Kent County ninth place among eighty-four agencies nationwide that raise more than four million dollars a year.

In 1986 United Way officials set a goal of $8.6 million, a 19.4 percent increase over 1985. By the time the fund drive ended, United Way of Kent County was congratulating the community for another record-breaking year—with pledges of $8.7 million representing a 20.5 percent increase over 1985. Not only was that increase the largest in the state, but it moved Kent County into first place nationwide among those agencies that collect more than four million dollars annually. United Way of Kent County also boasted the highest percentage increase in new pledges of any United Way fund drive in 1986.

The credit for the record-breaking effort belongs, said the campaign chairman, to the community. "This is not United Way's victory, this is a community victory. This is one more example of how we are 'the right place' and a community on the move with a commitment to excellence."

Because of that commitment, worthy causes such as United Way have traditionally found the Grand Rapids business community exceedingly generous with contributions of money, volunteer hours, and in-kind services. So, too, have charitable organizations been able to turn for funding to organizations such as the Grand Rapids Foundation. Established in 1923 through the auspices of the Association of Commerce, this foundation guards a perpetual trust whose funds have been donated in amounts large and small by members of the community. Using the income generated by the trust, the foundation helps support local nonprofit institutions. Three years after the foundation was organized, community historian William Etten wrote, "There is no doubt that within a short time this community trust will grow to large proportions and in future days will be of exceptional benefit to the people of this city." How correct he was. Since

its first grants were awarded in 1931, the Grand Rapids Foundation has distributed more than eighteen million dollars toward the betterment of the community.

The annals of charity in Grand Rapids testify to a history of cooperation between the private sector and the public sector. The early responsibility for providing care to the poor rested largely in private hands. But as the city's population grew and its needs increased, government, of necessity, began assuming a larger role; in 1916 a new city charter consolidated various relief efforts into a city department of welfare which remained in operation until the county and the state assumed responsibility.

In 1956 the County Welfare Department merged with the State Bureau of Social Aid to form the Kent County Department of Social Services (DSS), which administers a variety of welfare programs, including Aid to Dependent Children, General Assistance, Medicaid, Food Stamps, and Emergency Assistance. Over 50,000 county residents a year receive money or services at a cost of approximately $124 million, with the largest share going for medical services and nursing home care. In 1984-85, an improved economy and better employment picture lowered total welfare expenditures by more than two million dollars.

The DSS also offers a wide range of community social service programs including protective services for children; Child Haven, a temporary shelter for abused and neglected youngsters; foster care, day care, and adoption services; job training and placement for the unemployed; home help services for the handicapped and the elderly; and volunteer services of all kinds. In 1985 the department was honored nationally for its Teen Mother program, operated in conjunction with the Salvation Army.

Like public welfare and child welfare, public health has become a province of the public sector. Among the local government's earliest attempts to protect the health of its citizenry was the establishment in 1845 of a pesthouse outside village limits in which to quarantine smallpox victims. Later, city public health officials concentrated their efforts on better sewage control and safe drinking water to eliminate typhoid fever, higher milk standards to reduce the risk of tuberculosis, and the institution of a school nurse program to promote children's health. Concern over public health has placed Grand Rapids in the vanguard on more than one occasion. In 1928 Grand Rapids was the only U.S. city with a population of more than 5,000 that had no diphtheria deaths, and it was also the first city in the nation to fluoridate its drinking water.

Today's public health standards are the responsibility of the Kent County Health Department, which oversees a host of programs ranging from rabies control and the inspection of public facilities to health counseling and education, school vision, hearing, and scoliosis screening, family health services, and communicable disease clinics. The Kent County Health

Department is also the substance abuse coordinating agency for Kent, Ionia, Montcalm, and Newaygo counties.

Just as it was in its earliest days, Grand Rapids today is a city characterized by its concern for others. For over a century, local government and private citizens have worked hand-in-hand to provide generously for those less fortunate than themselves.

During the Great Depression the city welfare department operated a repair shop where unemployed men found work fixing furniture, baby carriages, and other items. Courtesy, Grand Rapids Public Library

11
Keeping in Touch

The art of communication, near the close of the twentieth century, has become an infinitely sophisticated pursuit, fueled by a technology that produces new wonders by the minute. But in the mid-nineteenth century, communication was confined primarily to discourse either by printed or written word, or by word of mouth.

The first signs of permanency in a pioneer settlement—land cleared for crops, cabins raised, corner posts driven, and commercial and public buildings erected—nearly always sparked among the citizenry of this newly developing country a yearning for a newspaper.

The first newspaper in Grand Rapids appeared a mere four years after the initial influx of settlers from the East. Before long there was not one paper but two, and by the 1860s there were a dozen or more weeklies, journals, and special-interest publications, including four or five in Dutch or German. Since the advent of the first newspaper in 1837, the town has not lacked for publications of a considerable variety and purpose, espousing myriad points of view.

Area residents are kept well informed by the wealth of newspapers, journals, and magazines written and published in and around Grand Rapids. Photo by Doug Diekman

The lively art of communication has been served well by technology, and every new mode of communicating has had its day in Grand Rapids. The city in the 1980s represents a large and lucrative newspaper, television, and radio market. Grand Rapids also has a remarkable number of advertising agencies and public relations and graphic arts firms, some with very large national accounts. The city has been a religious publishing center since the 1920s, with three major houses and one

325

Above: The *Grand River Times*, Grand Rapids' first newspaper, was produced on this Washington hand press. Courtesy, Grand Rapids Public Library

Facing page, top: The *Grand Rapids Herald*, delivered in trucks such as this one from the 1920s, brought the news to local residents for sixty-nine years. Courtesy, Grand Rapids Public Museum

Facing page, bottom: Pictured here is the *Grand Rapids Herald* composing room in 1890. Courtesy, Grand Rapids Public Library

smaller company specializing in Christian literature.

In the early days news and information were disseminated through the printed word—pamphlets, books, and newspapers. Grand Rapids newspaperman and historian Albert Baxter, admittedly not an impartial observer, wrote in 1890,

In the United States, newspapers are potent, if not the very chief, agents in the development of communi-

ties. . . . Reasoning from such premises, the surprising rapidity and solidity of growth which Grand Rapids has enjoyed, and the wide-awake spirit which has characterized her citizens, would seem to show that the newspaper had exerted its influence here at an early date. . . .

Certainly many newspapers were founded, and a few survived, to exert that influence. The first, *The Grand River Times,* appeared April 18, 1837. Most of the town turned out to see the first issue come off the hand-cranked press. Souvenir copies were printed on linen, and a special copy on silk was given to the city's founder, "Uncle" Louis Campau. Well might the occasion have excited such interest among the population. The twenty-three-year-old editor, George W. Pattison, and his printing press made it to Grand Rapids via the best tradition of harrowing experiences.

In 1836 Lucius Lyon and his Kent Company purchased the *Niagara Falls Journal* (N.Y.) for $4,000 and engaged its editor, young Pattison. Pattison and his Washington-brand press boarded the steamer, the *Don Quixote,* at Buffalo for the trip across Lake Erie, up the St. Clair River to Lake Huron, through the Straits of Mackinac, and down Lake Michigan to Grand Haven. The boat was wrecked off Thunder Bay, so the printing press and other paraphernalia were transferred to a sailing vessel and transported to Grand Haven. By this time it was winter, and the Grand River was frozen over, prohibiting shipping between Grand Haven and Grand Rapids. Undeterred, Pattison hired two dog-sled teams, loaded his press aboard, and started for Grand Rapids. Just below the rapids he encountered thin ice, and one sled and the press went to the bottom of the Grand. Pattison retrieved both from the river bottom, and in due time the little press was put into service in Grand Rapids' first newspaper office.

Louis Campau is said to have paid $1,000 in advance for 500 subscriptions for a year of the *Times;* the Kent Company also took, and paid for in advance, 500 subscriptions, and numerous others took from 10 to 25 copies each. The *Times* was the official paper of the county and so printed all the tax notices and other government information such as notices of meet-

ings and the minutes of the Board of Supervisors meetings. It did not, however, survive beyond 1840; in 1841, under its third owner, it was reorganized as the *Grand Rapids Enquirer* and continued as a weekly until 1855, when it became the county's first daily newspaper. Although it changed name and ownership often, the paper existed until, in its last reincarnation as the *Grand Rapids News*, it ceased publication in 1922.

Another weekly, the *Grand River Eagle*, was started in 1844 by a twenty-two-year-old apprentice from the *Times*, Aaron Turner. He later changed the name to *Grand Rapids Eagle*. After a number of uncertain years, when Turner occasionally had to suspend publication because he couldn't pay for newsprint, the *Eagle* became an evening daily in 1856 and was published by Turner until 1896, when he sold it to the *Grand Rapids Herald.* Turner was the first to introduce a Sunday edition and the first to bring, in 1859, a power-driven press to the city. Albert Baxter was a member of the *Eagle* staff for more than twenty years.

One source estimates that between 1837 and the 1980s in Grand Rapids, as many as 150 newspapers were launched and flourished or foundered. That number includes such special-interest papers as the *Agriculture World*, the *Medical Counsellor*, and the *Review*, a literary weekly printed in Polish, Swedish, Dutch, German, and other native languages.

At one time the city supported four daily newspapers, the *Grand Rapids Eagle*, the *Grand Rapids Herald*, the *Grand Rapids Democrat*, and the *Grand Rapids Press.* In the 1890s the *Eagle* and the *Democrat* succumbed to the twin ravages of the depression of 1893-1897 and overwhelming competition from the other two dailies.

The *Grand Rapids Herald* was at one time owned by William Alden Smith, who later was U.S. Congressman from the Fifth District from 1895 to 1905 and U.S. Senator from 1907 to 1919. He sold the *Herald* to Arthur H. Vandenberg, who served in the U.S. Senate from 1928 to 1951.

The *Grand Rapids Press*, founded as the *Morning Press* in 1890 by William J. Sproat, was the city's first penny paper. Two years later the paper was purchased by George G. Booth, a Canadian and son-in-law of the owner of the *Detroit News*. Booth also bought the *Eagle*, merged the two papers, and published as an evening daily, which he called the *Grand Rapids Evening Press.*

The afternoon *Press* and the morning *Herald* soon came to dominate the city news scene, and soon there were only two papers, the *Press* and the *Herald*. In 1906 the *Press* moved into a splendid new headquarters at 20 East Fulton, the first all-concrete building in the city and one of the first in the world; Edmund Booth, brother of George, became the paper's editor and manager. In 1913 the paper's name was changed to *Grand Rapids Press*. The *Press* and the *Herald* maintained an intense rivalry until 1958, when the *Herald*, suffering from declining advertising revenues, was sold to the *Press.*

The *Press* was the first and is the largest paper in a chain of eight Michigan dailies owned by Booth. In 1976 the Booth organization made newspaper history when it sold the Michigan chain to S.I. Newhouse, a New York communications conglomerate, for $300 million, the largest transaction in newspaper publishing history to that date.

The *Press*, whose slogan is "We've got you covered," has a daily circulation of 145,000 and a Sunday circulation of 172,000. The major paper in West Michigan, the *Press* is the third largest in the state, after the *Detroit News* and the *Detroit Free Press.*

Three weeklies serve the area: *Cadence*, published in East Grand Rapids; *Advance* Newspapers, a weekly news and shopper paper whose ten editions go into

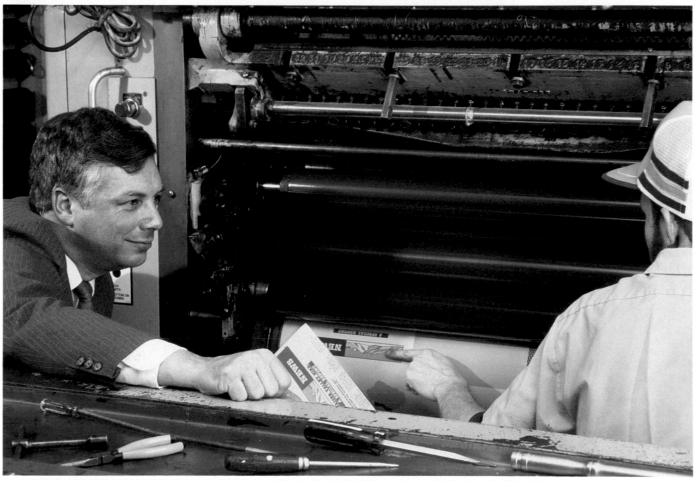

Facing page: New editions of the *Advance* speed over the presses at Jenison Printing Company. Courtesy, Advance Newspapers, Jenison Printing Company

Left: Grand Rapids residents have many newspapers available to keep them informed and abreast of world and local events. Photo by Jean Hoyle

Below: For the past 100 years, the presses at West Michigan Printing, Inc., have been rolling. Founded in 1886-1887 by Eber Rice and Horace J. Dibble, the company advertised itself as a "general commercial printer with facilities for first-class work." Owned by three generations of Rices until its purchase in 1936 by E. Jack Henningsen, the company also publishes the *Grand Rapids Legal News.* Photo by William Hebert

national news had to come to Grand Rapids newspapers by letter from Detroit or Chicago, or by special dispatch from Kalamazoo, which had had rail and telegraph service since the mid-1840s.

Grand Rapids' geographic and communications isolation was breached in November of 1858 when a Grand Rapids telegraph office was opened by the Western Union Telegraph Company. That event occurred just two months after the laying of the first transatlantic telegraph cable was completed. The wire was strung from Detroit over the line of the first railroad to reach the city, the Detroit, Grand Haven and Milwaukee. The mayors of Detroit and Grand Rapids sent congratulatory telegraph messages to each other, exchanging good wishes and expressing certainty that the transatlantic cable would "diffuse the blessings of civil and religious liberty throughout the world" and make "all nations one and mankind a brotherhood."

The telephone was a no less miraculous instrument than the telegraph, and its arrival in Grand Rapids was introduced by a "come here, Watson, I need you" sort of event in 1877. James Converse, president of the Grand Rapids Plaster Company, was a friend of Alexander Graham Bell and had been given a pair of crude wooden telephones by Bell. Converse put one phone in the company's headquarters on Monroe Avenue and the other in an office at his gypsum mines about three miles away. The plant manager, William S. Hovey, strung a telegraph wire between the two plants, and he and his assistant talked by telephone.

Such a demonstration made it obvious to local businessmen that the telephone could be a useful tool, and negotiations were begun to bring phone service to Grand Rapids. The Telephone and Telegraph Construction Company, a branch of the Michigan Telephone Company of Detroit, was opened in Grand Rapids in the fall of 1879, with one operator and twenty-five subscribers. By the end of the 1880s, the company had 1,100 subscribers, and nearly thirty new phones were being installed each month. Furthermore, the city had long distance service to more than 100 towns in western and northern Michigan.

In 1896, with Bell Telephone patents running out, independent phone companies were organized in com-

165,000 homes in Kent County and parts of Ottawa and Allegan counties; and the *Grand Rapids Times,* a newspaper for the black community.

When newspapers first appeared in Grand Rapids in the late 1830s, production was not an easy job. Baxter passionately described the process:

At that time the city had no railroad communication, no telegraph, no gaslight—not even kerosene light, not any of many other things now considered almost indispensable for the publication of a daily paper. Night after night, the compositors labored with straining eyeballs to decipher by the flickering light of 'burning fluid' lamps the . . . telegraphic dispatches received by stage from Kalamazoo.

Telegraph lines were strung along railroad lines, and because Grand Rapids had no railroad service until late in 1858, it had no telegraph service. All state and

Facing page: The dome of this telephone kiosk, located just outside the McKay Tower on Monroe Mall, was rescued from a Monroe Avenue building that was torn down during the 1960s urban renewal. Photo by David Jackson

Above: WCUZ invests in West Michigan by helping sponsor such community activities as the station's Home and Garden Show, the St. Jude Radiothon, Zoodaze, and Celebration on the Grand, which is pictured here. Courtesy, WCUZ

munities around the country. A group of local investors formed the Citizens Telephone Company, a move that resulted in intense competition for the next twenty-seven years between the Grand Rapids Bell Company and the new independent company.

Businesses had to subscribe to both services, because they had clients who subscribed to only one or the other. Citizens charged half what Bell charged, so Bell had to lower its rates.

In 1903 Citizens built a red brick building at 248 Louis Street N.W., and in 1904 put in automatic dialing, making Grand Rapids the first city in the country in which phone subscribers could call one another just by dialing the number. Citizens subscribers could not of course dial Bell subscribers, nor could Bell subscribers call Citizens customers.

The rivalry between the two companies finally ended in 1903 when Bell, which was buying out independent phone companies all over the country, bought Citizens and consolidated the two systems. The Louis Street building from that time on was known as the Bell Building and housed the company's installation department and later, for forty-six years, its accounting department. Bell built its present building on North Division in 1925 and put on an addition in 1956. The old Bell Building was purchased by the city in 1973 and was used as a warehouse for a number of years. Finally, it was sold in 1977 to a group of investors and was the first of the many downtown buildings to be renovated as an office building. It is now called the Oldtown Riverfront Building.

At about the same time that the two telephone

companies were merging, radio was becoming an international phenomenon. The city's first commercial radio station, WEBK, began broadcasting in October 1924, and about six months later a second station, WBDC, went on the air.

WEBK was financed by the local Furniture Manufacturers Association; WBDC was owned by State Senator Howard Baxter, who also owned Baxter Laundry Company. The WBDC call letters stood for Worldwide Baxter Dry Cleaning. A year after going on the air, WEBK's call letters were changed to WOOD, which, the FMA felt, better reflected the owners' interests. WBDC, following suit, changed its name to WASH. Eventually, after a series of ownership changes, the two stations came under joint ownership, and the WASH call letters disappeared from the scene. WOOD was the city's only radio station until 1940, when WLAV (named for owner Leonard A. Versluis, Sr.) went on the air. U.S. census figures that year marked Grand Rapids as the radio capital of Michigan. Ninety-six percent of the city's residents owned radios.

In 1946 WGRD and WFUR joined the airwaves, and many others followed in the ensuing decades. In the 1980s the city is served by more than two dozen radio AM and/or FM clear-channel, twenty-four-hour, or dawn-to-dusk stations catering to a variety of interests—easy listening, country, light rock, hit rock, Christian-, Hispanic-, and black-oriented broadcasting, community radio, news, and conversation.

Grand Rapids' two major television stations—WOTV-8 and WZZM-TV 13—are consistent award winners in local news and community-service programs. The city boasted Michigan's first television station outside of Detroit when Channel 7, owned and operated by WLAV, went on the air in 1949. WOOD applied for a license in 1950, bought WLAV-TV in 1951, and began broadcasting on Channel 7 in October 1951. Three years later the station changed to Channel 8, where it has been ever since. In 1971 WOOD radio was sold, and the television call letters were changed to WOTV-8.

WZZM-TV 13, the local ABC affiliate and the city's second TV station, began broadcasting on November 1, 1962, from studios in the Pantlind Hotel.

The area's Public Broadcasting Service station is WGVC 35/52, Grand Valley State College. Other regional stations that cover the Grand Rapids market are WWMT-TV Channel 3, West Michigan's CBS affiliate, broadcasting from Kalamazoo; WUHQ-TV Channel 41, Battle Creek, another ABC station; and the newest station, the independent WXMI-17 of Grand Rapids, which features movies, children's programming, and local and national sports.

GRTV-23, Grand Rapids Public Access Channel J, broadcasts city government proceedings and presents local organizations and would-be broadcasters with the opportunity to do their own television programming, and UA CableSystems gives the area access to most of the popular national commercial and pay-TV cable networks.

Informing and entertaining the public is the mission of the area's media, but all are equally committed to community service. All support charity and community causes through fund-raising campaigns and promotional events that not only benefit specific organizations or groups, but increase public awareness of the existence and needs of such groups. The media also sponsor public events that draw large crowds, are entertaining, and create much public good will.

Individuals from print and broadcast serve on committees and lend their names, time, and talent to dozens of community organizations and activities that need the extra boost that a celebrity can provide.

Broadcast media, by their nature, are a dominant force in the public mind, and they are certainly influential in the community. The production of the printed image, however, is the city's ninth largest industry. Grand Rapids is second to Chicago as a midwestern graphic arts center, and the fifth largest in the nation. The area's more than 4,000 printing trade craftsmen maintain a multimillion-dollar business. Many of the local printing and lithography companies serve the nation's publishing houses. Others specialize in items such as advertising specialties, business forms, maps or containers or labels for food products. Many offer general printing services, and, as in other cities, quick-print businesses are as numerous as gas stations.

Because of its strong ties to the Christian and Christian Reform denominations, it is no surprise that

Grand Rapids has become well known for its art displays in public places. The Kendall School of Design mural, seen through one of the sculptures that graces the Art Museum grounds, was designed by Ron Riksen, an associate professor at the school in 1985. Gannett Outdoor Advertising Company reproduced the design on the side of the building as a contribution to the school. Photo by Jack Standley

Grand Rapids has also become a religious-literature publishing center. William B. Eerdmans Publishing Company, established in 1910, for a brief period in recent years published Michigan-related books as well as religious publications. Zondervan Corporation was founded in 1931 and is the largest publisher of Christian literature in the world. Baker Book House began publishing in 1939 and currently publishes 150 new books annually and keeps about 1,500 titles a year in print.

Kregel Publications is an outgrowth of Kregel's Book Store, which was opened in 1909 by Louis Kregel as a secondhand book store. Louis' son, Robert, developed the business into one of the largest dealers in secondhand religious and theological books in the United States. Kregel Publications specializes in reprinting religious books.

Kendall School of Design, a four-year accredited art school teaching furniture design, illustration, advertising art, and fine art, has given the city a ready and constant pool of commercial artists. Many graduates enter local agencies and a few years later often leave to start their own agencies. The result is a high number of advertising and public relations firms in comparison to the total in other cities of the same size. Grand Rapids also has numerous printing and lithography companies, and many serve the nation's publishing houses.

The quality, diversity, and creativity of the advertising and graphic arts organizations in Grand Rapids have given the city a national reputation for excellence in the art of communication.

And communication, in all its forms, *is* an art in Grand Rapids—and a growth industry as well. "The wide-awake spirit" that Baxter attributed to early Grand Rapids citizens still prevails: his theory that the degree of enterprise and progress a community exhibits is in direct relationship to the success of its newspapers can be revised to fit the times. Rather, a community's success can be measured by how well it is served by the various manifestations of its communication industries. And Grand Rapids is most certainly well served.

12
An Enterprising City

Grand Rapids is, and has long been, the commercial center of West Michigan. Widely regarded by independent business owners and larger chains alike as a good place in which to conduct their business, Grand Rapids today is one of the fastest-growing metropolitan areas in the Midwest and in the nation.

From its earliest days Grand Rapids has valued entrepreneurship and has provided a hospitable business climate in which all manner of enterprises—from large industrial plants to small service businesses—have enjoyed the opportunity to flourish and grow. "The unique vitality and economic diversity" that characterize the city today have in fact been present virtually since the beginning. Now ranked among the top 100 cities in the United States in terms of population, household income, and retail sales, Grand Rapids promises to be one of the nation's most affluent markets in the decades to come.

Commerce has played a major role in the city's history since the time of the mound builders, whose widespread trading network provided them with exotic grave goods to be buried with their dead. Later came the fur-trading days, which brought Indians and traders together at the rapids of the Grand to exchange furs for manufactured items. The settlers from New England who arrived in the 1830s likewise required manufactured goods, and enterprising merchants set up shop in the downtown area to supply their needs.

The urban renewal of the 1960s was the harbinger of a new era in the history of downtown Grand Rapids. Photo by David Jackson

335

As the city's population doubled, redoubled, and doubled again in the three decades following the Civil War, the general stores of old gave way to more specialized mercantile establishments that elevated retailing to a prominent position on the local economic scale.

The retail business is big business in Grand Rapids and West Michigan, with thousands of establishments catering to every need, providing jobs to many thousands of workers, and accounting for billions of dollars in annual sales. In 1981, in the immediate Grand Rapids area alone, consumers spent a total of nearly a billion dollars. Almost $330 million was spent in grocery stores and $142 million in restaurants of all sorts. Local retail customers also bought more than $100 million worth of apparel in 1981 as well as nearly $33 million in household supplies and $63 million in appliances. Expenditures for liquor topped the $43 million mark, tobacco purchases added up to $25 million, and personal-care products came close to $20 million. In 1984 retail sales passed $3.5 billion, giving Grand Rapids a national ranking of sixty-sixth in annual sales.

For the first half of the twentieth century, downtown Grand Rapids remained the city's commercial and retail hub. But as the trend toward suburbanization picked up steam in the 1950s, businesses and population moved out of the center city, and much of the retail action shifted to suburban shopping centers. The Rogers Plaza, Woodland, Eastbrook, and Breton

Facing page: An increasing population meant escalating business for such downtown shops as these on the northwest corner of Monroe and Ottawa in the 1870s. Courtesy, Grand Rapids Public Library

Right: Getting set to march in a Labor Day parade, the Grand Rapids Typographical Union posed for this picture on Monroe Avenue in front of the Boston Store. Founded in 1885, the Boston Store was credited in 1911 with "occupying the largest commercial space in town." Courtesy, Grand Rapids Public Library

Village shopping malls and the stores and strip malls along 28th Street attracted a growing share of shoppers, and merchants found they had no choice but to adjust. Some, like the venerable Wurzburg's, did not survive the changes.

Today, while suburban shopping malls continue to play a major supporting role in the region's economy, the city has once again focused its attention on reviving downtown as a retail center. City Centre Plaza, a five-story downtown mall created by a multimillion-dollar renovation and remodeling of the old Herpolsheimer's department store, and the ten-million-dollar renovation of the Ledyard Building into an office and retail complex, attest to the faith that private developers and city officials have in the viability of downtown as a shopping area. And the establishment of the Downtown Management Board, made up of city officials and downtown merchants and given a budget of nearly $400,000 for its first nine months, further supports the efforts to revitalize downtown Grand Rapids by promoting and maintaining retail operations.

Concerned city involvement in the region's economic life is just one of the factors contributing to the congenial business climate. Grand Rapids also enjoys excellent transportation facilities and services, a skilled and productive labor force, relatively low labor costs, a quality educational system, an excellent sewage-treatment plant, abundant natural gas piped in from the Southwest and Canada by Michigan Consolidated Gas, and reliable electric power supplied by Consumers Power, the state's largest utility. Workers' compensation costs, moreover, are lower in Grand Rapids than in other parts of the state, medical costs

Above: Split Ring by Clement Meadmore can be seen in the Woodland Mall. Photo by Jean Hoyle

Right: Steketee's is one of the oldest retail stores in Grand Rapids. Founded in 1862, the business maintains six locations, one downtown and the other in Eastbrook, and has been operated by four generations of Steketees. Here, company CEO Richard Steketee is examining new merchandise with a member of the sales staff. Photo by William Hebert

Facing page: Downtown boosters are relying on City Centre Plaza to draw shoppers back into the center of Grand Rapids. Photo by William Hebert

Above: Grand Rapids area businesses make a major contribution to the quality of community life. Rogers Department Store, for example, takes a special interest in the handicapped, and sponsors a handicapped day at Ada Park as well as other events. Photo by John D. Strauss

Facing page: An intense Grand Rapids sunset silhouettes the towering power lines that bring light to the darkening city. Photo by William Hebert

been flocking to lending institutions to obtain new mortgages or refinance existing ones. The lower interest rates have also helped to stimulate local business expansion, and 1986 saw a significant increase in local business lending, spurred additionally by the national economic recovery and a sound overall business environment.

An examination of the city's business base reveals a remarkable diversity. The more than 11,400 businesses operating in the metropolitan Grand Rapids area include 1,021 manufacturers producing more than 250 different products. Of the nation's twenty major manufacturing-industry classifications, all but tobacco are represented here. Rolling out of Grand Rapids factories are a vast array of furniture, paper products, machinery, tools and dies, hardware, home-care products, household appliances, and electrical and transportation equipment, and a wealth of goods

are among the lowest in the Great Lakes region, and property tax rates are below the state average. All of these benefits considerably enhance the city's attractiveness as a regional commercial center.

Sound financial institutions are the backbone of a healthy economy, and West Michigan banks are prospering. In 1986 most of the area's banking institutions reported a substantial increase in profits in the wake of falling interest rates and a general economic upturn. As a result, consumers in record numbers have

made of plastic, rubber, stone, clay, glass, primary metals, and fabricated metals. Products made in Grand Rapids and designed for a multiplicity of applications reach national and worldwide markets every day.

Of the area's 330,000 workers, 30 percent are employed in manufacturing and 48 percent in nonmanufacturing jobs. Another 14 percent work in agriculture or are self-employed, and 9 percent are employed by government. More than 40 percent of the labor force falls into the professional, technical, and skilled-crafts categories; 30 percent of the balance is semiskilled; and the remainder is composed of management and clerical personnel.

Not only does Grand Rapids serve the Midwest as a distribution center for goods of all kinds, from durables to fashion merchandise, but the city is also a major regional wholesaling center. Such national retailers as Sears and J.C. Penney exist side by side with large discount chains, locally owned specialty shops, and branches of such Detroit-based operations as J.L. Hudson. Although the Grand Rapids area is home to many large companies, it also supports a host of family-owned businesses and numerous small enterprises owned and managed by local entrepreneurs, a growing number of whom are women. Four out of five business starts in the state of Michigan, in fact, are by women. No single corporation dominates the city's economy, but businesses large and small, publicly held or privately owned, are closely integrated into the fabric of community life as employers, as contributors to the city's economic prosperity, and as citizens committed to the welfare of the community as a whole.

While 93 percent of the city's workers are employed in firms of fewer than fifty workers each, the metropolitan area is also home to five companies that have made it onto the *Forbes* magazine list of the 400 largest privately held firms in the country. That number ties Grand Rapids with sixteen other cities for tenth place among cities with more than one *Forbes* 400 firm.

Steelcase, the largest private company in Grand Rapids and second largest in the state, ranks forty-ninth nationally, with sales in 1986 of $1.3 billion. The Meijer, Inc., supermarket chain, which is the second-

Facing page: Downtown retail sales were up and growing substantially in December 1986. Photo by Doug Diekman

Page 342: This view of downtown shows the Calder Plaza building (left) next to the Old Kent Center. Photo by William Hebert

Above: Founded in 1858 as J.S. Crosby & Co. to serve the city's property insurance needs, the Crosby and Henry insurance firm has remained in the Crosby family hands for five generations. Shown here, along with portraits of the preceding four generations of Crosby insurance men, are partners James Crosby, left, and William Henry, right. Photo by William Hebert

largest privately held company in Grand Rapids and third largest in the state, ranks sixty-ninth in the nation, with $1.1 billion in sales. The Ada-based Amway Corporation, manufacturer of personal-care products and the nation's second-largest direct-sales firm, ranks ninety-sixth on the *Forbes* list, with sales of $800 million (although company officials claim that $1.3 billion is a more likely figure). Gordon Food Service, a food wholesaler, and the Holland-based Haworth, Inc., furniture company rank 354th and 355th respectively.

Not as large as the giants, but noteworthy for their swift move upward are the privately held companies that have been singled out by *Michigan Business* magazine for its first annual "Michigan Private 100" list. Announced in May 1986, the list focuses on annual growth rates over the previous five years, and the only companies considered were those whose sales were between $100,000 and $30 million in base year 1981. Together, according to the magazine's statistics, these top 100 firms added more than $760.3 million to the state's economy and created 6,676 new jobs. Eight Grand Rapids companies made the list: Computer Strategies, specialists in computer hardware and software; American Annuity Life, insurance; C&F Stamping, manufacturers of metal and auto parts; DLP, producers of disposable medical devices; Nicholas Plastics, manufacturers of auto and furniture plastics; Comp-Aire Systems, microelectronic clean rooms; Wolverine Printing, commercial printers; and WBDC, architects and engineers.

Also contributing their measure to the overall economic health of the region are a number of publicly held firms whose top performances in 1985 have placed them on the West Michigan Top 40 list of the region's largest companies. Compiled by Buys-MacGregor, MacNaughton-Greenawalt and Company, West Michigan's largest brokerage firm, the list ranks manufacturing, high-tech, and retail organizations by sales, financial firms by assets, and service and insurance companies by revenues. Grand Rapids-based companies appear in every category. Like their privately owned counterparts, these firms, too, exemplify the city's economic diversity.

Included in the manufacturing and high-tech clas-sification are Zondervan Publishing Company, ranked tenth; Rospatch, a manufacturer of cloth labels, twelfth; Guardsman Chemicals, coatings and polishes, thirteenth; Knape and Vogt, specialty hardware, fifteenth; Corduroy Rubber, mechanical rubber goods, seventeenth; Autodie, dies for the automotive industry, eighteenth; and X-Rite, quality-control equipment for the photoelectronic industry, twenty-second.

Under the financial institutions heading, Old Kent Financial placed second; Union Bancorp, which recently merged with NBD (National Bank of Detroit) Bancorp, third; PrimeBank, formerly Mutual Home Federal Savings and Loan, seventh; and MetroBanc, eighth.

Two local companies—the sixty-three-store Gantos women's apparel chain and Holly's restaurants—were first and second, respectively, on the retail list; Care Corp., nursing home operator, topped the service list; and Foremost was recognized as West Michigan's largest insurance company.

Rankings such as these are more than a matter of prestige. The appearance of local companies on such lists paints a picture of overall business activity. Top-performing companies sell their products beyond the regional market, provide jobs, and generate a need for smaller support companies to serve as sources of supply. At the same time, prosperous, active financial institutions circulate the funds that act as a further stimulus to economic growth. All of this has a multiplier effect, promoting new business and industry and creating new jobs throughout the region.

Another prime indicator of the city's economic diversity is its list of leading employers. Of the eighteen area companies employing 1,000 workers or more, eight of them, led by Steelcase, General Motors, and Amway, are involved in the manufacture of products that run the gamut from soap to shoes, and hardware to home appliances. The other ten companies on the list are non-manufacturers. Of these, Meijer, Inc., food and general merchandise retailer, is the largest, with 4,600 employees. Also included among the area's leading employers are Spartan Stores, a food wholesaler; Old Kent Financial, banking; Foremost, insurance; Amway Grand Plaza Hotel, hospitality; and

Grand Rapids' urban landscape is distinguished by a remarkable array of sculpture. The many works of art that grace the city have gained national stature for Grand Rapids in the art world. Photo by William Hebert

Michigan Bell Telephone, communications, as well as Butterworth, Blodgett, and St. Mary's hospitals. Together with Metropolitan and Ferguson hospitals, these institutions account for $314 million in annual revenues and 7,638 employees. Medical care, in fact, has become a growth industry, according to many experts, that will serve in the future to help keep the region's economy strong.

Because of its diversity, the Grand Rapids economy has been able to weather the fiscal storms of recent recessionary years. As a result, according to a study undertaken by the Battelle Memorial Institute in 1985 at the request of GGREAT, "Grand Rapids did better than the state in employment and population growth during the 1970s." Between 1970 and 1980 Kent County grew by 8.1 percent, almost double the statewide growth rate of 4.4 percent. That growth continued into the 1980s.

Between 1980 and 1984 Kent County's population increased by about 4 percent, and overall employment rose by some 5,000 jobs. At the same time unemployment rates remained lower than the statewide average. According to a recent survey comparing Michigan's ten medium-sized metropolitan areas over the years between 1979 and 1985, Grand Rapids ranked second in employment growth, fourth in overall economic performance, and was the only metropolitan area in the state to see an increase in manu-

This night shot features the Amway Hotel tower on the right, and the Exhibitors Building at left. Photo by William Hebert

facturing jobs over the six-year period.

For the last three months of 1985, unemployment in Grand Rapids stood at a relatively low 6.5 percent. Ann Arbor, with 4 percent, had the state's lowest unemployment rate, while the upper peninsula, at 12.6 percent, weighed in with the highest. Grand Rapids' metropolitan area unemployment statistics continued improving in 1986, with totals dipping below the previous year's levels. Unlike the rest of the state, Kent County enjoyed significant growth across a majority of industrial sectors. And while the number of manufacturing jobs increased by 13,000 between 1982 and 1984, substantial growth occurred in the nonmanufacturing sector as well. The Grand Rapids area economy continued its expansion throughout 1986, with a slight decline in manufacturing employment offset by the growth of the service sector. Recent studies predict the creation of 111,100 new jobs in the Grand Rapids metropolitan area between 1985 and 2010, a 31.9 percent increase in overall employment levels that would make Kent and eastern Ottawa counties Michigan's third fastest-growing metropolitan area.

Diversity is only one of the keystones of Grand Rapids' economic foundation. Stability is another, as made evident by the substantial number of centennial businesses in the area that are still going strong. Such mercantile establishments as May's, Steketee's, Coye's, and Groskopf's, such industrial concerns as Monarch Hydraulics Company and Leitelt Iron Works, and such manufacturers as Wolverine World Wide of Rockford and Bissell were all established more than a century ago. And many of these old-line companies are still owned and operated by the descendants of their founders.

Perhaps the strongest attribute of all is the prevailing spirit of enterprise among Grand Rapids citizens, entrepreneurs, and officials. As the Battelle report put it, "Rather than having been overwhelmed by economic, social, and technical change, the people and institutions of Grand Rapids have learned to adapt and benefit from it." The transformation of the furniture industry, so the Battelle analyst noted, is a perfect example:

As the availability of furniture-grade lumber declined, so did a significant portion of the area's wood furniture production. That decline has been more than offset, however, by growth in the metal furniture industry. This transition, which combined the furniture design and marketing skills available in the wood furniture industry with the metal-forming and manufacturing skills available in the auto industry, was not simply good luck. It depended on the insight, intelligence, and hard work of many Grand Rapids residents.

The enormous effort that has been expended toward guaranteeing Grand Rapids' place as the region's tourist and convention center is another instance of the city's willingness and determination to anticipate change and turn it to advantage. While community leaders have long recognized the need for aggressive economic development, they have also been acutely aware that, unlike surrounding communities which have been able to concentrate on industrial growth and residential construction, Grand Rapids has virtually no land available for economic growth. Combining this reality with the fact that manufacturing is declining and leisure time is increasing nationwide, city officials have focused their attention on expanding regional business, transportation, and communication services and developing the downtown as an entertainment, cultural, and convention center.

That strategy has begun to pay substantial dividends. In the fiscal year that ended on September 30, 1986, 866 conventions brought more than 593,000 visitors to the city, a 4.6 percent increase over the previous year. Those visitors spent an estimated total of $97.2 million in the metropolitan area on food, lodging, entertainment, travel, gifts, and other items.

The spirit of enterprise that seeks to secure the city's future is also firmly anchored to the present with a can-do approach to problems. As a result, according to the Battelle analyst, ". . . local problems are manageable and are being addressed competently. There exists no discernible sense that the city of Grand Rapids is likely to confront any problem that is beyond its resources or capabilities." That being the case, the business community regards Grand Rapids as a "relatively risk-free, stable, and congenial place for investing and operating."

The need to address problems and cope with change has given rise to a high degree of cooperation among civic jurisdictions in the metropolitan area. Recognizing the benefits of working together for the common good, officials from Grand Rapids and the surrounding municipalities have adopted a cooperative strategy for future economic growth that will work to the advantage of the entire metro area. "While this cooperation is far from perfect," according to the Battelle report, "it has worked well enough to promote a surprisingly high quality of life and reasonable degree of economic opportunity. . . . Other political and corporate leaders in Michigan might look to the Grand Rapids model as one from which they could learn ways to cooperate constructively."

Because of its favorable business climate, enterprising citizenry, relatively low costs, spirit of cooperation among governments, and the many other factors operating in its favor, Grand Rapids, according to the Battelle study, can look forward to a "period of sustained growth for the next two decades." Change is inevitable, of course, but Grand Rapids has fixed its sights and its resources on a prosperous future, and is "better able to manage that change than virtually any other area in the state."

13
Quality in Education

A community's educational system not only is one of its greatest assets but also represents an essential investment in the future. In Grand Rapids that investment has been considerable. The Grand Rapids area possesses public and private educational resources in abundance, and the quality of local schooling is one in which residents take great and justifiable pride.

The city's first educational institution, the Baptist Indian mission, was founded on the west side of the Grand River, near the rapids, in 1825, to preach Christianity and teach American ways to the local Indian population. The early white settlers made use of the mission's educational services, too, ferrying their children across the river in canoes for a daily dose of the three Rs.

For nearly a decade, until Indian land cessions and federal treaties dispersed most of the native population from the vicinity, the mission served as the pioneer community's only school. Then, when the closing of the mission in the late 1830s left them to their own educational devices, the settlers converted available space in log cabins, warehouses, barns, and hotels into schoolrooms and pressed their young women into service as teachers. In many instances the only pupils attending these small, scattered, one-room schools were the teachers' younger brothers, sisters, and cousins. The establishment of the Grand Rapids Academy, a private secondary school, in 1843, afforded some

These students perform experiments in the chemistry lab at Grand Rapids' Creston High School. Photo by William Hebert

351

youngsters the opportunity to study English, Greek, and Latin for fees ranging from $3.50 to $5 a quarter; German was $4 extra. The academy, which "for a time furnished the only facilities in the village for obtaining a higher education," closed in 1851 in the wake of the establishment of the public school system.

Grand Rapids began organizing its first public school district in 1835, hired a teacher two years later, and in 1849 built its first stone school building, for elementary pupils, on Ransom and Lyon, where the Junior College Learning Center stands today. Like other schools throughout the city and the state, the Central School operated as an ungraded primary school until 1859 and the passage of a school grading act by the Michigan legislature. Beginning that same year, the ninth through eleventh grades were added at Central School, one each year, and in 1862 the city's oldest public high school was ready to graduate its first class. All thirteen graduates were girls; George Caulkins,

Above: One-room schoolhouses such as this one were common as late as the 1940s, but the economics of education made it impractical to continue such operations, and rural school districts began consolidating to afford students many more educational opportunities. Photo by James Glessner

Facing page: By the time these Central High School students were attending their study hall in the 1890s, the Grand Rapids public schools were operating free of charge. In 1869 the state legislature ended tuition fees for all Michigan public schools. Courtesy, Grand Rapids Public Library

the only boy in the class, had gone off to fight in the Civil War.

According to nineteenth-century historian Albert Baxter, the years 1853 to 1862 were:

a critical time in the history of the [Grand Rapids] schools. The fast-growing community began to require additional educational facilities, and the people were not yet wholly awakened and reconciled to the increased expenditures and more vigorous discipline necessary for the extension and management of a higher and more complex system of schools.

Ready or not to assume the necessary financial obligations entailed in running the schools, citizens then as now ultimately concluded that they had little choice.

Quality education costs money, and in Michigan that money has always come from two sources—state education funding and local property taxes. While all school districts in the state receive a guaranteed allocation of state funds based on attendance, the quality of education in each school district depends to a large extent on the district's ability to supplement state funds by raising money locally through property tax millages.

Because the power of the educational purse rests squarely in the hands of the voters, local schools have had to adapt to financial uncertainties over the years in the wake of millage failures and other budgetary restrictions. During the Depression, for example, citizens adopted a 15-mill property tax limit, and the Grand Rapids schools found themselves operating at an inadequate 5.1-mill levy. In 1950, two years after

the 15-mill limit was abolished, voters approved a special, two-mill, twenty-year building tax that would enable the district to proceed with a much-needed program of constructing new schools and remodeling and renovating older structures. Michigan's system of school financing has not changed over the years, and today's school programs and operations are still tied to voter willingness to say yes at the ballot box.

Until 1871 Grand Rapids had three separate public school districts, each with its own governing board. According to centennial historian William Etten, "there was considerable friction between the old districts, none of which had sufficient funds to employ the ablest educators." In a move described by Etten as "one of the most important events in the city's history," the three districts were consolidated into one by an act of the Michigan legislature in 1871 which required that all of the Grand Rapids public schools be under the jurisdiction of the municipal government and "under the direction and control of the board of education."

In the years following consolidation the school board was made up of the mayor plus two members

from each of the city's eight (soon to become twelve) wards. The injection of ward politics into school operations led to protests of patronage and a scandal involving kickbacks for textbook purchases, and in 1906 the board of education became a separate political entity, comprised of nine members elected by the city at large.

Along with consolidation came better teacher preparation. Between 1871 and 1878 Grand Rapids even had its own teacher-training institution, located in Primary School 3, later called Fountain Street

School. Would-be teachers spent ten weeks in each of the four classrooms, working under the guidance of the principal, who met with them at the end of each half-day teaching stint to offer criticisms and suggestions and evaluate the following day's lesson plans. In 1878 this far-from-ideal arrangement was replaced by the cadet system, an apprenticeship training program that was described by Baxter:

Each year, several cadet teachers are employed at $200 per annum, each of whom is assigned to some teacher whom she assists and by whom she is instructed. As soon as capable, the cadet is placed in charge of a room, which generally happens not later than the second year of her cadetship.

The cadet system sufficed until 1898, when the Grand Rapids Board of Education required all high school

Below: **These North Park School second-graders posed for a photo during the 1940s. Courtesy, Grand Rapids Public Library**

Facing page: **Four-year-olds take their first steps toward computer literacy at the Ridgemoor Park Child Development Center of the Grand Rapids Public Schools. Photo by William Hebert**

teachers to be college graduates. And by 1900, in keeping with a nationwide trend, the city was hiring as elementary-school teachers only those candidates who were trained in state normal schools.

Over the years the city has witnessed a vast increase in the number of students and buildings in the Grand Rapids public school system. In 1868 a total of 2,966 students attended public, private, and parochial schools in Grand Rapids. By 1872 the Grand Rapids public school district alone had grown to 11 buildings, 53 teachers, and 3,805 students. A decade later the number of students in the public schools had nearly tripled to almost 11,000, while the buildings had increased to eighteen. Along with growth has come a broadening of the curriculum to include art, music, business, and many other offerings designed to meet an ever-expanding range of student needs; the introduction of innovative programs and teaching methods; and an increasing commitment to educational excellence reflected in an enormous rise in costs. In 1887 the annual cost of educating a student was only $19.93; by 1985 the per capita cost had risen to $3,094. In the 1890s the maximum average annual salary for an elementary-school teacher with five years of experience was $500; in 1985 the average was a little over $27,000. Exactly a century ago property owners were taxed seven mills on the dollar to support the public schools. The 1986 rate in Grand Rapids, whose school system is the largest in Kent County, was thirty-four mills.

What those mills help to support is a system made up of forty-two elementary schools, five middle schools, and four senior high schools. Included in the district's services to its more than 23,000 students is an impressive array of programs designed to meet a host of needs. Academically talented and highly motivated students are afforded the opportunity to spend their sixth-grade year in special programs at the John Ball Zoo and Blandford Nature Center and to attend City High/Middle School, which features an accelerated curriculum. Nationally recognized special-education programs are available through the Grand Rapids public schools for the mentally impaired from early childhood through age twenty-six. The district offers special services to Native American students

and has instituted a bilingual-education program for the benefit of Hispanic students, who numbered 1,456 in 1985. Another program helps students from Southeast Asia learn English as a second language.

Also included among the myriad of services the district provides the community are vocational-education programs; alternative schools for troubled youngsters and pregnant teenagers; a federally funded Job Corps program; a citywide recreation program; and a community education program that serves 75,000 adults with leisure-time, basic-skills, and job-skills classes.

The Grand Rapids district is one of twenty Kent

Above: Playgrounds such as this one at Grand Rapids' Shawnee Park Elementary School provide colorful and innovative equipment to stimulate imaginative play and channel youthful spirits in constructive directions. Photo by David Jackson

Right: A student, recently arrived from Taiwan, learns English through the international English program offered by Grand Rapids Community Education. Photo by William Hebert

Facing page: Physics is just one of many academic courses offered by the Grand Rapids Public Schools, the largest of Kent County's twenty-eight school systems. Photo by William Hebert

County school systems served by the Kent Intermediate School District (KISD), an educational service agency dedicated to improving education by providing efficient and economical support services and acting as a link between local districts and the state board of education. Funded through state aid and a millage allocation, KISD operates the Kent Skills Centers for vocational education, coordinates staff-development programs, operates a media center, identifies and publicizes promising educational practices, runs the Howard Christiansen Nature Center, and offers a wide range of additional administrative and educational services.

While the costs of education continue to be a concern for citizens and school officials, the quality of education has also come in for an increasing share of attention in recent years, particularly in light of well-publicized reports testifying to a crisis in the nation's schools. As a result, school systems throughout the country have been reexamining their goals and methods in an all-out effort to upgrade instructional programs and turn out competent, capable graduates. The Grand Rapids public schools, along with other area public school districts, have been no exception.

Over the past several years the Grand Rapids district has lowered pupil-teacher ratios, increased graduation requirements, introduced minimum-competency testing, enforced a strong discipline policy, implemented a district-wide homework policy, established stricter attendance regulations, and set higher academic standards for students who participate in athletics and other extracurricular activities. In 1986 school officials were proud to point out that Grand Rapids students were performing above the national norm in standardized achievement tests and that state test scores in math and reading were on the rise as well.

The search for educational excellence has also led to the formation of the Grand Rapids Public Education Fund, a nonprofit corporation launched on June 26, 1986, with a $53,000 grant from the national Public Education Fund. Hoping to raise $150,000 by July

Above: The Reformed Bible College is one of a number of religiously affiliated institutions of higher learning in the Grand Rapids area. Photo by William Hebert

Facing page: Originally located in Central High School, Grand Rapids Junior College now boasts four classroom buildings, a learning center, pictured here, a library fieldhouse, natatorium, student center, and technical education center. Photo by Pat Bulthuis

1987, the Grand Rapids fund and its twenty-five-member board have already begun to award grants for classroom- and school-related projects that could not otherwise be funded. The purpose of the grants is to encourage educational innovations, strengthen community involvement in the educational process, and motivate teachers to seek new and better ways to teach and to create a more productive learning environment.

Operating alongside the broad-based, tax-supported public school system in Grand Rapids are the city's private and parochial schools. The Christian schools, linked through the Grand Rapids Christian School Association and affiliated with the Christian Schools International service agency, have an enrollment of 3,100 students in eighteen elementary and six high schools. Governed by parents and closely associated with the Christian Reformed Church, these schools teach academic subjects from a Christian per-

spective. The Grand Rapids Catholic Diocese operates eighteen grade schools and four high schools in the greater Grand Rapids area, serving approximately 9,000 students. Other parochial schools are run by the Baptist, Lutheran, and Seventh-day Adventist churches.

Not surprisingly, in light of Grand Rapids' strong religious orientation, attendance at the city's private, church-affiliated schools is twice the national average. Nor is it surprising that nearly 20 percent of all Kent

County students are enrolled in nonpublic schools.

Although the city's public and nonpublic schools have existed in mutual harmony for many years, adherents of each system have been finding themselves on opposite sides of a series of thorny issues of late. Parents of parochial school students, for example, are upset at the loss of the "shared time" program. Until the United States Supreme Court declared the practice unconstitutional in June 1985, the Grand Rapids Public Schools sent some of its own teachers into non-public-school classrooms to supply instruction in such subjects as art, music, and speech. While supporters of the ruling see the high court decision as a victory in maintaining the separation of church and state, opponents contend that their property tax payments entitle their children to receive such services from the public schools. Private-school tax vouchers are another bone of contention, and home schooling, on the

rise in Kent County, is in the public eye lately as well, as parents have become more vocal in protesting state attempts to require that home-schooled children be taught by state-certified teachers. Resolution of these issues will undoubtedly not be easy, nor will it be impossible, for the citizens of Grand Rapids understand full well the importance of providing quality education to all segments of the city's public and nonpublic school population.

Education in Grand Rapids doesn't stop at the secondary level. Today some 30,000 students attend nearly a dozen public and private institutions of higher learning in the Grand Rapids area. Although Grand Rapids is the largest metropolitan area in the country without a university, the city does offer students an educational spectrum that ranges from the fine arts to the liberal arts and from business courses to Bible studies.

Right: Students learn with hands-on experience at Grand Rapids Junior College. Photo by William Hebert

Facing page: Calvin College students pose in a residence hall lobby in this photo. Courtesy, Calvin College

Occupying an honored place in the city's educational roster is Grand Rapids Junior College, founded in 1914 as the nation's seventh junior college and the first in the state of Michigan. Only forty-nine students were enrolled when GRJC first began offering classes at Central High School, and only twenty-five received their two-year associate degrees at the school's first commencement exercises in 1918. But the institution addressed a definite community need, and expansion wasn't long in coming. In 1925 GRJC acquired the old Strong Junior High School building at Lyon and Ransom and later expanded into the facility at Bostwick and Fountain that once housed the Davis Technical High School, a vocational school that had opened in 1922, labored under the weight of the Depression, and closed before World War II ended.

In the beginning the emphasis at Junior College was on preparing students to continue their education at the University of Michigan and other four-year institutions, and the curriculum was structured so that course credit was readily transferable. Over the years, however, the college recognized the need to play a broader educational role and introduced a much wider range of programming, including technical training, commercial courses, industrial arts, a school of practical nursing, adult education, and a great deal more. Today numbering some 10,000 students, Grand Rapids Junior College remains highly regarded as one of the finest institutions of its kind in the nation.

The first bachelor's degrees awarded in Grand Rapids were conferred in 1921 by Calvin College, founded in 1876 as a theological seminary and at the time the only college in North America operated by the Christian Reformed Church. Originally intended as a training ground for ministers, the institution gradually evolved from a seminary that happened to have a "literary" department into a full-fledged, four-year, liberal arts institution with a separate seminary for which a bachelor's degree became a prerequisite. Situated on its present tree-lined East Beltline campus

since the late 1960s and known for its academic excellence, the college offers a broad liberal arts and sciences curriculum with majors in forty-five subject areas. Drawing more than 70 percent of its students from the Christian Reformed faith, Calvin College holds fast to the church's tenets. And because those tenets stress the idea of stewardship and the need to build a just society, a striking number of graduates and faculty members hold public office and play an active and prominent role in the life of the Grand Rapids community.

Aquinas College, another of the city's private colleges, also has religious roots. Founded by the Dominican Sisters of Grand Rapids as a school for women, it became a coeducational junior college in 1931 and a four-year, degree-granting institution more than a decade later. Today welcoming students of all faiths, Aquinas nevertheless retains much of its Catholic tradition.

To Dr. Norbert Hruby, recently retired president of Aquinas, goes much of the credit for transforming the institution from "an inward-looking, financially marginal school to one involved with the community and supported by a growing endowment." Under Hruby's seventeen-year tenure, which began in 1969, Aquinas increased its endowment from $8,500 to $5 million, became closely involved in the development of its Eastown neighborhood, instituted a nationally acclaimed career-development program, introduced a wealth of highly innovative programming, established its Emeritus Center for senior citizens, and opened its doors to a growing number of older and other nontraditional students. Today, in fact, more than half of the school's graduates are past thirty. As Hruby himself has noted, "We really were reaching out to a community that up to then didn't know we existed." Not only has Aquinas made its presence known to the local community, but the college has received national recognition as well. In July 1986 Aquinas College was one of twenty U.S. colleges singled out for "excellence

and leadership" by a published report entitled "Searching for Academic Excellence."

Just a few blocks from Aquinas is the Reformed Bible College, founded in 1940 and one of several such religious institutions in the area. Because religion has for so long played such a central role in the life of the community, it is entirely logical that Grand Rapids is home to a number of colleges and institutes of various denominations, whose programs focus on Bible studies and the training of missionaries and ministers. Among them are the Grand Rapids Baptist College and Seminary, Grand Rapids School of the Bible and Music, Grace Bible College, and the Great Lakes Institute of Bible Studies.

Students with a particular interest in business or the arts turn to Davenport College or Kendall School of Design. Not only does Davenport offer a well-rounded business curriculum leading to six bachelor of business administration degrees and a variety of associate degrees, but the school also administers an emergency medical services program to train paramedical personnel. About 3,500 students are enrolled at Davenport, which merged with the Detroit College of Business in 1985 and also has branches in Lansing and Kalamazoo. The school serves the community at large with a broad range of seminars and special programs, including the recently established Entrepreneurial Center, which provides customized training for businesses of any size and consulting and management expertise for small businesses.

Kendall School of Design, which has its origins in the city's furniture industry, was founded in 1928 by Helen M. Kendall as a memorial to her late husband, David, one of the industry's premier designers. Long known for its specialized training in furniture design, the school also offers programs in advertising, interior design, graphics, and illustration and has been conferring the Bachelor of Fine Arts degree since 1979.

Facing page: **The Aquinas College campus is situated on what was once a private estate belonging to Richard and Susan Lowe, well-known local benefactors. Photo by Boots Schmidt**

Until 1963 the only public institution of higher learning in Grand Rapids was Junior College. The lack of a public four-year institution empowered to grant bachelors' degrees was remedied with the establishment of Grand Valley State College, in Allendale, twelve miles west of Grand Rapids. Originally conceived as a commuter college, the school, which serves the greater West Michigan area, has enjoyed considerable growth over the past two decades. Current enrollment is about 7,600, and many students live on campus. Course offerings at Grand Valley's College of Arts and Sciences, Seidman School of Business, and William James College lead to undergraduate degrees in fifty-nine majors and graduate degrees in fourteen.

Always in tune with the needs of the community, Grand Valley has expanded its downtown presence with the new Grand Rapids Center, on the west bank of the Grand River. The center, which houses classrooms, computer laboratories, and a conference center, will help to strengthen the tie between education and the local economy by bringing services to working people and their employers in the downtown area. Designed to meet increasing demand for continuing and specialized education at a convenient place, Grand Valley's Downtown Center will be serving an estimated 12,000 students by the year 1990.

The college, in concert with GGREAT and The Right Place Program, has also announced plans to incorporate into its Grand Rapids Center a Center for Research and Technology because, as one official notes, "65 to 70 percent of the businesses that will grow in this area have a technical orientation, and that translates directly into the need for technical training." Established for the purpose of offering vital technological assistance to local industries through instructional programming and applied research, the proposed center will include facilities for industry-related research and development as well as an applied-technology laboratory for small and medium-sized companies. Underscoring the importance of research and technological services to the city's future, Steelcase announced in March 1987 the donation to the city and Grand Valley of ten acres of land and the former Stow/Davis furniture factory to serve as the site for the Center for Research and Technology. The

center, in cooperation with Michigan State University, will also offer undergraduate and graduate engineering programs. Technological services are to be provided in conjunction with Grand Rapids Junior College and Ferris State College of Big Rapids through their own Technology and Training Center, a separate technical assistance and training facility scheduled to open downtown in 1989.

Although Grand Rapids does not have a university of its own, it does have a College Consortium Assisting Business and Industry, CCASI. The presidents and representatives of the seven consortium institutions—Western Michigan University, Grand Valley State, Ferris State, Aquinas, Calvin, Grand Rapids Junior College and Kendall School of Design—meet regularly to discuss serving the needs of the Grand Rapids community. The consortium also functions as a clearinghouse for information and training.

College and university branch and extension pro-grams offered by Western Michigan University, Michigan State, Grand Valley, and others, also afford Grand Rapids students the opportunity to take courses locally, pursue degrees, and receive counseling. Jordan College, headquartered in Cedar Springs, has likewise brought its educational services to the students of Grand Rapids with the establishment of a campus on the city's southeast side.

The goal of education at any level—from preschool to postgraduate—is to prepare students for the future. Grand Rapids citizens, privately and as taxpayers, have made a substantial investment in that future through their support of local schools. And just as the community has had the wisdom to nurture its schools, the area's educational institutions have worked hard to address the needs of the community. Together, schools and community have committed their resources to an educational partnership dedicated to preserving and promoting the city's vitality.

Facing page: The Peter C. Cook Administrative Building, Davenport College, welcomes students to higher learning. Courtesy, Davenport College

Above: The Kirkhof Student Center of Grand Valley State College is pictured here. Photo by David Jackson

Right: These students were photographed on campus at Grand Valley State College. Courtesy, Grand Valley State College

14
The Downtown Renaissance

The area that is now downtown Grand Rapids has progressed through many incarnations ever since the land beside the rapids of the Grand became an Indian religious and trading center some 2,000 years ago. A rough-and-ready frontier outpost in the 1830s, the downtown grew into a thriving central business district that served the city's retail and commercial needs until the post-World War II exodus to the suburbs ushered in a period of decline and decay. In the late 1950s, backed by federal funds, the city embarked upon an urban renewal program that generated two additional decades of new building in the downtown area. Once again the centerpiece of the city's plans for its future, downtown has become the symbol of a prevailing spirit of renewal and rededication to growth and prosperity.

When Louis Campau first set up shop to trade with the Indians on the east side of the Grand River in 1826, downtown in his eyes was nothing more than a wilderness with possibilities. Seeing an opportunity to convert those possibilities to profit, Campau purchased seventy-two acres when the federal government offered the land for sale in 1831. Quick to follow suit was government surveyor Lucius Lyon, who bought his own tract of downtown property and with others formed the Proprietors of Kent, a land-speculating combine. By the time the tracts were platted—with Campau's streets running diagonally from the river

A skywalk connects the Amway Grand Plaza Hotel to a parking ramp on Pearl Street. Photo by David Jackson

and Lyon's according to compass directions—settlers in ever-increasing numbers were making their way west to the village beside the Grand, and Campau and Lyon were reaping profits from the sale of their properties.

Before long the little town became a boom town. Land prices skyrocketed, and wildcat speculation was the order of the day. While merchants, artisans, and tradespeople were setting up shop in a newly bustling downtown business district, the speculators continued to turn their tidy profits until, in the wake of the nationwide Panic of 1837, bust inevitably followed boom. Not until 1845 did Grand Rapids begin emerging from its economic doldrums to set its compass on a course of fiscal stability and economic growth.

Above and facing page: **Built in 1863, the Flatiron Building on Monroe Mall is one of the oldest commercial structures in the city today. Above, courtesy, Grand Rapids Public Library; facing page, photo by John D. Strauss**

By 1850, its population grown to 3,000, Grand Rapids boasted a profusion of businesses and commercial enterprises in the downtown area. According to a piece of promotional literature designed to attract even more settlers to the rapidly growing village:

there were twenty dry goods, two hardware, two clothing, four drug, two hat and cap and two book stores, twelve grocery and provision, ten boot and shoe stores, eight public houses and victualling establishments and

two printing offices [as well as] two tanneries, three flour mills, five sawmills, between 40 and 50 factories and mechanical shops of all kinds, three bakeries, two meat markets and about 100 carpenters and joiners.

Just as the Grand Rapids municipal charter of 1850 turned village into city, so did the 1850s and ensuing decades witness the transformation of downtown's primitive amenities into modern urban conveniences. Between 1850 and 1890 Prospect Hill was leveled, and lowlying swamplands and the channels between the river islands were filled in, creating more usable land. Brick buildings began replacing the wooden structures of old, and paved streets and sidewalks appeared where once there had been only mud

and dust. By 1869 shopkeepers were installing plateglass storefronts through which to display their wares, and streetlamps were lighting the way for pedestrians. The 1870s saw the building of a county jail on what had been Island No. 2, the raising of Sweet's Hotel four feet above its original ground level, and the straightening of the city's first S-curve, at Pearl and Monroe, where the amphitheater stands today. By 1892 sidewalk superintendents were monitoring construction of the city's first skyscraper, the ten-story Michigan Trust Building, on the corner of Ottawa and Pearl.

Change followed upon change as entrepreneurs tore down old structures and built new ones as monuments to their own success and in anticipation of even greater growth to come. With the city's reputation as

Right: Streetcars came to Campau Square in the 1890s. Sweet's Hotel, which became the Pantlind in 1902, is on the left, and the Wonderly Building is on the right. Courtesy, Grand Rapids Public Library

Facing page, left: In 1915, the two-story Grand Rapids National Bank Building, its Greek columns meant to convey the concept of a "temple of finance," replaced the old Wonderly Building. Now known as the McKay Tower, the building was extended to its present sixteen stories between 1926 and 1927. Five years after this picture was taken, the streetcars would be gone. Courtesy, Grand Rapids Public Library

the Furniture Capital of America indelibly etched in the aftermath of the Philadelphia Centennial Exposition of 1876, there seemed to be no limits to the city's prospects. And for a while, there weren't.

The furniture industry gave great impetus to downtown growth. Hotels expanded, exhibitors' buildings sprang up, restaurants opened, and theaters were built, not only to serve local needs but also to accommodate the throngs of buyers and exhibitors who flocked to the city's twice-yearly furniture markets. The furniture factories and their myriad support industries brought additional jobs and wealth to a city whose turn-of-the-century economy was showing signs of retail, commercial, and industrial growth. Downtown was the focus of that growth, and Monroe Avenue for decades occupied an honored position as the city's retail and commercial hub.

But the heyday of the residential furniture industry passed beneath the twin shadows of the Great Depression and competition from the South. Downtown's golden days clouded over, too, as the suburban development that followed World War II lured business owners and commercial and industrial enterprises out

of the center city.

Years of neglect took their toll, and by the late 1950s downtown Grand Rapids had lapsed into an unmistakable state of decline. Not one downtown office building had been constructed in nearly forty years, and the existing buildings wore a cloak of shabbiness and dilapidation that kept many shoppers, moviegoers, restaurant patrons, and prospective business owners away. Downtown had ceased to be the attraction it once was, except perhaps to convoys of teenagers who drove downtown on Friday and Saturday nights and cruised the empty streets in a motorized ritual known as "riding the circuit."

Grand Rapids was not the only city unable to marshal the enormous resources necessary to reverse the process of urban blight. Faced with a growing national problem, the federal government stepped in, offering a massive infusion of urban renewal funds as the prescription for solving urban woes. Under this new program the federal government and individual municipalities were to be partners, each putting up a share of the money that would be used for tearing down the old to make way for the new.

Above: **More than twenty styles of streetlights still grace the downtown area. Photo by Pat Bulthuis**

In 1960 voters in Grand Rapids and Kent County approved a millage increase to be applied to a $50 million downtown urban renewal project. With local funding committed, federal money came quickly, and the city prepared to demolish six square blocks of its history in order to erect a brand-new civic center. Among the landmark buildings—some more than a century old—that yielded to the wrecker's ball were the old City Hall, the County Building, and the Regent Theater. In their places over the next ten years rose a new post office, the City Hall/County Administration Building, state and federal office buildings, parking lots, a police headquarters and Hall of Justice complex, the Union Bank, Old Kent Bank, and Grand Rapids Press buildings, and a large central plaza.

The plaza was named in honor of the late Arthur H. Vandenberg, a Grand Rapids native who served with great distinction in the United States Senate from 1928 to 1951. An advocate of American isolationism early in his career, he later became the architect of America's bipartisan foreign policy and an ardent supporter of NATO, the United Nations, and the Marshall Plan. Today Vandenberg Plaza is most closely associated with Grand Rapids' best-known landmark, the bright-red stabile by world-renowned artist Alexander Calder. Called *La Grande Vitesse*—great swiftness, or Grand Rapids—by its creator, the forty-two-ton sculpture was the first piece of art in America to be financed entirely through a combination of private and federal funds. Since its dedication on June 14, 1969, the Calder, as it is popularly called, has been adopted as the symbol of a dynamic, progressive city.

Three years after the Calder was installed, the plaza became home to Festival, the city's lively, fun-filled, three-day celebration of the arts. Held on the first weekend of every June, Festival draws more than half a million people downtown to sample the best that the area's artists and performers have to offer. Festival

371

Above: Pictured here is the north side of Monroe Avenue, between Ottawa and Campau, in the 1920s. *Above, left:* This women's wear shop on the south side of Monroe between Ottawa and Market had an art deco facelift as the result of a 1930s' remodeling. *Left and facing page, top:* Downtown retailers such as Herpolsheimer's, Wurzburg's, and the Boston Store purveyed an impressive variety of goods. *Facing page, bottom:* F.W. Woolworth, the famous five-and-dime store chain, set up shop in downtown Grand Rapids in 1911. Courtesy, Grand Rapids Public Library and Grand Rapids Public Museum

373

Above: The Calder sculpture nestles beneath city buildings. Photo by William Hebert

Facing page: New construction continues in Grand Rapids, while old structures are preserved next door. Photo by Larry Heydenburg

features an astonishing array of local talent—from painters and sculptors to ethnic dancers, jazz combos, high-school chorales, rock bands, and storytellers. Sponsored by the Arts Council of Greater Grand Rapids and made possible by the contributions of time, cash, and equipment by countless businesses and volunteers, Festival has grown bigger and better over the years, a local showcase for the arts that has placed Grand Rapids under a national spotlight.

By the time the first downtown Festival had been launched, 1960s-type urban renewal projects calling for massive demolition were beginning to fall into widespread disfavor. With the growing realization that wholesale destruction led to undesirable social and economic disruption, a new philosophy was emerging, one that stressed restoration and rehabilitation instead of razing. The latest buzzword was "adaptive reuse," and Grand Rapids officials and citizens took that phrase to heart. By the 1970s a new era

of downtown revitalization had begun.

Like the first small detonation in a giant chain reaction, the urban renewal of the sixties had sparked an exciting downtown rebirth. Private efforts and public resources combined to meet the challenge of renewing the city. Old buildings were renovated, ambitious new construction projects were launched, and the racket of jackhammers was sweet music to the merchants, municipal officials, and business and cultural leaders who had placed their faith in downtown and directed their energies toward making the dream of a downtown renaissance come true.

Above, right, facing page, and following pages: The first weekend of every June the Calder sculpture becomes a backdrop for the city's Festival of the Arts. Balloons are launched, people crowd the streets, children experiment, and the Bethel Pentecostal Church Choir sings. Above, courtesy, Bethel Pentecostal Church; right, photo by John D. Strauss; following pages, photo by Marian L. Carter

Left: An Apollo Space Capsule, which rests on the site where the old City Hall once stood, is also the city's time capsule. Sealed on July 4, 1976, the capsule will be opened July 4, 2076, to reveal hundreds of objects considered representative of the city at the time of the nation's bicentennial. Photo by Marian L. Carter

Facing page, top: Work began in 1976 on transforming the old Monroe Avenue into a pedestrian mall and building a new Monroe Avenue extension. Courtesy, Grand Rapids Public Library

Facing page, bottom: The conversion of the old R.C. Allen office machine factory into Riverview Center, a first-class office complex, is a prime example of the private sector's commitment to the concept of adaptive reuse in the 1970s and 1980s. Photo by Larry Heydenburg

381

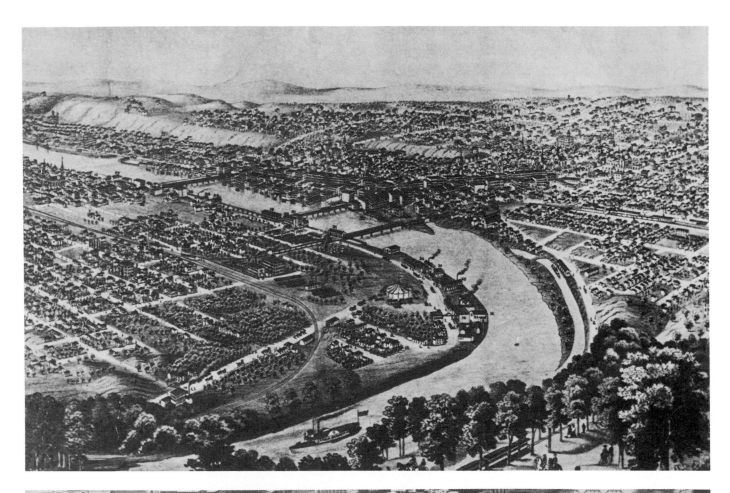

To counter the undeniable attractions of suburban shopping malls, the city focused its attention on converting Monroe Avenue into a pedestrian mall lined with trees and benches, closed to traffic, and complete with an amphitheater for entertainment in summer and ice skating in winter. Begun in 1976, the $9.4 million Monroe Mall was formally opened with much hoopla on September 12, 1980.

Exactly one month later the city staged a week-long "Celebration on the Grand" to mark the opening of Grand Center and DeVos Hall, the new convention facility and performing arts auditorium complex. Funded by bond issues, city parking fees, county hotel/motel tax revenues, and state and local grants, the convention center began living up almost immediately to its advance billing as a drawing card that would attract an increasing share of convention business. And DeVos Hall, too, has amply justified the faith of all those individuals, businesses, corporations, and foundations whose contributions, totaling five million dollars, covered the costs of construction. Named in honor of Richard and Helen DeVos, its principal benefactors, the 2,450-seat auditorium, home to the Grand Rapids Symphony Orchestra, Civic Ballet, and Opera Grand Rapids and host to innumerable touring productions, is a star in the firmament of the city's cultural life.

The excitement of that first Celebration on the Grand was magnified many times over just a year later in a jubilant week unequaled in the annals of Grand Rapids history. Not only did the festive occasion—complete with formal dinners and fireworks, balloon races and bicycle tours, heads of state and Hollywood personalities—herald the opening of the Amway Grand Plaza Hotel, the Grand Rapids Art Museum, and the Gerald R. Ford Presidential Museum, but the gala celebration also proclaimed in a splendidly appropriate way the city's enormous pride in what its citizens had accomplished.

Amway Corporation's multimillion-dollar investment in the dowdy old Pantlind had given Grand Rapids an elegantly appointed, beautifully restored, traditionally styled hotel that swiftly earned a five-star Mobil Guide rating and which would nearly double its capacity in two years with the completion of

Facing page: **This 1874 bird's-eye view of Grand Rapids, top, by an unknown artist shows a small city with commerce and transportation focusing along the river, while the modern view at bottom of downtown shows the dramatic changes that have taken place in the last 100 years. Top, courtesy, Grand Rapids Public Library; bottom, photo by Ernie Czetli**

Above: **This waterfall is a pleasure for all to see at the Monroe Mall Amphitheater. Photo by William Hebert**

its companion building, an ultramodern twenty-nine-story tower. The old Federal Building, completely refurbished, made a fitting downtown home for the Grand Rapids Art Museum's respected and growing collection. And thanks to the efforts of the dedicated volunteers who served on the Gerald R. Ford Commemorative Committee and the financial support of countless contributors, the Gerald R. Ford Presidential Museum, built entirely with private funds, graced the west bank of the Grand River.

The dedication of the Ford Museum brought favorite son Gerald Ford and Mrs. Ford to Grand Rapids,

Right and below: The Amway Grand Plaza East, shown below as it is today, traces its origins back to 1869 and the construction of Sweet's Hotel by local banker Martin Sweet. In 1898, J. Boyd Pantlind assumed ownership, renamed the hotel, shown at right in 1905, in honor of his uncle, A.V. Pantlind, and embarked on a remodeling process that culminated in the opening of a new, 550-room Pantlind Hotel in 1916. Several changes of ownership took place between 1922 and 1978, when the Amway Corporation purchased the historic structure and invested three years and millions of dollars in its restoration. Right, courtesy, Grand Rapids Public Library; below, photo by Larry Heydenburg

Facing page: Betty Ford accompanied her husband to Grand Rapids for the dedication of the Gerald R. Ford Presidential Museum. She later returned for a First Ladies symposium sponsored by the museum. Photo by J. Phillip Haven

along with a glittering contingent of other dignitaries, including President and Mrs. Ronald Reagan, Vice President and Mrs. George Bush, and the heads of state of Mexico, France, Japan, and Canada. Bob Hope taped a star-studded television special from DeVos Hall, and a media army was on hand throughout the week to record the proceedings. The eyes of the nation were fixed on Grand Rapids, and the city rose magnificently to the occasion.

Celebration on the Grand has since become an annual event, and each year has found the city with something more to celebrate in its continuing efforts to revitalize the downtown. The late 1970s and early 1980s saw construction of College Park Plaza on Division at Lyon, the Mutual Home (now PrimeBank) Building on Pearl and Monroe, and the Calder Plaza Building on Monroe opposite Grand Center. More recently the Campau Square Plaza and Square Center buildings have risen to take their places in the downtown skyline.

In 1985 a refurbished George Welsh Civic Auditorium was reopened to the public after being closed for nearly a year for remodeling. Originally financed by a $1.5 million bond issue passed the year after the stock market crashed, the building, completed in 1933, was the brainchild of then city manager George Welsh, who saw the project as a way to put the city's unemployed to work. For nearly fifty years, the Civic Auditorium, officially named in honor of George Welsh in 1975, did multiple duty as a sports arena, convention facility, concert hall, and entertainment center.

By the time the adjoining Grand Center and DeVos Hall opened in 1980, the Welsh Auditorium had seen better days. One proposed solution was to tear down the facility and replace it with an 8,000-seat multipurpose arena, complete with ice-making capability. Voters rejected the $13.9 million proposal, however, and in the end a more modest renovation was undertaken to improve the facility without destroying its art deco character.

Today the Welsh remains an important part of the Grand Center complex, host to the circus and the Ice Capades, rock concerts and sporting events, and numerous other convention and entertainment activities.

Other older structures—the Furniture Building (once Klingman's furniture store), 50 Monroe Center (the one-time Helmer Building), Two Fountain Place (formerly the Keeler Building), and the eighty-six-year-old Founders Building at the corner of Ottawa and Fountain (Union Bank's headquarters from 1929 to 1967)—have also been handsomely and carefully restored. In fact, thirty-one rehabilitation projects representing an investment of eighty-four million dollars and sixteen renovations totaling forty million dollars have been completed in Grand Rapids over the past seven years.

Financing has been one of the keys to the downtown revitalization, and funds for downtown development have been made available through a variety of sources. The 1981 passage of the federal Economic Recovery Tax Act provides investment and development tax credits for the rehabilitation of older structures. Certified rehabilitation work on buildings thirty years or older earns a 15 percent tax credit; work on buildings forty years or older a 20 percent credit; and work on historically significant buildings earns a 25

Right: The Grand Rapids Mutual Federal Savings and Loan became Metrobanc in the 1980s, but its old clock, on the corner of Monroe and Pearl, remains a downtown landmark. Photo by J. Phillip Haven

Facing page: One of the most extensive and unusual works of public art in Grand Rapids is *The Grand,* a mixed-media installation by California artist Alexis Smith. Dedicated on September 19, 1983, the work dominates all three levels of DeVos Hall's Keeler Grand Foyer, paying tribute through painted images and collage to the history and character of Grand Rapids. Photo by William Hebert

percent tax credit.

Other economic incentives include Economic Development Corporation tax-free bonding that guarantees mortgage money through local lenders, and twelve-year state tax abatements which freeze taxes for rehabilitation work and cut the tax levy in half for new construction. The Amway Grand Plaza Hotel project was a beneficiary in both categories, with a 50 percent tax cut for construction of the tower and a tax freeze for the renovation of the old Pantlind Hotel. Because private developers and city government have worked so effectively in partnership to plan projects and secure financing, Grand Rapids is now considered one of the country's leading cities when it comes to downtown development.

Much of the impetus for the recent downtown building boom has also come from the Downtown Development Authority (DDA,) a nine-member board appointed by the mayor that oversees the implementation of many downtown improvements. Incorporated in the late 1970s, the DDA—like similar groups in cities throughout the state—is empowered by an act of the Michigan legislature to stimulate downtown development through the use of tax revenues. These revenues come from the growth of the downtown tax base, and only money over and above an amount fixed by

law may be channeled by the city through the DDA. Over the past several years the DDA has played an active role in the development of City Centre Plaza, has acquired the land for an east-bank housing project and a west-bank hotel, and is in the process of acquiring land and arranging for a development package in the South Fulton area.

One strong indication that the investments in downtown revitalization are paying off is that rental space is going fast—so much so that one observer predicts a shortage of premium space in the near future. Downtown building and renovation projects completed within just the past two years account for 606,000 square feet of rental space, about 22 percent of the total market, and vacancy rates are below the national average.

What these figures demonstrate is downtown business growth. While some of that growth stems from the expansion of firms already established in the downtown area, a significant portion can be attributed to the arrival of new firms. Cigna Insurance, for exam-

ple, recently took 20,000 square feet at 678 Front Street, and Comerica, the state's second-largest bank holding company, now occupies the tenth floor of the Campau Square Building at 99 Monroe N.W. If the trend continues, so some business leaders say, downtown will be ready for another new office building within the next few years.

The key to the vitality of any downtown area is a healthy mix of commercial, retail, residential, and cultural uses. Downtown Grand Rapids has made great strides in nearly all of these categories. Construction of the Grand Center and DeVos Hall, renovation of the Welsh Civic Auditorium, and Civic Theatre's move into the remodeled Majestic Theater have created a fine downtown entertainment center. The completion of Grand Valley's Downtown Center has expanded downtown's already extensive educational services. Downtown commerce is thriving, and the tourist and convention businesses represent growth industries for the future.

Like a stone cast into a pond, the effect of down-

town revitalization has created ripples that extend throughout the region. Enhancing the downtown's attractions as a convention center, for example, has created new jobs, new tax revenues, and a host of other economic benefits. Since 1979, according to the *Grand Rapids Press,* ten new area hotels and motels, including the Hilton Inn and the Marriott Hotel on the city's southeast side, have added 1,674 rooms to bring the citywide total up to 4,270 rooms. Two additional hotels, one on the west bank of the Grand River, are under construction, and five more, one downtown and four on the southeast side, have been approved, for a total of more than 700 new rooms.

The money spent in Kent County by its hotel guests and conventioneers—an estimated $97.2 million in 1985—helps support approximately 18,000 hospitality jobs in the area (up from 11,489 in 1974), encourages investment in new hotels, and contributes to an expanding tax base. Revenues collected through Kent County's 3 percent hotel/motel room tax have increased 73 percent since 1982, and the 1986 total of more than $1.2 million represents a 15 percent increase since 1985. Used to fund the convention bureau and improve county tourism and convention facilities, the hotel/motel tax makes a significant contribution to the local economy by stimulating even further growth in the hospitality industry.

While downtown Grand Rapids has become a great place to visit, it is still not a neighborhood where many people live. Downtown housing, according to community leaders and civic planners, is a vital—and as yet missing—link in the completion of downtown revitalization. One of the city's major planning goals is to add between 800 and 1,000 new housing units downtown. Although a handful of urban pioneers have taken the plunge and made the move downtown, few others have followed their lead. For one thing, downtown is easy to reach from virtually any point in the greater Grand Rapids area, and although winter weather can make driving unpleasant, heavy traffic is seldom a problem. Second is the fact that downtown lacks such services as grocery stores and dry cleaners to support a substantial residential population. Perhaps most important of all, first-rate downtown housing is limited for the most part to the four-unit condominium opened in 1984 in the David Barney Building in Monroe Center and to the twenty-unit condominium in the Forslund Building on Pearl Street at the riverfront.

A number of plans now on the drawing board are aiming to increase the availability of downtown housing. United Development Corporation, for example, was selected in 1985 to develop a plan for housing to be constructed on four acres on the east bank of the Grand River north of West Fulton, along Monroe

Facing page: **The Forslund Condominiums offer residents spacious and luxurious living quarters conveniently located in the heart of downtown. Photo by William Hebert**

Above: **City Centre Plaza represents a multimillion-dollar investment in the downtown's future as a retail center. Photo by Pat Bulthuis**

N.W. The thirty-five-million-dollar project, unveiled in January 1987 and unanimously approved by the DDA, centers on a thirty-two-story, three-tiered tower complex that will combine hotel and residential facilities. The first seven floors of the new complex will house some 200 hotel rooms; the next four floors will be given over to 163 rental apartments; and the remainder of the space will be reserved for condominiums in the $80,000 to $100,000 price range.

Also included in the plans are a grocery store and a health-club facility complete with tennis courts, swimming pool, and running track. In order not to duplicate the services already supplied by the Amway Grand Plaza, the new hotel, to be run by the Compri chain of Phoenix, will not have restaurants or convention facilities; it will, however, be connected to the

Amway Grand Plaza by a skywalk. Construction of the new housing/hotel complex is expected to be completed by the fall of 1988.

Projects such as these, so developers and planners hope, will transform downtown into a virtual around-the-clock activity center by establishing a residential nucleus that will keep downtown vibrant after 5 p.m. and, as a significant side benefit, boost the retail trade.

Attracting shoppers to the downtown is a constant and prevailing concern. City Centre Plaza, which anchors the east end of Monroe Mall, has added immeasurably to downtown's retail appeal with its forty specialty shops and assortment of restaurants, but suburban malls still enjoy the majority of the city's retail business. Determined to change shoppers' perceptions of downtown, the city in 1985 engaged Project for Public Spaces (PPS), Inc., a nonprofit, New York-based consulting group, to study Monroe Mall operations and map out a blueprint for change.

PPS recommended a number of improvements, many of which were quickly implemented. In response to the PPS study, merchants are cooperating to lengthen and coordinate evening store hours to accommodate shoppers accustomed to daily 9 p.m. suburban mall closings. PPS also noted that Downtown Inc., the former downtown business association supported solely by member contributions, was understaffed and underbudgeted. The result was the establishment in 1986 of the Downtown Management Board, which is funded through assessments levied on downtown businesses, revenues from the city's general fund, and contributions from the Grand Rapids Economic Development Corporation.

Mall design likewise came under scrutiny. PPS recommended that the trees be pruned and the grassy knolls eliminated to convert the parklike setting into a more retail atmosphere. Other suggestions called for more tables and chairs for noon-hour diners and more attractive window displays. PPS also urged that plans for second-level skywalks be tabled until street-level retailing is revitalized.

Citizen committees appointed by the mayor in 1985 have also been examining and seeking solutions to the problems associated with mall design, maintenance and operations, marketing, and that perennially

Above: **Downtown workers and shoppers alike enjoy al fresco dining on Monroe Mall. Photo by William Hebert**

Facing page: **Celebration on the Grand fireworks light up the sky. Photo by David Jackson**

thorny issue—parking. The citizen parking task force made its report in the fall of 1986, and in November 1986 the City Commission voted to raise the rates substantially at downtown parking meters and city-operated ramps. At the same time the commissioners agreed to extend the number of free-parking hours made available to shoppers. The decision was tabled in the wake of an outcry from downtown workers, who felt that they were bearing the burden of the city's pol-

icy of financing ramp maintenance and operation solely through parking fees and violation fines. Once again the city has taken the matter under advisement as officials and citizens continue to seek a satisfactory solution to the downtown parking dilemma.

While downtown issues such as parking and the need to boost retail sales defy easy solutions, city officials and citizens remain undeterred in their desire to move ahead with downtown development plans. One proposal that has generated much excitement centers on the Wurzburg Block at the west end of Monroe Mall. Announced in the fall of 1986, the plan calls for a fifty-million-dollar, four-story, 240,000-square-foot complex that would combine 60,000 feet of retail space in the form of a festival marketplace with a new Public Museum. Officials are confident that the project will prove a major downtown drawing card to shoppers, museumgoers, and visitors; a feasibility study, financed by the Downtown Development Authority, is currently under way.

Other downtown plans focus on the river. In 1985 the city established a special tax district to promote development in a rundown area along the river north of Sixth Street Bridge Park, and a team of developers is proceeding with plans for an office building. Along with the ambitious projects that have emerged through the Grand River Edges policy, proposals have been made to link the Fish Ladder Park with Bicentennial Park and to renovate Sixth Bridge Park to include a Fish Ladder viewing chamber.

These plans are not mere pipedreams. They are instead incontrovertible evidence of a city with a vision of its future, a city not content to rest on the laurels of its previous achievements. For nearly thirty years, from the late 1920s through the 1950s, downtown Grand Rapids, like other downtowns in other cities across America, had stagnated, lacking the financial means to reverse urban blight and repair the urban infrastructure. The past three decades, however, have witnessed a remarkable turnaround, as a reenergized and revitalized center city emerged from the rubble of Depression and wartime-era neglect. Future decades will see further tangible evidence of the Grand Rapids rebirth as the downtown renaissance continues.

15
A Vast Horizon

Grand Rapids, like the rest of the country, faces a future that will be shaped to a large extent by several major forces at work in America today. For one thing, the shift from an industrial to a service economy is accelerating; non-manufacturing jobs, already at 70 percent of the national total, will continue to rise, while manufacturing employment falls even further. According to the Battelle Institute report of 1985:

By 2005 only about 22 percent of all jobs in Michigan will be in manufacturing compared to 29 percent today, with direct automotive manufacturing jobs dropping from 320,000 to 200,000. Health care, travel and tourism, retail trade, communications and other services are likely to become the dominant sources of employment throughout the state.

As the provision of services comes to occupy even greater importance in the economic scheme of things, knowledge, according to the Battelle study, will overtake and dominate capital resources as the nation's source of wealth. Therefore,

states that continue to focus primarily on landing manufacturing plants, rather than on attracting human capital (from artists to engineers), are positioning themselves on the trailing edge of economic change. Companies that continue to behave as though their competitive advantage depends primarily on

This view of Grand Rapids portrays the city aglow with the colors of autumn. Photo by William Hebert

393

their superior facilities or capital resources, rather than on the abilities and motivation of their research, marketing or production people, are likely to become losers in the marketplace.

Meanwhile, the marketplace itself is undergoing significant change as new technology, the deregulation of major industries, and federal cutbacks of subsidies to industries and aid to states and cities are leading to what the Battelle Institute calls a "wide array of competitive alternatives." At the same time, vastly improved communication and transportation networks are eliminating the constraints of geography, allowing businesses to relocate far from raw-materials sources and enabling residential communities to grow where no industry exists to support them. Combined with these trends is the fact that American life-style expectations are rising, and quality-of-life issues, from clean air and consumer protection to the demand for advanced, low-cost medical care, are in many instances taking precedence over economic factors in determining how and where Americans choose to live.

What all of this means for the future of Michigan and its cities can be summed up in a single word—*change.* The most significant change, of course, will be the decline in automotive manufacturing brought about by increased foreign competition and the relocation of domestic auto plants to other states. The coming years will also see a need for state government to take the lead in dealing with such life-style issues as crime, congestion, and medical benefits; for local school boards and institutions of higher learning to mobilize the resources necessary to attract and retain good teachers and provide quality educational programming; and for government officials at all levels to support and adopt measures that have a positive effect on the business climate.

Analyzing the future is the first step in planning

Left: **The Gerald R. Ford Presidential Museum reflects downtown Grand Rapids. Photo by Boots Schmidt**

Page 394: **Spring blossoms frame the glass-sided PrimeBank building. Photo by Jack Standley**

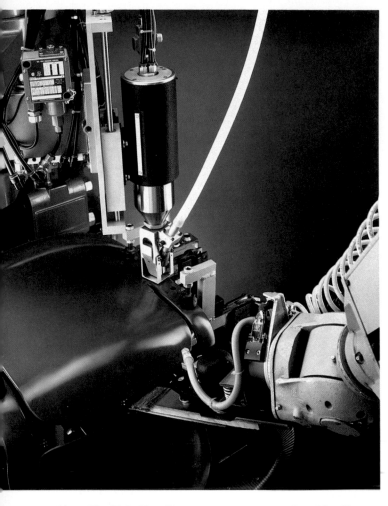

Above: **The Right Place Program hopes to attract such high-tech industries as robotics to the Grand Rapids area. Photo by Phil Schaafsma, courtesy, Cascade Engineering**

Facing page: **Grand Rapids towers above its reflection in the Ford Museum's fountain. Photo by William Hebert**

ing that same time period, and is expected to be among the top twenty fastest-growing areas in the nation in the coming decade.

Managing that growth is a task already under way. Local organizations such as GGREAT and The Right Place Program are not only working to bring new jobs to the area but are also advocating the formulation of an areawide land-use plan to unify goals for an expanding economy. One of GGREAT's aims is to identify areas to be retained for primarily agricultural, residential, and recreational uses, and to target other metropolitan-area sectors as candidates for business and industrial development. Working in conjunction with GGREAT, the Grand Rapids Area Chamber of Commerce's Right Place Program is seeking to attract the businesses needed for development to proceed.

Further diversification of the area's economic base is, and will continue to be, a high priority. Although the Grand Rapids economy of today is much less dependent on a single industry than is, say, the economy of Detroit or Flint, some analysts express concern that almost a third of the area's total employment is concentrated in manufacturing, and about 70 percent of the manufacturing jobs are concentrated, in turn, in the production of durable goods. With General Motors as one of the area's largest employers, and with many smaller firms relying on the auto industry for much or all of their business, Grand Rapids, as the Battelle report noted, "continues to be very sensitive to economic downturns." And because it is

for it, and how Grand Rapids fares in the decades to come will be determined in large measure by the preparations that are being made today. Mindful of the changes that lie ahead, and unwilling to leave the future to chance, Grand Rapids is already making provisions to secure a prosperous tomorrow.

With a population of over 600,000, the Grand Rapids metropolitan area is the second-largest metropolitan area in the state. Made up of thirty-five cities, villages, and townships in Kent and eastern Ottawa counties, the Grand Rapids metro area ranked first in the state in numerical population growth between 1970 and 1980, was second in percentage growth dur-

likely that auto-related employment will fall significantly over time, business and government leaders in the area must . . . be constantly on the lookout for development opportunities that will allow them to wean themselves away from dependence on the auto industry, particularly if those opportunities also involve reducing the area's concentration in durables manufacturing.

Area leaders are proceeding to do just what the Battelle analyst recommends, focusing their efforts on attracting to the Grand Rapids vicinity the kind of

Above and facing page: **Modern skyscrapers go up as Grand Rapids builds for its future. Above, photo by Pat Bulthuis; facing page, photo by J. Phillip Haven**

high-tech industries that experts perceive will be the wave of the future. They are also taking steps to support local entrepreneurs by assuring that capital funds, always a key to a healthy economy, are available for starting and expanding local businesses. A new program, called Venture Capital Resources Inc., (VCR) was organized in 1986 to "keep local investments locally invested." Funded through grants from the Grand Rapids Area Chamber of Commerce Foundation, The Right Place Program, and Grand Valley State College's Office for Economic Expansion, VCR uses a computerized network to match potential investors with local entrepreneurs.

As another step in the process of planning for the future, the Chamber of Commerce is actively seeking to move the West Michigan area back up to its previous ranking as one of the nation's top test markets for new products and services. Made up of fifteen counties and four major metropolitan areas—Grand Rapids,

Kalamazoo, Muskegon, and Battle Creek—the West Michigan market boasts a population of 1.6 million and a total effective buying income today ranked fortieth in the United States.

A number of advantages accrue to areas that are used as test markets. Not only do retailers receive distribution fees for the use of their facilities, but test marketing also brings sizable revenues to the region's advertising industry and mass communications media. Because these industries are certain to increase in economic importance over the years, any initiative that yields a positive impact now will continue to produce areawide dividends later.

Grand Rapids also expects to reap considerable dividends from the investments that have been made downtown, and are continuing to be made. The downtown renaissance, which shows no signs of slowing down, is a perfect illustration of the city's determination to control its own destiny by increasing the area's appeal to new business enterprises and the citizens needed to run them. And new projects already in the planning stages, such as the downtown Research and Technological Center, are addressing needs that will become critical in the future.

The concerted efforts of the past twenty years have paid off in downtown's reemergence as the region's commercial and cultural hub. Always known as a good place to live, Grand Rapids has become a great place to visit, a fact that will have increasing significance in future decades as tourism and the convention business continue their upward climb. Thanks to the time, energy, and funds—both public and pri-

vate—that have been lavished on the downtown, Grand Rapids proudly provides elegant hotel rooms, restaurants that offer gourmet dishes from the world's cuisines, a wealth of fine entertainment, and exceptional arts and cultural institutions.

Finding the funds to keep those institutions functioning in future decades will be a major concern to local officials. In light of the new tax code, Grand Rapids' cultural institutions, like those nationwide, may be facing a drop in private and corporate donations. At the same time, reductions in federal funding for the arts may lead to greater dependence on the state as a source of funds. Traditionally, however, Michigan has allocated a large part of its arts funding to Detroit. It has only been in recent years, as a result of pressure from local officials and West Michigan legislators, that the annual outstate equity funding package has given Grand Rapids and West Michigan a larger slice of the pie. A sign that Grand Rapids arts institutions will receive more state attention in the fu-

Left: This intricate ice sculpture celebrates the Christmas season in front of the Amway Grand Plaza Hotel. Photo by John D. Strauss

Facing page: Ice skating is a favorite winter pastime at the Monroe Mall Amphitheater. Photo by Jack Standley

Below: A horse-drawn buggy next to a contemporary building is a perfect blending of past and present. Photo by Larry Heydenburg

ture was Governor James Blanchard's announcement in September 1986 that the state would be willing to contribute the hefty sum of ten million dollars toward construction of a new Grand Rapids Public Museum.

As Grand Rapids moves toward the twenty-first century, changing times will bring forth new opportunities. New problems will also arise, and it will be up to the city's leaders to deal with them. Believing that knowledge is one of the keys to successful leadership, the Chamber of Commerce, through its Leadership Grand Rapids program, has already set about identifying the city's future leaders and preparing them for their roles.

Today's leaders, too, have their eyes on the future. Says Grand Rapids Mayor Gerald R. Helmholdt as he looks ahead to the coming decades:

The city of Grand Rapids is in a strong growth position. Expanding economic development combined with a strong sense of preserving our quality of life will contribute to that growth. Our real strength, however, lies with the people and their commitment to the greater Grand Rapids area community of which we are all a part.

Inherent in that commitment is the need to ensure that every community member shares in the prosperity that economic growth will bring, and that all groups are welcomed into the economic, social, and political mainstream. Regional cooperation among various governmental units and jurisdictions will likewise be essential to the efficient and economical provision of services that maintain and improve the quality of life.

Economic opportunities, quality of life, and its position as a regional business and service center have placed Grand Rapids high on the list of cities with significant growth potential. A 1982 survey cited Grand Rapids as a top growth city in the North Central region. In 1985 Grand Rapids was identified—along with Minneapolis, Chicago, Indianapolis, and Columbus, Ohio—as one of the five growth cities in the Midwest. Accompanying that growth will be a vast horizon of opportunities promising a future of stability, vitality, prosperity, and harmony for generations to come.

Above: **A reflection of the old in the new is captured in this photo of the McKay Tower shimmering in the PrimeBank building. Photo by J. Phillip Haven**

Facing page: **Grand Rapids is a city on the move, with endless opportunities for a future of prosperity, vitality, and harmony. Photo by William Hebert**

Patrons

The following individuals, companies, and organizations have made a valuable commitment to the quality of this publication. Windsor Publications and the Grand Rapids Area Chamber of Commerce gratefully acknowledge their participation in *In Celebration of Grand Rapids.*

Advance Newspapers*
American Acquest, Inc.*
American Seating*
Amway Corporation*
Amway Grand Plaza Hotel*
Aquinas College*
Atlas Truck Rental & Leasing
Autodie Corporation*
Bissell Incorporated*
Blodgett Memorial Medical Center*
Blue Cross and Blue Shield of Michigan*
The Bouma Corporation
Bulman Products Inc.
Butterworth Hospital*
Calvin College*
Clary, Nantz, Wood, Hoffius, Rankin & Cooper*
Clipper Belt Lacer Company*
Comerica Bank-Grand Rapids*
Consumers Power Company*
Country Fresh, Inc.*
C-Tec, Inc.*
Davenport College
    The W.A. Lettinga Entrepreneurial Center*
Daverman Associates, Inc.*
Dialcrafters, Inc.
Doyle & Ogden Insurance
Eberhard Foods*
Falcon Manufacturing*
Ferris State College*
First Michigan Bank Corporation*
Fishbeck, Thompson, Carr & Huber*
Gerald R. Ford Museum
Foremost Corporation of America*
Fryling Construction Company*
P.B. Gast & Sons Company*
Gemini Corporation*
General Motors*
Gerber Products Company*
Grand Rapids Junior College*
Grand Valley State College*
F.W. Grotenhuis Underwriters, Inc.*
Guardsman Chemicals, Inc.*
Hartger & Willard*
Haviland Enterprises, Inc.*
Heavyrope® by Bodyflex
Hope Rehabilitation Network*

Industrial Belting and Supply, Inc.*
Irwin Seating*
Jordan College*
Keebler Company*
Kendall College of Art and Design*
Klise Manufacturing Company
Knape & Vogt Manufacturing Company*
The Koeze Company*
Lacks Industries*
Mazda Distributors Great Lakes*
Metropolitan Hospital*
Michigan Litho*
Michigan National Bank*
Moss Telecommunications Services
NBD Union Bank*
Old Kent Bank and Trust Company*
Paragon Die & Engineering and Cascade Engineering*
Marvin L. Piersma
    MIKO Health Care Companies
Pine Rest Christian Hospital*
Prangley, Marks & Co. *
PrimeBank*
Quality Air Heating & Cooling, Inc.
Rapid Engineering, Inc.*
REALTY WORLD—Chase & Chase
Redco Manufacturing Division L.H.L. Incorporated*
Richland Mall Associates
Rospatch Corporation*
Ryder Truck Rental, Inc.*
Sackner Products, Inc.*
Seidman & Seidman*
H.B. Shaine & Co., Inc.*
Shearson Lehman Brothers
Silveri Company
Douglas J. Smith
Spartan Stores, Inc.*
Square Real Estate, Inc.*
Steelcase Inc.*
Steketee's*
Suspa Incorporated*
Sysco/Frost-Pack Food Services*
Thorn Apple Valley, Inc.*
TNT Holland Motor Express*
Travel Consultants, Inc.
Twohey, Maggini, Muldoon, Mudie & Sullivan*
Vans Delivery Service, Inc.
Varnum, Riddering, Schmidt and Howlett*
Warner, Norcross and Judd*
The WBDC Group*
Westinghouse Furniture Systems
West Michigan HealthCare Network (A Blue Care Network HMO)*

S.J. Wisinski and Company*
Wolverine World Wide, Inc.*
WZZM-TV Channel 13*
X-Rite, Inc.*
Yamaha Music Corporation, USA

*Corporate profiles of *In Celebration of Grand Rapids.* The histories of these companies and organizations appear in Part 2, beginning on page 177.

Grand Rapids Centennial Businesses

In continuous operation for at least 100 years, the following Kent County businesses have been recognized as centennial businesses by the Historical Society of Michigan:

Alexander Dodds Company (1882)

American Laundry & Cleaners, Inc. (1881)

American Seating (1886)

Barclay, Ayers & Bertsch Company (1875)

Bergen Brunswig Drug Corporation (1873)

Bissell, Inc. (1876)

Bixby Office Supply Company (1869)

Coye's, Inc. (1855)

Crescent Street Floral Company (1875)

Crosby & Henry (1858)

Davenport College of Business (1866)

Furniture Manufacturers Association of Grand Rapids (1881)

Grand Rapids Gypsum Company (1841)

Grand Rapids Label (1884)

Grinnell-Rowe Company (1875)

Groskopf's, Inc. (1881)

Hannah Floral Company (1880)

Herkner Jewelry Store (1867)

Herpolsheimer Company (1870)

Johnston Optical Company (1876)

Kutsche Hardware (1862)

Law, Weathers & Richardson (1868)

Leitelt Iron Works (1862)

Leonard Division of Kelvinator International (1881)

Monarch Hydraulics Company, Inc. (1856)

S.A. Morman and Company, Inc. (1857)

Old Kent Bank and Trust (1852)

Preusser Jewelers, Inc. (1850)

F. Raniville Company (1874)

Singer Manufacturing Company (1873)

Paul Steketee & Sons Co. (1862)

Stow and Davis Furniture Company (1880)

Wheeler, Upham, Bryant & Uhl (1883)

White and White Surgical Supply and Pharmacy, Inc. (1883)

John Widdicomb Company (1858)

Bibliography

"Accent On: City and County Parks." *Accent Magazine,* June 1979, pp. 11-15, 22-25.

"Accent On: City Planning." *Accent Magazine,* January-February 1979.

"Accent On: West Michigan's Furniture Systems Industry." *Accent Magazine,* March 1979, pp. 17-23.

Allen, Hugh. "Focus On: Fund Raising in West Michigan." *West Michigan,* September 1980, pp. 15-23.

An Analysis of the Grand Rapids-Kent County Area Strengths and Weaknesses. Columbus, Ohio: Battelle Institute, 1986 (Commissioned by the Greater Grand Rapids Economic Area Team and The Right Place Program).

Arlinsky, Ellen. "Citizens Designing Continuous Riverbank Park System for Future Generations." *Accent Magazine,* June 1979, pp. 19-21.

Arlinsky, Ellen. "Focus On: Grand Rapids Citywalk, A Walking Tour of Downtown Grand Rapids." *West Michigan,* July 1980, pp. 15-25.

Arlinsky, Ellen. "A New Era for Those Magic Nights at the Opera." *West Michigan,* November 1980, pp. 19-27.

Aves, John. "Grand Rapids: Public Furniture Capital of the World." *Accent Magazine,* March 1979, pp. 13-14, 49.

Ball, Michael. *Grand Rapids Statistical Abstract.* Information Brokers: Comstock Park, MI, 1983.

Baxter, Albert. *History of the City of Grand Rapids, Michigan.* New York and Grand Rapids: Munsell and Co., 1891 (reprint, Grand Rapids Historical Society, 1974).

Beyer, Eileen. "Getting There: The Economic Impact of Airports." *West Michigan Profile,* August 1986, pp. 7-9.

Beyer, Eileen. "The Office Space Market: How Much Room to Grow?" *West Michigan Profile,* February 1987, pp. 8-10.

Blaich, Jan. "Monroe Mall Gets Ready: An Interview With the Architect." *West Michigan,* July 1980, pp. 33, 55.

Brinks, Herbert. "The America Letters." *Grand River Valley Review,* Volume II, No. 2, Spring-Summer 1981, pp. 2-9, 28-35.

Brosky, John J., Jr. "Grand Slam." *Republic Scene,* May 1981, pp. 23-26, 38-40.

Cady, Marie Jay. "Senator Vandenberg Belonged to the State—and the World." *Advance,* January 20, 1987, p. 1.

Cleland, Charles E. *A Brief History of Michigan Indians.* Michigan History Division, Michigan Department of State. Lansing: 1975.

Clements, Richard. "Lost in the Search for Excellence." *Grand Rapids Business Journal,* Vol. IV, No. 6, July 7, 1986, pp. 5-6.

Conn, Marg Ed. "Accent On: The Grand Rapids Public Museum." *Accent Magazine,* November 1979, pp. 17-29.

Conn, Marg Ed. "Focus On: A Celebration of Ethnic Communities." *West Michigan,* August 1980, pp. 14-24.

Conn, Marg Ed. "The Calvin Connection: Making Room for Politics." *West Michigan,* December 1980, pp. 27-30.

Crawley, Nancy. "Area's Electricity Appetite Up, but Natural Gas Use Dropping." *Grand Rapids Press,* January 21, 1987, p. C26.

Crawley, Nancy, "Big Firms Put City in Good Company." *Grand Rapids Press,* November 1, 1986, p. A1.

Crawley, Nancy. "Irwin Seating Co. Enjoys Fruits of Success, Growing Prosperity." *Grand Rapids Press,* July 20, 1986, p. J1, 2.

Dunbar, Willis Frederick. *All Aboard! A History of Railroads in Michigan.* Grand Rapids: William B. Eerdmans Publishing Company, 1969.

Dunbar, Willis F., and George S. May. *A History of the Wolverine State,* revised ed. Grand Rapids: William B. Eerdmans Publishing Co., 1980.

Eberle, Gary. "The Strip: Fear and Loathing on 28th Street." *West Michigan,* October 1981, pp. 31-34.

"1887—C of C Diamond Jubilee Anniversary Year—1962." *Chamber of Commerce News Bulletin,* Vol. 50, No. 4, April 1962, pp. 1-2.

Elliott, Gerald. *Grand Rapids: Renaissance on the Grand.* Tulsa: Continental Heritage Press, 1982.

Etten, William J. *A Citizens' History of Grand Rapids, Michigan.* Grand Rapids: A.P. Johnson, 1926.

Everett, Franklin. *Memorials of the Grand River Valley.* Chicago: Chicago Legal News Co., 1878 (Reprinted, Grand Rapids Historical Society, 1984).

Fast, Doug. "How Much Is Grand Rapids Worth?" *Grand Rapids Business Journal,* October 15, 1985, p. 21.

Flanders, Richard. "Digging the Past," *Grand Rapids Past, Present and Future.* Grand Rapids: Urban Concern, Inc., 1981, pp. 2-8.

Gallasso, Joe, Ron Garbinski and Don Durocher. "The Premier Ranking: Michigan Private 100." *Michigan Business,* May 1986, pp. 38-45.

Gibson, Art. "Images of West Michigan Railroad History." *Grand River Valley Review,* Vol. V, No. 1, Winter 1984, pp. 21-28.

Gimborys, Kathleen. "To Market, to Market." *West Michigan Profile,* December 1986, pp. 11-13.

Grand Rapids Area Chamber of Commerce. *1986 Membership Directory and Area Guide.*

Grand Rapids Area Chamber of Commerce. *Regional Directory of Manufacturers.* Grand Rapids: 1985.

Grand Rapids Area Chamber of Commerce. "The Western Michigan Market: A Mirror of America," September 1986.

Grand Rapids Area Chamber of Commerce and Grand Rapids Real Estate Board. *Greater Grand Rapids, Michigan.* Woodland Hills, Calif.: Windsor Publications, 1980.

Grand Rapids Made: A Brief History of the Grand Rapids Furniture Industry. Grand Rapids: Grand Rapids Museum Association, 1985.

Grand Rapids Press Newcomers Guide, August 7, 1986.

"Grand Rapids Stars in Study of Housing Values," Grand Rapids Press, August 13, 1986, p. 1.

Harger, Jim. "Expansion Is a Vital Part

of Growth Alliance's Charter." *Grand Rapids Press,* June 29, 1986, p. F1.

Harger, Jim. "Robotic Work Hums as Hi-Tech Industry Grows in West State." *Grand Rapids Press,* June 22, 1986, pp. F1, F4.

"The Hispanics: A Story of Pride and Hope." *Grand Rapids Press,* July 27, 1986, pp. E1-4.

Honey, Charles. "There Are Schools for All Ages." *Grand Rapids Press Newcomers Guide,* July 7, 1986, pp. 22-24.

Hosey, Jeannie. "The West Michigan 40: Firm Foundation for Region's Economy." *West Michigan Profile,* September 1986, pp. 8-9.

Hostetler, Maggie. "Turning Back the Clock." *Grand Rapids Press,* February 16, 1986, pp. A19-20.

"The Immigrants," *Grand Rapids Press,* June 29, 1986, pp. B1-2.

Jennings, Carrie B. *The Grand Rapids Fire Department: History of Its Progress from Leathern Bucket to Steam Fire Engine and to the Present Time.* Grand Rapids: The Firemen's Fund Association, 1889 (Reprinted by Black Letter Press, 1971).

Kent County Department of Social Services. *1985 Annual Report.*

Knack, James. "The Grand Plan," *Grand Rapids Past, Present and Future.* Grand Rapids: Urban Concern, Inc., 1981.

Koopman, Leroy. "Books With Vision." *West Michigan,* June 1981, pp. 49-53.

Korreck, Gary F. "The Many Faces of Heartside." West Michigan, April 1981, pp. 19-22, 53-56.

Kurzhals, Richard. "The Community of the Bluff." *Grand River Valley Review,* Vol. V, No. 1, Winter 1984, pp. 6-18.

Kurzhals, Richard. "What Price Progress?" *Grand Rapids Past, Present and Future.* Grand Rapids: Urban Concern, Inc., 1981.

Kwapil, Marg Ed Conn and Ellen Arlinsky. "Grand Rapids Environment Since 1970." *Grand Rapids Press,* April 17, 1980, p. 4B.

Lohr, Mary. "Economic Prognosis Good for Grand Rapids Hospitals." *Grand Rapids Press,* January 21, 1987, p. C3.

Lohr, Mary. "Hospital Quality Is High, Costs Low." *The Grand Rapids Press Newcomers Guide,* August 7, 1986, pp. 11-12.

Lohr, Mary. "Record $8.6 Million Sought in United Way Fund Drive." *Grand Rapids Press,* June 25, 1986, p. B1.

Longcore, Kathleen. "State Food-Processing Industry Will Taste Success in 1987." *Grand Rapids Press,* January 21, 1987, p. C16.

Lydens, Z.Z., ed. *The Story of Grand Rapids.* Grand Rapids: Kregel Publications, 1967.

McCarthy, Tom. "Economic Firm Aims to Keep City Healthy." *Grand Rapids Press,* January 21, 1987, p. C27.

McCarthy, Tom. "Study Rates Grand Rapids High as Leader in Industry, But . . ." *Grand Rapids Press,* October 16, 1985, p. C3.

McClurken, James. "Strangers in Their Own Land." *Grand River Valley Review,* Volume VI, No. 1.

Mahoney, Cathie. "Smitty, 11,000-Year-Old Whodunit." *Grand Rapids Press,* February 23, 1986, Wonderland, pp. 6, 39-41.

Mapes, Lynn G. "A Century of Growth Through Annexation." *Grand Rapids Magazine,* May 1975, pp. 31-34.

Mapes, Lynn G. "The Great 1911 Furniture Strike." *Grand Rapids Magazine,* September 1975, pp. 19-22.

Mapes, Lynn G., and Anthony Travis. *A Pictorial History of Grand Rapids.* Grand Rapids: Kregel Publications, 1976.

Mapes, Lynn G., and Anthony Travis. "Clubs, Concerts, Social Issues and Suffrage." *Grand River Valley Review,* Vol. II, No. 1, Fall-Winter 1980, pp. 2-9.

Mencarelli, Jim. "A Life of Illusion and Fear." *Grand Rapids Press,* July 28, 1986, pp. 1, 4-5.

Meninga, Clarence. "What the Rocks and Rapids Tell Us." *Grand Rapids Press,* May 13, 1979, Wonderland, pp. 34-35.

"Monroe Center Opening Schedule of Events." *West Michigan,* September 1980, p. 37.

Narezo, Janet. "Landmark Furniture Buildings." *Grand River Valley Review,* Vol. III, No. 1, Fall/Winter 1981, pp. 28-31.

Narezo, Janet. "100 Years of Furniture." *West Michigan,* June 1981, pp. 27-35, 55-57.

"New Study Stresses Truth About Grand Rapids." *Grand Rapids Press,* October 25, 1985, p. A1.

Olson, Gordon L. "The Furniture Pioneers." *Grand River Valley Review,* Vol. I, No. 2, Spring/Summer 1980, pp. 1-4, 16-23.

Olson, Gordon L. "The Mound Builders of the Grand River Valley." *Grand River Valley Review,* Vol. V, No. 2, pp. 14-21.

"Railway Passenger Travel 1825-1880." *Americana Review,* 1962.

Realvesco Properties. *Real Estate Report,* Vol. I, No. 3, November 1986, p. 1.

Roeloffs, Barbara. "Living History." *Grand River Valley Review,* Vol. I, No. 1, Fall 1979, pp. 21-22.

Sinkevics, John. "Downtown's Missing Link." Grand Rapids Press, July 20, 1986, p. D1.

Sinkevics, John. "East bank Hotel Gets Go Ahead From City." *Grand Rapids Press,* June 17, 1986, p. 1.

Sinkevics, John. "Monroe Center—A Time of Transition." *Grand Rapids Press,* September 29, 1985, p. H1.

Smith, Denise L. "Real Estate Market Is Booming in Grand Rapids Area." *Grand Rapids Press,* September 18, 1986.

"Study: Metro Grand Rapids State's Fifth Most Segregated Area." *Grand Rapids Press,* October 10, 1985, p. C1.

Swierenga, Robert P. "The Dutch Transplanting in Michigan and the Midwest," The Clarence M. Burton Memorial Lecture, 1985. Historical Society of Michigan, 1986.

Sypert, Tracy L. "'Grand River Edges Policy' Is Slowly Becoming a Reality." *Grand Rapids Press,* October 6, 1986, p. C1.

Turner, Lynn. "City Looks at Linking Marketplace, Museum." *Grand Rapids Business Journal,* Vol. 4, No. 38, September 29, 1986, p. 1.

Tuttle, Charles Richard. *History of Grand Rapids 1874.* Grand Rapids: Black Letter Press, 1974 (reprint).

vanReken, Donald L. *The Interurban Era in Holland, Michigan.* Holland, MI: Donald L. vanReken, 1981.

Winter, John. "It's Everybody's Business." *Grand Rapids Past, Present and Future.* Grand Rapids: Urban Concern, Inc., 1981.

Index

D0791831

KATHARINE
HEPBURN

*An
Independent
Woman*

KATHARINE
HEPBURN

An
Independent
Woman

RONALD BERGAN

Arcade Publishing · New York

Copyright © 1996 by Ronald Bergan

All rights reserved. No part of this book may be reproduced in any
form or by any electronic or mechanical means, including information
storage and retrieval systems, without permission in writing from the
publisher, except by a reviewer who may quote brief passages in a
review.

FIRST U.S. EDITION

First published in the United Kingdom by Bloomsbury Publishing plc.
ISBN 1-55970-351-2
Library of Congress Catalog Card Number 95-83505
Library of Congress Cataloging-in-Publication information is available.

Published in the United States by Arcade Publishing, Inc., New York
Distributed by Little, Brown and Company

10 9 8 7 6 5 4 3 2 1

Designed by Bradbury and Williams
Picture research by Juliet Brightmore

PRINTED IN HONG KONG

Contents

Author's Note and Acknowledgements

Katharine Hepburn was eighty-seven years old when I visited her at her house on East 49th Street in New York in the spring of 1995. A few months previously, a biography of Katharine Hepburn by Barbara Leaming had been published. Although Kate herself refused to go into print on the subject, in private she was outraged and upset by the book's 'inaccuracies', and what she saw as a betrayal of her confidences. A number of people with special and personal knowledge, including Kate's niece Katharine Houghton, John Ford's grandson, and Selden West, the authorized biographer of Spencer Tracy, attacked the book's 'distortions'. Their main complaints were that Leaming had painted an erroneously negative picture of Tracy and his attitude towards Kate, and exaggerated the importance of Ford's relationship with the star, building a false psychological structure upon it.

It is not my intention to condemn the work of a fellow biographer, only to explain the book's effect on Kate and her family and friends when I approached her to comment on the pictures contained within these pages. In the light of the appearance of the Leaming book, Kate was naturally wary about talking to any other writer, and was reluctant to be drawn on this plainly disagreeable matter. Nevertheless, she was willing to allow me into her home, where she signed my copy of her autobiography, *Me*, and made a number of perceptive and penetrating remarks about her career, which I have included in this celebration of her life and work.

I have tried, as much as possible, to avoid speculation, and to weed out the myths that inevitably grow around a Hollywood legend. To this purpose, I have put my trust in much of what Kate has said in interviews and written about herself, and in those who knew her well, as well as in Anne Edwards' excellent biography (Hodder and Stoughton, 1985). But I was merely responsible for the text, and had only a small hand in the selection of the illustrative material in a book which, I feel, is eloquent proof of the adage that pictures speak louder than words.

I have cause to be grateful to the following people (in alphabetical order): Zelda Baron for choice anecdotes; Juliet Brightmore for her taste and eye for a good photograph; Howard and Ron Mandelbaum at Photofest, who anticipated my every need; Penny Phillips, who had the perspicacity to commission the book and supported me throughout; and Sharon Powers, Katharine Hepburn's congenial and most helpful secretary, who went out of her way to pave a way for my visit to Kate's home. Most of all, I am grateful to Katharine Hepburn, for her grace, intelligence, enduring beauty and radiant smile.

RONALD BERGAN, LONDON 1996

For Leslie, wherever you may be.

Introduction

―――――――――

I'm a personality as well as an actress.
Show me an actress who isn't a
personality, and you'll show me a
woman who isn't a star.

'A handsome woman of great temperament, authority, and presence. She has been a queen of international importance for forty-six years and you know it. Finally, she is that most unusual thing: a genuine feminine woman thoroughly capable of holding her own in a man's world.' This was how James Goldman pictured the character of Eleanor of Aquitaine in his play *The Lion in Winter*, an apt description of Katharine Hepburn herself at the peak of her profession. But it was not an easy or a straightforward climb to the top.

Given her nature, it is understandable that Katharine Hepburn, more than any other screen actress, has irritated as many people as she has enraptured. Among the great female movie stars, she is perhaps the most difficult to categorize. With her singular looks, the distinctive cadences of her voice and her complete disregard for the conventions of conservative Hollywood, she followed her own path, in films – where her choice of roles often reflected her own personality and beliefs – and in life.

As an actress, she was both robust and vulnerable, tough-minded yet sentimental, delivering lines in a voice that Hepburn herself described as 'a cross between Donald Duck and a Stradivarius'. She was a curious mixture of liberated and submissive woman, platonic and sexual beauty, scrawny spinster, waif and androgyne. Although she played the rebel daughter in many of her early successes, the Hepburn image seems always to have been of a slightly shocking, eccentric aunt. What she demonstrated, above all, on screen and off, were the pleasures, pains and possibilities of independence.

Katharine Hepburn at the beginning of her screen career in the early 1930s, when Hollywood was unsure how to present this singular personality to the public.

However, most of the men she fell for dominated her to a large extent, and she remained closely tied to her parents, heavily dependent on their approval. 'I'm like the girl who never grew up,' she once said. 'I just never really left home, so to speak. I always went back there almost every weekend of my life when I wasn't filming. I kept my life there... my roots.'

When Hepburn arrived in Hollywood in 1932, RKO studio executives described her as looking 'like a cross between a horse and a monkey', and George Cukor characterized her as 'a boa-constrictor on a fast'. She wasn't a long-stemmed American beauty, a seductive foreign vamp, a cute, golden-haired 'sweetheart', or a defenceless tragic heroine; she was decidedly a modern, emancipated woman, with a purposeful stride.

In a memo to his staff, David Selznick, rejecting her for the role of Scarlett O'Hara in his production of *Gone with the Wind*, wrote, 'Hepburn has two strikes against her – first, the unquestionable and very widespread intense public dislike of her at this moment, and second, the fact that she has yet to demonstrate the sex qualities that are probably the most important of all the many requisites of Scarlett.'

But she had confounded everyone, helped somewhat by Hollywood's glamour treatment, by emerging, with her high cheekbones and natural looks, as a stunning beauty. Her beauty grew out of her own belief in herself, exposing her own nerves and vulnerability, along with her intelligence and sensibility.

From her first appearance on the screen as John Barrymore's daughter in *A Bill of Divorcement* (1932), Hepburn was a breath of fresh air. She won her first Oscar in her third screen role in *Morning Glory* (1932), playing Eva Lovelace, a young actress who comes to New York determined to succeed on the stage and prove she is 'the finest actress in the world'. In her four films with Cary Grant – *Sylvia Scarlett, Holiday, Bringing Up Baby, The Philadelphia Story* – she was radiant, full of spirit and sexuality which he brought out in her, offering that rare combination of wit and emotional intensity.

Yet, for years, especially outside the big cities, she remained a minority or acquired taste, rarely appealing to Southern or Midwestern audiences. People couldn't relate to her. She wasn't selling sex or wholesomeness or glamour, the commodities most leading ladies dealt in, and her originality wasn't the sort that shopgirls could identify with or men fantasize about. She always appeared irreverent and very self-assured, threatening or challenging male supremacy. Children laughed at her diction and aristocratic airs. She had been dubbed 'Katharine of Arrogance'. Hepburn's fans came from the middle-aged, sophisticated portion of film audiences, but even this group was frequently put off by the fluttery mannerisms and pretensions of her worst films. Inevitably, in the 1930s, she gained the label of 'box-office poison'.

Richard Watts in the *Herald Tribune* spoke for many people when he began his review of *The Philadelphia Story* with a tribute to Hepburn's pluck. 'Few actresses have been so relentlessly assailed by critics, wits, columnists, magazine editors, and other professional assailers over so long a period of time, and even if you confess that some of the abuse had a certain amount of justification to it, you must admit she faced it gamely and unflinchingly and fought back with courage and gallantry.'

Katharine Hepburn's career straddled seven decades, proving that 'age cannot wither her, nor custom stale her infinite variety'. There are performers whose physique tends to type-cast them in historical roles, others who cannot appear anything but contemporary. Kate's style might be described as timeless. Thus there was no incongruity in her winning an Oscar for her suburban wife and mother in *Guess Who's Coming to Dinner?* as well as for her witty, patrician, strong-willed Queen Eleanor of Aquitaine, the estranged wife of King Henry II in *The Lion in Winter* in successive years. With *On Golden Pond*, she became the first performer to win four Best Actress Oscars, from a record twelve nominations, an achievement as yet unsurpassed.

As she matured, she was admired for the very reasons she had once been despised. Just as in life she had initially alienated many people by her haughty and assertive manner, and then won them over completely, so Katharine Hepburn finally conquered the movie-going public. She became a member of the select group of Hollywood favourites who are mythic embodiments of certain values such as independence and integrity, cherished by American audiences. How Katharine Hepburn moved from the awkward, flamboyant, tempestuous, self-opinionated girl and 'box-office poison' to become, in her own phrase, 'Saint Katharine', I hope the following pages will make clear.

Kate in 1975, after four decades in films, relaxing in her habitual casual clothes and manner at her New York home, surrounded by books and flowers.

*Two freckled-faced kids –
shy four-year-old Kate (left)
with older brother Tom,
whose tragic early death was
to leave a deep scar.*

1879 in Hanover County, Virginia. Of Scottish descent, the Hepburns could trace their ancestry back to James Hepburn, Earl of Bothwell, third husband of Mary, Queen of Scots. This was one of the reasons that Kate wished to play the doomed queen on screen many years later, despite her antipathy towards the character.

Tom Hepburn, an athletic, handsome red-head, was a graduate student at Johns Hopkins Medical School in Baltimore when he met Kit Houghton. Just after having been introduced to him, she told her sister Edith, 'That's the one!' When Edith pointed out that the man didn't have a penny, Kit replied, 'I'd marry him even if I knew it meant I'd die in a year – and go to hell!'

In 1904, after Kit had earned a master's degree in art at Radcliffe and Tom was an intern at Hartford Hospital, they were married. Within a year, they had their first child, Thomas Houghton Hepburn. When their second child, Katharine Houghton Hepburn, was born on 12 May 1907, at 22 Hudson Street, Hartford, Connecticut, Kit, who had hoped for a red-haired child, asked the nurse to hold the baby up to the window so she could see, and then exclaimed, 'Yes, it's red!' Her family called her 'Redtop', as well as 'Kat', 'Kate' or 'Kathy'.

Though Dr and Mrs Hepburn were not considered rich by Hartford's standards, they bought their own

home – an early Victorian house on Hawthorn Street – had servants and were one of the first families in the new neighbourhood to possess a car. Shaded by one of the eight giant cedars growing on the property, small Kate played by the brook that ran through her parents' land, and climbed trees.

One morning, her father opened the door to a policeman. 'Sir,' the officer reported, 'your little girl is in the top of that tallest cedar. I can see her red hair sticking out above the green.'

'For heaven's sake don't call to her,' Dr Hepburn retorted. 'You might make her fall.' He then shut the door and returned to his reading.

Shortly after Kate's birth, her mother attended a suffrage lecture given by Emmeline Pankhurst. In fact, Dr Hepburn encouraged her to go. He had read Shaw and Ibsen, who revealed to him the frustrations of the modern woman, and he knew that his wife, being a rebel at heart and dedicated to her own emancipation, would soon find the role of wife and mother too restrictive. Kate later interpreted her mother's thoughts as, 'Now this is great, and these two little things are fine, but is this the end of my contribution to the world?'

Mrs Hepburn was much impressed by the diminutive Mrs Pankhurst (they were later to become good friends), and she immediately decided to join the suffragist movement. It wasn't long before she was addressing meetings, marching and carrying banners demanding equality for women.

From the age of four, Kate was taken along to meetings and lectures with her mother. Seated either on the platform or in the front row, the child listened to her mother's booming voice as she rallied audiences to her cause. This impressed Kate no end, and throughout her life she was given to making speeches, not from a soap box, but in drawing rooms.

She would also devote a great deal of time, in her later years, to Planned Parenthood. Ironically, in the midst of her mother's campaigns for the practice of birth control, a further four Hepburn children were born: Richard (1911), Bob (1913), Marion (1918) and Peg (1920).

Dr and Mrs Hepburn taught their children that everything in life must be earned by their own efforts; nothing must be freely given or received. The children were never asked to leave the room no matter what the subject of the conversation. They sat in the parlour and listened to men and women of radical ideas discussing venereal disease, prostitution and the use of contraceptives. When Kate asked her mother, now President of the Connecticut Women's Suffrage Association, about her own birth, Mrs Hepburn explained to her 'scientifically and specifically'.

'Oh, then I can have a baby without getting married,' Kate replied. 'That's what I shall do.'

According to the author Nina Wilcox Putnam, an occasional visitor to the Hepburn household, the child was 'totally undisciplined by her clever mother'. 'I saw her take food from the plates of distinguished guests – at will and unreproved... I remember her interrupting the conversation of her elders – unreproved. I remember her snatching ladies' hats and putting them on her own head – unreproved.'

What bothered Kate most was her overabundance of freckles – they covered her from head to toe. Worried that because of them no one would want her, she confided her fears to her father.

'I want to tell you something, Kate, and you must never forget it,' he said. 'Jesus Christ, Alexander the Great and Leonardo da Vinci all had red hair and freckles, and they did all right.'

Yet, when she went to her first dance with her older brother Tom, she felt awkward, and overheard a boy ask Tom, 'Who's that goofy-looking wallflower standing over there?' An experience that,

unconsciously, must have stood her in good stead when she took on roles of a number of wallflowers, such as Alice Adams, from a young age.

At school Kate made few friends, depending mainly on Tom and her father for companionship. Every day their father led them in callisthenics, taught them wrestling holds and had them join his male friends in team matches of touch football, for which Kate had her hair cut so that the boys couldn't grab it. Winning was important to Kate, for it brought the highest praise from her father, who treated her on a par with the boys.

Dr Hepburn believed in cold baths, the colder the better, and all the children had to get used to them. 'That gave me the impression that the bitterer the medicine, the better it was for you,' Kate later commented. Cold showers were something she continued to practise into her old age.

Despite her mother's work for women's equality, and her independent nature, the Hepburn household was a classic patriarchy – though Mrs Hepburn did throw things at her husband when they argued about politics. Kate's description of her father defined her own ideal man. 'There are men of action and men of thought, and if you ever get a combination of the two – well – that's the top – you've got someone like Dad.'

Besides all sports, theatre and films interested her, and she idolized cowboy star William S. Hart. In the tiny theatre Dr Hepburn had built for her in the backyard, Kate dramatized Uncle Tom's Cabin, casting it with neighbourhood children. 'I wouldn't play Eva because Eva was too good. I played Topsy – and as there was a little girl in the neighbourhood who I wanted to get even with, I chose her for Eva – as Topsy played all the mean tricks on her.'

Up to the age of twelve, Kate was an uncomplicated, energetic, fun-loving, freckled tomboy. But then something happened that altered her character overnight, and indirectly contributed to the kind of actress and woman she was to become.

Left: *Such devoted sisters. Kate (left) with Marion (centre) and Peggy, her virtual double, at the Hepburn family home in 1940.*

Right: *Kit Hepburn flanked by her daughters, Marion (left) and Peggy, at the Radio City première of Kate's new picture,* Alice Adams *(1935).*

2

'Self-conscious Beauty!'

My father had been disgusted and heartsick over the fact that I wanted to act. Thought it a silly profession, closely allied to streetwalking. That I had developed into a cheap show-off and that I was entering a shabby profession which was based on youth and looks.

Kate and her brother Tom were virtually inseparable. He joined her in all her home theatricals. He played the banjo, loved to sing, and wrote some songs of his own. He was a good athlete and student, and his father was making plans for him to enter Yale as a medical student. On Tuesday 29 March 1920, during the Easter holidays, Mrs Hepburn took her two eldest children to New York, where they stayed with a family friend. Brother and sister saw Pavlova dance, explored Greenwich Village, Fifth Avenue and Central Park together, and went to see a play based on Mark Twain's *A Connecticut Yankee in King Arthur's Court*, in which a scene of a hanging plainly impressed Tom.

The next morning, Kate went upstairs to the studio attic to wake Tom, because they were getting the 10.20 from Grand Central back to Hartford. She got no reply when she called him. She screamed when she entered the bedroom and saw her brother's body suspended from a noose made from a torn bedsheet which had been placed around a beam. She frantically cut Tom down and lay him on the bed. Kate, who knew he was dead, was holding her brother in her arms when the doctor arrived fifteen minutes later. Tom had been dead for five hours.

Strangely, there was already a history of suicide on both sides of the family – Dr Hepburn's brother, and Mrs Hepburn's father and uncle. Kate remembered standing on the boat crossing the Hudson going to a crematorium in New Jersey with Tom's body, and seeing her mother crying. 'I'd never seen my mother cry before. And I never saw her cry again.'

Dr Hepburn believed that it was not suicide but a stunt that had gone horribly wrong. The *New York Times* ran a headline the next day: MYSTERY IN SUICIDE OF SURGEON'S SON. FATHER SAYS SON'S HANGING WAS BOYISH STUNT. Whatever the reasons, the tragedy had a severe and long-lasting

Kate as seen in her graduate year in the 1928 Bryn Mawr yearbook, far more at ease with herself than when she arrived at the college.

effect on Kate. A depression set in her, her schoolwork suffered and she found the company of her peers even more difficult. 'I felt isolated. I knew something that the girls did not know: tragedy.'

Because Kate had become a bitter, edgy, moody girl, she was taken out of school and given a tutor, Gradually, she attempted to replace or become her late brother. She spoke of taking up medical studies as Tom might have done and, knowing how much Tom's sporting prowess had pleased her father, she worked hard to equal his achievements. She became excellent at golf, her father's favourite pastime, coming second in the Connecticut Women's Open at fifteen. She won a junior ice-skating championship, and was a good tennis player and a competent swimmer and diver. Many of these athletic abilities were convincingly on display in *Pat and Mike* some decades later.

Kate was not much of a student – she flunked Latin, and had no notion of physics and chemistry. It became clear that becoming a doctor was out of the question, and for a time it seemed as if she would never pass college entrance exams at all. Her parents, however, were determined that she should obtain a degree in some field of study. After a crash course with private tutors, Kate arrived at Bryn Mawr College, her mother's alma mater, at the age of seventeen, totally undisciplined scholastically and with very few social graces. The other girls at the college found it difficult to warm to this oddball, snooty young woman. Kate took showers after midnight when the rest of the dormitory was asleep, bathed in the campus fountain and then rolled herself dry on the grass and once, during a blizzard, went out on to a roof in the nude, allowing herself to be covered with snow.

This exhibitionism might possibly be interpreted as a defence mechanism to conceal her feelings of inadequacy when dealing with girls of her own age. She made no effort to make friends, and had none.

Kate used to eat in her room as much as possible

to avoid going into the dining room. 'In the early part of the semester, I had gone into the dining room... I was dressed in a French blue flared skirt which buttoned up the front with big white buttons – and an Iceland blue and white sweater popular at the time. I certainly did not consider myself beautiful. I was just painfully self-conscious. To my horror, I heard a voice – a New York voice – from the vicinity of where I was supposed to sit: "Self-conscious beauty!" I nearly dropped dead... That year I never went back into that dining room.'

Kate was a poor student, cutting classes regularly, though she especially envied one girl her scholarship. 'I'd go to the library to study and sit next to her. I could hear the wheels whirring in her head. I was insanely jealous, and so, naturally, I loved her.' In her

The barefoot Pandora rests during rehearsals for the May Day college production of John Lyly's The Woman in the Moon.

sophomore year, the dean sent Dr Hepburn a letter suggesting that his daughter drop out of school.

'If I had a patient who was sick,' he replied, 'I wouldn't release him from the hospital.'

What kept her going was the dream of becoming an actress, although when she confided this to a friend, she received the reply, 'You! An actress? You're too skinny and funny-looking!' Unfazed, Kate studied night and day, aware that she would not be eligible for campus dramatics unless her grades improved greatly. They did, and she appeared as a leading man in A. A. Milne's *The Truth about Blayds*, and as Pandora in John Lyly's *The Woman in the Moon*, performed during the traditional May Day celebrations at the college. Barefoot and bare-armed, dressed in a white flowing gown, her red hair loose and blowing madly, Kate made a striking impression. However, her father, whose approval mattered beyond anyone else's, told her 'that all he could see in that performance were the soles of my dirty feet getting blacker and blacker. And my freckled face getting redder and redder.'

Kate's performance gained her a letter of introduction to Edwin H. Knopf, a young theatrical producer who was preparing a season of summer stock in Baltimore. Unfortunately, she was told there was no place for her in the season, and returned to college. But, the following year, on the eve of her graduation, Knopf offered her the part of a lady-in-waiting to Mary Boland in *The Czarina*.

At first, Mary Boland was dismayed by the skinny, red-haired, freckle-faced girl in the wings. She felt Kate's eyes burningly turned on her during rehearsals, and demanded that Knopf have her taken away. But when Boland saw her in a ball dress, she was surprised. 'The ugly duckling became a swan – it was incredible! I never saw anything like that eager girl, so proud to walk across a stage she seemed to be borne up by light.'

When Kate left the Knopf stock company, she

An unusual cheesecake pose from Kate at the beginning of her career – she never took kindly to this sort of thing.

headed for New York in search of an acting coach. She chose Frances Robinson-Duff, an imposing, white-haired woman, with whom Ina Claire, Helen Hayes and other great Broadway stars had studied. She had a classroom on the top floor of an East 62nd Street townhouse. 'I distinctly remember the day she came to me,' recalled Miss Robinson-Duff. 'It was raining. She had run up the stairs. She burst in the door, unannounced, and flung herself on the settee. Rain from her red hair and down her nose. She sat in a dripping huddle and stared. "I want to be an actress!" she explained. "I want to learn everything!" '

At the same time, Kate was being pursued by a young man whom she had met at a Bryn Mawr dance. Ludlow Ogden Smith was the son of wealthy parents, educated at exclusive boarding schools and a graduate of the University of Grenoble. Twenty-nine in 1928, tall and lean, 'Luddy', as Kate always called him, had a degree in industrial engineering that he never used, preferring to pursue a career as an insurance broker instead.

Though Kate described him later as 'an odd-looking man – dark hair, dark eyes far apart. He was foreign-looking. Pink cheeks. An odd nose, long with a hump in it. A long mouth, full-lipped', he possessed a quality of sophistication that she found attractive. In Luddy, Kate gained an attentive and elegant escort, an amusing companion, a sympathetic friend and a man who would never stand in the way of her career. She saw a great deal of him as she prepared for the role of the secretary in Knopf's New York production of *The Big Pond*. In fact, she lost her virginity to him. 'Luddy and I were in the apartment [a mutual friend's] and there was the bed and there didn't seem any reason not to... I mean we did it. I didn't object. And that was the end of my virtue. He was my beau from then on.'

About a week before the scheduled opening in Great Neck, Long Island, Knopf fired the leading lady and replaced her by Kate, just like a scene in *Morning Glory*. But unlike the 1933 RKO movie, the novice actress was totally unprepared for the part and terrified by it. Overcome by stage fright, she gave an appalling performance and was fired. Incredibly she was offered more work, in a flop called *These Days* and as understudy to the star, Hope Williams, in Philip Barry's *Holiday*, which had just opened successfully in New Haven. Williams was a popular light comedienne of the Twenties, whose arch mannerisms and boyish appeal may have influenced Kate's development as an actress. Philip Barry, the playwright, was to become a significant force in her career.

Two weeks later, Kate impetuously accepted a proposal of marriage from Luddy. 'If you want to sacrifice the admiration of many men for the criticism of one, go ahead, get married,' her mother had told her. They were married at her parents' West Hartford home on 12 December1928, and went to Bermuda on their honeymoon. But Kate soon realized that, whatever her histrionic abilities, playing a wife for real was a role that was beyond her.

A month after the Broadway production of *Holiday* closed in June 1929, without Kate ever having stepped on stage, she and Luddy crossed to France. Because difficulties arose between them, the vacation was cut short; they returned to New York within two weeks and took up separate residences. By that time *Holiday* was touring and, when Hope Williams took ill one night, Kate finally got the chance to play the role. This time she was more than adequate. Ten years later, now a glamorous movie star, she was able to make the part her own in George Cukor's dazzling screen version.

Although she got a few good reviews on the road in *Death Takes a Holiday*, in which she played Grazia, a young girl in love with Death, in the personification of Prince Sirki, a handsome man, one critic referred to her as 'a new girl looking for all the world like a death's head, with a metallic voice' and another thought her 'hoydenish and gaunt'. She was subsequently fired and, according to her brutally candid father, 'They were absolutely right. You are carrying on on that stage. You are galumphing there

like a maniac. Who's going to believe that my daughter, a big healthy girl like you, could fall in love with death? With death, for God's sakes!'

After a few more roles in summer stock, at the time when Kate felt her career was not going anywhere, she was spotted by theatre producer Gilbert Miller, who offered her the choice role of Leslie Howard's mistress in a Philip Barry play called *The Animal Kingdom* that he was bringing into New York. Rehearsals began in Boston, but Kate and Howard did not get on from the beginning. He hated her 'outrageous posturings' and 'insufferable bossiness'. She thought Howard disliked her because, at five foot seven, she was taller than him.

'I remember one hideous moment when I said, "What would you like me to do here, Mr Howard?" And he answered, "I really don't give a damn what you do, my dear."

Howard began to put pressure on Miller to have Kate removed, and she was replaced after the Pittsburgh opening. Devastated, she rang Philip Barry to complain about her treatment. When she asked him why she had been fired, to Kate's chagrin, the playwright replied, 'Well, to be brutally frank, you weren't very good.' This from a man, whose play *The Philadelphia Story*, written with her in mind, would later resuscitate her career, and who would become a great friend.

Then, in the vicissitudinous manner that typifies Kate's career, she was offered the part of Antiope, the energetic and athletic Queen of the Amazons (ideal casting) in Julian Thompson's *The Warrior's Husband*, loosely based on *Lysistrata*, which opened at the Morosco Theatre in March 1932. From the moment she entered in her short-skirted Greek costume, leaping spectacularly down a treacherous twenty-step stairway three steps at a time, a stuffed deer with an arrow in its back wrapped around her shoulders, she staked her claim to stardom.

The critics raved and Hollywood talent scouts started nosing around. 'Nobody ever noticed me until

Antiope, Queen of the Amazons, in The Warrior's Husband *at the Morosco Theatre in 1932, the stage role that brought Kate to the attention of Hollywood.*

scene from *Holiday*, which she had understudied for six months. She played it with desperate earnestness, miserably conscious of the camera, and overemphasizing all the wrong words.

As fate would have it, David O. Selznick was at that time struggling with the casting of the film version of Clemence Dane's *A Bill of Divorcement* at RKO, to be directed by George Cukor. Norma Shearer and Irene Dunne were among those considered for the key role of the daughter. To Cukor's astonishment, Selznick suddenly decided to cast his current girlfriend, 'a pretty little blonde *ingénue*'. Cukor, disgusted, threatened to quit. Hayward got word of the problem at RKO and persuaded Cukor to see Kate's test.

'She was quite unlike anybody I had ever seen... I thought, I suppose right away, "She's too odd. It won't work." But at one moment in a very emotional scene, she picked up a glass. The camera focused on her back. There was an enormous feeling, a weight about the manner in which she picked up the glass.'

I was in a leg show,' was Kate's comment. Halfway through the run of eighty-three performances, a Hollywood agent named Leland Hayward began to court her as a client. He thought that her vivacious personality and striking appearance would best be displayed on film, and he saw her as star potential. He talked to Paramount and they made a small offer for her services. Kate turned them down. With a shrewdness beyond her years and station, Kate insisted Hayward set $1500 a week as her price. RKO picked up the bait and asked her to take a screen test in New York. She chose a

Cukor had a terrible time persuading Selznick even to look at the test. He got top screenwriter Adela Rogers St John to back him up. Kate had just opened in a new play, *The Bride the Sun Shines on*, in summer stock when she received a telegram from Hayward telling her that not only would RKO meet her $1500-a-week demand, she was to leave for California immediately to appear opposite John Barrymore in her first film.

3

'My Star Will Never Set'

Everyone thought I was bold and fearless, and even arrogant... but inwardly I was always quaking... I've never cared about how afraid I may have been inside – I've always done what I thought I should.

In July 1932, Luddy saw Kate and her actress friend Laura Harding off to Hollywood on the Super Chief. In order to avoid the press, she stepped off the train in Pasadena, believing she looked quite elegant in an ill-fitting grey silk suit with a matching pancake hat, which she described as 'a sort of grey-blue straw dish upside down on my head'. To Leland Hayward and partner Myron Selznick, David's older brother, who had driven out from Los Angeles to meet her, her outfit appeared more bizarre than stylish. She also had a swollen eye from having got steel filings embedded in it on the train. Her hair was drawn tightly back, screwed into a casual knot and tucked under the band of her hat.

'This is what David's paying $1500 a week for?' Myron gasped.

Kate and Laura were then taken to the very smart Château Marmont Hotel above Sunset Boulevard. The next morning Kate arrived at the studio to be greeted by George Cukor, whose first reaction in seeing this 'boa constrictor on a fast' was even worse than Myron's. He thought he had made the most horrible mistake.

When Cukor showed her the sketches for her costumes for the film, Kate peered at them through red eyes and said, 'They're no good! I want my clothes designed by someone like Chanel.'

This got Cukor's dander up. 'Considering the way you look, I can hardly take your judgement seriously.'

'I thought these clothes were pretty fancy. I paid a great deal for them.'

'Well, they're terrible. You look ghastly. I think any woman who would wear such an outfit outside a bathroom wouldn't know what clothes are. Now what do you think of that?'

'You win. Pick out the clothes you want,' Kate acknowledged, extending her hand for Cukor to shake.

Cukor, then thirty-three, was a portly, bespectacled homosexual with

Kate made over by Hollywood in the Garbo mould. It took some time for them to exploit her own very special personality.

whom Kate was to become firm friends for life. He was also to prove one of her most sympathetic directors.

Kate's next studio appointment was with the RKO publicity department. The meeting lasted barely five minutes, during which time she announced that her private life was her own and that she did not believe in publicity. Nobody had any idea that she was married.

The make-up and hairdressing departments also threw up their hands in despair after an encounter with the studio's new acquisition. Kate told them she could do her own face and hair better than they could. Cukor agreed that her natural looks should be preserved but insisted the freckles and frizzy hair had to go. (For years heavy make-up blotted out her freckles on screen and they were removed from all stills.)

At the first encounter with her co-star in *A Bill of Divorcement*, former matinée idol John Barrymore, a notorious womanizer and drinker, he walked unsteadily over to Kate and peered into her inflamed eyes. 'I also hit the bottle occasionally, my dear. But I have a perfect disguise. You see this little phial of eyedrops? When I use it, it clears up the inflammation right away. People think I've been cold sober.'

'But, Mr Barrymore, I have a cinder in my eye!'

'That's what they all say, my dear.'

Later, Barrymore invited her to his dressing room and, without warning, threw all his clothes off. Kate was astonished and backed against the wall.

'My dear, any young girl would be thrilled to make love to the great John Barrymore.'

'Not me,' Kate said in terror. 'My father doesn't want me to make babies.'

On another occasion, Barrymore was said to have pinched her behind. 'If you do that again,' she said, 'I'm going to stop acting.'

'I wasn't aware you had started, my dear,' Barrymore snapped.

Kate enjoying the material benefits of stardom in her 1932 Bugatti, although she was never a showy person.

Above: *One of the many
vampish publicity stills to
which Kate had to submit in
her early years in Hollywood.*

Right: *Her strong
personality yet to emerge,
Kate is glamorized and
freckleless but instantly
recognizable in 1933.*

Rapidly making up on the set of Sylvia Scarlett, *in which George Cukor directed Kate for the third time.*

On the set of her second triumph, Morning Glory, *in her infamous dungarees, the cause of much disquiet in the publicity department. Director Lowell Sherman is the dark-haired man in the background.*

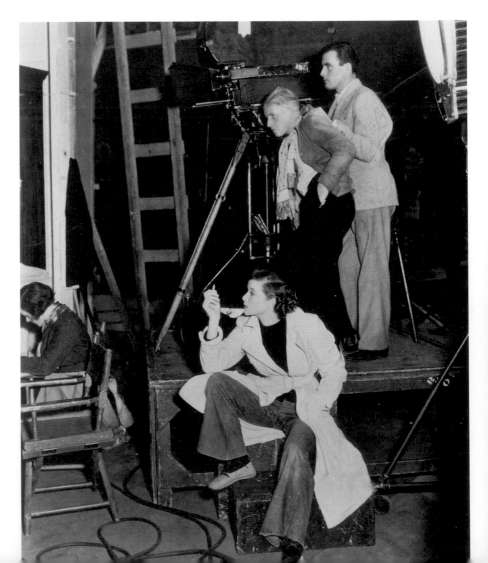

Kate denies this story. 'Barrymore never criticized me. He just shoved me before the cameras. He taught me all that could be poured into one greenhorn in that short a time.'

The press, having got wind that a new star was on the horizon, hung around the lot. The studio was dismayed because Kate would appear between scenes in her old dungarees, hardly befitting the glamorous image they were trying to disseminate. When she was asked to stopped wearing them, she refused. One day, she returned to her dressing room to find the offending garment gone. Thereupon, she walked through the lot in her underpants. It did the trick and, to Kate's delight, she was given back her pet dungarees.

Selznick's first reaction to the rushes of A Bill of Divorcement may have been 'Ye gods, that horse face!', but Cukor had no such qualms. Her freshness and directness made her ideal for the role of Sydney Fairfield, the daughter of a shell-shocked World War I victim (Barrymore) who escapes from an asylum, returning home on the very day his wife (Billie Burke), who has divorced him, is to marry again. His daughter, who also has plans to marry, gives up her own future to care for her father.

Although Kate was rather awkward in her movements and talked rapidly in a grating voice in the early scenes, it was still obvious to audiences that they were in the presence of a unique personality. Growing in confidence as the picture moves towards its climax, she conveys a tenderness mixed with aggressiveness that seems modern today in contrast with Barrymore's rather dated, theatrical style. It is doubtful, however, that anyone imagined that A Bill of Divorcement was the launching pad of the career of one of the greatest of screen actresses. As the actor Roddy McDowell has said, 'We take Katharine Hepburn for granted now. The sort of bravery, the wonderful lithe figure. But when she first appeared on the screen, they said, "What is this?" She defied

The débutante screen actress sharing a dramatic scene in A Bill of Divorcement *(1932) with Henry Stephenson (far left), John Barrymore (left) and Billie Burke.*

the law of possibility. She was a total original.'

The director Rouben Mamoulian once commented that few Hollywood actresses had a truly individual manner of walking. He mentioned Garbo, Cyd Charisse and Kate, who in her very first film demonstrated that distinctive cross between a stride and a lope, at the same time both stylish and gauche.

Before the film was previewed, Kate and Luddy decided they should go to Europe to see if they could make something of their marriage. Also, as Kate had not seen the final cut, she preferred to be far away at the opening in case she had made a fool of herself. The memory of her recent sackings and severe criticisms in the theatre was still fresh in her mind.

She need not have worried. A Bill of Divorcement was generally well received, but Kate's personal reviews were wonderful. The New Yorker called her 'half Botticelli page and half bobbed-hair bandit', and the Journal-American claimed she had 'flamed like opal, half-demon, half-madonna'. As a result, Selznick got RKO to pick up Kate's option.

Kate and Luddy were in Vienna when she received a telegram from Hayward urging her to return to New York. He had negotiated a new RKO contract, and the studio had a film planned for her, entitled Three Came Unarmed. When she arrived in New York, she denied to reporters that she was married, and answered a fan magazine's question of 'Have you any children?' with 'Yes, two white and three coloured.'

For the next four decades, Kate waged a vigorous battle to protect her privacy. She has said that on arrival in Hollywood she divided the world into two spheres; one was her private domain, the other was 'enemy territory'. She rarely went to parties or premières, and never dated Hollywood's eligible bachelors. Kate saw few people outside those of George Cukor's circle. At Cukor's famous Sunday lunches, however, she met a glittering array of film and literary celebrities, including Greta Garbo, her favourite actress.

At one of George Cukor's celebrated Sunday lunches for artists and intellectuals, with writers Hugh Walpole (left) and Roland Leigh.

Kate's clothes were also cause for comment in the Hollywood community. Apart from the gowns worn for glossy publicity stills, she had a few dresses for public appearances – many of them designed by Elizabeth Hawes – which somehow made her look dowdy. In private, she nearly always wore trousers.

Three Came Unarmed, which was to have paired her with Joel McCrea, was abandoned because of script problems. On the other hand, RKO had just purchased Gilbert Frankau's novel *Christopher Strong* and the role of the daredevil aviatrix Lady Cynthia Darrington seemed tailor-made for Kate. The story tells how the record-breaking pilot falls in love with Sir Christopher Strong (Colin Clive), a married man, becomes pregnant and kills herself by pulling off her oxygen mask while breaking the altitude record at 30,000 feet.

To Kate's delight, Selznick hired Dorothy Arzner, one of Hollywood's few women directors. But she was soon disillusioned. Although they developed a mutual respect, their relationship remained cool, distant and competitive. At one stage in the shooting, Arzner threatened to quit unless Kate stopped interfering with her direction. All this did not help the film, which turned out to be a creaky vehicle that never got off the ground, and it bombed at the box office. However, Kate, stalking around in aviator's gear, and mooning and swooning in the love scenes, laid the basis of her career-long screen persona – independent, intelligent, intrepid but, at the same time, extremely sensitive. She was still too self-conscious and fussy, and her voice was too shrill, but she held the eye. Brendan Gill, writing of Kate's early heroines, pronounced that 'they would make love after marriage and then only with a certain fastidious reluctance, nostrils flaring'. She plainly got up the noses of many a macho male, and it is ironic that the film's title is not the name of the leading character, but that of her rather stiff lover.

Soon after completing *Christopher Strong*, Kate was in the office of RKO producer Pandro Berman and happened to come across a script lying on his desk, which she idly began to read. 'I thought, "Oh, my God, that's the most wonderful part ever written for anyone." ' She slipped the

As aviatrix Lady Cynthia Darrington in Dorothy Arzner's Christopher Strong *(1933), a few years before Kate was taught to fly by Howard Hughes.*

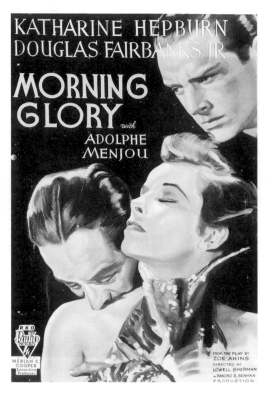

Adolphe Menjou demonstrating a vampire kiss on Kate as Douglas Fairbanks Jr looks on – RKO's idea of a come-on.

manuscript into her bag and took it home. After finishing it, she returned it in person to a nonplussed Berman, announcing, 'This is what I'd like to do next.'

Although Zoë Akins' script of her own play *Morning Glory* had been scheduled for Constance Bennett, Kate forced the studio to give her the part of the struggling young actress Eva Lovelace. One of the reasons for her hankering to play the role was its proximity to her own experiences.

Eva finds it difficult to get an acting job, until a friend and mentor takes her to a party given for a Broadway star, Rita Vernon. At the party she drinks too much champagne and, without warning, starts acting Juliet's balcony scene for the guests. However unconventional, her performance demonstrates her acting ability, and she becomes understudy to the star, taking over from her triumphantly when Vernon walks out of the show. 'Now you belong to no man. You belong to Broadway,' the producer (Adolphe Menjou) tells her.

Eva Lovelace was the role that really made Kate into a movie star. As a character burning with ambition, she was refreshing,

earnest and heart-breaking, even though she tottered on the edges of being embarrassing. When she said in her distinctive nasal voice, 'My star will never set,' it was not difficult to believe!

Within a week of the picture's opening, Kate knew that she had triumphed. Most of the reviews were ecstatic. The *New York Herald Tribune* commented that 'the striking and inescapably fascinating Miss Hepburn proves pretty conclusively in her new film that her fame in the cinema is not a mere flash across the screen... It is Miss Hepburn who makes *Morning Glory* something to be seen.'

As usual, there were a few detractors who found her too mannered, and she first began to be impersonated on radio and in nightclubs. As imitation is the greatest form of flattery, Kate knew she had really arrived.

Mean, moody and magnificent in a publicity still from the early 1930s.

Douglas Fairbanks Jr playing Romeo to Kate's Juliet in a scene from Morning Glory *(1933). It was a role Fairbanks would have liked to play to her in real life.*

4

'The Gamut of Emotion from A to B'

*Acting isn't a very high-class way of
making a living. Nobody ever won a
Nobel Prize for acting. You have to
remember that Shirley Temple could do
it at the age of four.*

During the making of *Morning Glory*, Douglas Fairbanks Jr, who was Kate's romantic lead, tried for days to get her to go out with him. Like many of her other leading men, after initially disliking her, he was completely captivated. Finally she accepted but, halfway through dinner, complained of a headache. Fairbanks drove her home, but didn't drive straight off, watching as she entered the house. 'Suddenly,' he recalled, 'the front door flew open and Kate came running out. Another car I hadn't noticed was hidden further up the driveway under some trees. She hopped in, and I saw a man at the wheel. They drove right past me without noticing me. She

Accompanied by Douglas Fairbanks Jr, an undelighted Kate is seen leaving producer Jess Lasky's Santa Monica home in December 1933, just after Fairbanks' divorce from Joan Crawford.

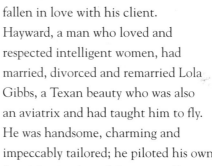

Top Hollywood agent Leland Hayward, an extremely important figure in both Kate's personal and her public life.

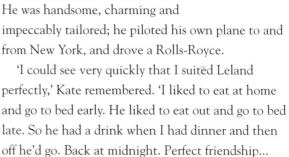

was laughing happily, her hair blowing over her face.'

The man at the wheel was Kate's agent, Leland Hayward, who had fallen in love with his client. Hayward, a man who loved and respected intelligent women, had married, divorced and remarried Lola Gibbs, a Texan beauty who was also an aviatrix and had taught him to fly. He was handsome, charming and impeccably tailored; he piloted his own plane to and from New York, and drove a Rolls-Royce.

'I could see very quickly that I suited Leland perfectly,' Kate remembered. 'I liked to eat at home and go to bed early. He liked to eat out and go to bed late. So he had a drink when I had dinner and then off he'd go. Back at midnight. Perfect friendship... Life with Leland had no problems... I don't remember any fights. We just enjoyed – enjoyed – enjoyed.'

But they were still both married and couldn't be seen alone together in public. Nevertheless, he would visit her often at her Cold Water Canyon house. It was while working on her next film, *Little Women*, directed by George Cukor, that Kate had to cope with her deep feelings for Leland, the responsibility of perhaps causing him to divorce his wife and marry her, and the issue of her own probable divorce from Luddy.

There had been a lot of Kate in *A Bill of Divorcement*, in the impatient and anti-establishment young woman, and in the idealistic New

Opposite: Kate beginning to look more like herself as a veteran of three feature films in 1933.

Ideally cast as Jo March in George Cukor's Little Women (1933), one of Kate's most cherished parts.

A hoop-skirted Kate taking time off from the filming of Little Women to watch others at work while being photographed from below.

England actress in *Morning Glory*, but in *Little Women* she was able to play an emancipated woman modelled on her mother. The Louisa May Alcott novel had always been a special favourite of Kate's, but Cukor, who had considered the book 'a story that little girls read', was startled when he read it for the first time. He found it a 'very strong-minded story, full of character and a wonderful picture of New England family life'; he felt that Kate was born to play Jo March because 'she's tender and odd and funny, sweet and yet tough, intensely loyal, with an enormous sense of family and all of Jo's burning ambition, and at heart a pure, clean simplicity and firmness'.

During a break in Little Women, *Kate lunches with George Cukor, her favourite director and one of her closest friends.*

There was, however, the occasional contretemps between star and director during the shooting. Walter Plunkett had made beautiful costumes out of authentic period material, and Kate was warned that they couldn't be replaced if she spoiled them. One shot required her to run up a flight of stairs carrying a dish of ice cream. Swept away by the scene, Kate forgot the warning and spilled ice cream on her skirt. Furious, Cukor slapped her face in front of the entire cast and crew – an insult that Kate accepted stoically, out of her respect for Cukor.

In this best of the three screen versions of *Little Women*, Kate gives a penetrating and subtly moving

Barefoot Kate trying to convince as an illiterate mountain girl in Spitfire *(1934) – audiences failed to respond.*

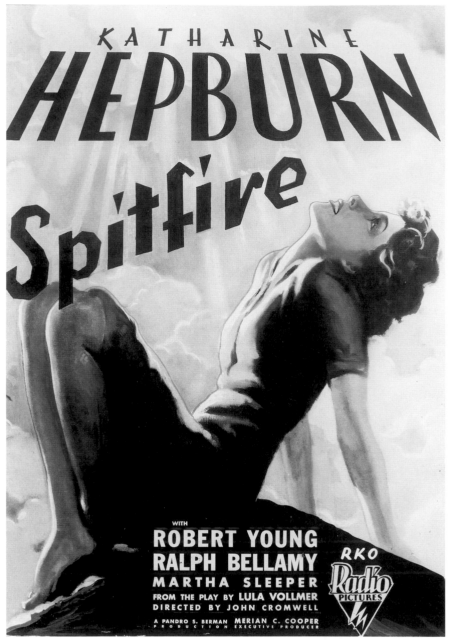

Kate's attempt to broaden her range resulted in one of her many flops in the 1930s.

Massingham and Murray MacDonald, to be produced by Jed Harris, the wizard of the Broadway theatre. Harris thought that Kate's current box-office popularity would help secure his investment. But RKO would only release her to do the play if she made another picture for them first. Perhaps she accepted *Spitfire* in order to prove that she could play a character other than blue-blooded East Coast types. It turned out to be a severe miscalculation. Although Kate made a spirited attempt at the role of a wild, quick-tempered, illiterate mountain girl who believes she has the gift in her hands to cure the lame, her natural elegance and breeding kept showing through the portrayal. The *New Yorker* thought 'her artistry does not extend to the primitive or uncouth'. The public did not appreciate it either, and *Spitfire* flopped.

On the personal side, Kate's pride was hurt when Leland Hayward began a relationship with Margaret Sullavan, a new young star. Jed Harris, too, had had an affair with Sullavan. In fact, Kate had no idea that the Harris-Sullavan affair was not quite over, nor that Sullavan had been

portrait of a resolute girl on the edge of womanhood. Beautifully lit, her expressive face is alive with joy, hope and despair.

Little Women was the first of her films to be an enormous box-office hit, and her stock stood high in Hollywood. RKO lined up numerous projects for her: Edith Wharton's *The Age of Innocence* and biopics of Sarah Bernhardt, Nell Gwyn and Queen Elizabeth. None of these inspired Kate and, buoyed up by her success in *Little Women*, she made a rash decision to return to the stage.

The play chosen was *The Lake* by Dorothy

Harris's first choice for the role in *The Lake*. With her relationship with Leland threatened, Kate was particularly susceptible to Harris's charm when she arrived in New York, believing that he would dedicate himself to her success in the play because of his respect for her as a stage actress. Nothing could have been further from the truth. He not only resented the fact that Kate, not Sullavan, was playing the role, he thought he had made a serious mistake in casting her.

Harris explained: 'I could see she was hopeless. I fought with her – I begged her to stop posing, striking attitudes, leaning against doorways, putting a limp hand to her forehead, to stop being a big movie star and feel the lines, feel the character. I was trying the impossible, to make an artificial showcase of an artificial star, and she couldn't handle it.'

But Harris drove her unmercifully. One witness remarked: 'If she turned her head to the left, he didn't like it. If she turned it to the right, he liked it still less.' The director's bullying did not diminish Kate's infatuation for him in the least. On the contrary. During one confrontation, she threw her arms around his neck and cried, 'I could have loved you so.'

In a way, Harris's instincts were correct. The role of a blighted young society woman whose husband drowns in a lake on the first day of their marriage, and suffers tremendous guilt because she loved a married man instead of him, would have been more suitable for Sullavan's delicate talents. The character is not a rebel, and Kate's quality was her strength.

The Lake was quite well received when it opened in Washington DC on 17 December 1933, but Harris, feeling Kate was not ready for Broadway, implored Kate to tour before going to New York. Kate stubbornly refused, arguing it would harm her career.

'My dear, the only interest I have in you is the money I can make out of you,' Harris told her.

Stunned, Kate stammered, 'How much will it cost you to open in New York?'.

'How much have you got?'

She opened her chequebook and said, 'I've got exactly $15,461 and 67 cents.'

'OK, I'll take that.'

Kate wrote the cheque for the full amount and the next day the company left for New York. On opening night, 26 December, the entire Hepburn family was there, plus Noël Coward, Gertrude Lawrence, Leland Hayward, George S. Kaufman, Amelia Earhart and Dorothy Parker. Kate started at such a fast pace that her timing was thrown off and her voice grew steadily more frenzied in decibel and pitch. It didn't help that she had to utter lines like 'The calla lilies are in bloom again. Such a strange flower. I carried them on my wedding day. And now I place them here, in memory of someone who is dead.'

Noël Coward came back stage and said, 'You mucked it up, but that happens to all of us. You'll get roasted. But keep at it. You'll find the way.' The next day, Dorothy Parker's barbed remark appeared in the press: 'Go to the Martin Beck Theatre and see Katharine Hepburn run the gamut of emotion from A to B.' This still famous quote was an albatross that hung around Kate's neck for years. To her relief, *The Lake* closed after fifty-five performances.

At the same time, Mrs Hepburn was courting notoriety after appearing on the stand of the House Caucus Room in Washington in passionate argument for a bill permitting the dissemination of birth-control information by physicians. An interview in the *New York Times* carried the headline STAR'S MOTHER FIRM IN STAND. Another event added to Kate's anxiety. When Margaret Sullavan married William Wyler, whom she had known for only a few weeks, Leland Hayward took the news harder than Kate would have wished.

With all this weighing upon her, Kate decided to take a trip to Europe, ostensibly to pick up her award for Best Actress in *Little Women* at Cannes. The day she sailed on the *Paris*, her career, seemingly in the doldrums, received a boost. She was informed that she had won the Best Actress Oscar for *Morning Glory*.

Unable to attend the ceremony, she wrote a telegram saying she didn't believe in acting contests and therefore felt it her duty to refuse the award. Hayward read the wire, tore it up and sent a thank-you note instead. 'He was right,' Kate said years later. 'I was being childish.' But she never picked up any of her four Oscars. 'I'm not proud that I didn't. I just never got round to it.'

Minister is the story of Lady Babbie, who is democratic at heart and loves to dress up as a gypsy, mingling with the humble weavers of the Scottish valley. She gets involved in the weavers' rebellion against her stern foster father and horrifies the villagers by falling in love with the prim young minister. With a second-league cast and director (Richard Wallace), Kate had to carry the whole picture, which she did to a large extent, creating a sympathetic and attractive non-conformist character. Although *The Little Minister* was perhaps too affected for Depression audiences, it did not fail entirely at the box office; it nevertheless lost $9000, because it was RKO's most expensive film of the year, and the most expensive in which Kate had appeared. According to Pandro Berman, 'Kate wasn't a movie star. She wasn't going to become a star, either, in the sense that Crawford and Shearer were – actresses able to drag an audience in by their own efforts. She was a hit only in hit pictures; she couldn't save a flop. And she almost invariably chose the wrong vehicles.'

After the completion of *The Little Minister*, Leland Hayward and Kate flew to New York. There they were hounded by reporters, who spread a rumour that they were married, something that the couple never bothered to deny. Both Kate and Leland were free and single, but marriage was not an option Kate ever thought of taking. As she later explained, 'For the independent woman the marriage problem is very great. If she falls in love with a strong man she loses him because she has to concentrate too much on her job. If she falls in love with a weakling, whom she can push around, she always falls out of love with him. A woman just has to have sense enough to handle a man well enough so he'll want to stay with her. How to keep him on a string is almost a full-time job.'

At Christmas in 1934, Leland was suddenly taken ill. Cancer of the prostate was suspected and Kate insisted they fly to West

John Beal in the title role of
The Little Minister *(1934), being comforted by Kate under the close eye of director Richard Wallace.*

James Barrie's 'immortal masterpiece' failed to survive in its screen version, which starred Kate in another period role.

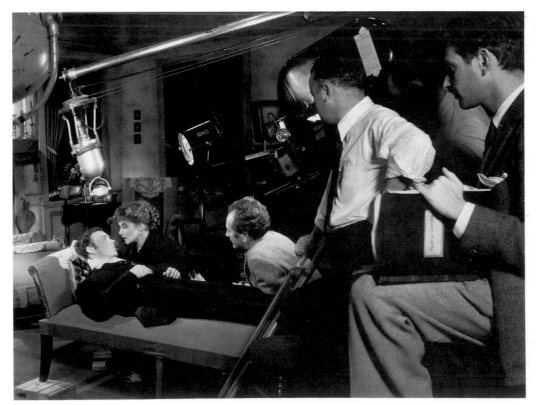

Hartford so that Dr Hepburn could perform the operation required. It was a story that the press found irresistible – 'Movie Star's Doctor Father Operates on Daughter's Fiancé – so reporters descended on the town. One day, when Kate was emerging from her house, flash-bulbs exploded in her face. Incensed, she grabbed the nearest photographer, and threw his camera to the ground. Then she turned and ran back into the house where she was met by her sister Peggy.

Charles Boyer and Kate made beautiful music together as conductor and composer in Break of Hearts (1935), *but the box-office takings sounded a sour note.*

'Where's the shotgun?' she shouted. 'Get it! Get it!' However, before more damage was done, Mrs Hepburn put the photographers to flight with a wire basket.

The operation on Leland was a success and, after a brief recuperation at the Hepburn house, he returned to California. Kate followed soon after, but they saw little of each other, and she was able to concentrate on her work. Unfortunately, her next film, *Break of Hearts*, turned out to be another critical and commercial disaster – and rightly so! Pandro Berman had persuaded Kate to star in this banal melodrama against her wishes. The film is about a temperamental and brilliant conductor (Charles Boyer) married to a struggling composer (Hepburn). When he becomes an alcoholic, she gives up her promising career to help him out of his drunken stupor. Again, as in most of her previous films, here was a woman in her own right, sacrificing herself for a man. During the filming Kate herself was rather smitten with the happily married Boyer and she could be seen, between takes, resting her head on his knee and looking up at him adoringly.

In an effort to save Kate's tarnished reputation, RKO cast her in the title role of *Alice Adams*, based on Booth Tarkington's touching story of small-town life. As Kate's contract had given her first choice of director, she considered George Cukor and William Wyler ideal for the subject. But Cukor was busy on David Copperfield, and William Wyler's marriage to Margaret Sullavan put him out of the running. She was forced to accept thirty-year-old George Stevens, whose only previous features had been routine comedies. Their relationship followed the pattern of so many prior ones, with the pair first being at odds, then gradually becoming attracted to each other.

One of the few happy moments in Break of Hearts, *during the filming of which Kate became briefly enamoured of Charles Boyer.*

GRETA GARBO'S TRUE LIFE STORY

Modern Screen

JANUARY
10 CENTS

THE LARGEST
CIRCULATION
OF ANY SCREEN
MAGAZINE

KATHARINE
HEPBURN

CHARLES BOYER TELLS ON HIMSELF!

Left: *Kate depicted as red-headed but unfreckled and green-eyed (hers were actually blue), making the fan-magazine covers, as she continued to do for years to come.*

Right: *Not the most accurate portrait of Kate for the cover of* Picture Play *in May 1933.*

Kate uncomfortably displaying one of Bernard Newman's costumes from Break of Hearts.

Smiling at co-star Fred MacMurray off set on Alice Adams *(1935). Director George Stevens is on MacMurray's left.*

As wallflower Alice Adams, desperately pretending she is the belle of the ball, Kate embarrasses her brother, played by Frank Albertson.

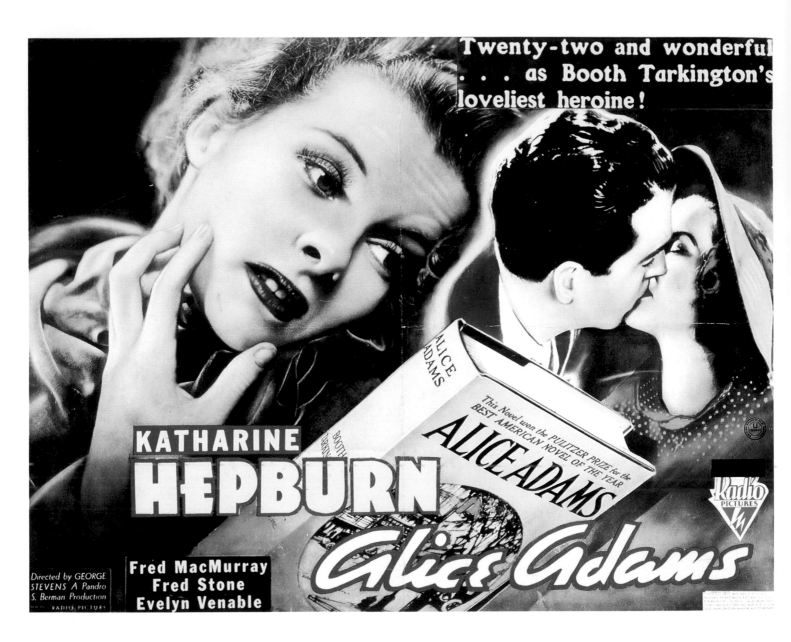

The film that gave Kate's screen career a temporary boost, as well as putting director George Stevens in the first division.

A lobby card for the film that plunged Kate down to the box-office depths, though it now enjoys cult status.

Kate as the doomed queen Mary Stuart with Fredric March as the Earl of Bothwell in John Ford's fustian drama.

55

An intense George Stevens directing a scene from Alice Adams *as Kate looks on. Director and actress were attracted to each other.*

56

Aged twenty-eight, in a publicity still dated 1935, when she was still hankering to play a contemporary American woman.

'A queer feeling.' Brian Aherne fails to understand his emotions when in the presence of a handsome young lad in Sylvia Scarlett.

George Cukor directing a travesty Kate in Sylvia Scarlett, *considered too sophisticated for audiences at the time.*

As a small-town girl snubbed by society because of her father's lack of money and ambition, Alice Adams was a character well-suited to Kate's talents, and she played her with a subtle mixture of acceptance and frustration, idealism and disenchantment, subduing most of her irritating mannerisms. She does have her affected moments, but Kate convinces us that these belong to the character rather than the actress. In the best scenes – when she invites her beau, Fred MacMurray, to a disastrous dinner with her family, or at the ball, anxiously glancing around for a man to ask her to dance – Kate reveals the pain and confusion that comes from rejection. The picture was a hit, and she recovered her good standing in Hollywood. Her next film, *Sylvia Scarlett*, was to undermine it again.

George Cukor had wanted to do *Sylvia Scarlett* for a number of years and gave Kate Compton Mackenzie's book to read, believing her special boyish quality made her perfect for the part. Kate agreed and she and Cukor finally (after much resistance) persuaded Pandro Berman to produce the film. He later called it 'by far the worst picture I ever made, and the greatest catastrophe of Kate's Thirties career'. He added that Cukor and Kate had 'conned me into it and had a script written. I said to them, "Jesus, this is awful, terrible, I don't understand a thing that's going on." I tried to stop them, but they wouldn't be stopped. They were hell-bent, claiming that this was the greatest thing they had ever found.'

Sylvia Scarlett was a daring choice for Kate, an off-beat story of a girl who disguises herself as a boy to help her father, who is a thief and a con man. They meet a crook (Cary Grant) and Sylvia falls in love with an artist (Brian Aherne). He is strangely attracted to her in her boy's disguise, and says, 'I don't know what it is that gives me a queer feeling when I look at you.'

The film, with its references to Shakespeare's travesty roles, was far too sophisticated for general audiences. They complained that they couldn't understand the English accents, especially Cary Grant's cockney, nor were they happy with the ambivalent sexuality, nor the fact that Kate masquerades as a boy through most of the action. Nevertheless, the public had accepted Greta Garbo in drag in *Queen Christina* two years before, though Kate's remarkable androgynous portrayal was more convincing. The *New York Herald Tribune* thought 'the dynamic Miss Hepburn is the handsomest boy of the season' and *Time* declared, '*Sylvia Scarlett* reveals the interesting fact that Katharine Hepburn is better looking as a boy than a woman.'

The picture was Kate's first of four pairings with Cary Grant, a seemingly perfect coming-together of two aristocrats of the cinema. But, as Kate's partnership with Spencer Tracy confirms, chalk and cheese can often be a better combination. Of his first meeting with Kate, Grant commented, 'She was this slip of a woman, skinny, and I never liked skinny women. But she had this thing, this air, you might call it, the most totally magnetic woman I'd ever seen, and probably have ever seen since. You had to look at her, you had to listen to her, there was no escaping her. But it wasn't just the beauty, it was the style. She's incredibly down to earth. She can see right through the nonsense in life. She cares, but about things that really matter.'

Sylvia Scarlett, which RKO held back for many months, harmed Kate's reputation again, but her choice of her next three films, all heavy period dramas, almost finished her career entirely. However, the first of the trio, *Mary of Scotland*, had a significant effect on her emotional life.

From the moment Kate saw Maxwell Anderson's play *Mary of Scotland* in New York starring Helen Hayes, she had been convinced she should play Mary Stuart on screen, and wanted Cukor to direct it. But after the disaster of *Sylvia Scarlett*, Berman refused to team them together again. Instead, the producer employed John Ford, a great director, but one totally unsuited to this kind of historical romance. Later,

Kate would say, 'I never cared for Mary. I thought she was a bit of an ass. I would have preferred to do a script on Elizabeth... The script was not very interesting. I never quite understood why Jack Ford was willing to direct it.'

In this heavy-handed but lush production, Kate seems rather remote and uncharacteristically passionless, though there is no lack of regal posturing. Little of Mary Stuart's or Kate's fervour creeps through. Instead the heroine becomes, in Andrew Sarris's words, 'a soft-focused unfairly slandered Madonna of the Scottish moors'.

As in her previous films, Kate insisted on executing most of her own stunts, still trying to prove, as she had done as a child to impress her father, that she could undertake the most difficult physical tasks. In this instance, Mary, wearing high-heeled pumps and a heavy, bulky gown, had to run down a flight of stone steps and then, without pausing, vault on to the back of a lively horse and ride away at breakneck speed side-saddle. Ford demanded a stunt woman do it. 'Mary of Scotland supposedly did it, and I'm a damn good horsewoman,'

Kate replied defiantly. Ford finally gave in, but he sadistically asked her to do the risky scene eleven times before he was satisfied.

Victor McLaglen, visiting the set of Mary of Scotland, *chats to Kate and his friend John Ford.*

Kate's courage delighted Ford, a rugged, hard-drinking, macho Irish Catholic, known to his friends by his real name, Sean. 'You're a hell of a fine girl,' he told her. 'If you'd just learn to shut up and knuckle under, you'd probably make somebody a nice wife.' Married, the father of two children, and twelve years Kate's senior, Ford found himself falling for her. Kate was soon responding to his attentions and began to allow him to dominate her.

After the completion of *Mary of Scotland*, instead of going on his usual week-long binge to Mexico with the boys, Ford followed Kate east to her family home in Fenwick, where they sailed and played golf together. Dr Hepburn considered Ford a philanderer who was taking advantage of his daughter. But Ford was serious enough to speak of divorcing his wife Mary. The fact that they had not been married in the

Roman Catholic Church would make a divorce easier. Yet Mary had once vowed that 'Jack is very religious; he'll never divorce me. I'm going to be Mrs John Ford until I die.'

It is ironic that two of Kate's greatest loves – Spencer Tracy and John Ford – should have been hard-drinking Catholic men, almost as if in rebellion against her father, a Protestant teetotaller. When Kate was a teenager, Dr Hepburn nearly had a fit when he discovered that one of her boyfriends was a Catholic. In his progressive eyes, Catholics were reactionaries, against birth control and votes for women. After her father had greeted the Catholic boy with what she described as 'chill politeness', Kate

Kate looks with disdain on Herbert Marshall in A Woman Rebels *(1936), the same attitude the public held towards the film.*

continued to meet him clandestinely.

When Ford was directing *The Plough and the Stars* at RKO, and Kate was making *A Woman Rebels* at the same studio, in the summer of 1936, they saw each other almost every day and night. Nevertheless, Ford refused to move out of the house he shared with his wife and children. At one stage, however, he did something he had never done before: he went on a bender in the midst of shooting a film. His producer, who found him at home in a drunken coma, phoned Kate (Mary was away), as he felt there was no one else to whom Ford would listen. She rushed to his home and, with considerable difficulty, got him up and drove him to the studio, where she smuggled him into her dressing room and tried to sober him up.

Ford eventually returned to his wife and Kate completed *A Woman Rebels*, about a suffragette of the 1870s, a story she wanted to do to pay homage to her mother's activities. The character, Pamela Thistlewaite, who fights for a woman's right to work, to live alone, to read whatever she pleases and to choose her own husband, suited Kate's personality perfectly. Unhappily, the film, ponderously directed by Mark Sandrich, turned out to be more interested in her relationships with two men (Van Heflin and Herbert Marshall) than in the subject of women's emancipation. Besides, the public were getting bored with this kind of fiery, non-conformist Hepburn heroine.

In *Quality Street*, Kate had the opportunity to play two sides of her screen persona, the self-righteous rebel and the self-conscious outsider. The film, based on a play by James Barrie and set in England during the Napoleonic Wars, tells of Phoebe Throssel, a young woman whose fiancé (Franchot Tone) goes off to war. On his return many years later, he fails to

George Stevens and Kate together again on Quality Street *(1937), vainly trying to repeat their success on* Alice Adams *two years earlier.*

Left: *Modelling a finely pleated gown of silver lamé, inspired by ancient Greek statuary.*

Right: *One of a range of unusual portraits taken of Kate by Cecil Beaton, the celebrated photographer of the famous.*

recognize Phoebe, who has become a schoolteacher teetering on the brink of spinsterhood. She decides to get her revenge on him by masquerading as her own, non-existent, flirtatious niece.

Quality Street reunited Kate with George Stevens in the hope that they might reproduce the success of *Alice Adams*. However, Stevens had very little sympathy with the subject, and failed to give Kate the direction she needed. 'She became precious, and preciousness was always her weakness,' explained Stevens. 'I should have helped her away from that, and I wasn't strong enough. *Quality Street* was a precious play about precious people, and that infected her.'

Whereas she had been tender and amusing in *Alice Adams*, her overwrought Phoebe Throssel lacked warmth and humour. The *New York Times* claimed that 'such flutterings and jitterings and twitchings, such hand-wringings and mouth-quiverings, such runnings about and eye-brow raisings have not been seen on a screen in many a moon'. Needless to say, *Quality Street* turned out to be another bomb, prompting serious discussions among the RKO brass about Kate's future with the studio.

With another box-office failure to her debit, the news of Leland Hayward's marriage to Margaret Sullavan, and John Ford out of reach, Kate's career and emotional life were at a low ebb. She was particularly susceptible when, to the surprise of many of her friends, she began seeing millionaire industrialist and aviator Howard Hughes on a regular basis.

They had first met during the shooting of *Sylvia Scarlett*. A biplane landed near the film's Malibu location, and out stepped RKO's backer, Howard Hughes. He came over to where Kate and Cukor sat eating during their lunch break and, in his curious high-pitched voice, introduced himself. Kate found him somewhat ridiculous, and displayed her old arrogance. He soon left, but flew back regularly. He then began sending Kate flowers and they saw each other a few times on her return to Hollywood. Gradually, she began to change her opinion of him.

'I don't know what she was doing with Howard Hughes,' commented Anita Loos. 'He had a whole stable of girls, and Kate simply wasn't the type to have anything to do with that kind of thing.' However, Kate was attracted to individualist men of action; she and Hughes shared a passion for aviation, golf and films, and both came from a wealthy background. Although Hughes was as taciturn as she was talkative, he became eloquent when he talked of aeroplanes, and taught Kate to fly.

With nothing planned for her at RKO, Kate announced she would return to the stage in an adaptation of Charlotte Bronte's *Jane Eyre* for the Theatre Guild at $1500 a week, with the hope that John Ford might later film it with her starring. While the play was on tour, Hughes followed in his private plane, attending some performances. In Chicago, he took a suite in the same hotel as Kate, which provoked the headline HUGHES AND HEPBURN TO MARRY.

Getting wind of this romance, John Ford was prompted to declare to Kate that he had decided to leave his wife for her. He then changed his mind again. When *Jane Eyre* was in Baltimore, Kate wrote to Ford to say she had had enough of his vacillations and demanded a final answer. But on her return to LA in May 1937, Ford was still wavering. As a result, Kate moved in with Hughes. On the way to visit her parents, Hughes proposed. She refused. 'Well, I'll never marry,' she recalled thinking at the time, although she had considered marrying Leland Hayward and might have married Ford. Hughes was another matter.

'I want to be a star, and I don't want to make my husband my victim. And I certainly don't want to make my children my victims.'

Speculation on the possible marriage between Kate and Howard Hughes reaches the covers of the movie magazines.

Exclusive! COMPLETE GUIDE TO ANSWERS IN $250,000 MOVIE QUIZ

Modern Screen

NOVEMBER
10 CENTS

THE LARGEST CIRCULATION OF ANY SCREEN MAGAZINE

WILL AMERICA'S HERO, HOWARD HUGHES, *Marry* KATHARINE HEPBURN?

Hedy Lamarr's LIFE STORY!

6

'Box-office Poison'

Two of an actress's greatest assets are love and pain. A great actress, even a good actress, must have plenty of both in her life.

On her return to Hollywood in the winter of 1937, Kate, now thirty years old, brooded on the failure of most of her movies to reach a mass audience. It was, therefore, with a great sense of relief that Leland Hayward was able to negotiate a new deal for her at RKO for $75,000 per picture, a miracle considering that she had been blamed for the low box-office returns on her last films.

For the first of the movies under the new contract, Kate suggested George S. Kaufman's *Stage Door*, which had been a huge hit on Broadway in 1936 with Margaret Sullavan. In order to hedge their bets, RKO cast Ginger Rogers in a part equal to Kate's in importance, giving the former higher billing. The

Friendly rivals. On the set of Stage Door *(1937) chatting to Ginger Rogers, with whom Kate shared top billing.*

two stars proved to be splendid foils for each other, and their barbed exchanges were a delight.

Kate's role was similar to her Oscar-winning characterization in *Morning Glory*, with Adolphe Menjou, also in the earlier film, again playing a Jed Harris-like producer. Like Kate, the character is a society girl who comes to New York determined to make it as an actress; she is well-off, domineering and opinionated; she has a father who disparages her choice of profession and yet gives her financial support; and she receives leading parts before she is capable of playing them. However, unlike the notorious fiasco of *The Lake*, her stage triumph comes in a play called *Enchanted April*, in which she enters clutching a bouquet, repeating the frequently sent-up line, 'The calla lilies are in

Opposite: Kate maturing into a great star despite a series of commercial disasters.

Katharine HEPBURN
Cary GRANT
in a
HOWARD HAWKS
production of
BRINGING UP BABY
with Charlie RUGGLES
BARRY FITZGERALD   MAY ROBSON   WALTER CATLETT   FRITZ FELD
Directed by HOWARD HAWKS • Associate Producer CLIFF REID •

In Stage Door *with the grand old actress Constance Collier, who became a great friend and drama coach.*

bloom again.' Kate plays the scene beautifully, without a trace of self-mockery.

Gregory La Cava, the director of *Stage Door*, said of Kate, 'She is completely the intellectual actress. She has to understand the why of everything before she can feel. Then, when the meaning has soaked in, emotion comes, and superb work.'

Unlike her last four films, *Stage Door* made a profit. As a test of her popularity it was inconclusive, because it was an ensemble picture, not a star vehicle. But it was significant in that a new Katharine Hepburn emerged, an actress who, after all the melodramas and costume pieces, proved she could play comedy and pathos in modern dress. *Stage Door* also introduced her to Constance Collier, who portrayed a splendid old actress in the picture.

Kate's only slapstick role – in Howard Hawks's Bringing Up Baby *(1938), acting for the second time with Cary Grant.*

Collier became Kate's mentor, drama coach, firm friend and confidante. When Kate began work on her next picture, she felt convinced that the bad times were behind her.

Impressed by her flair for comedy

in *Stage Door*, the studio cast Kate as a dizzy heiress pursuing a stuffy, bespectacled palaeontologist (Cary Grant) in *Bringing Up Baby*. The film's director, Howard Hawks, remarked of Kate, 'She has an amazing body – like a boxer. It's hard for her to make a wrong turn. She's always in perfect balance... This gives her an amazing sense of timing. I've never seen a girl that had that odd rhythm and control.'

Responding to Howard Hawks's rapid-fire direction, both Kate and Grant played at a break-neck speed suitable to the farcical situations, many involving the leopard of the title. Grant, taking his cue from Harold Lloyd, is hilarious, but Kate, though obviously communicating her enjoyment, is far too strident and unvarying for much of the time. A majority of critics now put *Bringing Up Baby* among the best screwball comedies ever made, though it sank in its day.

For her fifteenth motion picture, Kate moved away from RKO for the very first time. George Cukor was to direct *Holiday* at Columbia, and he persuaded studio head Harry Cohn, who had wanted to cast Irene Dunne, to sign Kate in the role she had understudied ten years before. On her first meeting with the infamous Cohn, he

Thought too off the wall for the period, Bringing Up Baby *is now considered the quintessential screwball Thirties comedy.*

The centre of attraction. Kate surrounded by the cast and crew of Holiday. *George Cukor and Cary Grant are on her immediate right.*

observed, 'Leland Hayward tells me you're great in the hay.' Kate went on talking rapidly as if she hadn't heard him. Cohn repeated himself. Kate still did not pause in her conversation, ignoring the remark completely, and Cohn gave up.

Holiday, one of the most stylish of romantic comedies, is about an impecunious noncomformist Johnny Case (Cary Grant) who becomes engaged to the snobby daughter of a millionaire banker, but discovers the girl he really loves is her unconventional sister Linda Seton (Hepburn). Instead of accepting the lucrative bank job offered him, Johnny decides to take a year's holiday with Linda in Europe, both of them giving up a gilded existence. 'Whatever he does is all right with me. If he wants to sit on his tail, he can sit on his tail. If he wants to come back and sell peanuts, Lord how I'll believe in those peanuts!' Kate says with exultant eloquence. As Linda is the archetypal Hepburn heroine – a rebellious society girl endowed with brains and beauty, strong yet unsure of herself – Kate played her with total conviction. The picture also revealed the new, glamorous Katharine Hepburn.

Working away from RKO for the first time, Kate teamed up again with Cary Grant and director George Cukor for Holiday *(1938) at Columbia.*

She had never looked more radiant on screen, with becoming make-up and hairdo, and the most flattering photography. Nevertheless, according to Kate, 'I was so terrible! It was heartbreaking to see how eager, how hard I was trying to impress – too eager. I turned to George [Cukor] and said, "Oh God, why did you hire me?" '

Despite good reviews, *Holiday* lost money, demonstrating that Depression audiences were unamused by the antics of the idle rich. It was around this time that the Independent Theatre Owners' Association published the names of performers who were, in their terminology, 'box-office poison'. Kate's name headed the list, which included Joan Crawford, Greta Garbo and Marlene Dietrich, all of them stars who portrayed mature, free-spirited women, while ten-year-old Shirley Temple and the teenage Deanna Durbin were the most popular female stars at the box office. Evidently, American cinema audiences in 1938 were looking for an escape into innocence. 'They say I'm a has-been. If I weren't laughing so much I might cry,' Kate commented.

She therefore decided to leave RKO for good, insulted when the studio offered her a role in a B picture called *Mother Carey's Chickens* (a part eventually taken by Ruby Keeler). Kate never worked for the studio again. In May 1938, she left

STAGE
THE MAGAZINE OF
After Dark
MARCH 15, 1939

15¢

Katharine Hepburn
in the
Theatre Guild Production

A lobby card for Holiday, *in which Kate, again as a rich girl, gave one of her most radiant performances.*

'Box-office poison' or not, Kate was still constantly featured on magazine covers like this one from March 1939.

Demonstrating her diving skills, just one of her sporting talents.

An all-round sportswoman, Kate was an excellent tennis player.

Left: *Kate in an uncharacteristic come-on publicity pose in the late 1930s.*

*No longer a false Hollywood
image, but her own woman.*

*The film that relaunched
Kate's career in a big way,
and over which she had
control for the first time.*

Left: *Although not yet seen
in a Technicolor film, Kate
shows herself as a natural
red-haired beauty as she
emerges into superstardom.*

Cary GRANT
Katharine HEPBURN
James STEWART
in
The Philadelphia Story

"It just offends my vanity as an ex-husband...
to have you marry a mugg like that!"

A Metro-Goldwyn-Mayer PICTURE

Hollywood for her family home in Connecticut, only to return in triumph.

Swimming and walking occupied most of her time there, and she still took about half a dozen cold showers a day. Looking the picture of health, Kate seemed to flourish away from Hollywood. There was one screen role, however, that she hankered for. Margaret Mitchell's epic novel of the American Civil War *Gone with the Wind* had been published the previous year and Kate had wanted to play Scarlett O'Hara from the time she read the proofs. But to her great disappointment, RKO rejected the book and it was passed on to David O. Selznick. She then pestered Selznick for a chance to play the part. George Cukor was signed to

With thirty-three-year-old Joseph Cotten as Dexter Haven in the hit stage production of Philip Barry's The Philadelphia Story *at the Shubert Theatre in 1939.*

Twenty-nine-year-old Van Heflin as Mike Connor in the stage production of The Philadelphia Story. *Heflin was bitter about being passed over in favour of James Stewart for the film version.*

direct the picture and he pressurized the producer to consider Kate. When Selznick finally agreed, she refused a screen test, telling him, 'You know what I look like on the screen. You know I can act. And you know this part was practically written for me. I am Scarlett O'Hara. So what's the matter?'

'Because, my dear, I can't see Rhett Butler chasing you for ten years.'

'Well, David, I may not appeal to you, but some people's idea of sex appeal is different from yours,' she retorted, and stormed out of his office.

Whatever Rhett Butler may have felt, Howard Hughes was still chasing her after two years, and Kate had succeeded in keeping him interested without any commitment on her part. Hughes courted her in high style, flying in and out with expensive gifts – including jewels, although Kate seldom wore jewellery.

In the summer of 1938, Philip Barry brought her a new play of his to read. The character of Tracy Lord in *The Philadelphia Story* bore a great resemblance to Kate, and there is no doubt that Barry had her in mind when he wrote it. She was enthusiastic and, putting up half the money with Hughes, got the Theatre Guild to produce it. Now owner of a quarter of the play, she bought the screen rights from Barry for an additional $25,000. Instead of a guaranteed salary, she took 10 per cent of the gross profits from the New York run and 12 per cent of profits on the road. For the first time in her professional career Kate had control over a play, and a possible film, in which she would star.

The Philadelphia Story went straight into rehearsals in the first week of January 1939. Van Heflin, who had appeared with her in *A Woman Rebels*, played Mike, the young newspaperman who falls in love with Tracy, and Joseph Cotten, from Orson Welles's Mercury Theatre, appeared as her ex-husband, C. K. Dexter Haven.

As opening night on Broadway – 28 March 1939 – approached, Kate grew increasingly nervous. She was carrying the label of 'box-office poison' around her neck, Philip Barry had had four flops in six years, and the Theatre Guild had had only one hit in three seasons. Her last appearance on the New York stage had been in the disastrous *The Lake*, six years previously, from which she still bore the

Kate, Cary Grant and James Stewart were at their sparkling best in The Philadelphia Story *(1940), George Cukor's sophisticated comedy of manners.*

scars. But all her fears proved to be unfounded. Both her performance and the play were rapturously received. Even more important to her was that her parents finally accepted that their movie-star daughter had become a fine stage actress.

Howard Hughes, weary of pursuing Kate, had turned to a succession of other women, though he remained a close friend and business partner. It was now Van Heflin who could be found most often in her company, and rumours abounded that they were having an affair. But when the run of the play entered its second year, he returned to Hollywood.

Within a few days of opening night, Kate received an offer from MGM for *The Philadelphia Story*. She sold them the rights for $250,000 with a guaranteed approval of director, co-stars and scriptwriter. To nobody's surprise, she chose her friends Cukor to direct and Donald Ogden Stewart to write the screenplay. As neither Joseph Cotten nor Van Heflin was then sufficiently known to movie audiences, she chose Cary Grant and James Stewart to star with her. (Heflin was to feel bitter about this 'betrayal'.) Against Kate's objections, Grant insisted on and received star billing above her.

Few retakes were required on *The Philadelphia Story*, which took eight weeks to shoot, five days under schedule. One of the few additions to the original play was the famous opening scene: a door opens, Grant walks out, Kate appears and heaves a bag of golf clubs after him; he turns around, shoves her in the face and she falls stiffly backwards into the house.

Right: *Kate in the wedding dress from* The Philadelphia Story, *designed by Adrian, MGM's top couturier.*

Left: *Katharine Hepburn now given the full, classy, MGM glamour treatment.*

refuses Mike's proposal and remarries Dexter.

In her Adrian frocks, Kate, looking glamorous and self-confident, portrayed Tracy with wit, wisdom and emotional intensity. Cukor said, 'She was perfect as Tracy Lord – she was arrogant but sensitive, she was tough but

George Cukor (behind the sofa) is amused by a rehearsal of The Philadelphia Story *with Kate, James Stewart and Ruth Hussey.*

Loyal as ever to the Theatre Guild, Kate went on tour with the play as soon as the filming finished. When the tour ended – appropriately, in Philadelphia – she gave a touching farewell speech, telling the audience, 'The curtain will never be rung down on this play.'

The plot of the film centres on Tracy Lord, a spoiled Philadelphia society girl about to marry a stuffy man. Ex-husband C.K. Dexter Haven (Cary Grant) arrives on the scene, as do reporters Mike Connor (James Stewart) and Liz Imbrie (Ruth Hussey) of *Spy Magazine* to cover the wedding. Tracy becomes infatuated with Mike, and the duo follow up a drinking session with a moonlight swim, an evening which transforms her from 'ice goddess' to 'real woman'. Earlier she had been told, 'You'll never be a first-class human being till you learn to have some regard for human frailty... but your sense of inner divinity won't allow it.' Now, realizing her deficiencies in her relationship with her ex-husband, whom she really loves, she breaks her engagement,

vulnerable, she didn't care what people thought of her, they had to accept her on her own terms or forget it. Of course, she was far more polished, more skilful than she had ever been before.'

Life magazine wrote, '*The Philadelphia Story* fits the curious talents of the red-headed Miss Hepburn like a coat of quick-dry enamel. It is said to have been written for her. Its shiny surface reflects perfectly from her gaunt, bony face. Its languid action becomes her lean, rangy body. Its brittle smart-talk suits her metallic voice. When Katharine Hepburn sets out to play Katharine Hepburn, she is a sight to behold. Nobody is her equal.'

The picture, which broke all records of the Radio City Music Hall after its première in November 1940, became Kate's professional vindication. She was to begin the new decade with a major triumph behind her, the complete confidence of Louis B. Mayer, a long-term MGM contract and the knowledge that she was part of the most powerful studio in the world.

In 1941, at the time of this MGM publicity still, Kate was gaining more power in the industry, and could make more of her own choices and decisions.

7

Love at Second Sight

It was a unique feeling that I had for
Spencer Tracy. I would have done
anything for him. My feelings — how
can I describe them? — the door between
us was always open. There were no
reservations of any kind.

Although they had never met, Katharine Hepburn idolized Spencer Tracy on screen. She admired his skill in not seeming to act at all, his directness and simplicity, his quiet humour and warm personality, his masculine qualities and his rugged yet sensitive features. She had seen most of his pictures, and, above all, cherished his role as Manuel, the Portuguese fisherman, in *Captains Courageous* (1937). 'I can never face the end without weeping so,' she said, after having seen it countless times.

Her heart was set on Spencer Tracy to play C. K. Dexter Haven in the film of *The Philadelphia Story*, certain that he would make a perfect foil for her Tracy Lord, but he had made four pictures in quick succession and needed a rest. Apart from that, he was the kind of man that attracted her most, like her father, not willing to take any guff, proud and strong – stronger than most women. She even mentioned that the name Tracy Lord appealed to her at the time because of her admiration for the actor.

When Kate went to MGM with Ring Lardner Jr's script of *Woman of the Year* in the summer of 1941, she insisted, as she owned the rights, that she would not sell it unless Spencer Tracy co-starred with her. However, Tracy was in Florida on location for *The Yearling* and would not be free for some time. Then the unexpected happened.

For various reasons *The Yearling* was postponed and Tracy was now willing and able to make the film opposite Hepburn. He admired her grace and style in *The Philadelphia Story* and proclaimed her 'a damn fine actress', even suggesting to Louis B. Mayer that she play both female leads in his *Dr Jekyll and Mr Hyde*, an idea Mayer immediately rejected. Nevertheless, Tracy was slightly wary of Kate's reputation for being uppity and her habit of wearing trousers in public. She was in awe of the man she was about to meet, although she had heard tales of the married Tracy's drinking and womanizing.

Kate, at five feet seven, was tall for a Hollywood actress, and with four-inch platform shoes, her hair piled high on her head and her rigid back, she seemed far taller. Tracy was

Opposite: At her peak, aged thirty-six, two years after meeting Spencer Tracy, the love of her life.

The beginning of a beautiful friendship. Tracy and Hepburn confront each other for the first time on screen in Woman of the Year *(1942), under the scrutiny of director George Stevens (centre).*

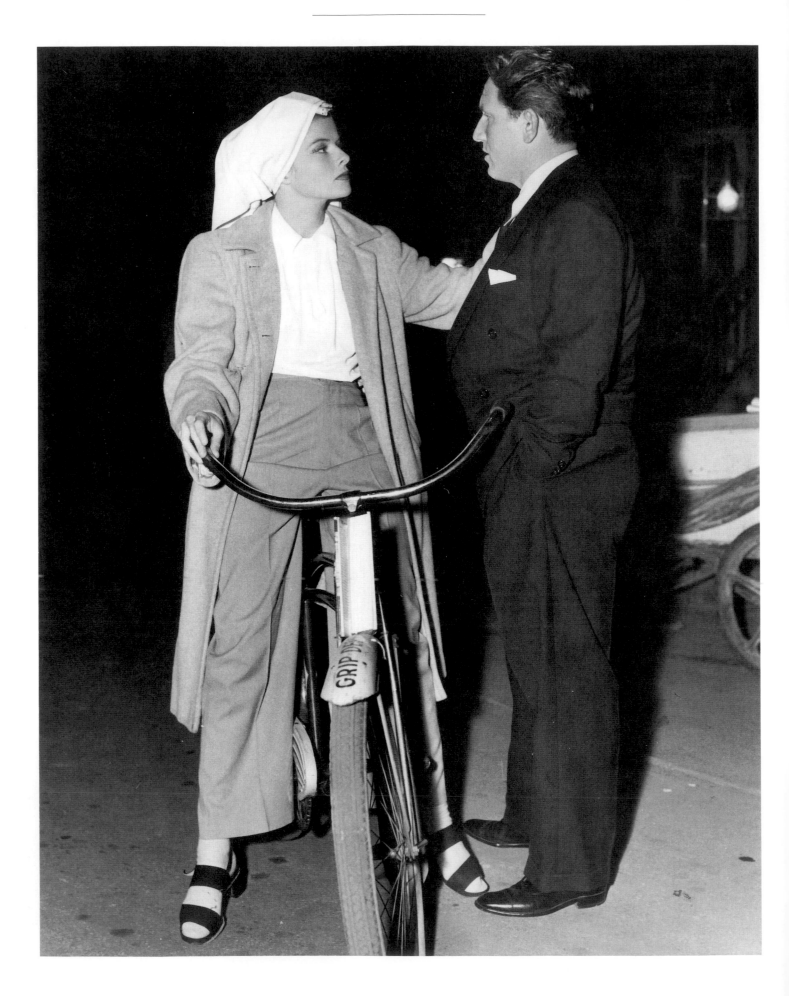

a big man, but not particularly tall at five feet ten and a half inches. On their first meeting, when the film's producer Joseph L. Mankiewicz introduced them, Kate remarked, 'I'm afraid I'm a little tall for you, Mr Tracy.' On seeing Spencer's abashed look, Mankiewicz quipped, 'Don't worry, baby, he'll soon cut you down to size.'

After she left, Tracy turned to Mankiewicz and said, 'Not me, boy, I don't want to get mixed up in anything like that.' Later, when she asked Tracy what he thought of the script, he replied, 'It's all right. Not much to do as it stands – but, Shorty, you better watch yourself in the clinches!' It was the beginning of a beautiful friendship.

From the moment shooting began under George Stevens' direction, something remarkable happened between Hepburn and Tracy. As the camera began to turn, it acted upon them like a magic ray: they fell in love. People around them and those working on the picture started to notice small things. In the first few days Tracy had called Hepburn 'Shorty' or 'that woman', but it gradually became 'Kate' or 'Kath'. She seemed to glow with a new feminine aura, and though she still always wore slacks or jeans, she took more care over her appearance. Stevens recognized the symptoms and backed away from his romantic attachment in a gentlemanly manner.

On the very first day of shooting, Kate's acting was subdued, her usually clear and distinctive diction mumbled. Tracy spoke his lines in an artificial and overstudied manner. 'My God!' cried Mankiewicz. 'They're imitating each other!' Stevens noted, 'From the very beginning of the picture, and their relationship, Spence's reaction to her was a total, pleasant but glacial put-down of her extreme effusiveness. He just didn't get disturbed about doing things immediately; she wanted to do a hundred and one things at once; he was never in a hurry.'

Woman of the Year proved to be

Kate with the characteristic towel wrapped around her head in an off-set moment with Tracy on Woman of the Year.

one of the top earners of the 1941-42 season. *Time* magazine wrote that 'actors Hepburn and Tracy have a fine old time... They take turns playing straight for each other...', and the *Baltimore Sun* recognized that 'his quiet masculine stubbornness and prosaic outlook on life is in striking contrast with her sparkle and brilliance. They make a fine team, and each complements the other.' The writer's comments could just as well have been applied to their real-life romance as well. Most of the nine pictures they did together reflected much of their personal rapport: humorous put-downs, amusing collisions and a mingling of desperation and joy.

Woman of the Year concerned the love-hate marriage of a sophisticated political columnist and a gruff sportswriter, based on Ring Lardner's real-life relationship with Dorothy Parker. The scenario emphasized the feminist angle until, at the rewritten ending, Kate's character submitted to domesticity in order to keep the man she loved. Kate used strong language about the reactionary finale, but it didn't offend Tracy's more conventional view of gender roles. Most of the films they made were really variations on *The Taming of the Shrew*, the message being that a woman who is really a woman must take second place to the man in her life. In all their films together, Kate took second billing. When the writer Garson Kanin once asked, 'Spencer, didn't you ever hear of ladies first?' Tracy replied, 'This is a movie, not a lifeboat.'

It was not long after their first meeting that Kate came brutally into contact with a part of her lover that she would spend the best part of her time fighting. Halfway through shooting of *Woman of the Year*, Tracy disappeared. Friends, and members of the crew who had worked with him before, knew that he had gone on one of his periodic binges. When he was not found at his usual drinking haunts, Kate went from bar to bar searching for him. She finally caught up with him, brought him home, fed him and sobered him up. On the set, for the rest of the

A scene from Woman of the Year, *the first and one of the best of the many Tracy–Hepburn pairings.*

A glamorous 1940 studio portrait presents a vivid contrast to Kate's everyday, more natural look.

picture, she brewed pots and pots of strong tea to serve him. It was all reminiscent of her attempts to keep John Ford off the bottle.

Kate was strongly advised against entering into an affair with Tracy. There were so many good reasons, if there had been a rational option, why it should never have happened. Tracy was only seven years her senior, but already had serious health problems at the age of forty-one. Mainly as a result of excessive drinking, his liver and kidneys had been affected, and his heart was not too strong either. He was often moody, rude and short-tempered, and suffered periods of melancholia.

Another negative aspect was the fact that, as a Catholic, he would never divorce his wife, Louise, though she was Episcopalian. The marriage had eroded, but it had turned into a dependent friendship with strong ties. The Tracys had been married nearly twenty years, through good and bad times. Louise had put aside her own acting career not long after their son of ten months had been diagnosed incurably deaf, dedicating her life to learning how to communicate with him and working for many years to help found and then fund the John Tracy Clinic for Deaf Children. A man of conscience

Sipping fish chowder with her idol President Roosevelt at Mrs Roosevelt's cottage in Hyde Park, New York, in 1940, where a group of artists gathered to give their support for the New Deal.

or character could never walk out on a woman like Louise. How many times had she welcomed him home either drunk or from the arms of another woman – or both – without recrimination?

This had not stopped him having affairs. Kate's friends reckoned that if Tracy had not left his wife for Loretta Young some years previously, he would never set up house with her. She would have to accept the terms of a clandestine relationship with all its pitfalls. But Kate was deeply in love with Tracy, and he saw her as his salvation – a woman who could share his work as well as his life, and accept him for what he was. By loving him, she became a less self-absorbed person and also a better actress.

They seemed an ill-assorted couple, the embodiment of the theory of the attraction of opposites. He was a devout Catholic, she was a free-thinker; he was hard drinking, she was virtually a teetotaller; he was a physical wreck, she was a superb sportswoman; he was of Irish stock born in Milwaukee, Wisconsin, she was the WASP personified born in Hartford, Connecticut; he was a pessimist, she was an optimist; his acting talent lay in doing as little as possible, her style was showy.

On the other hand, they shared the same brand of dry wit and humour, were equally dedicated to their chosen craft and could not tolerate flatterers or sycophants. They both had a no-nonsense attitude to life, did not suffer fools gladly, shunned publicity as much as possible, led extremely private lives and held strong convictions. Both were Democrats and great admirers of Franklin D. Roosevelt; both were repelled by the McCarthy witch-hunts of the 1950s. They loved reading, music and the theatre, were interested in sports, enjoyed discussing politics and had the same intellectual curiosity. They painted together – seascapes, landscapes and scenes through the windows of their hotel bedrooms. They fulfilled each other intellectually, artistically and spiritually. It was a love affair that was sustained and unwavering from 1941 to Tracy's death in 1967 and beyond.

The affection between the co-stars of Woman of the Year *was a genuine one, and this transmitted itself to audiences.*

8

Perfect
Partners

*We balanced each other's natures. We
were perfect representations of the
American male and female.*

Although rumours filtered through, the public at large was never fully aware of Kate and Spencer's affair until the early 1970s. It was Louella Parsons who called it 'the greatest love story never told'. But if Kate and Spencer's real relationship was a clandestine one, they could, at least, relive it in fictional terms for all the world to see. Therefore, they tried to work together as much as possible.

Following the success of *Woman of the Year*, the first Tracy–Hepburn pairing, MGM quickly put them into another vehicle. *Keeper of the Flame* was a competent melodrama, directed by George Cukor, that made the mistake of eliminating any love interest between the couple (the only one of their films to do so). Kate had managed to persuade MGM to make the film because she was fascinated by the character of a resolute woman placed in a tragic position on learning that her dead husband, whom she thought a hero, had been a traitor to his country. Tracy played the investigative reporter who discovers the truth. Because the film pointed to the dangers of creeping fascism in the USA, Kate thought that it would be of valuable assistance to the war effort. But it turned out to have what Cukor called a 'waxwork quality'. Kate herself felt that *Keeper of the Flame* was pretentious and unconvincing. Photographed by William Daniels, Garbo's favourite cameraman, she was made to resemble the Swedish star. 'I didn't like the glamour side of Kate,' Cukor commented. 'I loved the fresh, natural Kate when she forgot to be a movie queen. The subject brought out the movie queen in her, and that wasn't good.'

Not long after Kate and Tracy's return from a trip east, where Kate introduced Spencer to her family, they agreed to make *The Sea of Grass*. Tracy played Colonel James Brewton, a nineteenth-century New Mexico cattle tycoon, obsessed with the grasslands of his family estate, and

A relationship both playful and erotic, it mirrored Tracy and Hepburn's real-life one.

Kate was Lutie Cameron, the strong-willed, sensitive young woman who marries him. Elia Kazan, who had made only one previous feature, was signed to direct. 'I was scared of Kate – I was overpowered by her,' Kazan recalled. 'After all, she was "royalty".' He found her 'a very cool person'. To break down her reserve, Kazan asked her to cry in one scene, and Kate was happy to oblige. However, Louis B. Mayer didn't like the scene. 'The channel of tears is wrong,' he told Kazan. 'They go too near her nostrils.' The director tried to explain that Kate's face was made

The fine horsewoman with Spencer in George Cukor's melodrama Keeper of the Flame *(1942), their second pairing.*

Relaxing while listening to
George Cukor on the set of
Keeper of the Flame.

that way, but Mayer shouted him down. 'Some people cry with their voice, some with their throat, some with their eyes, but she cries with everything, and that is excessive.'

The stilted film reflects the director's inexperience and failure to get more than adequate performances from the two leads. It also suffered from being filmed in a studio, when it cried out for authentic open spaces.

In those early years of the 1940s, Tracy was still battling against the alcoholism which had plagued him during the latter part of the previous decade, and Kate made it her bounden duty to break him of the habit. She conducted a vigorous campaign to separate Tracy from his drinking companions, and succeeded to some degree. He had moved into a modest guest cottage that Cukor had on his grounds and Kate into a hilltop house that had once belonged to silent-screen star John Gilbert.

Kate's routine remained virtually unchanged. She still rose early each morning and was always the first on the set. She always wore the same military student's cap, which she had picked up on a trip to Europe with Luddy in 1932, and an old army fatigue jacket which her brother Richard had left behind on a visit years before. She had a succession of dogs, which she adored, taking them with her on her constant walks around Hollywood. She refused to eat out. 'Whenever I eat out, I pass out – sounds funny, but it's true. I've only been to a restaurant five or six times in my life, and each time I've passed out. My nerves are terrible – if people are watching me, I gobble my food, and then I get sick. So I always eat at home.'

Private as ever, she rarely gave an autograph. On one occasion, some fans begged her. She refused. When one said, 'How dare you refuse? We made you what you are today,' Kate replied, 'Like hell you did!'

Jack Dawn's oriental make-up for Kate in Dragon Seed *(1944) went some way to help her convince as a Chinese peasant.*

In September 1942, Luddy filed for divorce in Hartford under the name of Ogden Ludlow. He claimed desertion and told the court that he doubted the legality of the decree Kate had received in Mexico in 1934. The case appeared on the docket simply as 'Ogden Ludlow v. Katharine H. Ludlow'. Not until the hearing was over did the judge realize the identity of the defendant. A week later, Luddy married a divorced Boston socialite, Elizabeth Albers.

Now at MGM, Pandro Berman, who had once sworn he would never do another film with Kate, came to her with an adaptation of Pearl S. Buck's *Dragon Seed*. The role of the idealistic yet realistic Chinese girl, Jade, appealed to Kate, perhaps because of the challenge of portraying a woman of another culture, but also because the theme was that of the Chinese peasant's long struggle against Japanese aggression.

The $3 million production was filmed largely on location in the San Fernando Valley, where an entire Chinese peasant village was constructed on a 120-acre tract of land. Kate's high cheek-boned features lent themselves well to the Chinese make-up, but her Bostonian voice was less convincing. Yet, despite James Agee's remarks about her 'Peck and Peckish pajamas' and 'her twangy New England Oriental accent', she managed, against all the odds, to create a sympathetic character, even overcoming such risible lines such 'I don't want my baby teethed on Japanese bullets.'

Although she enjoyed making *Dragon Seed*, Kate really wanted to work with Spencer again, as the partnership was good for both of them. With the failure of the dramas *Keeper of the Flame* and *The Sea of Grass*, Kate looked around for a vehicle in which they could return to the lighter bantering mood of *Woman of the Year*. She found it in *Without Love*, the Philip Barry play in which she had starred in a moderately successful fourteen-week limited run in New York towards the end of 1942. On stage, Kate had been the centre of attraction, delivering witty lines while swanning around in her Valentina costumes. With Tracy's considerable presence, the plot gained in substance, becoming a more balanced piece. It is a comedy about a scientist and a rich woman who offers him the basement of her mansion to use as a laboratory. They therefore agree to marry 'without love'.

Towel-headed again, Kate pours herself tea off the set of The Sea of Grass.

Unfortunately, the picture suffered from mediocre direction (Harold S. Bucquet), and a retrograde performance from Kate – full of girlish mannerisms, frequently exclaiming, 'By gum!', grinning and clutching at her throat. She was beginning to be self-conscious about her 'scrawny' neck, which she would cover with scarves and high collars.

With Tracy off the booze and working, Kate took on a couple more parts without him, though neither enhanced her reputation. *Undercurrent*, a reasonably entertaining piece of hokum, directed by Vincente Minnelli, is about a young, rather naive woman who marries a charming and wealthy industrialist (Robert Taylor). Her husband confesses to her that he has a psychopathic brother (Robert Mitchum), who has committed murder and is a constant threat. When the brother finally appears, she becomes convinced that it is her husband who is the killer. Kate was woefully miscast in the role of a defenceless wife, more

Tracy and Hepburn, suspicious of Elia Kazan's 'Method' training, gave the director a hard time on The Sea of Grass.

Above: *A still aptly demonstrating the title of* The Sea of Grass, *though it was actually shot on the MGM back lot.*

Right: *Not one of Tracy and Hepburn's best efforts,* The Sea of Grass *was held back from release by MGM for over a year.*

Overleaf: *Kate in a typically informal pose in slacks and sweater on the set of* Undercurrent (1946).

It's a wrap. Kate celebrating with the crew and director Vincente Minnelli (third from left) on the soundstage of Undercurrent.

Smiling again in Without Love *(1945), after two unsuitably dour dramas together.*

109

suited to the talents of Ingrid Bergman. She mentioned that her greatest difficulty was 'getting the right horrified reaction'.

During the making of *Undercurrent*, Kate became very friendly with Minnelli's wife, Judy Garland. She forced Judy to get up early and take morning walks, and tried, unsuccessfully, to stop her from drinking and taking drugs.

Song of Love was an over-romanticized story based on the marriage of Clara and Robert Schumann. For her role, Kate studied daily with pianist Laura

Dubman, a pupil of Artur Rubinstein (who made the recordings for the film), and mastered 'the proper techniques of playing difficult compositions for close-up shooting'.

Artur Rubenstein supplied the music, while Kate displayed pianistic skills in Song of Love.

Rubinstein commented, 'If I hadn't seen it with my own eyes and ears, I wouldn't have believed it! That woman is incredible! She actually does play almost as well as I do! And when she ends and I begin, only I in the whole world could tell the difference!' Actually, Kate was well cast as the determined Clara, who gives up her career to marry the struggling composer (Paul Henreid) and have seven children.

During the war years, Kate was a Roosevelt partisan, but lost faith in the Democratic Party when Truman inherited the office. In 1947, she switched her allegiance to Henry Wallace, who was campaigning for the Presidency on a third party, Progressive, ticket. He was labelled 'a Communist dupe'. In May 1947, when Wallace was barred from using the Hollywood Bowl for a political

For her role as piano virtuoso Clara Schumann in Song of Love *(1947), Kate took lessons from Laura Dubman, former pupil of Artur Rubenstein.*

The Tracy–Hepburn union was in good fettle during the shooting of Frank Capra's political comedy–drama State of the Union *(1948).*

address, Kate agreed to participate in an anti-censorship rally held in Los Angeles. In her speech, she attacked the House UnAmerican Activities Committee. 'The artist since the beginning of time has always expressed the aspirations and dreams of his people. Silence the artist and you have silenced the most articulate voice the people have.'

Poles apart politically off screen, Kate and Adolphe Menjou had to put enmity aside while working together on State of the Union.

Kate's speech was impressive and carefully prepared, but she was negligent about her clothes. 'At first I was going to wear white,' she recalled. 'And then I decided they'd think I was the dove of peace, so I wore pink. Pink! How could I have been so dumb?' Although her name came up at the HUAC, she was never called before it. In 1947, she joined a group of actors and directors, led by John Huston and William Wyler, who formed the Committee for the First Amendment, a group dedicated to combating 'the unfavorable picture of the film industry arising from testimony before the House Committee on UnAmerican Activities'. Like France during the Dreyfus case, Hollywood was divided into two enemy camps. This became apparent while Kate was shooting her next film.

It was time for her to have another success. It

came with Tracy again in *State of the Union*, directed by Frank Capra. Claudette Colbert was originally cast as the estranged wife of a presidential candidate, but when she refused to work beyond 5 p.m., the director sacked her. Capra phoned Tracy to tell him the bad news. Tracy, of course, knew someone who could fill the role. 'The bag of bones has been helping me rehearse. Kinda stops you, Frank, the way she reads the woman's part... She might do it for the hell of it.'

By Monday morning, Kate was on the set ready to start shooting. There was, however, a touchy problem. Adolphe Menjou, who played the crafty campaign manager, had co-operated with the HUAC, while Kate had spoken out against the committee's 'smear campaign'. Capra ordered the soundstage closed as she and Menjou performed their scenes, because the press were anxious to report any friction between them on the set. As professionals, they refused to let their personal rancour show, but it was a sad contrast to their pleasant working rapport years before in *Morning Glory* and *Stage Door*.

Tracy portrays a liberal Republican seeking the Presidency, and living apart from his wife. In order to show the electorate that he is a solid citizen, she is asked to return and masquerade as his loving spouse. But she watches her husband alter his values and decides to speak up, pointing out that the people with whom he has chosen to throw in his lot are greedy, grasping and corrupt. He listens to her and understands what he has done. On the radio, he announces he is taking his name off the nominating slate because he feels he is not worthy of consideration on the voters' part.

Of Tracy and Hepburn, Capra commented that when they 'played a scene, cameras, lights, microphones, and written scripts ceased to exist. And the director did just what the crews and other actors did – sat, watched, and marveled.' Though Kate played the non-flashy part with a nice balance of humour and conviction, *Time* magazine thought

that 'Hepburn's affectation of talking like a woman simultaneously trying to steady a loose dental brace sharply limits her range of expression.' *State of the Union*, though taking itself a little too seriously, cemented Tracy and Hepburn as a team in the public eye.

During the halcyon days between 1942 and 1949, when they were paired six times, Kate and Spencer continued to live in separate homes. Kate ran both households in her capacity as Tracy's companion, secretary, nurse, cook and chauffeur. She even managed to stop his drinking. On weekends when they were not working she kept him as occupied as she could. They walked, swam, talked and painted. Everything in her life, including her choice of film roles, was dictated by Tracy's needs. On pictures in which she did not appear with him, she would still drive him to the studio, remain with him on the set, drive him home and cook him a meal.

In 1948, taking the opportunity to spend a stretch of time in England with Kate, Tracy accepted the lead in *Edward My Son*. During the shooting, he was a guest of Laurence Olivier and Vivien Leigh at their huge thirteenth-century mansion, Notley Abbey, while Kate had a suite at Claridge's. He could not stay with her at the hotel, and they would not have felt at ease together at Notley. It was one of the coldest English winters for decades, and Spencer shivered in the cavernous rooms of the abbey. As a result he and Kate were glad to be able to film *Adam's Rib* in New York in the spring, under George Cukor's direction. During the amiable atmosphere of shooting, Kate was able to live in her house on East 49th Street, while Spencer stayed at the Waldorf Towers.

Adam's Rib (the original title *Man and Wife* was vetoed by the MGM front office as being indiscreet) was written by Garson Kanin and his wife Ruth Gordon with Tracy and Hepburn in mind. It concerned a pair of lawyers, husband and wife, who find themselves on opposite sides in a court case. The

Cole Porter (at the piano) composed the lovely song 'Farewell, Amanda' especially for Adam's Rib, *in which it is sung to Kate.*

film, heralded by the billboards as 'The Hilarious Answer to Who Wears the Pants!!', helped give MGM a financial shot in the arm. The *New York Times* wrote that Tracy and Hepburn's 'perfect compatibility in comic capers is delightful to see. A line thrown away, a lifted eyebrow, a smile or a sharp, resounding slap on a tender part of the anatomy is as natural as breathing to them. Plainly, they took pleasure in playing this rambunctious spoof.'

At the end of the picture, Kate delivers a speech which could well have been made by her mother. 'An unwritten law stands back of a man who fights to defend his home. Apply the same to this maltreated mother. We ask no more. Equality! Deep in the interior of South America, there thrives a civilization, older than ours... In this vast tribe, members of the female sex rule and govern and systematically deny equal rights to the men – made weak and puny by years of subservience. Too weak to revolt. And yet how long have we lived in the shadow of like injustice?'

Adam's Rib, probably their most sparkling picture as a team, had them doing what they did best together, sparring affectionately and wittily in a bouncy battle of the sexes. The tailor-made dialogue by the Kanins, who knew Kate and Spencer very well, suited the stars' personalities admirably and underscored both their on- and their off-screen relationship. A home-movie sequence was very much modelled on how the couple behaved 'at home'.

For some months following *Adam's Rib* they looked for another script that would be right for both of them. When nothing suitable materialized, Tracy went into *Malaya*, an uninspiring action melodrama. Kate, meanwhile, was delighted to be able to take up an offer to play Rosalind in a Broadway production of *As You Like It*, as she had never tackled Shakespeare

Turning on the waterworks – an effective weapon in the battle of the sexes waged in George Cukor's delightful comedy Adam's Rib *(1949).*

before. 'I realize I'm putting my head on the line,' she said. 'But for me, the personal satisfaction justifies the risk.'

She brought Michael Benthall from England to direct, and her dear friend Constance Collier to coach her in the role, working with the older actress for three hours a day for eight months.

Proud of working on a project she considered

worthwhile, Kate invited her mother to accompany her to a few of the cities on tour. Mrs Hepburn agreed, and Kate played to her mother as much as she did to her audiences. However, she knew she was taking a risk in leaving Tracy, who was finding it increasingly difficult to cope without her during a nine-week pre-New York tour and then a longish run. While she was away, he started drinking again and phoned

Kate listening intently to her screen mentor George Cukor on the set of Adam's Rib, *considered the best of the team's comedies.*

'From the east to western Inde, No jewel is like Rosalind.' Kate in As You Like It *at the Cort Theatre, New York, in 1950.*

her about three times a day.

As soon as *Malaya* was completed, Tracy caught up with Kate in Cleveland, where he promised to give up alcohol. But during *As You Like It*'s 145 performances on Broadway, Spencer was seen reeling into and out of Kate's apartment night after night. None of the cast ever saw Spencer, who was smuggled in and out of tour hotels in the freight elevator, because he and Kate were determined to keep their loving relationship a secret from almost everyone.

In March 1951, Kate came home to West Hartford. The tour with *As You Like It* had left her physically exhausted but feeling more at ease about her future. Life in Hartford, despite the fact that her brothers and sisters were all married and living away, had not changed. At seventy-five, her father still went to his office on weekdays. Her mother's devotion to birth control and women's rights had not wavered.

On 17 March Kate and Dr Hepburn came in from a brisk walk a few minutes late for afternoon tea. They found the table set, the teapot filled with hot, freshly brewed tea, and the house unnaturally quiet. Exchanging frightened glances, they ran upstairs without a word. Mrs Hepburn had recently had a small heart infarction, and they were not wrong in suspecting what they would find. Kit Houghton Hepburn, at seventy-three, was dead, lying gracefully across her bed. Kate had adored her, and it was painful to realize that this brilliant woman was gone.

'The thing about life is that you must survive,' Kate later said. 'Life is going to be difficult and dreadful things will happen. What you do is to move along, get on with it and be tough. Not in the sense of being mean to others, but tough with yourself and making a deadly effort not to be defeated.'

9

An Unmarried Woman

I never was a child and I never was a mother. I was an Aunt Kat. Sometimes the oldest in a big family turns out that way. I helped raise the others.

Spencer Tracy still considered it a matter of principle that he and Kate lived apart, although both of his children were grown and his son John, despite his deafness, had married. Kate was eager to find a script that would enable her to return to Hollywood, but suitable ones were hard to come by. At forty-four, she realized there were few screenplays that centred on women entering or in middle age, whereas such roles for men were bountiful. She finally found what she was looking for in *The African Queen*, opposite Humphrey Bogart and directed by John Huston, although it meant going all the way to the Belgian Congo to make it.

The African Queen was the name of the rusty old river steamer which took scruffy, profane, unshaven, gin-drinking captain Charlie Allnut (Bogart, winning his only Oscar) and prim, scrawny, Bible-quoting spinster missionary Rose Sayer (Hepburn) down the Congo River during World War I. On the trip, during which they negotiate rapids, shallows and storms, finally succeeding in blowing up a German gunboat, the ill-matched pair learn from each other and fall in love.

At first Kate behaved towards Bogart with a certain disdain, as if out of habit, until he shook her and said, 'You ugly, skinny old bag of bones! Why don't you come down to earth?' Kate, staring him right in the eye, replied, 'Down where you're crawling? All right!' She laughed, everyone laughed, and from that moment, she and Bogart (and Lauren Bacall, who had come along for the ride) became close friends.

Gracefully entering early middle age and a new phase in her career in 1952.

'Bogie hated Africa, but for me it was a glorious adventure,' Kate wrote. It was also a hazardous one. There was a moment when Kate had to go into the water to release the boat, which was stuck in the reeds. 'Oh!' she said, when Huston asked her to do this. 'The river's full of crocodiles!'

'Don't worry. I'll have my prop men fire a few rounds of ammunition into the water. You'll find the

The hard drinker and the tee-totaller, the sinner and the missionary. The inspired pairing of Bogie and Kate in John Huston's The African Queen *(1951).*

crocodiles get scared by the noise, and they'll vanish,' Huston assured her.

'Yes, but what about the deaf ones?' Kate retorted. She went in anyway.

Ironically, because of her temperance, she got dysentery. 'I was so busy complaining about Bogie and John drinking hard liquor I tried to shame them by drinking water in their presence at mealtimes. Well, the water was full of germs! They never got sick, and I had the Mexican trots, and was in bed every day for weeks! I thought I was going to die – and in the Belgian Congo!'

Out of Africa. Lauren Bacall, Humphrey Bogart and Kate return to London looking reasonably refreshed after a gruelling time in the Congo filming The African Queen.

She found Huston brilliant in flashes, as when he told her to base her character of Rose Sayer on Eleanor Roosevelt when she visited the hospitals of the wounded soldiers, always with a smile on her face. 'He had felt that I was playing Rosie too seriously, and that since my mouth turned down anyway it was making the scenes heavy. Since I (as Rosie) was the sister of a minister, my approach to everyone and everything had to be full of hope... In short, he told me exactly how to play the part.'

Wearing little if any make-up to cover her abundant freckles, and exposing her scraggy neck, her gaunt face smudged with mud, Kate bravely abandoned all semblance of glamour, presenting herself exactly as she was. The box-office triumph of this first Technicolor feature for Huston, Bogart and Hepburn could be attributed to its skilful blending of comedy, drama and thrills, its authentic exotic setting, and the inspired pairing of Hepburn and Bogart, the missionary and the sinner, between whom an unlikely romance begins to blossom. They both gave among their most appealing performances, and the film carried the stars to new success in what were essentially character parts.

While in Africa, Kate wrote daily letters to Tracy; these were taken back to the village once a week by native runners, and then picked up by launch, finally reaching Léopoldville, where there was a post office. John Huston relates in his autobiography, 'I remember the many nights I sat with Kate on the top deck of the paddle boat and watched the eyes of the hippos in the water all around us... We talked about nothing and everything. But there was never any idea of romance – Spencer Tracy was the only man in Kate's life.'

But if Tracy was the man in her life, she was the

life in her man. Depressed by Kate's absence, he began drinking heavily again. After location shooting on *The African Queen* was completed on 17 July 1951, Hepburn and Bogart had to spend an extra six weeks filming in England. Tracy had arrived in London earlier to await her. There he met Joan Fontaine at a dinner party and later phoned the actress to ask her out. Fontaine declined the invitation out of respect for Kate, and also reminded Tracy that he was a married man. 'I can get a divorce whenever I want to,' he told her. 'But my wife and Kate like things just as they are.'

Back in America, Kate rolled up her sleeves and got to work on Tracy again, brewing endless cups of coffee, insisting he take cold showers, go for walks and swim every day. Now completely grey, Spencer looked much older than his fifty-one years, but Kate got him into reasonable shape again. She was greatly helped in her efforts by the fact that their good friends Garson Kanin and Ruth Gordon had another made-to-order script ready for the two of them.

Husband-and-wife writers Garson Kanin and Ruth Gordon discuss their screenplay of Pat and Mike *with the friends for whom they wrote it. It was a happy experience for both stars.*

Pat and Mike was a happy experience for both stars and for audiences everywhere. Filmed almost entirely at the Riviera Country Club in Pacific Palisades, it concerned the loving and bantering relationship between a sports promoter and an all-round sportswoman. A favourite line has Tracy saying in a broad Brooklyn accent, when he first claps eyes on Kate, 'Not much meat on her, but what there is, is cherce [choice].'

Looking ten years younger than she had in *The African Queen*, Kate got a rare chance to show off her legs in a short white tennis skirt. She plays a professional golfer and tennis player, but whenever her sexist fiancé is around she feels inferior and her game deteriorates. By the end of the picture, she has dumped him and married sports promoter Tracy, although she has to prove she's weaker than him in order to protect his male ego. *Pat and Mike* is another example in a 1950s Hollywood movie of struggling feminism, manacled in the end by patriarchal ideology.

With her MGM contract at an end (Tracy remained with the studio for three more years until his erratic behaviour got him fired), Kate became obsessed with playing the role of Epifania, Shaw's outrageously spoiled madcap heiress in *The Millionairess*, on stage. 'I adored the play. Everyone kept saying, "Why do you want to do it? It's such a bad play." Well, I thought it was fun, and I still do. It portrays a wonderful character. My mother worshipped Shaw. She knew everything he'd ever written. Backwards. So did my

A rare glimpse of Kate's shapely legs during a practice game for her role as a tennis champ in Pat and Mike *(1952).*

father. A great deal of Shaw was read out loud at home. He was sort of a god.'

Epifania, one of Shaw's 'superwomen', is a role that provides ample scope for an intelligent and vibrant actress. The London opening of The

Millionairess at the New Theatre in June 1952 was a triumph, being ecstatically received by Kenneth Tynan in the Observer, while another newspaper was headlined 'HEPBURN PLAYS SHAW – AND WINS'. Michael Benthall, who had directed Kate in

Ready to take on real-life tennis star 'Gorgeous' Gussie Moran in Pat and Mike, in which Kate was able to display her sporting prowess.

127

Robert Helpmann as the Egyptian doctor and Kate as Epifania in Michael Benthall's production of George Bernard Shaw's The Millionairess *at the Shubert Theater, New York, in October 1952.*

As *You Like It,* disguised the play's weaknesses by mounting a glamorous production, with the star dressed in Pierre Balmain gowns, one of which was an eye-catching jewel-encrusted organdie ball gown.

Kate was joined by Tracy, who flew in to be with her during much of

the limited season of twelve weeks in London. When *The Millionairess* reached New York, it was greeted coldly, many of the reviewers accusing Kate of storming, fuming and carrying on excessively in a role that inclined to highlight the more strident side of her personality. Despite this, Kate tried to get the play made into a film, in which she would co-star with Alec Guinness; the director was to be Preston

Sturges, who was in very poor physical shape at the time and drinking heavily. When finances were not forthcoming for the project, Kate decided to give up work for a couple of years in order to keep an eye on Spencer, while he made a number of movies.

Once Kate was confident that her loved one could be left alone again, she took up the tempting offer to make *Summertime*, for David Lean in Venice. There she stayed in a splendidly furnished apartment on the Grand Canal, with a beautiful garden on the river, a cook, butler and maid, and a private gondola. But her absence again created a deep void for Tracy.

He was set to make *Tribute to a Bad Man* opposite Grace Kelly. Rumours reached Kate in Italy of a romance between Tracy and the cool, blonde beauty. When reproached by Kate, Spencer flew over to visit her in Venice for a short period to reassure her that his dinner dates with the future Princess Grace of Monaco had been strictly business.

Summertime concerns a brief encounter between a married antique dealer (Rossano Brazzi) and an unmarried midwestern schoolteacher (Hepburn). The suave Latin lover tells her, 'You Americans think too much about sex instead of doing something about it,' just before she succumbs to his kiss. The romance ends when she breaks it off on moral grounds. Having had her illicit cake, she leaves Venice clutching her crumbs of comfort. As Jane Hudson, Kate overdoes her scrawny, tearful spinster bit, coming to Venice eager to take in all the sights, and hoping to find a 'magic explosion', an expression hardly applicable to the finished film, given David Lean's tame direction. Upstaging everyone was La Serenissima, the city of Venice, well-photographed in Technicolor by Jack Hildyard, which contributed to the film's great success.

The technical difficulties of filming in Venice were endless; even Kate found it exhausting, not having entirely recovered from the dysentery she had contracted in Africa. All the equipment had to be floated on launches or barges, and noisy crowds often ruined key scenes. The most difficult sequence in the picture, and the most famous, was the one in which Kate, photographing an antique shop, backs too

The famous scene in David Lean's Summertime *(1955) in which Kate falls into a filthy Venice canal, watched by little Gaitano Audiero. Her eyes never fully recovered from the infection she picked up.*

close to the edge of a canal and falls into it. It took four takes.

'I knew how dirty the water was, so I took all kinds of precautions – even washed my mouth with antiseptic, put special dressing on my hair, wore shoes that wouldn't waterlog. But like an idiot I forgot my eyes. When I fell in, I had a startled look, with my eyes open... Well, the water was a sewer! Filthy, brackish, full of trash! When I got out, my eyes were running. They've been running ever since. I have the most ghastly infection – I'll never lose it till the day I die. When people ask me why I cry a lot in pictures, I say, mysteriously, "Canal in Venice." '

Uncomfortable in the muggy heat that settled on Venice in that summer of 1954, sometimes weak and ill, upset by her distance from Tracy and irritated by the slowness of the crew, Kate made herself unpopular. After Tracy's departure, she complained, 'Nobody asked me to dinner. They went off and left me alone. I felt rather angry about that. I wandered off by myself through Venice feeling very lonely and neglected, and sat down by the canal and looked in the water, and while I was sitting like that, a man came over to me and said, "May I come and talk to you?" Only it wasn't Rossano Brazzi. It was a French plumber... It was my own fault entirely. I have brought it upon myself. I am rather a sharp person. I have a sharp face and a sharp voice. When I speak on the telephone, I snap into it. It puts people off, I suppose.'

On her return from Venice, Kate found it impossible to resist the offer of a tour of Australia in three Shakespeare plays, *The Taming of the Shrew*, *Measure for Measure* and *The Merchant of Venice*, playing opposite her friend Robert Helpmann, who had co-starred with her in *The Millionairess*. Tracy took her acceptance of the tour as a personal affront. On the day she left for Australia in May 1955 he began to drink heavily. Shooting on *Tribute to a Bad Man* was due to start on 1 June. Tracy arrived at the Colorado desert location six days late, without any

explanation to director Robert Wise. Two days later he disappeared again, causing panic among the crew. Calls were placed to Kate in Australia. Soon after, Tracy was fired and his twenty-one-year MGM contract terminated. Thereafter, he spent much of his time drowning his sorrows and calling Kate, a situation not calculated to help her concentration during her demanding Australian tour. She determined on her return never again to leave him for any length of time. She also took the rumours about Tracy and other women seriously enough to make sure he didn't stray.

The gossip that Tracy would never be hired again in Hollywood was silenced when he was nominated for an Oscar in 1955 for *Bad Day at Black Rock*. (Kate was nominated in the same year for *Summertime*.) But he was a very sick man from then onwards. His liver had deteriorated, his heart and lungs were weak. Kate cut down her own smoking drastically in an effort to help him stop, and she made sure he ate healthily, took exercise and lost weight. She nursed him, cheered him up and encouraged him to keep working. When Paramount signed him to do *The Mountain*, she accompanied him to Chamonix in France for the location shooting. It was not the best choice of subject for Tracy, not only because he was unconvincing as a Swiss shepherd, but also because the high altitude and the climbing gave him breathing difficulties and put a strain on his heart and lungs. Kate managed to remain discreetly in the background during filming, but hardly left his side when the day's work was done.

With *The Mountain* being completed at Paramount in Hollywood, Kate accepted *The Rainmaker*, opposite Burt Lancaster, at the same time and at the same studio so they could be together as much as possible. The story concerns a tense twenty-seven-year-old spinster Lizzie Curry (forty-something Hepburn), who cares for her father and two brothers on a south-western farm plagued by drought. A charming conman, Starbuck (Lancaster), arrives,

Kate and co-star Burt Lancaster confer on the set of The Rainmaker (1956), *though their relationship was relatively cool.*

other, and each resented the other's power over Kate.

In January 1956, Kate flew to London to film a *Ninotchka*-type comedy, *The Iron Petticoat*, at Pinewood Studios with Bob Hope. Hope arrived with an entourage of gag writers who immediately began rewriting the script, weighting the film in his favour. Despite her great care in learning a Russian accent for the role of the stiff Soviet airwoman who falls for the frivolities of capitalism (such as Balmain dresses), Kate was plainly ill at ease playing Bob Hope's stooge.

In the spring, Spencer and Kate flew to Cuba where he was to start filming *The Old Man and the Sea* under Fred Zinnemann's direction. Leland Hayward, Kate's ex-agent and ex-lover, now a producer, had persuaded Tracy that he was the only man to play the ancient Mexican fisherman of Ernest

giving Lizzie more self-confidence and claiming he can bring rain.

Kate made a brave attempt to play a rough, awkward, uneducated farm woman, but, although some genuine passion and humour emerged, it remained a deft, rather theatrical performance from too mature, too knowing an actress. Anyway, it was her third plain spinster act in a row, and it was beginning to pall.

The Rainmaker was finished shortly before Christmas 1955, and Tracy accompanied Kate to Fenwick for the holidays. Some competitiveness existed between him and Dr Hepburn. In fact, the two men were too similar in many ways to like each

Hemingway's novella. Unhappy about the film, Tracy began to tour the Havana bars, after which Kate would get him back to the rambling, fourteen-room villa where they were staying. Between watching Tracy on set and off, Kate managed to find time to paint a number of colourful Cuban seascapes.

The shooting proved arduous for Tracy, who was forced to play many scenes in an open boat, sometimes in difficult weather conditions, with Zinnemann driving him on relentlessly. After watching some of the rushes, Hayward and Hemingway, with some prodding from Kate, had Zinnemann fired, and the whole project was postponed. (It was later shot in a tank in Hollywood

Playing straight woman to Bob Hope in The Iron Petticoat *(1956) was not to Kate's liking.*

by John Sturges.) On their return to California, Kate was determined that Spencer would never again have to endure any gruelling location work.

Happily, they were soon given an opportunity to make their first film together since *Pat and Mike* five years earlier. At first Tracy was against making *The Desk Set,* but he didn't want to deprive Kate of the pleasure of doing another film with him. Kate played an extremely intelligent woman in charge of a library who can answer the most abstruse questions immediately. She and her staff are convinced they will be made redundant when Tracy installs a computer in their office.

Although enjoyable, the picture, directed by Walter Lang, lacked the oomph of Hepburn and Tracy's previous confrontations, being a rather more leisurely affair. But, supremely at ease with each other, they demonstrated they had lost nothing of their comic timing.

Working in Hollywood again, going for long walks, painting, reading and listening to music in Kate's company gave Tracy a new lease of life. They were closer to each other than ever, but Kate was still an actress who needed to stretch herself.

Happily on screen again together after five years, in The Desk Set *(1957).*

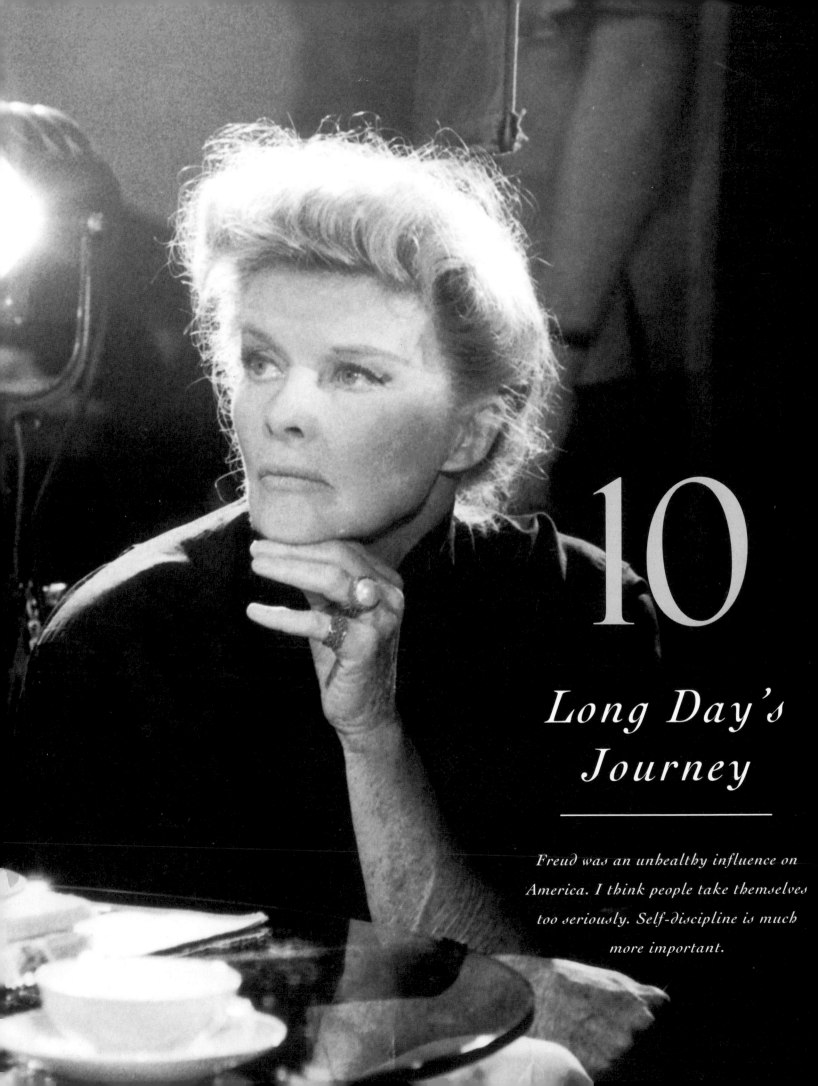

10

Long Day's Journey

Freud was an unhealthy influence on America. I think people take themselves too seriously. Self-discipline is much more important.

The year 1957 began with the news that Humphrey Bogart was terminally ill with cancer. On 13 January1957, Spencer and Kate paid their last visit to him. Emaciated and in great pain, Bogie still managed to smile and joke. After half an hour by his bedside, Kate stood up and leaned over and kissed him. Tracy took his hand. 'Goodbye, Spence. Goodbye, Kate,' Bogart said, instead of 'Goodnight.' When they were leaving, Tracy turned to Kate and said, 'Bogie's going to die.' In fact, he lapsed into a coma the next day, and was dead twenty-four hours later.

Although Kate was now fifty, at the peak of her powers, no films she wanted to do came her way. Consequently she decided to appear in two productions for the American Shakespeare Theatre in Stratford, Connecticut, in the summer of 1957, as Portia in *The Merchant of Venice* and as Beatrice in *Much Ado About Nothing*. John Houseman, the artistic director of the festival, recalled, in his book *Final Dress*, how Kate kept talking about Tracy 'with a mingling of loyalty, tenderness and admiration' during the whole season. She also spoke continually of his imminent arrival from Los Angeles to see her. 'Finally,' Houseman writes, 'the great day came when Kate, with a young girl's enthusiasm, proclaimed that this time Spencer was really coming. His plane ticket was bought and all arrangements were made. On the evening of his arrival... she drove off alone, in a state of high excitement, that she made no attempt to conceal, to Idlewild, to meet him. Soon after she had left, there was a phone call from California. Somehow, on the way to Burbank, Spencer had got lost and missed his plane. He never did appear.'

Kate got mixed reviews for her Shakespearian heroines, but, as always, many in the audience came just to see the movie star. During one performance, someone stood up and took a flash photograph. Kate stopped centre stage and faced the audience.

Kate, entering her sixtieth year, waits patiently for a shot to be set up on Guess Who's Coming to Dinner? *(1967).*

'There will be no more of that or we won't go on,' she said in a stentorian voice, before returning to her scene. When criticized for interrupting the flow of the play, Kate replied with a laugh, 'Well, I guess I would have been a great school principal.'

After the Shakespeare tour, Kate continued to keep fit by jogging and playing tennis wherever she was. She read assiduously and painted her seascapes of both coasts. Her experiences with the flora and fauna in Africa and Australia had

Between rehearsals for The Merchant of Venice, *in which she played Portia, at the American Shakespeare Festival in Stratford, Connecticut, in July 1957.*

enhanced her feeling for nature. She had begun to understand herself more, and had come to terms with her faults. 'Stone-cold sober, I found myself absolutely fascinating,' she said years later.

Watched by Montgomery Clift and Joseph L. Mankiewicz, Kate manages a laugh on the set of Suddenly Last Summer *(1960), although she hated making the film.*

Aware that Tracy would need constant attention, Kate began to think seriously in 1957 and 1958 of retiring from the screen for good. For eighteen months, she spent most of her time caring for him. Uppermost in her mind was finding suitable scripts worthy of his great talent. She looked no further than *The Last Hurrah*, directed by John Ford. Kate was especially watchful on the set at Columbia, as the supporting cast was made up almost exclusively of members of his old Wednesday night drinking circle. She needn't have worried, as by now they had all reformed.

There was, however, a slight uneasiness on the set, because both Ford and Kate still retained a deep affection for each other. According to Barbara Leaming's highly speculative biography of Hepburn,

As the monstrous Mrs

Venable, facing the wrath of

her daughter-in-law

Elizabeth Taylor in

Suddenly Last Summer,

passively observed by

Montgomery Clift.

'Kate seemed frightened of his feelings, and of her own. He loved that in private she still addressed him as Sean. He cherished her visits to his office... He leapt on every reference to their shared past... she remembered all that had passed between them.'

A short while later, Kate decided to make another film, reuniting herself with two old and valued associates, producer Sam Spiegel and director Joseph L. Mankiewicz, for a version of Tennessee Williams' one-act play *Suddenly Last Summer*, adapted by Gore Vidal. She was asked to play the role of Mrs Venable, a monstrous, bloodsucking caricature of an American mother,

whose homosexual son, Sebastian, has been 'cannibalized' by youths. In order to conceal the secret, she has Sebastian's cousin Catherine (top-billed Elizabeth Taylor), who witnessed the assault and murder, committed to a sanitarium and insists on the girl's having a lobotomy to destroy her memory.

This often ludicrous Gothic melodrama was unlike anything Kate had done hitherto, and she thoroughly disliked the character she was playing. On top of which, for reasons of economy, the film was shot in England, and Spencer was in Hollywood suffering from emphysema. As always, her separation from him was unsettling. In addition, she spent her time duelling with Mankiewicz over the interpretation of the matriarch and what she felt was the director's cruel behaviour towards an ailing and

Opposite: *A contemplative portrait taken in London in 1959 at the time of* Suddenly Last Summer.

Left: *Kate joking around by rolling up the leg of her celebrated slacks during the making of* Suddenly Last Summer.

both she and Elizabeth Taylor were nominated for Best Actress Oscars.

Kate was vastly relieved to return to America and her beloved Spencer. Apart from two months playing Cleopatra and Viola at the Shakespeare Festival in Connecticut in the summer of 1960, Kate seldom left his side. It was around that period that stories began to appear in print implying that Tracy and Hepburn were romantically involved, but little else was revealed. Insinuations were generally ignored, people preferring to see them as good companions of long standing. Until 1962, Tracy and his wife were still being photographed together. The deification of Mrs Spencer Tracy and her husband, nicknamed 'The Pope' by David Niven, prevented public gossip and censure.

'Age cannot wither her.' In Antony and Cleopatra with Robert Ryan at Stratford, Connecticut, in July 1960.

distressed Montgomery Clift, who was existing on a diet of codeine tablets washed down with brandy. It was also the first time in her career that she was supporting another woman star.

Mankiewicz recalled that 'on the last day of shooting, Kate came up to me, looked me in the eye, and spat. On the floor. Then she went into Sam Spiegel's office and spat on his floor. She never worked with either of us again.' Another witness, the actor Gary Raymond, remembered her spitting in the director's face. Kate claimed never to have seen the film, and never discussed it, though

In 1960 producer-director Stanley Kramer, who worshipped Tracy, offered him the meaty role of the defence lawyer in the notorious 1925 'monkey' trial in *Inherit the Wind*. Kate sat in the corner of the set knitting and peering over the rims of her spectacles from time to time to watch a scene. She was as protective of him as ever. So splendid was Tracy in the role that Kramer implored him to take the part of the American judge in *Judgment at Nuremberg*, to be filmed in the city of the title in 1961.

Because of his admiration for

Kate applying her make-up in preparation for her role as Mary Tyrone in Long Day's Journey into Night *(1962), directed by Sidney Lumet.*

Kramer, Tracy agreed, although he hated travelling. But at the airport, as Kate and he were ready to leave, he suddenly had second thoughts. He hadn't been well for some weeks and wondered whether he could withstand the flight (he had difficulty breathing at high altitudes) and the location shooting. Kate took him aside for a few minutes, kissed him on the cheek and helped him board the plane. When they arrived at Berlin Airport a car was waiting to take them to their hotel. A few blocks away from the Hilton Kate ordered the driver to stop. She got out, walked the rest of the way, entered the hotel by the service entrance and went up to her suite – a common ruse to prevent photographers from snapping her in Spencer's company. She then joined him in Nuremberg.

Soon after their return to America they were approached by producer Ely Landau to play James and Mary Tyrone in a low-budget film version of Eugene O'Neill's mammoth autobiographical play, *Long Day's Journey into Night*, to be directed by Sidney Lumet. Tracy said he would only consider playing it for $500,000, which he knew to be an impossible demand. Perhaps it was his way of turning down a role he would have found too mentally and physically exhausting. (Ralph Richardson was cast instead.) Kate readily accepted $25,000 for about the best role she had been offered for many years.

She had to give a lot of herself, and by the end of the thirty-seven days' shoot, it was she who was physically and mentally exhausted. She made no objection to being photographed unbecomingly, without filters, artful lighting or flattering camera angles. Yet Lumet in his memoirs, *Making Movies*, tells how Kate refused to go to the rushes. ' "Sidney," she said. "I can see how you work... You're...dead honest. You can't protect me. If I go to the rushes all that I'll see is this' – and she reached under her chin and pinched the slightly sagging flesh – "and this" – she did the same thing

Kate as nature intended during rehearsals for Long Day's Journey into Night.

under her arm – "And I need all my strength and concentration to just play the part." '

Kate, brilliantly in command of the role of the tragic mother, later revealed to be a drug addict, never shies away from the ugly realities of the character. The four principals (Hepburn, Richardson, Jason Robards, Dean Stockwell) were awarded a joint best acting award at Cannes, and Kate gained a ninth Oscar nomination.

A short while after the intense shooting of the film, Dr Hepburn died with all his children at his bedside. Kate wrote to Leland Hayward, 'Dad had a stink of a time for nine months. He said, "Thank God it was me and not your mother." He heaved a sigh and was gone with a little sigh... How lucky I have been to have been handed such a remarkable pair in the great shuffle.'

Her mother's death had been more difficult to cope with than her father's. Dr Hepburn's remarriage to Madelaine Santa Croce, the nurse who had worked with him for many years, within months of her mother's death, was seen by Kate as a kind of betrayal of Mrs Hepburn. The great reverence she had felt for him had transferred itself to Tracy.

When Ely Landau went to breakfast with the couple, he found it 'extraordinary to watch her with Spence. She was a totally different person. She turned really submissive – it's the only word I can use – and hardly opened her mouth, other than introducing us.' Once, when they had guests, Kate picked up a log and threw it on the fire. Tracy reprimanded her sharply in front of everybody. She had intruded upon his territory. The guests were astonished to see she was not shamed but sat down beside him more loving than ever. He would call her names like 'bag of bones' or 'Olive Oyl', and ask her to 'shut up for once', and she would accept it from him alone.

In January 1962, *Look* magazine revealed that Tracy was an alcoholic, that he had been living separately from his wife for years and that he and

Kate were 'something more than frequent co-stars'. The article made no impact on the way they lived. They still maintained two homes as a matter of principle, always stayed in separate hotel suites when travelling, and were almost never seen dining out together. They led a quiet life, entertaining only a few intimate friends. Tracy's physical condition improved noticeably, thanks to his abstention from cigarettes and alcohol.

But, in July 1963, something happened to make Kate retire from acting for five years. One afternoon, she and Spencer were on their way to a picnic when he suffered a heart attack. She gave him mouth-to-mouth resuscitation until the ambulance arrived. She remembered that on the way to the hospital, Spencer suddenly smiled and said, 'Kate. Isn't this a hell of a way to go to a picnic?' Once he was installed at St Vincent's, she called Mrs Tracy. It was then that each took turns to keep vigil by his bedside. Gradually, Tracy recovered and on his release from hospital Louise left him in Kate's care.

For the next few years, the couple were able to enjoy each other's company without the interruption of work. Although Kate was offered roles which would have satisfied her artistically, she opted to remain beside the man she loved, helping to extend

The last hurrah. The final teaming of Tracy and Hepburn, in Stanley Kramer's Guess Who's Coming to Dinner? *(1967).*

his life as long as possible and be with him at the end. On days when he visited Louise or she had errands to run, Kate would pack his lunch or dinner in a basket and leave it on his front doorstep. She was also to see that her fridge had a plentiful supply of milk, which Tracy drank, and the daily amount of beer the doctor permitted him. She made him exercise by going for bike rides, or flying kites on windy days.

In September 1965 Tracy was hospitalized again, this time with an inflamed prostate gland requiring surgery. Once again Louise and Kate took it in turns to be with him. All reports of his health were issued to the press by Mrs Tracy. The film colony was prepared for Tracy's imminent death, and spoke in admiring tones of the two women's devotion to him. Miraculously, Tracy improved, so much so that when he had been home for little over a month, Stanley Kramer proposed a script for a film in which Kate and Tracy could co-star again.

The story of *Guess Who's Coming to Dinner?*, about a middle-class WASP couple coming to terms with their daughter's wish to marry a black man, appealed to Kate's liberal sentiments. Spencer left it to Kate to make the decision, and agreed to work on the picture without having read the script. It was good enough

Kate and Spencer waiting around during the making of Guess Who's Coming to Dinner?

145

Left: *Kate transforming her usual towelled head-dress into Arab wear on the set of* Guess Who's Coming to Dinner?

Right: *With her niece Katharine Houghton, her sister Marion's daughter, seen together as mother and daughter in* Guess Who's Coming to Dinner?

Auntie and niece enjoying a bike ride around the movie lot during the making of Guess Who's Coming to Dinner?

A Life *magazine cover feature captures Kate in buoyant mood to relaunch her career with gusto.*

151

With Katharine Houghton in Kate's studio in Hollywood, studying one of her paintings. The photos suspended are of one of Kate's nephews.

for him that Kate was enthusiastic, and that the film urged racial tolerance and understanding, a theme that was dear to his heart. Kate also got Kramer to cast Katharine Houghton, her twenty-three-year-old niece (Marion's daughter), as their daughter.

Stanley Kramer knew that he was taking an enormous risk by hiring Tracy. The insurance company refused to cover the star, whose health they knew to be precarious. Therefore, Kramer personally accepted the responsibility for any financial loss engendered and both he and Kate put up their salaries in lieu of the insurance money, should Tracy die during shooting. Employing the ailing actor became an enormous task of courage for everyone connected with the film. Kate was risking losing Spencer, and Kramer was risking his bank balance and his career.

It was typical of Tracy that he was able to marshal his forces and use all his considerable skills and experience to fulfil his contract admirably. When he delivered the last line of the screenplay to Kate, 'If what they feel for each other is even half what we felt, then that is everything,' she was moved to genuine tears.

When the rather soft-centred *Guess Who's Coming to Dinner?* opened in December 1967 it carried an extra resonance. The critic of the *New York Morning Telegraph* wrote, 'Both of them are splendid, both of them are so beautifully matched... that a lump rises in the throat on the realization that they will never appear together again,' and the *New Yorker* observed that 'when, at its climax, he turns to her and tells her what an old man remembers having loved, it is, for us who are permitted to overhear him, an experience that transcends the theatrical'.

Guess Who's Coming to Dinner? proved to be one of Kate's greatest successes. It grossed many millions of dollars and helped Columbia, which was in

financial difficulties. In the weeks following the conclusion of the shooting, Kate made it a practice to sleep in a small room at the end of a corridor from Spencer's bedroom. She would often leave a light on so that she could get up quickly if he needed anything.

At around 6 a.m. on Saturday 10 June 1967, Tracy had a massive heart attack and died while drinking milk in the kitchen of his home. Kate found him a short time later hunched over the kitchen table. She telephoned the doctor, their friend George Cukor and Tracy's brother Carroll, who in turn contacted Louise. Tracy was moved to the bedroom, where Kate sat alone with him. Ten minutes later, she emerged, her eyes moist with tears, and walked out of the house.

She was not among the congregation that crowded into the Immaculate Heart of Mary Roman Catholic Church to hear the requiem mass held for Tracy, nor among the hundreds of people at the burial at Forest Lawn Cemetery. While Louise stood at the graveside, veiled and in black, Kate remained at home in seclusion. She had debated whether or not to go, but decided that her presence might provoke a field day for reporters and photographers. Forty-eight hours later she went to offer her condolences to Louise and flew back to her family's summer home on the east coast for peace and consolation.

Both Tracy and Hepburn were nominated for Academy Awards in April 1968. Louise, accompanied by her son and daughter, was present at the Oscar ceremony, hoping she would accept the posthumous award for her husband. Kate was in Nice filming *The Madwoman of Chaillot* when the news came that she had won the Academy Award, making her the first three-times winner of the Best Actress Oscar.

'Did Spencer win, too?' she asked. When told he did not, she replied, 'Well, that's OK. I'm sure mine is for the two of us.'

A Lioness in Winter

I'm like the Statue of Liberty to a lot of people. When you've been around so long, people identify their whole lives with you. They identify particularly their moments of hope and confidence. It's rather the style now to romanticize certain of the older actors.

The end of Kate's life with Spencer was also a beginning. Faced with the agony of separation by death, she had to take stock. She still had her beloved brothers and sisters, and her friends. There was speculation that Kate would now retire permanently from the screen, but her Puritan temperament wouldn't allow her to surrender to grief, and she turned to work as an antidote to her pain. She felt ready for another good role, which she soon found in the screen adaptation of James Goldman's sub-Shavian historical play *The Lion in Winter*, in which she would portray Eleanor of Aquitaine, the estranged wife of the English king Henry II in twelfth-century France.

Kate carried off her second successive Oscar-winning performance with aplomb, though she occasionally added dollops of sentimentality to her portrayal of the overbearing queen. Certainly, she was able to empathize with the character of a strong-minded, ageing woman, bemoaning her fading beauty, forced to share her husband with another. The *New York Times* thought her 'triumphant in her creation of a complete and womanly queen... a sophisticate whose shrewdness is matched only by her humour'.

Rehearsals for *The Lion in Winter* took place at the Haymarket Theatre in London in October 1967. So enthusiastic was Kate about the project that on one of the first days she rushed through a heavy iron stage door so fast that she slammed it on her hand and smashed her thumb. Hearing her scream, Anthony Harvey, the director, and Peter O'Toole, her co-star, ran over. She was in agony, but she refused to be taken to hospital and insisted on continuing with the rehearsal. Not only had her thumbnail been crushed, but a deep cut ran all the way down her hand. She was out of pain and well enough when *The Lion in Winter* started shooting in Ireland, before shifting to Wales, and then to

A few months after Tracy's death, Kate plunged into work again on The Lion in Winter.

France. The filming was marked by the good-natured but vigorous sparring between Kate and Peter O'Toole, twenty-four years her junior. Witnesses remarked how Kate reduced O'Toole to a shadow of his normally rebellious self. 'She is terrifying,' he remarked. 'It is sheer masochism working with her. She has been sent by some dark fate to nag and torment me.'

Kate dismissed this. 'Don't be silly,' she told him. 'We are going to get on very well. You are Irish and make me laugh. In any case I am on to you and you to me.'

While on location, Kate was indefatigable, constantly showering, swimming, cycling and painting. She had the same routine in the South of France where she had rented a villa in St Jean-Cap Ferrat while making *The Madwoman of Chaillot*. Wearing Spencer Tracy's old

Rehearsing A Lion in Winter *in October 1967 at the Haymarket Theatre in London.*

Right: On location in France, preparing to bundle up against the medieval cold while shooting A Lion in Winter.

Opposite: In the South of France during the making of The Madwoman of Chaillot *(1969). Nice settings, pity about the film.*

Kate winning her third Best Actress Oscar in the role of the formidable Eleanor of Aquitaine in A Lion in Winter.

*All dolled up on the banks of
the Seine for the title role of*
The Madwoman of
Chaillot.

sweater, she pedalled about in her slacks and tennis shoes, going to bed every night at 8.30. To Kate's disappointment John Huston had walked off the film just before it went into production, and Bryan Forbes had been signed only eighteen days before shooting began.

Supported by a cast that included Charles Boyer, Paul Henreid, Yul Brynner and Danny Kaye, Kate softened and sentimentalized the central role of the madwoman living in the past, going against the grain of the more caustic character of Jean Giraudoux's play. Tennessee Williams commented, 'Kate Hepburn was just not quite old enough or mad enough to suggest the charisma of lunacy.'

In 1968, Kate announced that she would soon direct a film called *Martha*, an adaptation of two related Margery Sharpe novels, about the career of a gifted girl who goes to France to become a painter. 'This isn't a fantasy,' she told a reporter on the *New York Times*. 'The fact is that I've always been interested in directing. Louis B. Mayer quite seriously asked me to direct films twenty years ago, as did John Ford, but I've never had a real opportunity to do so before this.' But although she worked hard to have a script written and get the film off the ground, it never came to fruition.

Her next major venture was a return to Broadway in a musical. Alan Jay Lerner called Garson Kanin to ask if he could persuade Kate to play the role of the world-renowned Parisian couturier Coco Chanel. She was both horrified and intrigued, claiming that she had never even seen a Broadway musical. But the challenge was too good a one to pass up.

In preparation, she went to meet Chanel, then in her mid-eighties, in Paris. 'I was scared to death to meet her. I had worn the same clothes for forty years, literally, even the shoes. I thought, "If I don't like her, it will be agony." ' She need not

With co-stars Yul Brynner (standing) and Danny Kaye on location at Chez Francis in Paris for The Madwoman of Chaillot.

*Kate in a typical black
Chanel dress, posing for Cecil
Beaton's camera in Paris in
1969 in preparation for her
role in the musical* Coco.

As 'the mobled queen' Hecuba in Euripides' tragedy The Trojan Women, *shot in Spain in 1970.*

have worried, and they took to each other immediately, although Coco commented in private to Lerner, 'She's too old for the role. Why, she must be close to sixty!'

On Chanel, Kate remarked, 'She got to me. The essence of her style was simplicity. Exactly what I appreciate most.' Ironically, *Coco* was one of the most expensive shows in Broadway history, far from this essence of simplicity. Although most reviewers attacked the show, Kate's forceful personality, which overcame the limitations of her minimal dancing and her squawking singing voice, won plaudits and

Bewigged and in full song in the title role of Coco *at the Mark Hellinger Theatre in 1969, Kate's one and only musical.*

packed the theatre for seven months. When the far more suitable Danielle Darrieux took over, audience attendance diminished.

After the Broadway run, Kate made the cast album. When she got home with the disc, she realized she couldn't play it as she didn't own a record player. She called co-star George Rose and said, 'I can't find a Victrolla! Father never believed in them, you know!' Despite her knowledge of contemporary events, and her professional and

Hecuba, Queen of Troy, in The Trojan Women *(1971), directed by Michael Cacoyannis, in which Kate outranked a distinguished cast of women.*

private contact with much younger people, Kate often seemed to be stuck in the era of her childhood.

In 1970, Kate left for Spain to co-star with Vanessa Redgrave, Irene Papas and Genevieve Bujold in *The Trojan Women* for Greek director Michael Cacoyannis. Asked why she took on the role of Hecuba, the old queen of Troy, she replied, 'My time is running out. And one wants to do everything.' Wearing a torn, dusty, black widow's dress throughout, Kate played up the arrogance of the queen over the more melancholy side. She rarely touched the tragic heights, though when she hisses, 'Kill her!' to decide the fate of Helen of Troy, Kate reveals the power of which she was capable.

Back in the USA, she opened a tour of *Coco* in her home town of Hartford. Returning after an evening performance, Kate, her father's widow and others noticed that a ground-floor window that had previously been closed was open. They went stealthily into the dark house. When Kate reached an upstairs bedroom, a woman jumped out of the closet wielding a hammer. They struggled, and the intruder bit off the end of the index finger of Kate's left hand. The woman made her escape, but Kate recognized her as Luella West, whom she had earlier sacked as a chauffeur. A doctor was called, and the finger, hanging by a thread, was grafted back on.

Kate spent much of her time during the tour planning to appear in a film version of Graham Greene's *Travels with My Aunt*, thrilled at the prospect of working with George Cukor again. But she was fired before shooting began, when the producer felt the role needed a younger woman and cast Maggie Smith instead. Kate thought of suing because 'I don't feel things like that should be allowed to happen. But I thought it was a bore, trying to prove that you've been

misused. One thing that really offended me was to write me a letter to "Katherine". I thought the least he could do when he fired me was to spell my name right.'

In 1971, Garson Kanin's *Tracy and Hepburn – An Intimate Memoir* was published. It was full of personally observed anecdotes that revealed much about the romantic friendship. Kate reeled from the blow. To her, its publication marked a public betrayal by Kanin, placing, as she said, 'a great strain on our friendship'.

Her friendship with John Ford, however, continued as strongly as ever. They had kept in touch over the years, and Ford had even come to New York to see her in *Coco*. In March 1973, as soon as Kate heard Ford had terminal cancer, she went down to see him in Palm Desert, a vacation and retirement community 140 miles from LA, where he had been living a reclusive life for years. He had been married for more than forty-five years to Mary, who had accepted his infidelities just as long as he kept his affairs from becoming public

Tony Richardson (right) directs Kate, Joseph Cotten and Betsy Blair in the TV production of Edward Albee's A Delicate Balance *(1974).*

Laurence Olivier cracks up on the set of the TV movie Love among the Ruins *(1975), directed by George Cukor (right).*

knowledge. However, she knew his real vice had always been alcohol, not women.

Shocked by Ford's skeletal appearance, and deeply affected by his courage and remaining acerbic wit, Kate spent a week in Palm Desert, talking to him for hours about the old times. The great director was to die five months after Kate's visit.

Now in her mid-sixties, Kate was beginning to get more offers of work, mostly for TV films. The first of three made in London was Edward Albee's *A Delicate Balance*, a savage play about a Connecticut family which fights against the intrusion of two unwanted people. With great intensity, Kate played Agnes, an extremely unsympathetic suburban matron on the verge of insanity. Later, she was to say she accepted the assignment because she wanted to discover what Albee was trying to say in the play.

The entire film was shot in sequence by director Tony Richardson in a large, empty Victorian house near Crystal Palace. The production team tried to make it as comfortable as possible, but there was no running water, which prevented Kate from taking her constant cold baths and showers. One day, during a break in filming, Kate walked down the hill, and knocked at the door of a house. A woman answered the door.

'Excuse me,' said Kate. 'We're filming in the house up the road, but there is no running water. I wondered whether I could take a bath in your bathroom.' The astonished woman, who recognized the star, asked whether it was a *Candid Camera* prank. Reassured, she allowed Kate to use her bathroom every day throughout the shoot.

Kate was more at ease in Tennessee Williams' *The Glass Menagerie*, but was miscast as Amanda Wingfield, the faded Southern belle. In the scene when Amanda remembers the South, Kate wore the same wedding dress she had worn for the stage performances of *The Philadelphia Story*.

Not long afterwards, George Cukor sent her a script for *Love among the Ruins*, which he had agreed to make for ABC and for which he hoped she might consent to play opposite Laurence Olivier. Osteoarthritis in Kate's hip had been giving her progressive trouble and she had recently submitted to a hip-replacement operation. But the prospect of working with Cukor for the first time in twenty years, and with Olivier for the first time ever, was too irresistible for her to decline. Six months after the surgery, she returned to London to make the film, which had a twenty-day shooting schedule.

To please Kate, Cukor engaged Spencer's daughter, Susie Tracy, as the unit's stills photographer. Kate, who had made a speedy recovery from hip surgery, stayed in the country near the studio and after a day's work would jump on her bicycle and pedal down the nearest country lane. In the extremely slight, old-fashioned but pleasant romantic comedy, Kate played a world-famous Shakespearian actress and Olivier an English barrister. It might have carried more conviction if the roles had been reversed.

In the autumn of 1974, less than a year after her hip surgery, Kate found herself riding a horse and shooting rapids on location in Oregon for *Rooster Cogburn*, opposite John Wayne, Ford's favourite star. Though they were diametrically opposed politically, a deep affection grew up between Kate and 'Duke'. She knew that he had had a lung removed and was being monitored for any sign of the return of the cancer that had been cut away, but he asked for no pity or privileges. Kate spoke of Wayne as 'Self-made. Hardworking. Independent. Of the style of man who blazed trails across our country... They seem to have no patience and no understanding of the more timid and dependent type of person... They don't need or want protection. They dish it out. They take it. Total personal responsibility.' This description might have

fitted the other men in her life such as Tracy, Ford and Hughes.

Wayne commented of his co-star, 'She wants to do everything, too much really, because she can't ride worth a damn and I gotta keep reining in so she can keep up. How she must have been at age twenty-five or thirty! How lucky a man would have been to find her then!'

Rooster Cogburn, in which Kate played a Bible-thumping spinster who learns to use a rifle against marauding bandits to aid a demoted marshal (Wayne), turned out to be a weak retread of *The African Queen*. It was only watchable for the two elderly stars, giving rather self-indulgent performances.

Not long after *Rooster Cogburn*, Kate, as energetic as ever, agreed to appear on Broadway in Enid Bagnold's *A Matter of Gravity* for twelve weeks, as well as touring for a few months before and after the New York engagement. The play was about a wealthy and eccentric woman in her late seventies, with a grandson, a socialist sympathizer, to whom she wishes to leave her estate. A young Christopher Reeve, in his first Broadway play, was cast as the grandson. The future Superman said that Kate greatly influenced him. 'What I learned from her was simplicity. She's a living example that stardom doesn't have to be synonymous with affectation or ego.'

When the play opened in Philadelphia, she and Luddy, who had moved back to his family home a few years earlier, held a reunion after the show. The following morning Luddy met her at her hotel and they had breakfast in her suite. Her ex-husband, now seventy-seven, was ill and ageing, but he was still smartly dressed, and his devotion to Kate had never wavered.

That summer, Kate went to California to make *Olly Olly Oxen Free*, because 'I've always wanted to fly a balloon.' It was charming enough kiddie fare about an

On location in Oregon in Rooster Cogburn *(1975) with John Wayne, with whom Kate had a happy time competing.*

Kate as Bible-toting spinster Eula Goodnight in Rooster Cogburn.

In Love among the Ruins, *filmed in London for ABC TV.*

Seventy-five-year-old George Cukor directing sixty-five-year-old Kate and sixty-seven-year-old Laurence Olivier in Love among the Ruins.

Still wearing the military student's cap which she had picked up on a trip to Europe with Luddy four decades earlier.

eccentric (an adjective continually used for her later roles) old junkyard proprietress who befriends two adventurous youngsters and helps them repair a hot-air balloon, which accidentally takes the three of them aloft for the trip of a lifetime. At the picture's finale, Kate and the two boys descend in the balloon on the Hollywood Bowl concert stage during a rendition of the *1812 Overture*. After the scene was shot, Kate climbed out of the balloon and addressed the audience that filled the Bowl: 'This should prove to all of you that if you're silly enough you can do anything.'

Late in the summer of 1977, Kate went on a visit to London on the invitation of Enid Bagnold, with whom she had struck up a friendship. Bagnold, eighty-six at the time, told Kate frankly that she should have a facelift. After much persuading, Kate travelled incognito up to Scotland to a Glasgow plastic surgeon, who raised the skin beneath her eyes and gave her a slight tuck.

In January 1978, George Cukor came to visit Kate to see if she would work with him once more on another TV production. Cukor, now almost eighty, did not feel he could stand the pressures of a major film. Kate found it difficult to deny Cukor anything, and he suggested they collaborate on Emlyn Williams' *The Corn Is Green*, the inspiring story of an unmarried schoolteacher who helps a young miner gain a scholarship to Oxford. She agreed immediately and pressed to have it filmed in its proper locale – Wales. All the exteriors were shot in Ysbyty Ifan, a small, bleak Welsh village, near the town of Wrexham. Typically, Kate insisted on going down a mine with some of the film crew. They descended 1300 feet in the pitch dark in an open-cage elevator, each carrying a lamp, a gas detector and a gas mask. She talked to the men for a few minutes and then started back up. As they rose in the elevator, 'We heard a beautiful tenor voice start a song. Then

others gradually joined in... It was, in a curious way, both moving and eerie.'

One scene in the film called for Kate to ride a heavy 1890 bicycle up to the top of a steep hill. 'I was humiliated. Nearly had a stroke. But I just could not pump up that hill. Infuriating failure. I have always been able to do my own stuff. But my legs just could not push hard enough to keep that bike from a drunken wobble.' As a result, a twenty-four-year-old woman doubled for Kate. 'They thought that I was silly to be so mad that she could and I couldn't. Yes, I suppose so. But there it is. I still am mad. Damned old legs!'

Although Kate imbued her portrayal of Miss Moffat with idealism and passion, she in no way effaced the memory of Bette Davis's performance in the same role in the 1945 film. Davis had been thirty-seven years old at the time, while Kate, at seventy-two, was too old for the part, and the shaking of her head, due to incipient palsy, was becoming noticeable.

A little later, Cukor sold his house and Tracy's old bungalow. He begged Kate to buy it, but she could not see herself making any more films in California. With John Wayne's death in 1979, there were few of the great old stars left. Two of the survivors were Kate and Henry Fonda. Not only had Kate never acted with Fonda, they had never even met. *On Golden Pond* was to bring them together at last. At their first meeting, Kate walked straight over to Fonda, held out her hand and said, 'Well, it's about time.'

The director, Mark Rydell, and the producers were concerned about Kate's health as well as about Fonda's. Her palsy had progressed, and her head shook involuntarily at more frequent intervals. They finally decided that Kate's palsy would give the elderly wife authenticity, and the starting date was set for June 1980.

Two months before, Kate dislocated her shoulder while playing tennis. The doctors claimed she would

Henry Fonda wearing Spencer Tracy's old hat in On Golden Pond *(1981), Fonda's last film, in which the two old-timers played a bickering but devoted couple.*

Kate protecting herself from the New Hampshire sun on location for On Golden Pond.

As Ethel Thayer in On Golden Pond, Kate won a record-breaking fourth Best Actress Oscar.

need a full three months to convalesce and even then a film would be out of the question. 'I knew the film was dependent on the Fonda part being lazy and not working and not wanting to do a lot of physical things. The wife, my part, had to carry all the luggage, do everything, and here I am with an arm that's really bad. Well, I tried to get out of the picture, but Fonda said, "No, you'll be fine. You'll do it. We won't get anyone else." '

With Dorothy Loudon in Ernest Thompson's play West Side Waltz *at the Ethel Barrymore Theatre, New York, in November 1981.*

Amazingly, only two weeks later than planned, filming began on location in New Hampshire. Kate's shoulder healed during the filming, although some days she was in such pain that they had to shoot around her. On the first day, Kate came up to Fonda and said, 'I want you to have this. This was Spencer's favourite hat.' He was moved to tears and wore it throughout the film.

On Golden Pond turned out to be a gentle movie, loved by gerontophiles, anglers and those who cherished the memory of Fonda and Hepburn in films of Hollywood's past. It was also a persuasive look at the fear of approaching death. Fonda, seldom so moving as when he shows his terror of losing his faculties, was exceptional in his last screen role, and Kate, the spiritual centre of the story, was marvellous, too, doddery but placid, full of wisdom, and the quiet strength in the family, although she does seem to be on the verge of tears most of the time and her head shaking is quite noticeable.

Soon after, Kate agreed to return to the stage in *West Side Waltz* by Ernest Thompson, the author of *On Golden Pond*, which dealt with the same theme of ageing. Kate portrayed a widowed former concert pianist living alone in an apartment on the West Side of Manhattan, until a somewhat vulgar middle-aged violinist (Dorothy Loudon) becomes her flat-mate. Playing the piano was marvellous therapy for her shoulder, but at the same time it was difficult, uncomfortable and frustrating. She and Loudon rehearsed daily at Kate's house, practising the piano and violin together as well. Determinedly, Kate practised three to four hours a day, regaining the mobility of her fingers, memorizing the intricacies of each piece, striving to achieve the appearance of a professional pianist at work.

The conventional Broadway play opened in New York on 8 November 1981 for a limited three-month engagement, and received lukewarm reviews. Again, despite the material, Kate gained praise. Walter Kerr in the *New York Times* wrote, 'One mysterious thing she has learned to do is breathe unchallengeable life into lifeless lines. She does it, or seems to do it, by giving the most serious consideration to every syllable she utters. There may have been a time when she coasted on mannerisms, turned on her rhythms into a form of rapid transit. That time is long gone.'

A little over a year later Kate suffered another accident. Driving on slippery icy roads in Fenwick, she hit a pole. The impact crumpled the front end of the car and a piece of steel nearly severed her right foot. When help came and Kate was extricated from the car and transferred to an ambulance, her foot 'was hanging just from a tendon'.

She insisted she be taken to Hartford Hospital, an hour's ride over icy roads, where the surgeon who had saved her finger was on the staff. He was alerted and immediately performed intricate surgery to reattach the foot. The foot was saved, but for the next eight months she spent equal time in and out of hospital. After six more months of therapy (and the news that Luddy had just died), she decided to go back to work.

Kate had long wanted to do *The Ultimate Solution of Grace Quigley*, a black comedy about an elderly woman who hires a hit man (Nick Nolte) to help her put an end to the lives of her ageing companions, who no longer care to live. The script, by Martin Zweiback, had been literally dumped on her back doorstep when she had occupied the California bungalow eleven years earlier. She had tried to get it produced, but euthanasia was considered too controversial a subject.

The film finally started shooting in October 1983. Nolte called Kate 'a cranky old broad, but a lot of fun'. She had to tackle without a double a scene that called for her to ride a motorcycle with Nolte, but she did it, as well as braving harsh conditions of shooting on location in New York during a particularly cold autumn.

Unfortunately, the film fails to come off, either as a plea for mercy killing or as a black comedy, being neither pointed nor funny enough. But Kate's glowing eyes, wobbly head and shaky voice bring an element of otherworldliness to the role. On the theme of the film, Kate commented that she personally had no fear of death. 'What release! To sleep is the greatest joy there is... If I were a burden to myself and I could leave my money to younger people who could really use it, I would feel it was my privilege to do what I could do... If my own mother had been desperately ill and attached to a lot of humiliating machines, I think I would have shot her.'

However, despite the themes of her last two films, Kate, a comparatively healthy seventy-seven-year-old, was not ready to contemplate death, or even retirement, just yet.

Always ready to try something new, seventy-seven-year-old Kate clings to Nick Nolte in The Ultimate Solution of Grace Quigley *(1984).*

Left: *In the title role of* The Ultimate Solution of Grace Quigley, *a black comedy on the theme of euthanasia, a subject close to Kate's heart.*

Right: *Still holding the screen in one of her last TV movies,* The Man Upstairs *(1992).*

12

Twilight of a Goddess

Isn't it fun getting older is really a terrible fallacy. That's like saying I prefer driving an old car with a flat tyre.

Few people passing the four-storey Manhattan brownstone house on East 49th Street would suspect that it is the New York home of one of the cinema's greatest stars. This East Side area, known as Turtle Bay – the original bay has long been filled in – may be an elite area now, but it was considerably run down when Katharine Hepburn moved there in the early 1930s.

Huge windows look out on to a back garden of trees and flowers, most of it upkept by Kate herself. Although she has a cook, a chauffeur and a secretary, she prefers to do much of her own cooking, shopping and organizing herself, and to be alone for a good deal of the day. The comfortable yet simply furnished living room, always filled with vases of freshly picked flowers, has two large white sofas, a few antique chairs, Persian rugs and, on the walls, besides a portrait of Ethel Barrymore by John Singer Sargent, hang many oil paintings executed by Kate herself. A vast bald eagle stands on the mantelpiece. None of her four Oscars is anywhere to be seen.

On the dressing table of her third-floor bedroom is a framed photograph of Dr Hepburn; a photograph of Spencer Tracy sits on the bedside table. On the wall is a portrait of Tracy painted by Kate in the Sixties, as well as a small bronze bust she made of him. In the small basement kitchen are more photographs of friends and co-stars of yesteryear.

The composer Stephen Sondheim, a next-door neighbour, shares the communal garden. Some years ago, Kate was woken up in the early hours of the morning by Sondheim, who was busy working at the piano on the score of *Pacific Overtures*. Wrapping a robe around her, Kate went out into the garden and placed her nose against one of Sondheim's windows. The composer and a companion froze when they caught sight of her, standing and staring at them. Kate disappeared as quickly as she had appeared, but she had made her point. From then on,

In serene old age, Kate continued to lead a full life, even acting from time to time.

Sondheim was careful not to play the piano late at night.

Never one to shy away from controversy, Kate spent a great deal of her time working for Planned Parenthood, thus carrying on the work of her mother. 'Things are getting worse,' she proclaimed. 'Now they've even changed the rules about when a foetus is alive – although I've never seen a religious service for a miscarriage, have you?'

As she entered her eighties, Kate began to limit her acting appearances to the odd television role. She was only seen in public on rare occasions. When she did go to the theatre or a movie, she generally made sure few people would recognize her. Ironically, however, there were two well-reported occasions when she drew attention to herself in public.

One evening, she and her director friend Anthony Harvey attended a performance of a minimalist production of Leonard Bernstein's *Candide*. Like the rest of the audience, she was forced to sit on one of the rows of wooden seats. At the intermission, Kate rose from her seat, walked on the stage and reclined on a canopied bed that was part of the set. She had been suffering back pain, and it was her way of protesting at the discomfort of the seating. It added to her reputation of being slightly dotty. However, she told a reporter, 'The young always think their elders are eccentric.'

The other of her very public displays was when she came out of a movie on 58th Street to find her car hemmed in by a double-parked truck. She decided that her only means of escape was to drive her car on to the sidewalk and make a sharp turn. Many of the people waiting to get into the theatre recognized her, and they stood back to make room for her and see what she would do. 'I gave it the gas,' she explained, 'aimed at the crowd and turned amid cheers – "That's it, Katie, ride 'em!" It was thrilling.'

Although Kate would have enjoyed working more, she found the scripts she was offered far too

Happily relaxing in her comfortable New York home on East 49th Street, where she has lived since the 1930s.

Portrait of the most unpretentious of Hollywood legends.

With Anthony Quinn in the semi-autobiographical TV movie This Can't Be Love *(1993), in which she played an Oscar-winning film star in retirement.*

Kate enjoys a secret with her niece Patricia at New York's Madison Square Garden at a concert by the Jackson Five in August 1981.

distasteful or exploitative. When many actresses of her age were reduced to playing Grande Guignol murderesses in tawdry horror movies, pathetic old people or bit parts, Kate had continued to play leading roles in prestigious films. Now she refused to appear in anything that offended her professional and personal standards. 'The assumption is that the audience is totally uninspired, and that pornography and depravity are all they want to see. I find it offensive and very sad that producers and actors are so willing to sell out for the money... It's awfully easy in the entertainment field to talk yourself into justifying the degrading things you do.'

She had been uncomfortable with a speech in *A*

Delicate Balance in which she had to express her distress at her husband's predilection for coitus interruptus, and the only 'four-letter' word she had uttered in her career had been in *Coco*. As the curtain went up at the beginning of the second act, Kate strode down a staircase, crossed over to the footlights, stared at the audience and exclaimed, 'Shit!' Then she turned on her heel and walked off the stage to gales of laughter and applause. The amused reaction came about merely because the word had been uttered by Katharine Hepburn.

Kate, with false naivety, even seemed to deny the existence of homosexuality. This from someone with advanced views, a close friend

Fighting off photographers while attending a performance of 42nd Street *at the Winter Garden Theatre in October 1980.*

185

of George Cukor, an intimate of Noël Coward, Tennessee Williams and Robert Helpmann, a participant in *Suddenly Last Summer*, and an actress whose gay fans were legion.

One script for a TV movie that appealed to her greatly was *This Can't Be Love*, which was written for her and which verged on the autobiographical. With natural warmth and humour, Kate played an Oscar-winning film star in retirement, who spends many of her days painting. She mourns the death of her elder brother (in World War I), talks about growing up a tomboy, reminisces about working with George Cukor and John Ford, and acting with John Wayne, recalls her affection for George Bernard Shaw, and when she looks in the mirror says, 'No one ever knew what to do with this face.'

When Warren Beatty first called Kate to ask if she would play the cameo role of his Aunt Ginny in the second remake of *Love Affair*, she answered the phone by saying, 'What do *you* want?' in an abrupt manner. She refused the offer, explaining that she had never taken a supporting role or a small one. Undeterred, Beatty showered her with presents and flowers, and flew to New York to see her on a number of occasions. After he had promised to send his private jet to take her from New York to the Warner Bros studio set in California, she finally capitulated. Looking remarkably spry, though her head shook badly, Kate gamely did her bit in a scene when would-be married couple Beatty and Annette Bening pay her a visit on a Pacific island, in order to obtain her blessing. Critics failed to give the redundant and soppy film their blessing, but Kate escaped unscathed by the experience. It was to be her swan song.

Kate was now happy to spend her days reading, doing the gardening, and visiting her family in Connecticut at weekends. 'We're very limited by this box we came in,' she once said. 'The box is me and it is gradually rotting away... When the vital things go, it dissolves. You'd have to be a fool not to recognize that.' She continued to see death as 'the big sleep', an idea she found not at all frightening.

Katharine Hepburn had been a star for over six decades, and generation after generation of movie-goers has been aware of her. In 1995, in a poll conducted among fifty critics worldwide and the general public by the *Guardian* newspaper, Kate was selected as the greatest woman film star ever, alive or dead. She topped a similar poll among film-makers in *Time Out* magazine a few months later. She achieved this reputation through her innate talent, but also through a tenacious character, possibly formed by her upbringing in an atmosphere of complete spiritual freedom and Spartan physical discipline. She was determined to have her own way in an industry noted for compromise and commercial priorities. Even when at her lowest ebb, she refused to accept defeat, nor was she willing to pander to the media's insatiable appetite for prurient gossip. She had pursued her career on her own honourable, dignified and exacting terms, and it paid off.

'Go out and make life interesting,' Dr Hepburn once told his daughter. By following his advice, Katharine Houghton Hepburn made our lives more interesting as well.

Leaving the Ethel Barrymore
Theatre after a performance
of West Side Waltz *in*
November 1981. Au revoir,
Kate!

(N.B. Dates given are release dates in USA. Names in parentheses are roles played by K.H.)

1932
A Bill of Divorcement (Sydney Fairfield)
Director: George Cukor
(RKO)

1933
Christopher Strong (Lady Cynthia Darrington)
Director: Dorothy Arzner
(RKO)
Morning Glory (Eva Lovelace)
Director: Lowell Sherman
(RKO)
Little Women (Jo March)
Director: George Cukor
(RKO)

1934
Spitfire (Trigger Hicks)
Director: John Cromwell
(RKO)
The Little Minister (Babbie)
Director: Richard Wallace
(RKO)

1935
Break of Hearts (Constance Dane)
Director: Philip Moeller
(RKO)
Alice Adams (Alice Adams)
Director: George Stevens
(RKO)

1936
Sylvia Scarlett (Sylvia Scarlett)
Director: George Cukor
(RKO)
Mary of Scotland (Mary Stuart)
Director: John Ford
(RKO)
A Woman Rebels (Pamela Thistlewaite)
Director: Mark Sandrich
(RKO)

1937
Quality Street (Phoebe Throssel)
Director: George Stevens
(RKO)
Stage Door (Terry Randall)
Director: Gregory La Cava
(RKO)

1938
Bringing Up Baby (Susan Vance)
Director: Howard Hawks
(RKO)
Holiday (Linda Seton)
Director: George Cukor
(Columbia)

1940
The Philadelphia Story (Tracy Lord)
Director: George Cukor
(MGM)

1942
Woman of the Year (Tess Harding)
Director: George Stevens
(MGM)
Keeper of the Flame (Christine Forrest)
Director: George Cukor

1943
Stage Door Canteen (Herself)
Director: Frank Borzage
(United Artists)

1944
Dragon Seed (Jade)
Directors: Jack Conway and Harold S. Bucquet
(MGM)

1945
Without Love (Jamie Rowan)
Director: Harold S. Bucquet
(MGM)

1946
Undercurrent (Ann Hamilton)
Director: Vincente Minnelli
(MGM)

1947
The Sea of Grass (Lutie Cameron)
Director: Elia Kazan
(MGM)
Song of Love (Clara Wieck Schumann)
Director: Clarence Brown
(MGM)

1948
State of the Union (Mary Matthews)
Director: Frank Capra
(MGM)

1949
Adam's Rib (Amanda Bonner)
Director: George Cukor
(MGM)

1951
The African Queen (Rose Sayer)
Director: John Huston
(United Artists)

1952
Pat and Mike (Pat Pemberton)
Director: George Cukor
(MGM)

1955
Summertime (Jane Hudson)
Director: David Lean
(United Artists)

1956
The Rainmaker (Lizzie Curry)
Director: Joseph Anthony
(Paramount)
The Iron Petticoat (Vinka Kovelenko)
Director: Ralph Thomas
(MGM)

1957
The Desk Set (Bunny Watson)
Director: Walter Lang
(Twentieth Century-Fox)

1959
Suddenly Last Summer (Mrs Venable)
Director: Joseph L. Mankiewicz
(Columbia)

1962
Long Day's Journey into Night (Mary Tyrone)
Director: Sidney Lumet
(Embassy)

1967
Guess Who's Coming to Dinner? (Christina Drayton)
Director: Stanley Kramer
(Columbia)

1968
The Lion in Winter (Eleanor of Aquitaine)
Director: Anthony Harvey
(Avco Embassy)

1969
The Madwoman of Chaillot (Aurelia)
Director: Bryan Forbes
(Warner Bros–Seven Arts)

1971
The Trojan Women (Hecuba)
Director: Michael Cacoyannis
(Cinerama Releasing)

1975
Rooster Cogburn (Eula Goodnight)
Director: Stuart Miller
(Universal)

1978
Olly Olly Oxen Free (Miss Pudd)
Director: Richard A. Colla
(Sanrio Film Distribution)

1981
On Golden Pond (Ethel Thayer)
Director: Mark Rydell
(Universal)

1984
The Ultimate Solution of Grace Quigley (Grace Quigley)
Director: Anthony Harvey
(MGM/UA)

1994
Love Affair (Aunt Ginny)
Director: Glen Gordon Caron
(Warner Bros)

THEATRE

1928
The Czarina (Lady-in-Waiting)
by Melchior Lengyel and Lajos Biro
The Cradle Snatchers (Flapper)
by Russell Medcraft and Norma Mitchell
The Big Pond (Barbara. Fired after one performance)
by George Middleton and A. E. Thomas
These Days (Veronica Sims)
by Katharine Clugston
Holiday (understudy to Hope Williams. Played one performance as Linda Seton)
by Philip Barry

1929
Death Takes a Holiday (Grazia)
by Alberto Casella

1930
A Month in the Country (Katia)
by Ivan Turgenev
The Admirable Crichton (Lady Agatha Lasenby)
by J. M. Barrie
The Romantic Young Lady (Amalia)
by Martinez Sierra
Romeo and Juliet (Kinswoman to the Capulets)
by William Shakespeare
Art and Mrs Bottle (Judy Bottle)
by Benn W. Levy

1931
The Animal Kingdom (Daisy Sage)
by Philip Barry

1932
The Warrior's Husband (Antiope)
by Julian Thompson
The Bride the Sun Shines on (Psyche Marbury)
by Will Cotton

1933
The Lake (Stella Surrege)
by Dorothy Massingham and Murray MacDonald

1936
Jane Eyre (Jane Eyre)
by Charlotte Brontë

1939
The Philadelphia Story (Tracy Lord)
by Philip Barry

1942
Without Love (Jamie Coe Rowan)
by Philip Barry

1950
As You Like It (Rosalind)
by William Shakespeare

1952
The Millionairess (Epifania)
by George Bernard Shaw

1957
The Merchant of Venice (Portia)
by William Shakespeare
Much Ado About Nothing (Beatrice)
by William Shakespeare

1960
Twelfth Night (Viola)
by William Shakespeare
Antony and Cleopatra (Cleopatra)
by William Shakespeare

1969
Coco ('Coco' Chanel)
by Alan Jay Lerner (book and lyrics) and André Previn (music)

1976
A Matter of Gravity (Mrs Basil)
by Enid Bagnold

1981
West Side Waltz (Margaret Mary Elderdice)
by Ernest Thompson

TELEVISION

1973
The Glass Menagerie (Amanda Wingfield)
Director: Anthony Harvey
A Delicate Balance (Agnes)
Director: Tony Richardson

1975
Love among the Ruins (Jessica Medlicott)
Director: George Cukor

1979
The Corn Is Green (Miss Moffat)
Director: George Cukor

1986
Mrs Delafield Wants to Marry (Mrs Delafield)
Director: George Schaefer

1992
The Man Upstairs (Victoria)
Director: George Schaefer

1993
This Can't Be Love (Marion Bennett)
Director: Anthony Harvey

ACADEMY AWARDS AND NOMINATIONS
(Winning titles in bold)

1932-33 **Morning Glory**
1935 Alice Adams
1940 The Philadelphia Story
1942 Woman of the Year
1951 The African Queen
1955 Summertime
1956 The Rainmaker
1959 Suddenly Last Summer
1962 Long Day's Journey into Night
1967 **Guess Who's Coming to Dinner?**
1968 **The Lion in Winter**
1981 **On Golden Pond**

INDEX

PICTURE ACKNOWLEDGEMENTS

Archive Photos Stock Photo Library, New York
Associated Press, London
Photograph by Cecil Beaton courtesy of Sotheby's,
        London
Camera Press, London, with acknowledgement to: Cecil
        Beaton, John Bryson
Joel Finler
Burt Glinn/Magnum Photos
Bob Henriques/Magnum Photos
George Hoyningen-Huene
David Hurn/Magnum Photos
The Kobal Collection, London
London Features International
David McGough/LFI
Photofest, New York
Pictorial Press, London
Range/UPI/Bettmann
Rex Features, London, with acknowledgement to: Araldo
        di Crollalanza, Joel Elkings, Globe, Sipa Press,
        Ruan O'Lochlainn, Don Ornitz, Anita Weber
Terence Spencer/*Life* magazine © Time Warner Inc.
Dennis Stock/Magnum Photos

BFI Stills, Posters and Designs, London, with acknowl-
edgement to: ABC/TV, American Film Theater, Avco-
Embassy, Cannon Film Inc., Cinerama Releasing
Corporation, Columbia Pictures, Embassy Pictures,
Metro-Goldwyn-Mayer, MGM/UA/Cannon Films,
Paramount Pictures, PNC TV, RKO Radio Pictures Inc.,
Time Warner Inc., Turner Entertainment Corporation,
Twentieth Century-Fox, United Artists Corporation,
Universal/AFD, Universal Pictures, Warner Brothers,
Warner Brothers-Seven Arts

Every reasonable effort has been made to acknowledge
the ownership of copyrighted photographs included in
this volume. Any errors that have inadvertently occurred
will be corrected in subsequent editions provided notifica-
tion is sent to the publisher.